WAKEFIELD PRESS

# encountering
## TERRA AUSTRALIS

Jean Fornasiero is Associate Professor of French Studies at the University of Adelaide and a member of the ARC Baudin Legacy Project team. She has a particular interest in the place of the Baudin voyage in the history of science, including anthropology. Her recent publications focus on the opposing concepts that the different leaders of the expedition brought to the role of scientific voyager.

Peter Monteath is Associate Professor in the History Department at Flinders University, where he teaches European history. He is the author or editor of several books, including *Sailing with Flinders: The Journal of Seaman Smith*. As chance would have it, he is also a descendant of Philip Gidley King, Governor of New South Wales at the time of the voyages of Flinders and Baudin

John West-Sooby is Associate Professor of French Studies at the University of Adelaide and a member of the ARC Baudin Legacy Project team. His recent work on the Baudin expedition includes studies of the scientific reputation, the hydrographic achievements and the personality of its commander. He has also published widely on the nineteenth-century French novel.

Puv J.M.H. Jan 2017

In. 02

# encountering
# TERRA AUSTRALIS

The Australian
Voyages of
Nicolas Baudin and
Matthew Flinders

*Jean Fornasiero,*
*Peter Monteath and*
*John West-Sooby*

Wakefield Press
1 The Parade West
Kent Town
South Australia 5067
www.wakefieldpress.com.au

First published 2004
Reprinted in this new edition 2010

The illustrations in this book have been reproduced with the kind permission of the
following institutions: Art Gallery of South Australia; Barr Smith Library, Adelaide;
Mitchell Library, Sydney; Muséum d'histoire naturelle, Le Havre; National Library of
Australia, Canberra; National Maritime Museum, Greenwich; Natural History Museum,
London; Naturhistorisches Museum, Vienna; Royal Geographical Society of South Australia;
State Library of New South Wales.

Designed by Liz Nicholson, designBITE
Typeset by Clinton Ellicott, Wakefield Press
Printed in China at Everbest Printing Co. Ltd

National Library of Australia Cataloguing-in-Publication entry
Fornasiero, F. J. (F. Jean).
Encountering Terra Australis: the Australian voyages of Nicolas Baudin
and Matthew Flinders.

Bibliography.
Includes index.
ISBN 978 1 86254 874 9.

1. Flinders, Matthew, 1774–1814 – Journeys – Australia. 2. Baudin, Nicolas, 1754–1803 –
Journeys – Australia. 3. Explorers – Australia. 4. Australia – Discovery and exploration.
I. Monteath, Peter, 1961– . II. West-Sooby, John. III. Title.

994.02

**Government
of South Australia**

Arts SA

Publication of this book was assisted by the
Commonwealth Government through the
Australia Council, its arts funding and advisory body.

# CONTENTS

# PREFACE

## *The Encounter of Nicolas Baudin and Matthew Flinders: Meeting Them Half Way*

Between 1801 and 1803, two rival voyages were engaged in charting the last missing sections of the Australian coastline. Of the two navigators chosen to complete the task, it seemed that History could designate only one winner. This was to be Matthew Flinders, the commander of the British voyage. His remarkable exploits have been recorded in novels, history books and in place names; he has achieved heroic status through the use of epithet ('Indefatigable', 'the Great Denominator'); the facts of his life, his love and his tragedy are widely known. Above all he is associated with one specific and remarkable achievement: the circumnavigation of the continent he was to name. Regardless of whether one could or should quibble over details of the portrait and the mythology, such is his reputation.

On the other hand, if the commander of the rival expedition is remembered at all by the public at large, it is as a cantankerous and incompetent leader who failed dismally in his task. Informed historians know better, but there are those who, in defiance of certain facts, still perpetuate the image of Nicolas Baudin the Incompetent, the archetypal loser. Why are his weaknesses seen to be so great that they cannot be offset by his achievements, as are those of his fellow navigators, and indeed of Flinders himself?

We can well understand the process by which Baudin was seen to be an unworthy second to Flinders. In the early nineteenth century, the race to colonise Australia and to counter Napoleon's global ambitions was a sufficient pretext for defending the cause of British navigation and belittling the endeavours of the French rivals. A hundred years further on, the canonisation of Flinders corresponded to the young Australian nation's need to establish heroic tradition. Two hundred years after the events, with Australians more interested in the plurality of the experiences that make up their history, are they now prepared to view the two expeditions in an equal light?

It was this question and our own affirmative response that led to our choice of presentation of the two voyages of discovery. We are not attempting to prove what has already been the subject of learned and fascinating accounts by the historians; our aim is to present readers with the means of comparing the two voyages for themselves. We have taken what is common to both voyages and drawn the parallels between them, from the narrative of places visited to the artistic and scientific record of specimens collected. In the first part, *Voyages*, where the stories of the the two journeys are told, we have juxtaposed the captains' narratives in order to highlight their encounters and their common experiences at particular sites. We have followed the French itinerary, not only for chronological reasons – to start and finish with the voyage that departed first and returned home first – but also to ensure that we have given due recognition to Baudin's achievements as a navigator, since he is so often treated as a poor second to Flinders. Wherever possible, we have chosen complementary illustrations from the artwork of the two voyages, so that the interests of the scientists and the accomplishments of the artists are similarly seen in parallel. In the second part, *Legacies*, we have summarised the current state of opinion on the achievements of the two voyages in the areas of navigation, art and science, paying particular attention to anthropology.

Throughout, we have made our own translations of the French documents used. Although we make occasional reference to the journals kept by a number of officers and midshipmen on the Baudin expedition, it is Baudin's own account of his voyage that is the basis for our story. Our aim is to present Baudin's words in parallel with those of Flinders, in order to emphasise the commonality of their experience and to establish the events as experienced first hand by the French captain. Part of the reason for Baudin's obscurity is undoubtedly the fact that the official account of the voyage was made by his enemies, who painted a damning and often untruthful picture of their commander. The official account commissioned by the French Government after Baudin's death is the *Voyage de découvertes aux Terres Australes* prepared by François Péron and Louis Freycinet and translated into English, as early as 1809, as *A Voyage of Discovery to the Southern Hemisphere*. We recommend it as a fascinating document in itself, but we have only occasionally used it, mainly where it has been necessary to resolve discrepancies with Baudin's journal. Baudin's own version of events appeared in French for the first time only in

2000, in the illustrated edition prepared by Jacqueline Bonnemains and entitled *Mon voyage aux Terres Australes*. This version of Baudin's narrative is most often referred to as the fair copy; the other version is his sea log, which has been translated into English in its entirety, in the magnificent translation by Christine Cornell. For those who wish to read the complete story of Baudin, this remains the indispensable reference.

We have translated Baudin's story largely from these two narratives, the fair copy and the sea log, using microfilms available in the State Library of South Australia, themselves copies of the original documents that are held in the French National Archives; for the first part of the voyage, we have at times drawn on the fair copy, which is of great interest, but unfortunately incomplete, covering only the first year of the four-year journey. For the most part, we have translated extracts of the sea log. However, there is a large gap in Baudin's narrative corresponding to the stay in Port Jackson. For this period, we have retranslated the letters of Baudin contained in the *Historical Records of New South Wales*. Since we found in Baudin's philosophy, humour and talent for human observation a quality that strikes a contemporary note, this is what we have attempted to bring out in our translations.

In order to tell the story of Flinders' voyage, we have drawn on his official account, *A Voyage to Terra Australis*, published in London in 1814. Flinders too had kept rough and fair logs during his voyage but had ample time to work on the draft of his narrative during his six and a half years of imprisonment on the island of Mauritius. On his return to England in 1810, he devoted all his energies to revising and refining his text and his charts. Flinders' account is therefore a carefully wrought document compiled at a distance – both spatial and temporal – from the events themselves.

In contrast, neither of Baudin's texts is a finished product. The sea log was the commander's record of events as they happened and included essential navigational information. It would form the basis of Baudin's report to the authorities and was not meant for public consumption in its raw state. The frank and often blunt tone that characterises Baudin's assessment of his officers, crew and scientific staff can be attributed, at least in part, to the immediacy of his observations. There is already a difference, however, between Baudin's sea log, in which he jotted down details of daily occurrences on board, and the fair copy, which was exquisitely illustrated and contained many official reports.

If he had lived to write the official account of his voyage, as Flinders did, it is likely that Baudin's third writing of the events may also have been slightly different in tone and content from its two predecessors. Baudin may well have removed many of the musings and the criticisms that make his sea log quite a personal document. We can only speculate. What we do know is that Baudin, unlike Flinders, had no opportunity to distance himself from the frustration of daily setbacks or to write an officially sanctioned narrative in which he could show the polish and statesmanship that come through in his correspondence; nor could Baudin give a complete overview of the final achievements of his project. Flinders, on the other hand, was able to give due prominence to his many accomplishments. Indeed, his narrative can be seen on one level as an exercise in self-affirmation – hardly surprising given the frustration of his imprisonment in Mauritius and his struggle for recognition on his return to England. Circumstances have thus partly contributed to the fact that the writings of the two commanders do not correspond strictly to the same genre.

This does not, however, invalidate the juxtaposition of the narratives in question – it simply makes allowance for the difference in tone and content. More importantly, this juxtaposition enables us to give the French captain a distinctive voice that can be heard alongside that of Flinders. The personal tone of Baudin's writings conveys directly to the reader something of his courage, sensibility and humour – qualities in which he is much closer to Flinders than one might have imagined. There is more than a hint of irony here: the personal qualities with which Flinders is readily associated are often difficult to detect behind the matter-of-fact tone of *A Voyage to Terra Australis*; Baudin's less polished sea log puts both his leadership qualities, and his shortcomings, more plainly into view. Beyond the differences in temperament and narrative purpose, the journals tell nonetheless of remarkably parallel experiences.

By bringing out all that is parallel in the Australian encounters of the two captains, we hope to contribute to the process whereby the journeys of Baudin and Flinders will eventually lead them to the same destination: to the full and equal recognition of their discoveries in Terra Australis. Only then can we finally determine whether they were engaged in a race that either of them could really win – or accept that they did indeed meet half way.

# PREFACE TO THE SECOND EDITION

For a book to enter into its second life is indeed a happy moment for all who have been involved in its creation and production. For the authors, it provides a second chance to thank all of those who appear in our acknowledgments – the appreciation of whose input has in no way diminished over time – and to add to their number the readers who, since this work's appearance in 2004, have responded so positively to our account of the intertwined stories and histories of Matthew Flinders and Nicolas Baudin. Where we have been able to take up our readers' suggestions, we have happily done so, although we have obviously not sought to make major changes to a format that has been so warmly received. One notable addition is a full list of the illustrations used throughout our text. Although we had already provided a complete description within our text of the source of each image, we certainly appreciate the usefulness of a consolidated list, which has now been included at the end of the volume. We have also taken the opportunity to amend some minor points in order to improve the clarity of expression or exposition. We have not, however, fundamentally altered the text or our argument.

Since our narrative and our analyses were based on primary sources which are not, in the usual course of events, subject to fluctuation we trust that our work will remain as reliable as that base. While new and finer details can emerge at any time where two such complex voyages are concerned, the itineraries of the two captains and their companions are well established. The story of where the expeditioners went and what they did, as told in our Part One, thus remains essentially the same. Our decision to focus on the narratives of Baudin and Flinders in the telling of that story is also just as important now as it ever was: the existence of competing narratives and the reliance on these shown by some commentators, particularly where the French expedition is concerned, are confirmation for us of the ongoing need to assert the primacy and authority of the captains' voices. The comparative approach we have taken in Part Two of this book, where we have provided an assessment of the relative merits of the two expeditions in various fields of scientific endeavour, likewise remains pertinent, since the achievements of the French expedition, though they are slowly obtaining wider recognition, still do not have the currency of those of Flinders.

Naturally, scholarly activity has not diminished since 2004, or indeed since the bicentennial 'moment' of 2002, which raised the profile of Nicolas Baudin while at the same time reminding us of the achievements of Matthew Flinders, whose works and deeds were once more widely celebrated. Indeed, in the intervening years research into the two captains and their voyages has continued apace. This ongoing interest has led, in particular, to the publication of a number of primary source texts that were previously available only in archives and rare book collections. Plans for further publications of manuscript material are also well advanced.

In 2005, for instance, the Friends of the State Library of South Australia published the private journal of Matthew Flinders, edited by Gillian Dooley and Anthony J. Brown, thereby adding to the stock of Flinders' writings that have been made more readily accessible in recent times. Another example is Marc Serge Rivière's 2003 publication of the correspondence between Flinders and Thomi Pitot, the French merchant with whom the English navigator struck up a friendship during his imprisonment at Mauritius. There has clearly been no decline in the reading public's fascination with the life and friendships of Matthew Flinders, a subject to which Miriam Estensen has once more contributed with her lively biography of George Bass (2005).

It is interesting to note that Australian historians are not alone these days in placing Flinders' achievements firmly alongside those of the pioneers in Pacific exploration, as maritime historians worldwide delve more deeply into his case (see, for example, the book by Nigel Rigby et al., *Pioneers of the Pacific: Voyages of Exploration, 1787–1810*, published in London by the National Maritime Museum in 2005).

As for Baudin and his companions, the many textual records they left are attracting increasing attention on the part of researchers, both in Australia and in France, though for the most part the original documents themselves remain unpublished. The notable exceptions are François Péron's official account of the expedition, the complete version of which, in Christine Cornell's updated translation, was published by the Friends of the State Library of South Australia in 2003 (vol. II), 2006 (vol. I) and 2007 (Book 5 or *Dissertations*), to which we must of course add Baudin's sea log, republished by the same team in 2004 (updating the 1974 edition). It is to be regretted that Baudin's sea log has still not found a publisher in France, though 2009 will see the publication in French of his journal from the scientific expedition he led to the West Indies in 1796–1798. It is to be hoped that Michel Jangoux's edition of the *Journal of the Belle Angélique* will soon find its way into English translation, as it will add significantly to our appreciation of the French commander's character, seamanship and commitment to science.

It seems 2009 will in fact be a significant year for Baudin scholars. The Friends of the State Library of South Australia have plans to publish François Péron's famous 'spy report' on Port Jackson, translated and edited by Jean Fornasiero and John West-Sooby. The same year also marks the appearance of a website that will provide access to all of the journals kept by the officers and scientists on the Baudin expedition, in the original French and in English translation – the result of a project funded by the Australian Research Council and undertaken by Margaret Sankey, Jean Fornasiero, Michel Jangoux and John West-Sooby. This is a major breakthrough, not only for historians and the general public, but also for scientists in a range of fields who might wish to study the contribution made by the Baudin expedition to the history of their discipline. This is, of course, not the only web-based resource that is helping to change the mode of access to primary sources; the websites of the State Library of New South Wales, the National Maritime Museum at Greenwich and the Muséum d'histoire naturelle in Le Havre provide access to a wealth of resources relating to the Flinders and Baudin voyages, and more such material is set to become available in the near future.

Little wonder, then, that scholarly work on the two expeditions continues to grow. Several specialist conferences devoted to Baudin and Flinders have taken place in the last few years, in Australia and Europe, as well as Mauritius, and others are in preparation. There are doctoral students now actively engaged in new research and analysis. Specialists in domains such as geology, zoology, hydrography and anthropology continue to investigate the work undertaken by the scientists who accompanied Baudin and Flinders to Australia. Last but not least, the expeditioners themselves, and the relationships between them, remain a subject of fascination, as the imminent publication in France of the journal of captain Pierre-Bernard Milius amply demonstrates. Further, as the exquisite artwork of Charles-Alexandre Lesueur and Nicolas-Martin Petit becomes more widely known, through publications and new exhibitions (such as *Littoral*, planned for 2010), the Baudin voyage will not only have emerged from relative obscurity but will eventually leave its own indelible mark.

This is not to suggest, however, that everything about these stories inspires absolute unanimity or that there is no room for scholarly disagreement and debate. One case in point is that of the anthropological work of the French and the role played by Baudin's trainee zoologist, François Péron. The interactions between the French explorers and Australia's indigenous peoples undoubtedly raise many complex and challenging questions, both in their own right, as specific and personalised encounters, and more generally, for the place they occupy in the wider history of contact between Europeans and native populations during the Age of Discovery. It is hardly surprising, then, to note that anthropology remains one of the main topics of inquiry and debate amongst commentators on the Baudin expedition. We nevertheless stand by the analysis we have presented in our Chapter 17 ('The Clash of Cultures'). While it is by no means an exhaustive account of the subject, it is informed by a close reading of the voyage narratives and other primary sources, as well as by a thorough study of all the relevant scholarly literature. It is, moreover, based on the same approach we have adopted throughout this multilayered history, in which we have allowed the protagonists to speak for themselves as a prelude to our discussion of their legacy. Reviewers have responded favourably to this approach, though one commentator took exception to our portrait of François Péron, deeming that we identified him as racist. We leave it to our readers to form their own opinion on whether or not our account is biased against Péron. As for branding him a racist, we have not used that term, nor have we sought to imply any such attitude on Péron's part. Indeed, we fail to see the pertinence or the interest in doing so. What we have sought to do is identify the key ideas that he succeeded in passing on to others, principally through his official account of the voyage, which acquired an international readership and proved to be extremely influential. The regret that we have expressed regarding Péron's anthropological legacy is not that we deem him personally responsible for the fate that eventually befell the inhabitants of Tasmania – we actually end our chapter by remarking that 'the anthropologist was not to blame' – but that his conclusions regarding the inferiority of the Aborigines and the inevitability of the colonial project in Australia were to be so widely shared. It is our own close reading of Péron's writings, and of the history of their reception, that has informed our assessment of his anthropological observations and their controversial legacy. We have as yet found no reason to change the views expressed in this book, either on Péron's ideas and their influence or on the anthropological work of the Baudin expedition more generally.

Clearly, then, the two expeditions and the men who embarked on them still have the potential to court controversy and to stir the passions. It is indeed a subject of some fascination for us that the echoes of old disputes and rivalries continue to resonate so strongly with contemporary readers. We take this to be a sign that the story of these voyages and the contribution they made to our understanding of Australia's geography, its peoples and its flora and fauna will always make for compelling reading. We also remain convinced of the need for a contemporary retelling of this story that incorporates difference and debate. For the new readers of this story, we hope that we shall succeed in bringing to life the experiences and achievements of Baudin, Flinders and the host of colourful characters who accompanied them on their navigations to the Southern Lands, those lands that, after their passage, and because of it, became Australia.

April 2009

# AUTHORS' NOTE

All translations from the original French texts are our own. In translating from Baudin's journal, we have sought as far as possible to remain faithful to his style, which is characterised by long, fluid sentences. This has necessitated the addition of punctuation markers which are often lacking in the original. The spelling in Flinders' narrative has been modernised for ease of reading.

Other aspects of the two narratives have, however, been retained for the sake of authenticity. The place names given in Baudin's journal have been preserved, despite the fact that they differ in a number of instances from those in current usage. In such cases, modern nomenclature is indicated in brackets. The terms used to refer to distances and weights may also be unfamiliar to modern readers. Flinders, of course, was working with the imperial system of weights and measures. The French Revolutionary government had introduced the metric system of weights and measures in the 1790s, but this had yet to enter common usage (it was not until 1 January 1840 that the use of the metric system became compulsory in France). Consequently, Baudin and Flinders used terminology that was largely the same, although there are slight variations in the lengths and distances that some of these terms designated.

| BAUDIN | | FLINDERS | |
|---|---|---|---|
| 1 nautical mile | 1.852 kilometres | 1 nautical mile | 1.852 kilometres |
| 1 knot | 1 nautical mile per hour | 1 knot | 1 nautical mile per hour |
| 1 league ('lieue') | 5.556 kilometres (3 nautical miles) | 1 league | 5.889 kilometres (3.18 nautical miles) |
| 1 inch ('pouce') | 2.71 centimetres | 1 inch | 2.54 centimetres |
| 1 foot ('pied') | 32.48 centimetres (12 inches) | 1 foot | 30.48 centimetres (12 inches) |
| 1 fathom ('brasse') | 1.624 metres (5 French feet) | 1 fathom | 1.829 metres (6 English feet) |
| 1 pound ('livre') | 0.454 kilograms | 1 pound | 0.454 kilograms |

One further peculiarity of Baudin's text is his use of the French Republican Calendar to record dates. According to this calendar, which was instituted in 1793 (to be abandoned in 1806), the year began at the autumn equinox (22 September) and was divided into 12 months of 30 days, to which were added 5 or 6 complementary days devoted to various Republican celebrations and festivities. The names of the months reflected seasonal changes and events: the winter months, for example, were given the names *nivôse* (snow), *pluviôse* (rain) and *ventôse* (wind). As an illustration, the entry in Baudin's journal recounting the departure of the *Géographe* and the *Naturaliste* from the port of Le Havre on 19 October 1800 bears the date of *27 vendémiaire, Year IX of the French Republic*.

We have transposed these Republican dates to the corresponding Gregorian dates throughout, but have maintained Baudin's original terminology in the passages we have translated from his narrative, in order to give something of the flavour of the French revolutionary spirit that prevailed at the time. The use of the egalitarian term 'Citizen' as a universal form of address also communicates something of that spirit.

Finally, a word on the illustrations and maps. The images chosen provide a visual record of the places visited, the peoples encountered, and the animal and plant life that the expeditioners collected and studied. These images have been included in the body of the text, as close as possible to the relevant sections of the narrative or of our commentary. The maps are those that were drawn up as a result of the two expeditions. In some cases, we have cropped original maps in order to provide more detail of a particular section of coast. The animal and plant sketches are similarly those made by members of the expedition. A number of them represent the precise specimens mentioned in the text; where this has not been possible, sketches of specimens typical of a particular area have been provided. Where the Latin name of an animal or plant is given, it is generally followed, in brackets, by the name of the person who identified and classified it, and the year when this was recorded. The guiding principle adopted for the colour plates is that of comparison and contrast. Wherever possible, we have identified like images from the two voyages and placed them side by side, or on facing pages. In this way, the artwork of the French and the British expeditions can more readily be compared. This is the first time, to our knowledge, that these drawings have been presented in this way.

Reference is occasionally made to the work of other scholars, particularly in Part Two. In such cases, the name of the person is always indicated, and the source of the information quoted or referred to can be identified by looking up the 'Works Cited' section of the Bibliography.

# INTRODUCTION

## *The Lure of the South*

European exploration in the southern oceans was driven from the outset by both scientific curiosity and the pursuit of commercial interests. From a geographical point of view, the ancients had speculated that there must be a great southern land that would balance the land mass of the northern hemisphere. But it was not until the 15th century that the nations of Europe set about solving the question. In addition to the honour of discovery, other glittering prizes were dangling before their eyes. Exploration of the southern seas had the potential to open up a sea route to India and the east, thereby creating new opportunities for trade. Untold riches might also be found in lands as yet undiscovered. Geographical exploration and empire building would go hand in hand.

Sailing into uncharted waters with only the most rudimentary of navigational instruments to guide them was a perilous enterprise for these early explorers. Their vessels were subject to the vagaries of the weather and the sea currents, knowledge of which would take time to accumulate. To these practical difficulties were added threats of a human kind: apart from the ever-present danger of pirates, sailors also ran the risk of encountering hostile native populations. Undeterred, they continued their explorations with the result that, over time, the southern hemisphere gradually began to reveal some of its secrets. The Portuguese and the Spanish are acknowledged as the pioneers in this bold undertaking, but the Dutch, the English and the French also took up the challenge that eventually brought about the settlement of European Australia.

It was in fact a Frenchman, Binot Paulmier de Gonneville, whose travels caused a stir in Europe reminiscent of the excitement generated in 1492 when Christopher Columbus discovered the New World. Sailing south from the

Normandy port of Honfleur in 1503, Gonneville believed he had discovered the great unknown south land, or *Terra Australis Incognita*, when he sighted a coast after six months at sea. The precise location of this land is still a subject of debate – all of the documentation on board was apparently lost when Gonneville, just a short distance from home, drove his ship onto a reef off France's Atlantic coast in order to avoid being taken by pirates. Based on the report he subsequently made on the land and the peoples he encountered, current wisdom has it that the place he visited is situated somewhere in Brazil. Nevertheless, his voyage served to fuel speculation in Europe regarding the existence of a great south land.

Shortly afterwards, the Portuguese came close to discovering a new land mass in the south seas – if not the vast mythical continent imagined by Europeans – when they settled in Timor in the early 16th century. From there, they explored the coasts of the neighbouring islands, including New Guinea, and may even have sighted the shores of northern Australia. The maps of the day – drawn up, oddly enough, by French cartographers working from stolen Portuguese charts – hint tantalisingly at the existence of a land mass in the waters south of Java. But these maps are inconclusive. The first recorded sighting of the Australian coast was made at the beginning of the 17th century by a Dutchman, Willem Jansz, sailing in the *Duyfken*. Travelling east from the islands of Indonesia in 1606, he was driven south and soon came upon a particularly inhospitable coast whose native inhabitants proved to be even more hostile. These negative first impressions were confirmed when, a short time later, several of his crew were killed, though his talk of 'man-eaters' might suggest New Guinea rather than northern Australia.

Despite his frightening experience and his less than glowing reports of the land he had seen, Jansz set a new navigational trend for his countrymen. During the 17th century and into the 18th, navigators sailing for the Dutch East India Company made a series of landings on the northern, western and south-western coasts of what soon came to be known as New Holland. Their quest for new trading opportunities with the indigenous people of this largely desolate land proved vain, but the Dutch did leave a lasting legacy in the many names they conferred on the coastline from Nuyts Archipelago in the south to the islands and other features of the Gulf of Carpentaria in the north.

One particular Dutch navigator ventured further south and east than his compatriots in the search for more fertile and productive lands. Many still believed that there existed south of New Holland an even larger continent with a more temperate and agreeable climate. In 1642 Abel Tasman did indeed discover a wooded land in the higher latitudes of the southern seas. He named this land after the man who had sent him on his voyage, Governor Van Diemen, but its name was later changed to honour Tasman himself. Sailing further east, he made landfall once again in a place he named New Zealand. In neither case did he realise the lands he had discovered were in fact islands. It was still possible to think that they belonged to a hypothetical southern continent more vast than New Holland. Tasman's voyage therefore raised more questions than it answered. Most disappointing was the fact that Tasman had found no new trade opportunities for his country. Though more pleasant to the European eye, the wooded and mountainous lands he had discovered were just as unhospitable in their own way as the barren coasts of New Holland. The local inhabitants were similarly 'uncultivated' and hostile – four of Tasman's crew were killed by natives in New Zealand. The southern lands were decidedly unfriendly places to visit.

## The British and French in Southern Waters

The first Englishman to sight the shores of New Holland was, like the Dutch, unimpressed by what he saw. In 1688, and again in 1699, William Dampier spent some time exploring the north-west coast of New Holland. The unusual flora and fauna excited his interest, but his assessment of the land and its peoples was overwhelmingly negative. Little wonder, then, that the English did not hasten to send ships to New Holland in his wake.

It was not until the second half of the 18th century that Britain turned her attention once more to the south seas. Intellectual curiosity in the Age of Enlightenment was not the sole driving force in this – more practical commercial and geopolitical realities too played their role. The Seven Years War gave the British the upper hand in North America over their long-standing rivals the French. The Treaty of Paris, signed in 1763, not only sealed British pre-eminence in America, it also stripped France of most of her colonial possessions in India. Building on this momentum, Britain turned her attention to the Pacific, sending a number of ships in search of the unknown south land during the 1760s. These reported little of interest, with the notable exception of the discovery of Tahiti in 1767 by Samuel Wallis. A follow-up expedition to the island was promptly organised, to be led by a certain James Cook. Its primary purpose was scientific – to observe the transit of Venus across the sun in 1769. But Cook's instructions also required him to look in the latitude of 40° for the elusive southern continent – a requirement that had the interests of both science and empire in mind.

Cook was no more successful in this enterprise than his predecessors. The great southern land, he mused, might simply not exist. During that same voyage, however, he made a discovery that, while not accorded great importance at the time, would soon change the course of history. In 1770 Cook sighted the east coast of Australia. He proceeded to explore and map this coastline, naming the land New South Wales and claiming it in the name of his king – an act of possession that would lead to the establishment, 18 years later, of a convict settlement and to a rekindling of interest in the real Terra Australis.

This was the first of Cook's three great voyages of exploration. Thanks to his efforts over the course of a decade, he all but dispelled the notion that there existed a vast land mass in the south equivalent to that of Europe and Asia in the north. This conclusion may have disappointed the scientists and philosophers, not to mention those with more mercantile interests. Nevertheless, Cook's exploits had earned him universal respect and admiration as the most accomplished navigator of his day and one of the greatest in the history of maritime exploration. As impressive as his achievements were, however, Cook was not able to avoid the perils to which so many of his fellow seamen from all nations had succumbed. His resourcefulness had allowed him to overcome a serious incident during his first great Pacific voyage, when the *Endeavour* ran onto a reef in the treacherous waters off the coast of present-day Queensland. But his third voyage ended in tragedy when Cook and several of his crew were killed in the Sandwich Islands (Hawaii).

This was an all too familiar scenario, as Cook's French counterparts had also been learning. Like Britain, France was looking to the antipodean south for new strategic and commercial opportunities in the latter part of the 18th century. This was particularly important in the wake of the Seven Years War and the humiliating losses the French had incurred. Voyages of exploration, with their promise of new scientific and geographical discoveries, would be instrumental in restoring national pride and re-establishing France's credentials as a major world power.

Louis Antoine de Bougainville (1729–1811), who himself had suffered the pain of defeat at the hands of the British in Quebec, was among the first to try to rebuild French interests elsewhere. After an aborted attempt to establish a French colony in the Falklands, he responded to his government's call to explore the Pacific and to find out whether the rumoured southern continent, *Terra Australis Incognita*, really existed. The fame of discovery was not the only prize dangled before his eyes – at stake too was the opportunity of extending French trade routes into largely unknown territory. The intrepid Bougainville sailed into the Pacific from the east in late 1767, visiting Tahiti and the New Hebrides before making his way further to the west. In June of 1768 he found himself not far from the Queensland coast, heading directly towards it, and curious to learn what might lie on the other side of the breakers thrown up by the Barrier Reef. Wisely, perhaps, he chose not to negotiate the reef and, with a famishing crew, he turned north past Bougainville Island and the northern coast of New Guinea. Deprived of a view of the Australian coast, he returned to France with his life and his health quite intact. Moreover, he was widely feted on his arrival there, in large part because he had also managed to keep alive and bring to Paris an indigenous Tahitian by the name of Ahu-toru or Aoutourou. At last the French could attach a face and a name to philosopher Jean-Jacques Rousseau's concept of 'le bon sauvage' (the noble savage).

Bougainville's voyage was not the only occasion on which the French stopped unwittingly short of Australian shores. Like James Cook, and indeed at the same time as Cook, Charles de Surville explored the coast of New Zealand, known to Europeans since Abel Tasman's time. But whereas Cook had then headed to the west, knowing that at some point he must run into the eastern extremity of the Dutch-discovered New Holland, Surville had gone east and suffered an all too common end. He died on the Peruvian coast on 7 April 1770 while attempting to land a boat through surf. Less than two weeks later, Cook sighted the Australian coast.

The voyage of Marc Joseph Marion-Dufresne in the years 1771–1773 was another that was to stop short of the Australian continent and end in tragedy. Designed to discover the purported great southern land – the French spoke of Gonneville Land – but also to return Ahu-toru to his Tahitian home, the expedition led by Marion-Dufresne sailed on 18 October 1771 from Mauritius, a key possession in the Indian Ocean, which the French had re-named Ile de France after taking it from the Dutch in 1715. Marion-Dufresne followed a very southern latitude on his way to Tasmania, which he reached in March 1772, having found no great land on the way. He then headed east to New Zealand, which proved his undoing. He and a number of his crew were killed and then apparently eaten by Maoris after joining a fishing party in the Bay of Islands – thereafter called by the French the 'Baie des Assassins'.

Similarly driven by a desire to find the non-existent Gonneville Land, and like Marion-Dufresne beginning his quest in Mauritius, Yves Joseph de Kerguelen de Trémarec made his way east across the Indian Ocean in early 1772. Unlike his compatriot, Kerguelen *did* set his eyes upon an unknown coastline in the higher latitudes of the ocean, which he was convinced must be the fabled great southern land. However, his eyes deceived him. The coastline was merely that of what Cook was to name Desolation Island, now Kerguelen Island. But Kerguelen's consort, the *Gros Ventre*, under the command of Louis François Marie Alesno de St Allouarn, chose to proceed further to the east, where the French did finally come across continental Australia.

St Allouarn made landfall in present-day Flinders Bay, on the eastern side of Cape Leeuwin at the south-western tip of the continent. After exploring and charting the bay, he turned north and headed for Shark Bay, which he sighted on 28 March 1772. He promptly organised a shore party to visit Turtle Bay on Dirk Hartog Island, where he raised the French flag and claimed possession of this section of western Australia in the name of King Louis XV. Following his survey of Shark Bay, St Allouarn resumed his northerly course, keeping at a cautious distance from the little-known and treacherous coast of north-western Australia. St Allouarn was not able to penetrate all of the mysteries of this coastline, but he did succeed in charting a number of its important features such as the numerous shoals and archipelagos to be found there. In so doing, he added significantly to the maps produced by the Dutch and by William Dampier in the previous century. In desperate need of food and water, he finally broke off his survey near present-day Darwin and headed for Timor. Special though St Allouarn's achievements might have been, his fate was sadly more common – he died of illness soon after returning to Mauritius.

Jean-François de Galaup de La Pérouse might well have had the fate of his predecessors in mind when he set sail in 1785. He had been set the extra-ordinarily ambitious task of exploring both the north and the south of the Pacific. His aims were primarily scientific, and to this end he carried aboard a complement of scientists, but he was also asked to ascertain the activities of the European powers in that vast region. Cook's third voyage (1776–1780) had paved the way for a lucrative fur trade between north-western America and China, and France needed to complete its knowledge of the Pacific in order to establish its own share in this and other commercial enterprises. La Pérouse also wanted to find out if the British were establishing a colony in New Zealand. Like Bougainville he approached the Pacific from the east; he rounded Cape Horn and proceeded to explore the North Pacific. While in a Russian port, he received orders to make his way to New South Wales to find out what the British were doing there. The British were, as we well know, establishing a penal colony, and La Pérouse famously arrived in Botany Bay on 26 January 1788, just in time to witness the founding of a settlement. From Botany Bay he set out for New Caledonia and islands to the north of there. He was never seen alive again; it was only in 1827 that the wreckage of his two vessels was found by an Irishman, Captain Peter Dillon, on reefs off the island of Vanikoro in the Santa Cruz group.

The unexplained disappearance of the widely admired La Pérouse caused great concern in France. In the vain hope that he might yet be found, an expedition was established in 1791 to go in search of him. Led by Antoine Raymond Joseph de Bruni d'Entrecasteaux, it has gone down in history as the failed attempt to find La Pérouse, though in fact it was much more than that. D'Entrecasteaux had a scientific and exploratory agenda of his own, and indeed he achieved much in this regard, including the discovery in south-eastern Tasmania of the channel that now bears his name. Importantly, the impressive charts drawn up by his geographer-hydrographer Charles François Beautemps-Beaupré, which showed the existence of safe harbours in D'Entrecasteaux Channel and near the entrance to the Derwent River, aroused French interests in establishing a settlement in this area.

One might by now guess that the commander's ineluctable fate was premature death: in the middle of 1793, on his way to Java, d'Entrecasteaux succumbed to scurvy and dysentery. By that time the expedition had at least covered south-western Australia and south-east Tasmania, before heading north into the Pacific. But after the captain's demise, and under the strain of political tensions whose origins lay on the other side of the world – royalist officers and republican sympathisers were bitterly opposed – the expedition soon fell apart with the mystery of La Pérouse unsolved.

## Antipodean Antipathies

The sustained presence of the French in the Pacific and Indian oceans was a clear sign that they were keen to establish themselves as a major player in the region. Traditional Anglo-French rivalry alone would guarantee the British great pleasure in stealing the march on France in the southern hemisphere. But the sense of rivalry, and with it the sweetness of victory, grew all the stronger after the British in turn were evicted from North America. Two decades after the 1763 Treaty of Paris the Americans won their struggle for independence, with not a little help from France. The British remained without question the dominant sea-power in the world; but, like the French before them, they now had to refocus their energies elsewhere. And, in the aftermath of Cook's dis-coveries, they redoubled their efforts in the southern seas. With their powerful navy to support the venture, they expected to spread throughout the world the unquestioned benefits of British commerce and civilisation. In that endeavour, it was raw power that counted most, and the British were well accustomed to wielding it without compromise.

The occupation of lands considered to be 'vacant' was the method by which Britain asserted new territorial claims. Thanks to the efforts of Cook, New South Wales was known by the time the American colonies were lost. In due course, and with the engagement of Cook's former botanist Joseph Banks, his New South Wales was established as a penal colony. From this base further exploration could be pursued, both north and south of Port Jackson, but also in New Holland to the west. At that time it was still not clear whether New South Wales and New Holland were part of one and the same land mass. This was just one of a number of geographical mysteries that remained to be solved. Once again, the British would vie with the French for the honour of unlocking these secrets.

Shortly after the east had been colonised by his countrymen, George Vancouver explored the southern coast in the west, where he discovered and named King George Sound. That was in 1791, when he followed the coast from Cape Leeuwin to Termination Island before breaking south to head for Tasmania. On this occasion, too, the British had beaten the French, since Bruni d'Entrecasteaux did not arrive in that part of the world until the end of the following year.

Not to be outdone, the French decided to return to the fray at the turn of the century, organising yet another expedition to the southern oceans. To be led by Nicolas Baudin, this expedition was designed to continue the rich tradition of French scientific exploration. One of its principal objectives was to solve the riddle of the south coast, much of which was still uncharted. As if on cue, the British, upon learning of this new French expedition, quickly set about organising one of their own, to be entrusted to Matthew Flinders. The stage was set for a new episode to be played out in the history of maritime exploration and Anglo-French competition.

## Revolution and War in Europe

If the rivalry between France and Britain was a drama performed on a world stage, its plot was written in Europe, and even before the voyages of Vancouver and d'Entrecasteaux that plot had taken a very dramatic turn. France was plunged into revolution in the summer of 1789. The prison of the Bastille was stormed on 14 July and the Declaration of the Rights of Man, with its radical insistence on *liberté*, *égalité* and *fraternité*, was pronounced the following month to the jubilation of many and the shock of others.

For conservatives throughout the European continent, this was a profoundly vile and seditious document. But if a mere declaration would not shock them into action, then the course of events soon did. The fervour of the revolution seemed to magnify with time, so that by September of 1792 France had become a Republic. Four months later both king and queen had lost not just their crowns but their heads; a brutal reign of terror began. Overwhelmed in France, conservatives banded together elsewhere. A coalition of European forces was assembled as early as 1792, and by February of 1793 Britain too had entered the fray against its old foe.

Having reorganised their system of government and transformed the whole fabric of their society along revolutionary lines, the French proved a formidable force, both on land and at sea. Moreover, their efforts were soon bolstered by the military genius of Napoleon Bonaparte, the 'little corporal', who followed initial successes in Italy with stunning victories in other parts of Europe. True, he had to suffer the ignominy of defeat against Nelson's forces at Aboukir, which eventually forced the French out of Egypt. But when the young Bonaparte made his way back to France in 1799 he overthrew the government and, in an act of naked opportunism, seized power for himself. In name he was First Consul, in reality he was a military dictator – albeit one who enjoyed great popular support. In 1804 he had himself crowned Emperor of the French, a role in which he imposed his presence upon Europe and the world for years to come. During his time in power he oversaw many victories, both in the field and on the waters of battle, but none were sweeter than those won against the British. For their part, the British despised no other enemy of the day more intensely than Napoleon, but they had to wait until 1815 to put an end to his reign.

## National Pride and Scientific Internationalism

Napoleon Bonaparte's battles were fought in the name of the Revolution and its principles. Force was required to overthrow unenlightened reactionary regimes and to liberate the peoples of Europe from the yoke of oppression. Science and the pursuit of knowledge, however, were equally vital weapons in the struggle against traditional religious beliefs and intellectual servitude. Accordingly, scientists were held in great esteem in the new Republic, not least by Bonaparte himself. The Egyptian campaign that was launched in 1798, though a failure in military terms, brought great intellectual prestige to France and helped to establish its leader's credentials as a friend of science. Its strategic objective had been to block the English route to India, but Bonaparte, in defiance of convention, had also taken with him nearly 150 scientists whose task it was to investigate all facets of this land including its rich and exotic cultural heritage. Once Cairo was taken, these scientists formed a society and met regularly to discuss their work. Bonaparte, who was himself a member, is reported to have enjoyed the company of these scientists and to have taken a genuine interest in their discussions. Though he returned to France in 1799, many of the scientists remained until the end of the campaign in 1801, ensuring that their nation would enjoy the fruits of their labours for years to come. The discovery of the Rosetta Stone in particular would later allow Champollion to unlock the secrets of Egyptian hieroglyphics.

The scientific successes of the Egyptian campaign confirmed for Bonaparte the utility of such large scale projects. When he received the proposal for an ambitious new voyage of scientific discovery he was readily convinced of its merits. The Baudin expedition held the promise of exciting discoveries in geography, natural history and the study of indigenous peoples, and therefore presented the opportunity to add significantly to the nation's prestige. There is no reason to doubt the sincerity of Bonaparte's commitment to science; it would be naive, however, to suggest that this was his sole motivation in approving the expedition. The recent history of maritime exploration and the state of political affairs in the Pacific and Indian oceans would almost certainly have contributed to his decision. No evidence has been found to suggest that Bonaparte had any particular plans for settlement at that stage, but he would have been mindful of the fact that new and improved knowledge of the southern oceans and the lands they contained would, directly or indirectly, serve France's commercial and strategic interests. While the instructions drawn up for the expedition clearly established its scientific purpose, the potential political benefits were difficult to ignore. This voyage of discovery would have the delicate task of fulfilling its explicit objectives while remaining conscious of the strategic uses to which its discoveries might be put.

Curiously, the pursuit of this nationalistic agenda would rely upon the spirit of international cooperation that characterised the scientific community of Europe at the end of the 18th century. The scientists of France and Britain had remained in constant contact with one another, despite the outbreak of hostilities between their two nations. They were well served in this by their respective national bodies: the Royal Society of London, whose president was none other than Cook's former botanist Sir Joseph Banks, and the Institut National de France, to which France's most prominent scientists and intellectuals belonged. A mutual respect and admiration existed between the two groups. Banks was a corresponding member of the French Institute and cultivated relations with its professors. He maintained a particularly cordial correspondence with Antoine-Laurent de Jussieu – a botanist like Banks, and the director of the Muséum d'histoire naturelle in Paris. Their relationship would be instrumental in securing safe-conducts for the voyages of Baudin and Flinders. In times of war, the pursuit of human knowledge was felt by scientists of all nations to be more important than ever. Banks and Jussieu, like their colleagues throughout Europe, were determined to ensure that this knowledge was freely shared. The 'commonwealth of learning' knew no borders – though this did not necessarily mean that national interests were always relegated to the background.

## Class Politics

At the end of the 18th century, scientists in Europe had to fight against a climate of international conflict in order to maintain the neutrality of their endeavours. For the French, that spirit of cooperation was further tested by politics of a domestic nature. Traditional class relations in France had been thrown on their head by the events of 1789. In the true spirit of equality, the Revolution had abolished the privileges enjoyed by the aristocracy under the ancien régime. This led to profound social and institutional changes that affected every facet of life in France. In some domains, however, change would take longer to effect. The navy is a case in point. It drew heavily for its supply of officers from the ranks of the nobility. The great voyages of discovery had been led by aristocrats of note – Bougainville and La Pérouse were Counts, no less. This recruitment practice could hardly be changed overnight: in addition to the inertia caused by the weight of tradition, time was needed to produce well-trained and skilled officers. It was barely a decade after the Revolution that the Baudin expedition was approved and organised. The republican government consequently found itself sponsoring a voyage that relied for its success on a complement of officers drawn to a considerable extent from the nobility.

Though slow to change, the navy was by no means immune to the new spirit of the times. Its officers had to accustom themselves to subtle but significant changes to shipboard life. These extended to the use of language: everyone on board the ships of the new Republic – scientists, officers and ordinary crewmen – was addressed indiscriminately as 'citizen'. Such changes may have rankled. But the officers recruited for the Baudin expedition had a much more bitter pill to swallow: they would be led by a man who was not of noble birth and who did not belong to the naval establishment. From the outset, Nicolas Baudin was faced with the task of having to earn what he should have been able to take for granted: the goodwill and respect of his officers.

On the other side of the Channel, life in the Royal Navy, however difficult it may have been, was spared this added complication. British society had not experienced the sudden and violent upheavals that had wracked France. Its highly effective and formidable naval tradition, though it had experienced its own problems, did not have to deal with the sudden intrusion of class politics. In fact, the Royal Navy had shown that class was not necessarily a barrier to success: while there did exist a strong naval establishment, this did not prevent those of more modest origins from rising through the ranks and achieving greatness. The most striking example is provided by James Cook: son of a Yorkshire farm labourer, he rose to become his nation's greatest maritime explorer. Matthew Flinders was similarly able to pursue a career in the navy, unimpeded by his middle-class origins. And when he set sail in the wake of Nicolas Baudin, he did not have to contend with the same climate of mistrust and resentment that, from the outset, clouded relations on board the ships of his French counterpart. It was therefore in contrasting circumstances that two expeditions left Europe for Terra Australis at the turn of the century to fulfil remarkably similar objectives.

Amid war and revolution in Europe, two such voyages of discovery to far-flung regions of the globe might appear as little more than jottings in the margins of history. But if they are jottings, they are remarkably informative ones. They tell us a great deal about the world at that time as they present to us a most remarkable paradox.

After all, Baudin and Flinders should have been bitterly uncompromising rivals. Their countries had competed since time immemorial for ascendancy both on land and on the high seas. Each had fought to squeeze the other out of every corner of the globe, and they had adopted it as a national mission to beat the other to claiming as their possessions whatever it was that their voyages to the antipodes might reveal. If the great southern land did exist, then each wanted it for themselves. If it did not exist – as indeed it did not, at least not as the European mind conceived it – then each wanted to be the first to complete the map of the southern land that was already known to exist: *Terra Australis*. On top of all that, Baudin's France and Flinders' Britain from 1793 were engaged in what was seen universally as a life and death struggle.

Instead, their meetings were marked by cordiality and respect. The ugly international politics of their day should by rights have pulled them apart, but the spirit of science that drove them both on long and dangerous voyages united them. If there is much in the stories told below that gives expression to the bitter rivalries of their day, there is also in the character of these two remarkable men a nobility of spirit that both defines their age and transcends it.

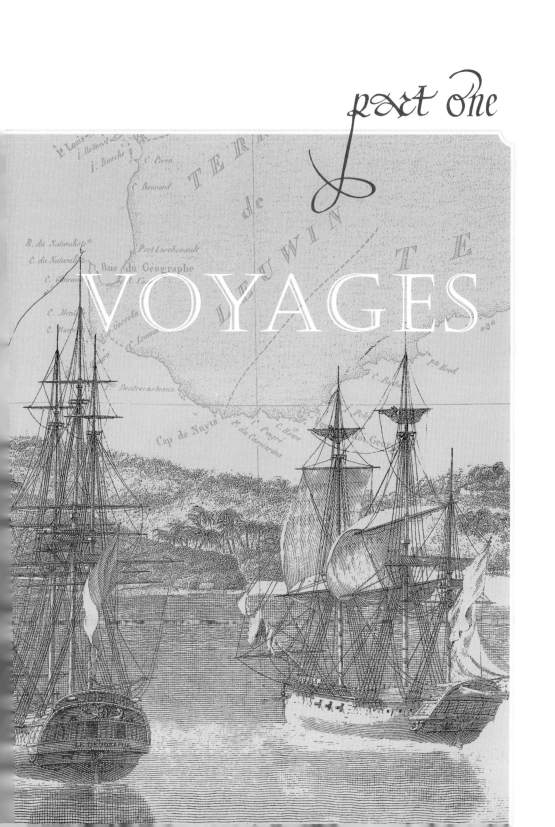

# part one

# VOYAGES

Post-Captain Nicolas Baudin, Joseph Jauffret (c1800).
Muséum d'histoire naturelle, Le Havre – n° 06 152

Portrait of Matthew Flinders. Reproduced from the
*Naval Chronicle* (1814)

# chapter one

# THE JOURNEY OUT

Those who embrace the rigours of a seafaring career are of a particularly hardy and single-minded breed, and neither Nicolas Baudin nor Matthew Flinders proved to be an exception to this rule. Perhaps the call of the sea inspired different dreams and ambitions in the two men, whose relatively modest origins would not immediately open doors to the higher echelons of the naval establishment. Yet it was clear that they intended to reach them and that, for both of these aspiring navigators, the sea offered a pathway to an illustrious destiny. This is no doubt the conviction that sustained their courage in the face of the severe hardships of their voyages of discovery. Setting out in 1800, Nicolas Baudin was the first of the two captains to verify the adage that there is always worse at sea. His difficult passage to Terra Australis was to set the tone for his entire voyage.

## *The Obstacle Course of Nicolas Baudin*

We know little of the early life of Nicolas Baudin beyond the barest details. He was born in 1754 into a family of merchants on the Ile de Ré, a small island off La Rochelle on France's Atlantic coast. He went to sea as an adolescent, serving out his apprenticeship on merchant ships, and later enlisted in the French Navy. By 1778, at the beginning of the American War of Independence, he had become an officer. He obtained his first command in 1780, but was soon replaced in this role by an officer of noble birth who had better connections. Baudin took this badly: he resigned in disgust and complained bitterly of the injustice he had suffered. Some claims have been made suggesting that his prickly character may have been responsible for this indignity, but there is no evidence to suggest any professional failings. Indeed, Baudin was soon to make his mark as a merchant seaman.

He had been plying the route between the Americas and Europe in this capacity when a stopover at the Cape of Good Hope in 1787 brought him into contact with Franz Boos, gardener to Joseph II, Emperor of Austria. This was a decisive encounter. Baudin would assist Boos in bringing his important botanical collections safely back to Austria, while Boos would awaken Baudin's interest not only in the natural sciences but also in the techniques required to transport living specimens on long sea voyages. This first successful voyage on the *Pepita* brought Baudin the admiration of professional botanists and the patronage of the Emperor. He made three other voyages for the Austrians, on ships now aptly named for the floating plant boxes they had become – all three named the *Jardinière*. However, Baudin's initial luck had vanished. Perhaps as an ominous sign of what was to come for the naturalist seaman, these botanical voyages ended in shipwreck: the first of the *Jardinières* foundered when, during Baudin's absence, his second in command was in charge; the second was lost in a cyclone while sitting in port in Mauritius; and the third was similarly wrecked during a frightening storm near the Cape of Good Hope.

In spite of the hostility that these misadventures caused him with the Austrians – who, like the English, were now at war with the French – Baudin pursued his career as a botanical voyager with his reputation seemingly unscathed. On his next voyage he sailed under French colours, in an expedition that was warmly supported by Antoine-Laurent de Jussieu, director of the Muséum d'histoire naturelle in Paris. Baudin would merit Jussieu's confidence by the splendid results he achieved. Departing in the *Belle Angélique* in 1796, Baudin travelled to the West Indies, accompanied by four naturalists from the Museum with whom he enjoyed the close personal and working relationship that finally confirmed him in his taste for botanising and for scientific expeditions generally. He greatly admired the 'zeal and the tireless activity' shown by his closely knit team of Riédlé, Maugé, Levillain and Ledru. They admired the same traits in Baudin, who preferred to lead by example. They were particularly impressed by the seamanship he displayed when battling violent storms before bringing them safely to port. His strength of character also served them well as he made his way through the British blockade of French ports. He made a triumphant return to France in 1798 – just in time for his exotic cargo to be paraded in the streets of Paris on 28 July, the Republican Day of Freedom. The commoner who had been slighted in favour of an aristocrat could at last enjoy his moment in the sun. He was reinstated as post-captain in the French Navy and Jussieu was anxious to support him in his next ambitious project – a scientific voyage of discovery around the world.

Although the scientific and naval establishment gave its full support to Baudin's proposal, the revolutionary wars prevented the immediate execution of his plans. He continued to lobby the authorities and, on 7 and 8 March 1800, presented a detailed outline to the Institut National. He no doubt hoped to take with him the naturalists who had accompanied him on the *Belle Angélique* – and all of them expressed a wish to go – although his new plans included doubling the complement of scientific staff on board in order to cover the expanded range of scientific research that he now envisaged. His aims were:

> to check on certain doubtful points of geography; to chart unknown coasts; to visit the peoples who inhabit them; to explore, if possible, the interior of their countries; to increase their wealth by exchanging objects with them or by making them gifts of animals or plants that can adapt to their soil, and subsequently offer resources to navigators; to accept in return from these nations such gifts of products that will increase our national wealth; to undertake in these unknown places, or in others that have not been properly visited by scientific travellers, the natural history research and the collections that will complement in every respect those held in the museum.

Exploration, trade and botany were Baudin's principal objects of interest, but he also mentioned specifically his intention to contribute to ethnographical research.

> Everywhere we go, we shall undertake the detailed study of the monuments of the countries we are able to visit. The writing, hieroglyphics, books, language, clothing of the peoples we encounter on our travels, will be a tribute we can offer upon our return to the Third Class of the Institute . . .

This orientation for the projected voyage was later confirmed in the detailed instructions addressed to Baudin by the secretary of the Society of the Observers of Man. On behalf of the Society, the author recommended not only that the expedition study the different physical, spiritual and social aspects of the peoples they encountered, but also that it bring home some living human specimens – to be treated with great kindness, but whose remains, if they chose to see out the rest of their days in France under the care of the

Society, would be destined for a new museum. This suggestion, shocking to the modern sensibility, was modelled on the example set by James Cook and Louis Antoine de Bougainville, who had brought two Tahitians back to Europe from their great Pacific expeditions of the mid-1770s. In any case, the Society's insructions reinforced the growing importance of the fledgling science of anthropology.

In the meantime, Baudin had put his point across to the French scientific establishment. So successful was he in his presentation that the Institute agreed to recommend his project to the First Consul. The outcome of the audience with Bonaparte on 25 March – an audience at which Baudin was present – was also highly favourable. Baudin may therefore have imagined an early departure, but he soon encountered the first of many frustrations. Fearing the hostile reaction of the English to Bonaparte's campaign in Italy, the Minister of Marine, Pierre Forfait, refused to equip the vessels for departure before he had received their British passport. The delays in receiving this and other foreign passports, in addition to the problems encountered in identifying the ships finally found to be most fitted to the task – now named the *Géographe* and the *Naturaliste* – meant that, in August 1800, Baudin was still engaged in fitting out and loading his two ships, and chafing his heels.

His projected departure had already begun to attract widespread attention from the scientific community, as we can see from the instructions and advice he received from both the Ministry and the Institute. Some of these papers were addressed to Baudin by well-known personalities, such as the German doctor, Franz Mesmer, or the novelist and former Director of the Jardin des Plantes, Bernardin de Saint-Pierre, each of whom stressed the importance of subjects close to his own interests: animal magnetism, in the case of Mesmer, but also the relation between the severance of the umbilical cord and resistance to smallpox; and for Bernardin de Saint-Pierre, the direction of sea currents, but also dancing to the bagpipes as a means of combating low morale and scurvy on board. The latter concern was also the subject of instructions from the Ministry. The detail of the instructions concerning sleeping conditions, food, water, exercise and general hygiene, especially when these are compared with the supplies actually taken on board and the practices established by Baudin, belie the suggestion later made by his enemies that the commander was unaware of the dangers of scurvy or that he had disobeyed the orders pertaining to the health and well-being of his men. We know now that the incidence of the disease on his ships was relatively low and that it broke out mainly when fresh food was in short supply. It is correct, however, to say that food supplies – both their quantity and their quality – were an issue during certain stages of the journey. In spite of the care and thought that went into the planning of the voyage, the rigours of seafaring sometimes meant that this essential aspect of the crew's well-being could not be assured – a situation that was not helped initially by the malfunctioning of the kitchens constructed especially for the expedition.

These problems were still a long way off when Baudin received final instructions on 24 September 1800. Not only was his voyage to follow a shorter itinerary, but it would include a far greater contingent of scientists than the commander thought appropriate. He commented that there were 22 names, where he had requested only eight per vessel – and he had suggested that number envisaging a much longer voyage encompassing the Americas. Since his instructions were now merely to take two ships to New Holland, his opinion was that four scientists per vessel was the ideal number – a judgment that was no doubt founded on the happy experience on the *Belle Angélique*, but also one that history would find to be accurate.

However, in terms of professional qualities, Baudin was not badly served in the choice of scientists, artists and crew who accompanied him. Many of his officers and midshipmen later pursued distinguished naval careers. Among these were Emmanuel Hamelin, who captained the *Naturaliste*, the Freycinet brothers, Henri and Louis, Pierre-Bernard Milius and Charles Baudin. His geographers, Boullanger and Faure, were highly competent hydrographers, and his astronomer, Bernier, although a difficult man, performed his duties well. Of course, there was also François Péron, who would later commence the official account of the voyage, completed by Louis Freycinet. Péron would acquire a well-merited reputation as an anthropologist and zoologist.

Many of the artists and scientists selected by the Institute proved temperamentally unsuited for a long sea voyage, but Baudin could rely upon the skills of his companions from the *Belle Angélique* to build up the natural science collections, as well as the talents of the two young men, Lesueur and Petit, whom he had hired ostensibly as assistant gunners, but whose artistic services he had in fact acquired for the illustration of his private journal. It is interesting to speculate how different the climate on board may have been if Baudin had had more say in his choice of companions – those whom he chose, he chose well. This hard task-master did have a gift for friendship and inspired loyalty amongst those who came to know him. These included Jussieu, whose support had ensured that the voyage became a reality and to whom Baudin wrote faithfully throughout the entire campaign.

François PÉRON.

Né à Cérilly, département de l'Allier, le 22 août 1775.

Mort le 10 décembre 1810.

François Péron, engraving by Choubard from a drawing by Charles-Alexandre Lesueur. Muséum d'histoire naturelle, Le Havre – n° 06 105

With his crew selected and on board the *Géographe* and the *Naturaliste*, Baudin was finally ready to set sail from the Normandy port of Le Havre. The lateness of the departure on 19 October 1800 would already make it difficult for him to respect the letter of his instructions, which included a very tight timetable. He was permitted to vary his itinerary when it was absolutely essential, but only on condition that he return to it as quickly as possible after any variation. Time was obviously of the essence if the expedition was going to fulfil one of its major objectives: to beat the English in the race to chart the unknown south coast of New Holland.

On the day of departure, the expedition set out from the docks of Le Havre amid much patriotic enthusiasm. Baudin no doubt reflected on the glory that was now his lot: his dry humour was certainly aroused by the interest that his voyage inspired in officers 'of distinction' or in women who once may well have disdained a man of his modest origins. His remarks combine the cynicism of the professional seaman with the satisfaction of an ambition fulfilled.

> The interest that each of [the officers] took in the success of our campaign had inspired their [trip to Le Havre] and we had the satisfaction of seeing they were happy with the situation of the two corvettes.

> We were also favoured by the visit of several beautiful ladies who appeared
> to be distressed to know where we were headed, since we would be deprived for
> so long of the company of women. However, as not a single one of them agreed
> to come with us, sadly we were to possess them for only one brief moment.

Baudin appeared to have been more deeply moved by the acclaim of the
citizens of Le Havre, who shouted their farewells 'in a manner that was
unprecedented. May the memory that I shall keep of this moment apprise
them of how moved I was by their expressions of friendship!'

As the ships commenced their journey, two incidents seemed to announce
the difficulties that were in store: the *Naturaliste* ran aground in the harbour
(through no fault of her captain) and, shortly after, the expedition encountered
an English frigate that detained the two ships until they had examined their
passports. Even though everything turned out well, this second incident
reminds us of the background of rivalry between the English and the French,
particularly during the time of the French Revolution and Napoleon
Bonaparte's rise to power, and, on a more immediately practical level, of the
problems of keeping two vastly different ships together during a long and
difficult campaign. A storm that they successfully negotiated in the English
Channel convinced Baudin that both vessels handled well, but he noted that
the inferior speed of the *Naturaliste*, in spite of Captain Hamelin's best efforts
to compensate for it, would have 'extreme consequences'.

Nonetheless, progress towards their first port of call was rapid, which
brought happy relief to the many scientists suffering from sea sickness. They
were greatly cheered by their arrival at Tenerife, in the Canary Islands, on
2 November 1800 and enjoyed their time ashore, particularly in the beautiful
gardens of Orotava. The expedition was received by the Spanish authorities in
a most amicable manner, but it soon became apparent that the commander
would be frustrated in his plans to purchase wine supplies because of the
low stock of quality wine and the high prices. Although purchasing wine
was the principal reason for their stopover, Baudin decided to take on only a
small amount, along with some beer, and to move on to Mauritius. This
revised plan was in turn delayed by the late arrival of fresh supplies. In the
meantime, various incidents added to Baudin's sense of frustration. His head
gardener, Riédlé, was badly injured in a fall, a mishap which touched Baudin
personally but also caused him anxiety because of his friend's prime importance to the expedition. One of the *Géographe*'s cables was damaged by the
faulty manoeuvre of an English vessel and, more importantly, problems of

The *Géographe* and the *Naturaliste* at anchor, detail of an engraving by Pillement and Née from a drawing by Charles-Alexandre Lesueur. Published in the *Atlas* of the *Voyage de découvertes aux Terres Australes* (1807). Muséum d'histoire naturelle, Le Havre – n° 17 033

discipline affected morale. Baudin's impatience to depart increased daily: he had lost 11 precious days and derived no positive benefit from his stay, except for the gift of fresh supplies from another trusted friend, the Marquis of Nava, to whose Orotava gardens he had himself brought plants and seeds. Decidedly, it was the natural science connection that united him most closely with others.

On 14 November the expedition set out for Mauritius. This leg of the journey is often cited by Baudin's critics, beginning with François Péron, as evidence of his poor seamanship. Against this, three main points preserve Baudin's reputation. Firstly, Baudin took less time to reach the Cape of Good

Tenerife Woman, Nicolas-Martin Petit. Muséum d'histoire naturelle, Le Havre – n° 14 005. The notebook of zoologist Stanislas Levillain contains a description of this costume: 'A red or purple dress, a yellow veil, a hat and a parcel or bundle carried on the head form the costume generally adopted by women who come from the countryside to buy provisions at the markets. No distinction is made between young and old; all wear the same dress.'

Hope from Tenerife than his predecessor, d'Entrecasteaux, even though he was held back by the slow pace of the *Naturaliste*; secondly, his chosen route was similar to those taken by such English navigators as James Cook before him and Matthew Flinders after him, and his time to reach the equator compares favourably with theirs; thirdly, even though the expedition experienced strong currents and contrary winds, the main reason for Baudin's failure to respect the schedule set out for him was the time he was forced – against his will and through no fault of his own – to remain idle in the port of Tenerife and later in Mauritius.

It is true that the passage to Mauritius was long and tedious, but health on board was good and some memorable celebrations took place, including the ceremony of the crossing of the equator and a Christmas Eve binge when some of the crew drank a cask of wine belonging to the artist Lebrun. Baudin seems to have been more indulgent on such occasions than Hamelin, who refused to allow the men on the *Naturaliste* to celebrate the equator crossing, but both captains respected the practice of evening dances to keep the crew active and in good spirits.

The scientists were also kept busy, with Baudin reporting that 100 new specimens were taken on board by the time the ships reached the latitude of the Cape of Good Hope, and that Petit and Lesueur had completed many fine drawings of them. His own happiness with the achievements of the expedition was soon soured, however. A seemingly harmless compliment he paid to the young artists Petit and Lesueur offended one of the distinguished official artists, Milbert, who assumed from this that his own work was not valued by the captain. Baudin apparently explained to him in a kindly manner that no offence was intended, but it was perhaps already too late to recover his position with the official artist. Or indeed with anyone else. Baudin's mail was being read by mischief-makers who were attempting to discredit him. Baudin's friend Riédlé the gardener was touched when the commander attempted to defuse the situation by appealing to his men to cease their disruptive behaviour in the name of their glorious mission. The captain's appeal had little effect, however, and others on board recorded Baudin's speech in a completely negative manner. It was only too evident that the poisonous climate would prevail.

By the time the expedition anchored at Mauritius on 16 March 1801, the scene was set for numerous desertions. The stopover commenced pleasantly enough – the scientists took lodgings on shore while Baudin commenced his official round of visits and presented the list of supplies he needed. Before long, however, Baudin became aware of the unwillingness of the French colony's administrators to render him any assistance at all. After further negotiations, he was offered a meagre supply of wheat, but little else. He soon learned how to procure his provisions from other sources, in particular his friend the Danish consul. However, it took nearly a month before all supplies had been finally stowed and by then the desertions had commenced. No doubt existing problems had been aggravated by the commander's running battle with the colony's administrators, but it appears that certain colonists had also been actively encouraging the crew to desert. At this point began the real combat between the determined commander and those who wished to see his expedition come to a grinding halt.

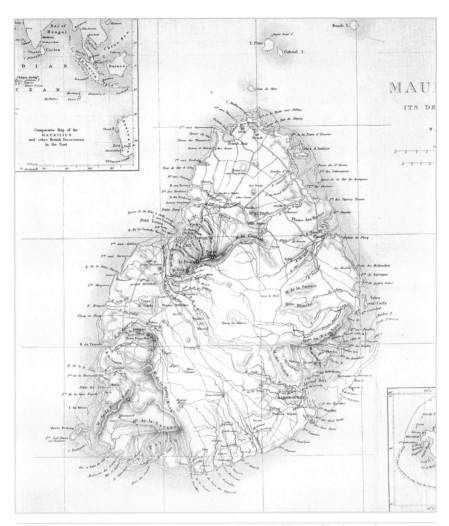

Map of *Ile de France* (Mauritius) by Flemying (1862). Royal Geographical Society of South Australia

Baudin's determination served him well. By holding hostage the Mauritians who had come to work on his ships, he eventually ensured that most of his deserters were returned or replaced. He was not so lucky with the officers and scientists, although perhaps he thought he was at the time. He was certainly glad to see many of them go, having so poor an opinion of their competence and usefulness. What should have been of greater concern – and what he could not know – was that two of the deserters, Gicquel and Bory de Saint-Vincent, would spread rumours of his own incompetence and that these mainly baseless rumours would prove difficult to dispel.

In the course of his earlier voyages, Baudin had endured difficult dealings with the colonists of Mauritius and it is possible that his troubles were due, at least in part, to these previous encounters. It is also certain that Gicquel and Bory de Saint-Vincent were malicious in their reporting of various incidents at sea. Besides, desertions affected the *Naturaliste* and the *Géographe* in a similar fashion, which means that Baudin's gruffness cannot be used as an all-encompassing argument to condemn him in comparison to the more genial Hamelin. In his letters to Jussieu and the Minister, Baudin shows restraint when he discusses the deserters or the behaviour of the administrators. At this stage in his journey, his relief at overcoming the obstacles he encountered was more palpable than any desire to justify himself at the expense of others. A lesser man, or the venal man that he was now said to be, would surely have given up. Perhaps even he would have done so if he had known that worse was to come.

To add to the list of his sins now being collected by his growing number of detractors – many of whom were attempting to escape the consequences of their own desertion – Baudin was about to depart from his strict orders. On leaving Mauritius on 25 April 1801, already slowed down by the delays suffered at two ports of call, he had decided to make for the western coast of New Holland instead of attempting to survey the coasts of Tasmania. This was perhaps Baudin's real error of judgment; but, then again, how could he suspect what its consequences would be? As he set his course for Cape Leeuwin, he was still unaware of the rival expedition that would shortly be bound for the same destination.

## *Matthew Flinders: Separations and Smooth Sailing*

In comparison with his French counterpart, Matthew Flinders was an unlikely seafarer. Not only his father but his grandfather too was a surgeon, and it was expected that young Matthew, who was born in 1774, would follow in their footsteps. He did, though, have an uncle, John Flinders, who had opted for a career at sea. Whether it was John's example which persuaded Matthew to join the Royal Navy at the age of 15 is unclear. If anything, John's experience might have proved cautionary, since, after nine years of service, he had still not achieved promotion to lieutenant.

If it was not John, then it might well have been a fictional character who proved decisive. In Daniel Defoe's *Robinson Crusoe*, a book Flinders knew from an early age, the hero resolves as a boy to go to sea against his father's vigorously stated commands and his mother's entreaties. The place they envisioned for him in life was the 'middle station', where one 'was not exposed to so many vicissitudes as the higher or lower part of mankind'. The thought of a life of mediocrity struck Flinders with horror, with the result that, having completed his education, at free school at his native Donington in Lincolnshire, and later at the Horbling grammar school, he sought a path into the navy. Little did he suspect that, like his fictional hero, his choice would lead him to spend a good part of his life, quite against his will, on an island far from home.

Like Robinson Crusoe, Flinders found a patron in the navy who cleared a path into it. Through a cousin, he gained an introduction to a naval captain by the name of Thomas Pasley, who tutored Flinders in the basics of navigation and mathematics, and then, impressed with his charge's talents, found him a position as a lieutenant's servant on HMS *Alert*. This was in the year of the French Revolution, 1789. In the following year, Pasley intervened again, taking Flinders into service on his own ship, the *Scipio*, before arranging a transfer to the *Bellerophon*, where he was promoted to midshipman.

Pasley again played the role of mentor in enabling Flinders, still just 17 years of age, to join an expedition under the command of Captain William Bligh. By that time, Bligh already had the experience of mutiny on the *Bounty* behind him. On this occasion, his mission was to transport breadfruit trees from the south Pacific to the West Indies. If Flinders' mind was still occupied with the fictional world of Robinson Crusoe, the expedition must have seemed deeply attractive. It would take him for the first time into the sorts of tropical waters where his hero had been stranded; it also gave him the opportunity to learn the art of seamanship from an acknowledged master. When Flinders returned to England on the *Providence* in August 1793, he had two further years of invaluable sailing and navigational experience behind him, and he had set foot in such far-flung places as Tahiti, St Helena, St Vincent's and Jamaica. Moreover, the voyage had given him the first sighting of the country which ultimately he was to name, since the *Providence* spent a short time charting part of the south-east coast of Van Diemen's Land.

The encounter with the South Seas, exoticised and romanticised in British art and literature, proved for Flinders an exciting experience. Although his relationship with the autocratic Bligh became strained, his appetite for further exploration and adventure knew no limits. A second voyage to the Pacific became his dream, though for a time war delayed its realisation. Flinders again turned to his patron, Thomas Pasley, who took him once more aboard the *Bellerophon*.

It was then, in 1794, that Flinders experienced his first and only naval battle – the so-called 'Glorious First of June', in which British forces delivered a crushing blow to the French Navy in the waters off Brest. The story has it that Flinders, serving at the time as Pasley's aide-de-camp, overrode Pasley's orders when he 'had a shot' at the French. Presumably any displeasure felt by his superiors was quickly dissipated in the glory of victory.

During his service on the *Bellerophon* Flinders became acquainted with Henry Waterhouse, fifth lieutenant aboard the ship. Waterhouse was promoted to commander of the *Reliance*, which received the task of transporting the newly appointed second governor of New South Wales, John Hunter, to his post. As good fortune and Pasley's blessing would have it, Flinders was able to apply for and gain the position of master's mate aboard the *Reliance*.

After his arrival in the troubled fledgling colony in September 1795, Flinders barely paused to take breath, immediately expressing a keen desire to explore the adjacent coast. His enthusiasm for the task was shared by a man whose acquaintance he had made aboard the *Reliance*, namely the ship's surgeon, George Bass. Like Flinders, the slightly older Bass was a native of Lincolnshire, and there was much else that they had in common. Bass, too, had joined the Royal Navy in 1789 enchanted by Robinson Crusoe and allured by the prospect of exploring the south seas. It was Bass who provided the boat in which the by now close friends could venture out through Sydney Heads to follow the coastline to the south. At just two-and-a-half metres, the *Tom Thumb* was not much longer than Bass was tall, and yet they were able to take with them Bass's servant, William Martin. In October 1795, just seven weeks after their arrival in Port Jackson on the *Reliance*, Bass, Flinders and Martin explored Botany Bay and the George's River, about which they delivered a favourable report to the new governor. In the following year, and after a tour of duty to Norfolk Island, the same threesome made a more ambitious voyage aboard a slightly larger *Tom Thumb* further down the coast, examining Port Hacking and reaching Lake Illawarra.

During this journey, Flinders made his first contact with Aborigines unaccustomed to Europeans. The *Tom Thumb* capsized and waves washed its drenched occupants, along with their provisions, onto the beach. After eventually beaching the boat on the banks of a small creek they set about drying their clothes and provisions. Soon, a number of Aborigines assembled, curious at the behaviour of the intruders. As Bass and Martin continued their work, Flinders amused the Aborigines, members of the Tharawal tribe, by clipping their hair and beards with a pair of scissors. The incident provided yet another demonstration of Flinders' resourcefulness.

After that journey, the ways of Bass and Flinders were provisionally parted. Bass made an unsuccessful attempt to cross the Blue Mountains, followed by a more fruitful expedition to find coal south of Port Jackson. Then Governor Hunter commissioned him to make a voyage further south than the two *Tom Thumb* expeditions had taken him, this time in a whaleboat crewed by six oarsmen. For three months from December 1797, Bass and his crew pressed south and then, following the line of the coast, west to Wilson's Promontory and Western Port. The strong westerly swell and the tides of the southern coast led Bass to surmise that he had entered a strait, and that the land mass that lay further south, still known then as Van Diemen's Land, must therefore be an island. But without the opportunity to circumnavigate the island, he lacked definitive proof.

Flinders, in the meantime, had travelled as a passenger aboard the schooner *Francis* to the Furneaux group of islands, off the north-east coast of Tasmania, to visit the wreck of the *Sydney Cove*, beached there in February 1797. Happily, he had been promoted to lieutenant, and by joining the *Francis* with the governor's permission he was able to refine further his navigational and charting skills. His account of the voyage, *Narrative of an Expedition to Furneaux Islands*, confirms his own view that the insularity of Van Diemen's Land was 'almost past conjecture'.

The chance to prove this hypothesis came later that year when, with the approval of Governor Hunter and the use of the Norfolk Island-built sloop *Norfolk*, Bass and Flinders sailed south with the clear intention of circumnavigating Van Diemen's Land. They reached Port Dalrymple on the north coast of the island in November 1798, then followed the coast west until eventually, as they had both expected, the coastline turned to the south. They reached the Derwent River just before Christmas of that year, before returning to Port Jackson.

For Bass, the voyage had been invaluable in allowing him to pursue his keen scientific interests. He observed some of the island's plants and animals in great detail, even employing his surgical skills to perform a dissection on a wombat. Governor Hunter's gratitude to the charismatic Bass for discovering a strait that would shorten voyages to Australia was so great that he named the strait after him. For Flinders, too, the expedition was enormously beneficial. It had been his first command, carried out without a hitch, and with a detailed narrative as well as an impressive set of charts to show for it.

Just as their shared success reached its pinnacle, the ways of Bass and Flinders parted for good. Now a proven navigator and explorer, Flinders was

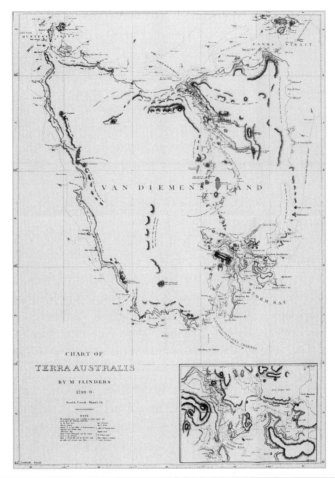

Map of Van Diemen's Land by Matthew Flinders (1798–1799). Published in *A Voyage to Terra Australis* (1814)

sent north by Governor Hunter to survey the coast of what is now Queensland, following it as far as Hervey Bay. Bass, in contrast, had few duties to perform in his official capacity as ship's surgeon on the *Reliance*. He resigned in order to undertake a more entrepreneurial activity that entailed supplying the colony with much needed goods. He returned to England to raise money for his venture only to find that, by the time he made his way back to New South Wales, shortages had given way to a glut; the bottom had fallen out of his potential market. Undaunted, he chose to pursue his business ideas by trading with South America but, after leaving Port Jackson in February 1803 bound for Chile, he was never heard of again.

In his own manner, Flinders was just as enterprising. He wished to pursue his explorations of the Australian coast, large parts of which remained uncharted or only very roughly charted. Governor Hunter was acutely aware of the practical and strategic benefits that might come from further exploration, whether by following the coast or by penetrating inland into a continent which still held its share of mystery for Europeans. But the resources of the colony were insufficient to underwrite the kind of wide-ranging exploratory work required; they would have to be found in England. The great hurdle to be cleared there was the fact that naval resources, in particular, were being stretched to the limit in war against post-revolutionary France. If assistance were to be gained, it would have to be from a person of influence who was able to look beyond the political and financial exigencies of the day.

That person was Joseph Banks. For Banks, of course, Terra Australis held special significance. He had travelled as botanist aboard the *Endeavour* when James Cook explored the east coast of New South Wales in 1770 and claimed it for Britain on his first great voyage (1768–1771). Thereafter, Banks had been one of the most vigorous proponents of Botany Bay as a site for a penal colony. With the establishment of the Port Jackson colony in 1788, Banks gradually cemented himself, as historian Sidney Baker puts it, as 'the great arbiter on all matters dealing with Terra Australis'. Moreover, as a result of the high regard in which his scientific work was held, Banks in 1778 accepted the respected and influential position of President of the Royal Society.

Sir Joseph Banks, hand-coloured stipple engraving by Antoine Cardor (1772–1813). Courtesy of the Royal Geographical Society of South Australia

There was another reason for the British Admiralty to pay heed to Banks's supplications for a naval exploratory expedition, and that was the sure knowledge that the French had already prepared such an expedition. That fact was well known, because the British had issued Baudin's expedition with a passport guaranteeing it safe passage in the event that it should encounter an armed British vessel. To that sure knowledge was added the fear that, aside from its scientific purpose, the French expedition might well have been allotted the corollary task of aiding in the establishment of a French settlement somewhere in the south. With that perturbing prospect in mind, the Admiralty even managed to exercise some haste in agreeing to Banks's proposal and

HMS *Investigator*, drawing by R.T. Sexton. Reproduced courtesy of the artist

setting the groundwork. Because of the state of war, naval vessels were at a premium, but a 334-ton sloop bearing the name *Xenophon* was identified as suitable for the task. Renamed the *Investigator*, to signify its scientific and hydrographic brief, it was prepared for sailing even before the end of 1800.

It is a measure of the influence of Banks and of the regard in which he was held that he received the responsibility of appointing an appropriate commander. His choice fell on the youthful shoulders of Matthew Flinders – a decision that had much to do with Flinders' own foresight and enterprise. Before leaving Port Jackson for England, Flinders was informed that Banks had plans for an exploratory expedition, and that he had Flinders in mind for the role of commander. When Flinders returned to England on the *Reliance* in 1800, his record spoke for itself: he had already carried out substantial exploratory and hydrographic work on the coast of New South Wales as far south as Van Diemen's Land, which to his great credit he had proved to be an island, and as far north as Hervey Bay. He had written narratives of his voyages, published charts and proven himself in many regards an exemplary leader. Beyond that, he had little hesitation in putting himself forward as the ideal leader of an exploratory expedition.

Immediately upon his arrival back in England, Flinders wrote perhaps the most important letter of his career. 'Presuming' to address Sir Joseph Banks, Flinders mounted the case for leading a circumnavigatory expedition of discovery back to the continent from which he had just returned.

It cannot be doubted, but that a very great part of that still extensive country remains either totally unknown, or has been partially examined at a time when navigation was much less advanced than at present. The interests of geography and natural history in general, and of the British nation in particular, seem to require, that this only remaining considerable part of the globe should be thoroughly explored. The brig *Lady Nelson* has lately been sent out partly with this view, as reported: but, if Sir Joseph Banks will excuse me, I presume she must be very inadequate to the task, as perhaps would any single vessel. A further knowledge of the strait between New Holland and New Guinea and of the south coast of the latter, are perhaps desiderata of importance, and might possibly be explored during the circumnavigation of New Holland without much loss of time . . .

If His Majesty should be so far desirous to have the discovery of New Holland completed, as to send out a vessel after the *Lady Nelson* proper for the execution of it, and the late discoveries in that country should so far meet approbation as to induce the execution of it to be committed to me, I should enter upon it with that zeal which I hope has hitherto characterised my services.

Flinders' enthusiasm for the idea apparently knew no bounds. He went on to offer to visit Sir Joseph at his residence in Soho Square to argue his case more fully.

Banks did not need much convincing. He had met his fellow Lincolnshireman Flinders on a number of occasions in 1793 and 1794 and gained a very favourable impression. When, in 1798, Banks proposed an inland exploratory expedition in New South Wales, to be carried out by the renowned African explorer Mungo Park, it was Flinders he put forward as the man to act as commander. That plan collapsed, but on receiving Flinders' missive a couple of years later, Banks wasted little time in replying. He told him that he could visit him at Soho Square any time he liked.

When Flinders was put in charge of the *Investigator* in January 1801, he was just 26 years of age. Like the Lords of Admiralty, who had urged the 'utmost dispatch', he was keen to expedite preparations and thereby keep the advantage of the French expedition to a minimum. For a combination of reasons, the process took much longer than anticipated; the months dragged by. The delay had at least one advantage for Flinders: on 17 April, he married Ann Chappelle. Given that the *Investigator*'s voyage was expected to be of at least three years' duration, the timing of the marriage seems odd. But Flinders had plans of his own – plans which, for reasons that soon became apparent, he chose to keep to himself. They involved, in effect, smuggling his new bride aboard the *Investigator* and taking her with him on the voyage, at least as far as Port Jackson, which would serve as a base while Flinders carried out his exploratory work. Even while the *Investigator* was still preparing to sail, Flinders took Ann on board, an incident that did not go unobserved.

All went awry, as perhaps was inevitable, when Banks himself got word of Flinders' indiscretion. Banks wrote a letter informing Flinders that he had read of his recent marriage in a Lincoln paper, and that he had been told of Mrs Flinders' presence aboard the *Investigator*. He proceeded to issue an unveiled threat that, if this contravention of Royal Navy regulations were to continue, then the displeasure of the Lords of the Admiralty would unavoidably be incurred. The necessary consequence for Flinders would be the loss of his newly won command even before he had managed to leave England's shores.

Flinders does not appear to have wasted much time in choosing between his wife and his great chance at glory. Soon after receiving Banks's letter, he responded:

> If their Lordships' sentiments should continue the same, whatever may be my disappointment, I shall give up the wife for the voyage of discovery; and I would beg of you Sir Joseph, to be assured that even this circumstance will not damp the ardour I feel to accomplish the important purpose of the present voyage, and in a way that shall preclude the necessity of anyone following after me to explore.

Before the expedition finally departed, a couple of other incidents might also have served to scratch the previously unsullied image of Flinders. When Flinders sailed the *Investigator* from the Nore, at the mouth of the Thames, to Spithead (near Portsmouth) in preparation for departure, he ran it aground in Hythe Bay off the coast of Kent. Fortunately no damage was done, but he felt obliged to report the accident. His excuse that the charts with which he had been provided were outdated and inaccurate was plausible and duly accepted. There followed the desertion of a small number of crewmen and the flight of a prisoner entrusted to Flinders' care, for which he was able to offer similarly credible excuses. But for Banks, there was just one simple explanation: the indiscipline caused by the presence of the captain's wife.

When the *Investigator* finally received its French passport, guaranteeing it the same free passage that the English had guaranteed Baudin and his ships, and when its master, John Thistle, finally became available, Flinders could depart at last. The *Investigator* sailed on 18 July 1801, giving the French expedition a headstart of nine months. Ann Flinders might well have been sorely missed, but Matthew was not entirely deprived of the company of family. His younger brother, Samuel, was also aboard. Samuel would play an important role in the expedition's scientific and hydrographic work, though not always with the level of dedication and commitment his brother expected.

Joseph Banks was in very large part responsible for the presence of the eminent naturalist Robert Brown. In his botanising exploits, Brown was to be assisted by the similarly eminent, Austrian-born botanical draughtsman, Ferdinand Bauer, and by the appropriately named gardener, Peter Good. Completing the complement of those whom Flinders often referred to as 'the scientific gentlemen' was the miner, John Allen, and the astronomer, John Crosley, though the latter was to leave the expedition in Cape Town. The official landscape artist for the voyage was William Westall. Aged just 19 at the time, he was a gamble, since, although clearly gifted, he was a mere probationary student at the Royal Academy when offered the opportunity of a lifetime. Indeed, it would eventually become apparent that Westall did not always find the barren shores of Terra Australis to his liking. Beyond these nonnaval 'supernumeraries' there were altogether 83 men, including 15 marines.

If the mishap in Hythe Bay might have raised some concerns about Flinders' abilities, they were put to rest on the voyage south. The ship reached the Portuguese island of Madeira, to the west of Morocco, without incident and reprovisioned as planned. Thereafter, it pressed further south, crossing the equator on 8 September – an event that Flinders allowed to be celebrated with the long established antics of the crossing-the-line ceremony. The Cape of Good Hope was reached, to Flinders' immense satisfaction, 'without having a single man on the sick list.'

The journey did, however, raise concerns of a different kind. Although the *Investigator* moved well enough, it became apparent alarmingly early in the piece that she leaked badly. A leak below the waterline meant frequent deployment of her pumps from then until her eventual abandonment. Contemplating the inevitable rigours of the voyage ahead, Flinders noted with understandable trepidation that the leakiness 'indicated a degree of weakness which in a ship destined to encounter every hazard could not be contemplated without uneasiness.' The trepidation was fully justified, since the leaks were to present him with ongoing dilemmas. For the time being, though, the best that could be done was to give the vessel a thorough caulking during the scheduled visit to Cape Town. Thereafter, the run east in favourable conditions across the Indian Ocean to the New Holland coast was smooth, giving an overall time for the voyage there of 142 days – in contrast with the 220 days taken by the French to reach their destination. The signs now pointed to a race to the unknown south coast that would be closer run than first thought.

# chapter two

# CHARTING THE WESTERN COAST

*Baudin from Cape Leeuwin to the Bonaparte*
*Archipelago, 27 May to 19 August 1801*

By the beginning of the nineteenth century, the western coast of Australia was by no means unknown territory for European sailors. From the early part of the seventeenth century, many Dutch ships had sailed directly to the east across the Indian Ocean after rounding the Cape of Good Hope on their way to the Dutch East Indies. Some of them, though, were blown so far to the east that they sighted and occasionally made landings on the coast of what the Dutch called New Holland.

Typically, the ships would then head north to their destination. Such was the case, for example, with the voyage undertaken by Frederick de Houtman in 1619. He initially sighted land in the south-west of the continent near modern-day Bunbury before proceeding north to Rottnest Island, Houtman Abrolhos and eventually Java. Similarly, just three years later, the *Leeuwin* sighted land in the far south-west near the cape to which it gave its name. As its predecessors had done, it then turned north. But when one Dutch ship, the *Gulden Zeepaard*, arrived on the southern coast of western Australia in 1627, its captain decided to take a different route. Instead of turning to the north, François Thijssen chose to head south and east. After rounding the south-western corner of the continent he followed the line of the coast for some 1500 kilometres. There he reached a group of islands that to this day bears the name Nuyts Archipelago, after Pieter Nuyts, a member of the Council of India who happened to be on board the ship. At that point, just south-east of where Ceduna now stands, the *Gulden Zeepaard* departed from the coast, so that everything to the east remained unknown to Europeans until the *Investigator* arrived nearly two centuries later.

Before then, the western coast of Australia had become known to British navigators as well. William Dampier, a British buccaneer-cum-scientist, landed in the north-west in 1688 on board the *Cygnet*. While the ship was careened, Dampier took the opportunity to make observations on the natural history of the continent and the people he encountered there. In the account of his journey, *A New Voyage Round the World*, he famously described the Aborigines as the 'miserablest people in the world'. The arid sandhills and lowlands he found equally lamentable. Eleven years later, and with the respectability of the command of a British exploratory expedition conferred upon him, he returned with the *Roebuck*. This time his landfall in Shark Bay lasted about five weeks before water shortages forced him north to Timor, his dim view of the coast apparently unchanged. A century later, in 1791, Dampier's countryman George Vancouver followed him to the western coast. Unlike Dampier, Vancouver's focus was on the south, where he explored and named King George Sound and its extensions, Princess Royal Harbour and Oyster Harbour. He then followed in the wake of the *Gulden Zeepaard* along the southern coast to the east as far as Termination Island, at which point he sailed south past Tasmania on his way to New Zealand.

As for the French, they too had some direct knowledge of these shores. Like the Dutch and the British before them, they had found them sadly inhospitable. A ship under the command of Louis François Marie Alesno de St Allouarn left Mauritius in early 1772 in search of the fabled continent of 'Australasie'. Despite separation from its consort, the *Gros Ventre* struck boldly to the east, sighting Cape Leeuwin in March and then following the coast north to Shark Bay. On Dirk Hartog Island, St Allouarn took possession of the land in the name of the French king. Whatever glory might have attached to this act proved short-lived, however – St Allouarn died soon after his return to Mauritius. The next French expedition to western Australian waters pursued quite a different goal. Commanded by Rear Admiral Bruni d'Entrecasteaux, it set sail in September 1791 in search of a lost maritime hero. Unfortunately, La Pérouse, the hero in question, eluded d'Entrecasteaux, who could not have known that his countryman had long since come to grief on the island of Vanikoro north of Vanuatu; but the rescue expedition did make its way along the south-western coast of the Australian continent in early 1793, until lack of water persuaded d'Entrecasteaux to leave the coast for Recherche Bay in Tasmania.

When Baudin and Flinders arrived in western Australian waters in 1801, they were well armed with the charts of those who had gone before them – Dutch, British and French. But those charts were in large parts patchy and unreliable, put together with the aid of unsophisticated and by now outmoded navigational equipment. The task of charting such an immense stretch of coastline to the north and to the east was huge. Moreover, an array of flora and fauna with which previous visitors had made only the most fleeting and pro-visional acquaintance awaited the expeditions' scientists who, after the long voyage, were straining at their leads to commence their work on dry ground. There was much to be done.

———————

The Baudin expedition arrived on the Australian continent first, in May 1801, after a relatively swift and uneventful crossing from Mauritius. Tension still reigned on board the *Géographe*, where the scientists and officers had been unsettled by the desertions and by the climate of intrigue that had marked their five-week stay in the French colony. They also remained aggrieved by what they claimed to be an unfair distribution of provisions. The long shore delays experienced at different points of the journey, including a 17-day hold up in Le Havre prior to departure, had caused the expedition to fall signifi-cantly behind schedule. The advanced season and the prevailing southerlies would, according to Baudin, make it difficult to proceed directly to his survey of Tasmania. He consequently decided to depart from the plan set out for him by Count Fleurieu – the former Minister of Marine who, as member of the Commission of the Institute of France, had drawn up the itinerary for the expedition – and to make for Cape Leeuwin, putting off his explorations of Van Diemen's Land and of the southern coast of New Holland until after the winter months had passed.

At eight o'clock on the morning of 27 May 1801, Terra Australis finally came into view.

## 27 MAY 1801

The first sight we had of the land corresponds exactly to the coloured drawing that I have had made of it, and any ship making landfall in the same latitude we did will recognise it without difficulty. The southern part of Cape Leeuwin, when seen from a distance, presents a fairly uniform coastline and appears from nine or ten leagues out to form several islands, or indentations at least, the depth of which cannot be seen.

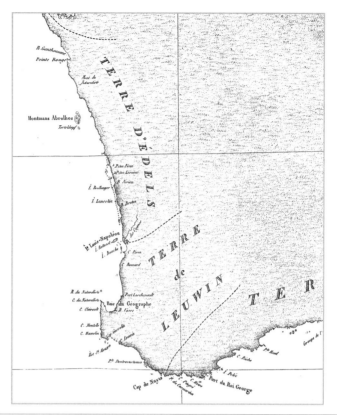

*Terre de Leeuwin* (Leeuwin's Land), detail of the French map of New Holland (1804). Published in the *Atlas* of the *Voyage de découvertes aux Terres Australes* (1811)

Over the next three days, Baudin and his scientists continued their careful observations of the land, with a special eye to any natural resources it might offer and to signs of any human presence.

## 29 MAY 1801

While we were sailing along the coast, the astronomers and geographers kept themselves busy taking angles and bearings for the map they were making. I think this work will be well done, judging from the pains they took with it and our short distance from the shore.

All of the countryside we have inspected looked arid to us. As for the coastal land nearest to us, the most prominent hills were covered mainly by a type of heath that did not grow to any great height. From time to time we could make out a few plateaux with trees of a rather lovely green, which only made the treeless parts more unpleasant to look at. One of the things that most

Coastal profiles of Cape Leeuwin, Charles-Alexandre Lesueur or Nicolas-Martin Petit. The coastal profiles are most likely the work of Petit, though some plates are signed by Lesueur. This set of profiles is from Baudin's personal journal. French National Archives, Paris

struck me was that, along the quite considerable stretch of land that we had so closely examined, we could see no ravine that appeared to offer an outlet for water flowing into the sea.

The mountains (for there are many that bear the name without being high enough) did not extend far inland and came down to the sea in what seemed to us a rather gentle slope; along the shoreline, as I have already said, sheer cliffs made the coast inaccessible . . .

We had thought for some time that this coast was deserted, but we did not take long to find proof to the contrary, for at night we noticed fires in various places which showed that it was not uninhabited.

Baudin notes that the naturalists, in particular the botanists, were most anxious to make their way to shore to pursue their study at closer quarters. To their regret, however, no safe anchorage could be found.

If, during the day, I had noticed a few places that were suitable for taking ships into, I would have made sure I returned the next day. But apart from the fact that there is no anchorage, the bottom is foul. Almost everywhere, we have found nothing but sand mixed with large corals, or a hard bottom of pure coral and rock . . .

I do not know if the coast we have just examined can offer anything of interest to Natural History, since we made no landing at all. But what does at least appear rather extraordinary to me is that not a single land-bird has dropped in on us. And the only sea-birds we have encountered have been two Cape pigeons, which is almost sufficient indication of the aridity of the land and of the few resources that the sea can offer these creatures.

A most pleasant surprise awaited the expedition, however, on the morning of 30 May. Following the coast north from Cape Leeuwin, they came to another large cape – later to be named Cape Naturaliste. Upon rounding this, they found that the coast, instead of continuing northwards, cut back towards the south-east. They had made their first significant discovery: Geographe Bay, so named by Baudin to commemorate his ship. Moreover, it was to offer them several safe anchoring points and so the opportunity to set foot on the continent for the first time.

## 30 MAY 1801

As we approached the land, we saw two sandy coves in which the sea appeared fairly calm; it was in the more easterly one that I anchored in 23 fathoms on a bottom of fine sand mixed with a little clay, no more than 4 miles off the coast. The *Naturaliste* being a long way to leeward of us, but easily able to see our manoeuvre since it was still light, I was not concerned about the one she would make to come and join us. And indeed, at eight o'clock, she dropped anchor abeam of us.

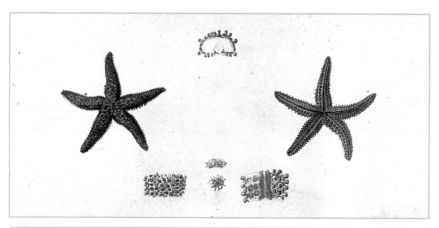

Starfish, *Uniophora aff. granifera* (Lamarck, 1816), Charles-Alexandre Lesueur. Muséum d'histoire naturelle, Le Havre – n° 74 048

As soon as I was at anchor, I sent my dinghy out to sound all round the ship, and, even a fairly long way off, all of the soundings it took indicated an excellent bottom, so I had no fears for my anchor. When this was done, not wanting to spend a night doing nothing, I sent the dinghy out to put down the dredge about 250 fathoms [sic] from the ship. We were not very lucky, however, making a rather curious catch: a sea-urchin, star-fish and plants.

During the night we got a dinghy ready to depart before dawn the following day in order to go reconnoitring on shore. I put Citizen Freycinet

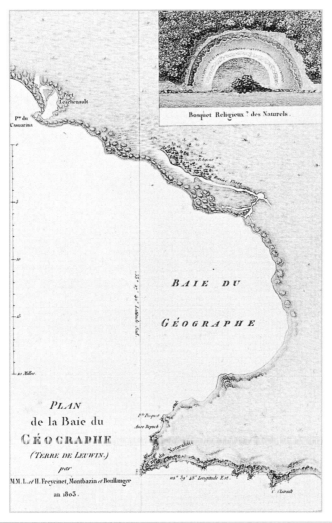

*Map of Geographe Bay*, L. & H. Freycinet, Montbazin and Boullanger (1803). Inset: Aboriginal ceremonial ground (possibly a sacred grove). Published in the *Atlas* of the *Voyage de découvertes aux Terres Australes* (1811)

in command of it. All the scientists wanted to go with him, but as the boat could take only eight men in all, there were some dissatisfied customers, as will often be the case on such occasions in the future. Riédlé, the gardener, and Depuch, the mineralogist, were the only ones chosen to go ashore; one to give us an idea of the land and the other to determine the nature of the soil, in an area that looked much nicer than the parts we had sighted up till now.

The shore party accomplished its mission without incident and the reports produced for their captain by Henri Freycinet, Riédlé and Depuch bear witness to their scientific zeal and alertness to detail. Depuch ends his report with a number of keen observations on the native flora and fauna:

– In several places I noticed what looked like rabbit burrows. Several of them seemed to me to have been freshly dug. I looked carefully to see if I could see any foot-prints but there were no traces of any in the fine soil.
– On the beach, however, there were definite prints of a cloven hoof. We found large numbers of droppings everywhere; they are in differing stages of freshness and have the consistency and shape of horse-dung. At their largest, they are barely an inch, or even three quarters of an inch long.
– A type of tree that I can compare to nothing better than the screw-pine of Ile de France [Mauritius], although the leaves are not nearly so wide, contains a resin of a very pleasant reddish-yellow colour that gives off a nasty smell when burning. This tree and several other full-grown resinous trees seem to have been burnt by a fire of some violence. Was it started by the heat of summer?
– Finally, Commander, I saw nothing to make me suspect that the district was inhabited by anything other than animals.

Several other shore parties were organised in Geographe Bay. One of these, which included the zoologist Péron and the botanist Leschenault, caused Baudin anxiety and frustration, since it was considerably overdue in returning – partly because of some poor seamanship, according to Baudin, and more particularly because Péron, having gone off exploring by himself, over-stayed his visit (a scenario that would be repeated on several occasions over the course of the voyage).

The excursion led by Baudin himself, however, also on 4 June, proved fruitful: in addition to the observations made by the astronomer and the geographer, numerous specimens were collected, including some samples of animal excrement that aroused much curiosity and speculation. Most notably,

Baudin's shore party was the first to encounter one of the native inhabitants from the local Wardandi tribe – a 'very old man', thought Baudin, 'judging by the colour of his beard, which was very long and grey.' Their approach interrupted his spear fishing and, much to Baudin's disappointment, he beat a hasty retreat over the sand dunes and into the nearby bushland. This excursion lasted for three hours, at the end of which various fruit and vegetable seeds were planted in the plain behind the dunes, in order to provide 'additional sustenance for the individuals in this part of New Holland, whose existence seemed very miserable to me'.

On that same day the captain of the *Naturaliste*, Hamelin, had sent a small crew led by Sub-Lieutenant Heirisson to examine the coast further south of their anchorage. Heirisson discovered by chance what he believed to be a large river, but which the impending night-fall had not permitted him to explore at any length. Acting on Heirisson's report, which had 'inflamed the imagination' of the naturalists, but whose importance he also immediately understood, Baudin ordered that a more substantial excursion be organised. To be led by Hamelin, it was to comprise two of the smaller boats from the *Naturaliste* and Baudin's own longboat with Commander Le Bas de Sainte Croix in charge. Along with 19 men, the longboat took a good store of provisions. Furthermore, 'as this expedition could be delicate and even dangerous, since I was certain that there was no lack of natives in the vicinity', Baudin ensured that it was well armed.

This ill-fated excursion began, naturally enough, in high spirits, with the naturalists so impatient to get to shore that they set off well before daybreak, at three o'clock. The day passed uneventfully for those on board the *Géographe*, the major preoccupation being the accuracy of the measurements of longitude and latitude that the captain had ordered. Then, towards sunset, Baudin caught sight of the sails of the shore party's boats and presumed that they were returning early. Sadly this was not the case and by the end of the next day, with strong northerlies and rough seas prevailing, Baudin had become anxious. When the mineralogist Bailly and later Hamelin himself finally brought news, it was far from reassuring.

## 6 JUNE 1801

Around four o'clock in the afternoon the *Naturaliste*'s boat, which had come back to the ship during the night, came across to the *Géographe*; the mineralogist who was in it and who had gone ashore the day before reported to me that what had been mistaken for a river was little more than a lagoon into which the sea-water flowed. He confirmed that he had been to the mouth, which is barred by a number of wooden stakes that the natives place across the opening to catch fish brought in by the rising tide. He had considered this place of so little importance that he had not wanted to wait there for his companions to return. He added that some of those who were ashore had communicated with the natives of the region, and particularly with a woman who was pregnant and aged about forty. According to his report, our people apparently did not cause her any alarm and she waited most patiently for them at the place where she had stopped. The same was not true of a man accompanying her, who took to his heels. They gave this woman various presents which she appeared to like very much and they noticed that she set more value on a small mirror than on all the other things offered to her.

From the report that the *Naturaliste*'s mineralogist had just given me, I found it difficult to imagine why my longboat was so late returning. The only plausible reason was that M. Le Bas de Sainte Croix, whom I had put in command, had allowed himself to be led astray by the smooth talk of the naturalists who were with him; and that, taking no account of his situation, and being uncertain of the ship's whereabouts, he had let himself be won over, with no thought of the consequences, and given them more time than he should. In line with this conviction, I made a solemn vow that such a thing would never happen again and, whether these gentlemen like it or not, that's too bad: they shall not go ashore again, except when the ship is no longer in danger of being driven out to sea and when they themselves are in no danger of being wrecked and abandoned on a deserted, unknown shore . . .

At half past nine at night, with the wind having moderated considerably, M. Hamelin came aboard. He had been at sea for about twenty-two [hours] in his dinghy with four men. When the wind was at its strongest – from eight in the morning until four in the afternoon – he had spent the whole time at anchor on his grapnel, in danger of being swamped a thousand times over. The waves broke over them with such violence that he could do nothing but keep bailing out the water that came in. He told me that my longboat had been stranded on the beach, but did not know precisely how this accident had occurred. This news struck like a thunderbolt, when I considered the plight of those who had been on board. Before leaving his travelling companions, M. Hamelin had given them all the arms and ammunition he had, so that they would be in a better position to defend themselves. They still had two days' supplies with them. We agreed to send out his large boat and mine at four in the morning in order to transport to the place he had indicated all that was needed to refloat the longboat, and, at the very least, to bring back the men on shore, if we had to abandon it. After ten o'clock the winds had changed to east and the sky was fairly clear, but in the middle of the night the winds changed to south-west and then to north and a stiff breeze blew again. It would be difficult to convey all that I suffered when I saw that it would be impossible for me to send any help the next day to the men in my longboat; I imagined that they were perhaps already in the hands of the natives of the region, who, upon seeing their distress, would surely have tried something.

The next day, notwithstanding the strong winds, Baudin approached the coast and sent one of his boats to see if contact could be made with the shore party. This boat also carried with it a rather terse note addressed to Le Bas, expressing the captain's displeasure and giving orders to try to save the long-boat, but only if this could be done without further risk. Finally, around mid-afternoon, several figures were seen on the beach. This was good news in one sense, but not enough to quell Baudin's fears or solve the mystery of why they had not previously responded to the signal rockets in order to make their presence known. Had some grave misfortune befallen them? Or was Baudin to put their conduct down, as he says, to 'carelessness and apathy'? At last, at half past seven, an answering rocket was fired from the shore and Baudin was afforded some peace of mind – but for a short time only.

## 7 JUNE 1801

At nine o'clock at night my boat returned, bringing only Citizen Péron, who was more dead than alive and who had been forced to swim to the boat, which had not been able to reach the shore. Citizen Le Bas would not allow the other naturalists to embark on the pretext that he needed them to help him refloat the longboat. But I think that it was perhaps to keep up numbers and make a stronger impression on the natives in case they decided to try anything.

On the following day, with the barometer falling and Baudin's agitation mounting, all of the men in the shore party were finally brought back on board. Quite apart from the loss of the longboat, along with some precious equipment, the excursion had also proved to be a scientific disaster: not only had Heirisson's 'river' turned out to be nothing but a lagoon, but none of the specimens collected by the naturalists could be saved.

## 8 JUNE 1801

At last [my boat] returned about four o'clock with all my men. But, in order to get them all on board, they had had to leave everything else behind, so that, quite apart from my longboat, which was completely equipped and rigged, I lost all the gear that had been requested in the hope of refloating it. Almost all the objects that the naturalists had collected and assembled while on shore suffered the same fate and, in this regard, Riédlé fared worse than the others; apart from the boxes he had left on the shore, he lost the tin box in which he had placed the most precious things he had; as he was climbing into the *Naturaliste*'s boat, a wave washed over his head and carried it off.

As soon as M. Le Bas de Sainte Croix came aboard, he did not fail to come and apologise for the accident that had befallen him, continuing to insist that it was no one's fault and that if the sea had not been so rough he would have saved the longboat. I listened to his excuses without replying, for his condition did not permit me to reproach him in the manner he deserved.

Worse news was yet to come, however, as Baudin was to be denied even the satisfaction of having at least saved all his men.

Given that the boat was empty, I had it hauled on board, but my worries were not yet over, for the *Naturaliste* still had two boats ashore: her large dinghy, which I had sent out so that mine should be less encumbered, and her small one, which I had seen going ashore in the morning with one of her officers . . . By eight o'clock they had still not appeared, although every quarter of an hour we lit very bright port-fires to indicate the ship's position to them and the *Naturaliste* sent up rockets now and then.

Finally, between half past eight and nine, they both arrived. M. Milius, who was in the small boat, told me that, having gone to the place where the longboat was, to see if he could be of some use, he had found nobody there; but, upon seeing many of our belongings on the beach, he had attempted to salvage some of them and this attempt had cost the life of one of his helmsmen, who was carried away by a wave and drowned. The fear of endangering his other men made him abandon any further attempts. Without this calamity, I could at least have been consoled in my misfortune by the fact that no one had been a casualty of the rashness of two officers. But this happiness was not for me and, by a remarkable stroke of fate, it so happened that he who least deserved to be struck down should become its victim.

Baudin was not to be allowed to dwell on the tragic loss of Timothée Vasse: gale force winds from the north, 'without doubt the worst weather we had had since leaving France', kept him busy on a night in which he was also to lose contact with the *Naturaliste*, not to be seen again until more than three months later, in Timor.

Contrary winds forced Baudin out to sea over the next few days, though he was able to re-enter Geographe Bay from time to time to continue his survey of the coast. The first rendezvous point in case of separation of the two ships was Rottnest Island, and Baudin, having achieved all that he could in Geographe Bay, decided to head north in the hope that he would soon be reunited with his consort.

## 15 JUNE 1801

While sailing along the coast in the evening, we found ourselves abeam of a large bay, whose northern tip no doubt ends in the headland that must form the entrance to the Swan River. We were only 5 or 6 leagues away, according

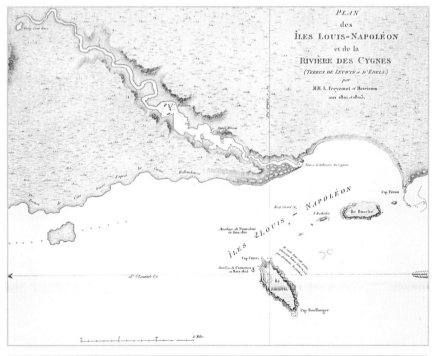

*Plan des Iles Louis-Napoléon et de la Rivière des Cygnes* (Rottnest and Garden Islands and the Swan River), L. Freycinet and Heirisson (1801, 1803). Published in the *Atlas* of the *Voyage de découvertes aux Terres Australes* (1811)

to our calculation of the distance covered since midday and the observation we made of our latitude at that time. But we had no hope of seeing it in the short term, for we had to turn back the moment the weather permitted in order to inspect the coast that we had just gone past, as we had not been able to determine its bearings and tortuous outline.

### 18 JUNE 1801

According to the latitude observed at midday, we were not very far from Rottnest Island; I even think that our sighting of it was accurate because, at about two o'clock, we could make out land that seemed separate from the continent and lay 6 to 7 leagues to the north-east. This land looked higher to us than any we had seen till now, but the weather was too unsettled to allow us closer access. I thus went on the other tack so that I would have no trouble rounding before nightfall the headland of a rather deep bay on our beam, the northern tip of which no doubt ends near Rottnest Island and perhaps forms the entrance to the Swan River. Although we were then fairly close to the coast, which was on our beam, the depth continually increased from 25 to 30 fathoms, with a bottom of greyish, and sometimes red, sand.

Unfortunately, the persistent bad weather drove the *Géographe* out to sea, where it remained battling the adverse conditions for some time.

During the night of the 29th to the 30th [Prairial – 18–19 June] the weather was extremely bad. A howling gale blew until midnight, at which time the winds changed to south-east and the rain began to pelt down, accompanied by thunder and lightning, as if the elements were in torment . . . As we wore ship, we rang the bell, and the entire crew was immediately ready for action. Even though we were at the height of a squall, the manoeuvre was quickly executed and I am pleased to give the crew the recognition it deserves on this occasion.

In the face of such unfavourable weather, Baudin decided to sail further north to the second rendezvous point in the sheltered conditions of Shark Bay – a decision that was to draw criticism from Péron and later commentators (the *Naturaliste*, as it happened, was anchored in wait off the north-east tip of Rottnest Island), although it appears to have attracted little or no adverse comment from any of the others on board, judging by the accounts they have left.

## 19 JUNE 1801

At eight o'clock, seeing no sign of a change in the weather, I decided to head north-west by north in order to reach a latitude that was more suitable for navigation and for our work, reserving the possibility of coming back from north to south, and returning to the tasks that I was abandoning, in the event the weather eased up.

Despite this sense of unfinished business, Baudin's summing up of the sojourn in Geographe Bay testifies to the importance and the diversity of the expedition's accomplishments there:

On the 7th [Prairial – 27 May] we had sighted land and on the 8th had started taking bearings of it, from both far out and close in, and had continued to do so until the evening of the 29th [18 June]. However, the bad weather had not allowed us to do much good work up till then; except for the stretch of coast between the western point of Leeuwin Land and the point forming the entrance to the beautiful bay that I have called Geographe Bay, all the rest is represented by rough, incomplete drafts, which the slightest amount of fine weather would have enabled us to complete in two days, if we had been fortunate enough to have them. It was this expectation, and the fact that little remained to be done, that had persuaded me to stay there until this point and to endure all the foul weather to which we were exposed. This weather twice chased us from the bay and caused us to drift south of Cape Leeuwin, so that for 23 days we did nothing but beat about gunwhale under so as to claw off from the coast on to which the winds continuously drove us whenever we went in close enough to examine it thoroughly.

Our four anchorages in the bay provided us with some quite interesting details on the quality of the soil, the lie of a section of the coastline, the population occupying it and the resources that navigators can find in terms of timber, fishing and hunting. But they must not expect to find water in any shape or form, and what may occur through seepage, if you dig for it, is only a very poor resource. However, anchorage in Geographe Bay is good and solid everywhere . . .

It is with regret that I leave a place which must be extremely pleasant during the good season and where, while we went about our geographical work, we collected in our dredge a large number of Natural History specimens, some absolutely new to science. But since I am determined to come back this way at some point to complete the exploration of this coast, I shall have another chance to get the best I possibly can out of it.

## SPECIFIC REMARKS

Our landfall off the cape or point of Leeuwin Land took place during the finest weather you could imagine, day or night. The winds from both on and off shore seemed essentially regular and even. In the morning they were generally from the east, varying to north, and in the afternoon they almost always came from south to south-east, where they remained for most of the night. During that time the breezes were moderate and very pleasant. The sky was almost always clear and the nights were moonlit. This fine weather accompanied us as far as Geographe Bay, where we enjoyed it for a few more days. But during the last quarter of the moon the weather changed completely and, from the time we were forced to leave the bay, we had a period of bad weather that lasted longer than the good weather had done, with scarcely a fine day from 16 Prairial to 1 Messidor [5–20 June], when I made the decision to head north . . .

During our stay in Geographe Bay we found few resources. Fish were very rare, but whales, on the other hand, were very common. Likewise, we saw no more than one or two turtles. The land does not appear to provide much in the way of food for the natives, who seemed to obtain it mainly from the sea. Nowhere we went did we find a single tree bearing edible fruit or a single vegetable plant. The only food that we found was some wild celery and a type of purslane,* but the second was not as good as the first.

On 23 June, with night about to fall, Baudin prudently decided against entering Shark Bay through the channel to the south of Dorre Island, as Dirk Hartog had done in 1699, preferring instead to sail north and make his way round the northern tip of Bernier Island.

## 26 JUNE 1801

The northern entrance to Shark Bay is easy to recognise. At the mouth of the bay the land is high with steep cliffs. The Dutch chart gives a very accurate and well-drawn view of it. Of all our maps, it is the most accurate and the best done. It seems that the Dutch were most painstaking in the bearings they took of this whole coastline, which they may very well have designs on for whaling – the only resource it has to offer. Those creatures are so plentiful here that they often get in the way, and sometimes they come in so close that they put the boats in danger. Also, when you are tacking in the bay they are a constant problem; the enormous masses of water that they stirred up made them look like reefs, with waves breaking violently over them.

---

* A fleshy-leaved trailing plant with small yellow flowers; can be eaten in salads.

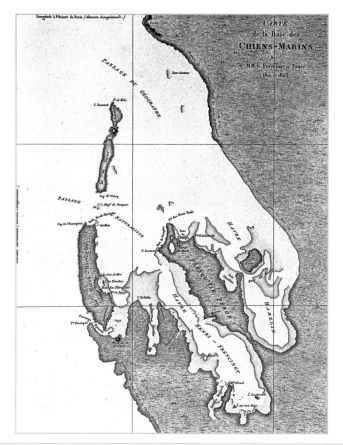

*Carte de la Baie des Chiens-Marins* (Shark Bay), L. Freycinet and Faure (1801, 1803). Published in the *Atlas* of the *Voyage de découvertes aux Terres Australes* (1811)

The *Géographe* spent two weeks in Shark Bay, anchored for the most part off the northern tip of Bernier Island. During this time, numerous shore parties were organised to visit the island (though none to the mainland), affording the crew some respite and providing the naturalists with a rich source of material for collection and observation.

## 28 JUNE 1801

On the morning of the 9th [Messidor] Citizen Bonnefoi, to whom I had given the command of my dinghy to survey the coast, told me that he had had no trouble landing in two accessible coves. I immediately had the large and small dinghies manned, and all the naturalists got in. The gardener, who had accompanied Bonnefoi the day before, had brought back two packets of

Striped wallaby (Shark Bay), *Lagostrophus fasciatus* (Péron and Lesueur, 1807), Nicolas-Martin Petit. Muséum d'histoire naturelle, Le Havre – n° 80 055

Bird of the Meliphagidae family (Western Australia), *Meliphaga virescens* (Vieillot, 1817), Charles-Alexandre Lesueur. Muséum d'histoire naturelle, Le Havre – n° 79 007

various plants he had collected by moonlight and that he thought to be quite new, which meant that, even after spending the greater part of the night ashore, he was keen to go back . . .

When we left, the sky was clear and the wind was calm. We took two hours to reach land because there were oarsmen in the boats whom we had not chosen and who were unable to row. About eleven o'clock the sky clouded over, although it did not look threatening. I was all the more annoyed by this, in that it would prevent me from observing the latitude on shore and taking hour-angles there. But the others were delighted, for they considered this weather better for the fishing and hunting expeditions they all planned to engage in . . .

The gardener and the other naturalists went further inland to examine the island's natural resources. Maugé and I went chasing after birds. Everybody had orders to be back on the beach by five o'clock at the latest so that we could dine before returning to the ship.

Our various excursions into the island's interior gave us 12 or 15 new species of plants, two very handsome lizards and seven birds, two of which are particularly remarkable for the beauty of their plumage. We also saw some kangaroos. I even fired a shot at one, but probably only frightened it, for after being hit it made off faster than ever . . .

Upon returning to the beach, we were pleased to see that the boatmen had caught about a hundred fish. Amongst them were some that were very pretty

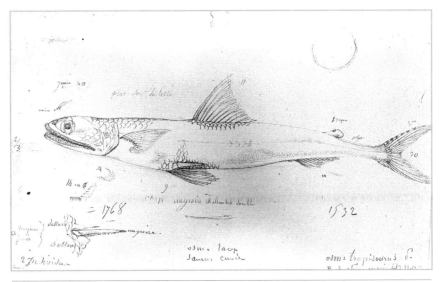

Fish of the Synodontidae family drawn from a specimen caught in Shark Bay, *Saurida undosquamis* (Richardson, 1848). Charles-Alexandre Lesueur. Muséum d'histoire naturelle, Le Havre – n° 76 188

Front view of a fish of the Scorpaenidae family (found in the northern half of Australia, down to Rottnest Island), *Pterois volitans* (Linnaeus, 1758). Charles-Alexandre Lesueur. Muséum d'histoire naturelle, Le Havre – n° 76 320

Left profile of *Pterois volitans* (Linnaeus, 1758). Charles-Alexandre Lesueur. Muséum d'histoire naturelle, Le Havre – n° 76 321

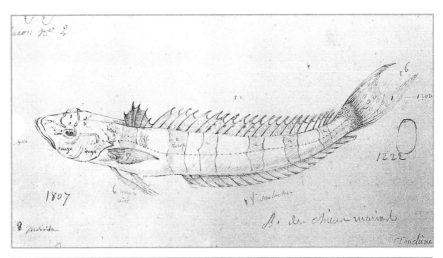

Fish of the Mugiloididae family drawn from a specimen caught in Shark Bay, *Parapercis nebulosus* (Quoy and Gaimard, 1825). Charles-Alexandre Lesueur. Muséum d'histoire naturelle, Le Havre – n° 76 274

because of the variety of their colours, but generally they were all small and much like sardines. That was in fact the name we gave them. The largest closely resembled the European whiting in shape and flavour, although we thought its head seemed longer.

When they had been distributed, we cooked our share for dinner and found it all very good. As there were not many fish, I filled up on oysters and crabs, which were plentiful.

At low tide, on the reef that ran along the beach in various places, we found some very beautiful turban-shells, a few common shells and a lovely cone shell with its fish, which is no doubt unknown in Europe and of which I have had a drawing done. We also collected some rather fine

Various gastropods from north and north-west Australia, *Terebralia sulcata* (Born, 1778), *Conus victoriae* (Reeve, 1843), *Aplustrum amplustre* (Linnaeus, 1758). Charles-Alexandre Lesueur. Muséum d'histoire naturelle, Le Havre – n° 72 057

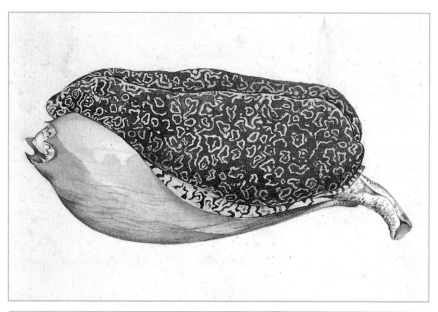

Shell found on the west coast of Australia, *Melo miltonis* (Griffith and Pigeon, 1834). Nicolas-Martin Petit (?).
Muséum d'histoire naturelle, Le Havre – n° 72 054

Volute found on the south and west coasts of Australia, *Aulicina nivosa* (Lamarck, 1804). Charles-Alexandre
Lesueur. Muséum d'histoire naturelle, Le Havre – n° 72 062

mussels, several other ordinary shells and, above all, clams, on which the sailors feasted.

By five o'clock everyone was back except Citizen Péron, who was no doubt carried away by his enthusiasm and had gone too far to be able to get back by the specified time. While we waited for him, we sat down to our meal and dined without him, for he did not return.

After dinner Baudin, noting drily that Péron 'had in all probability become lost on the island', took most of the men back to the ship in the larger of the two boats, leaving one of the officers, Sub-Lieutenant Picquet, with a search party to continue looking for the intrepid naturalist. On a more positive note, when Baudin arrived back on board he was informed that 'during the day more than 600 pounds of good fish had been caught on the line, without counting two or three dog-fish which everyone found very good to eat'.

At daybreak next morning there was still no sign that Péron had been found.

## 29 JUNE 1801

A stiff south-south-easterly breeze was blowing on the morning of the 10th [Messidor] and at sunrise there was still no sign of the boat returning – proof that Citizen Péron had not rejoined it during the night and that he had spent the night somewhere on the island without knowing where he was.

At last, after keeping constant watch, we noticed the boat at about ten o'clock. It was under sail and tacking to return to the ship, which it reached with some difficulty by one in the afternoon. Fortunately, Citizen Péron was in it. On coming aboard, he presented himself to me in the most pitiful state. He had not eaten for 24 hours and was utterly worn out, having wandered about nearly all night until he dropped from exhaustion and fell into a sound sleep at the foot of a shrub. At daylight he regained his bearings and returned to the beach, where he found the men who were looking for him.

Since he is to make me a report on his adventure, I shall not say everything I might want to say about it, but I did make him a firm promise that when he went ashore again I would send someone with him who would not let him out of his sight and who would be responsible to me for getting him back to the place of departure at the specified time.

The need to keep a closer watch on Péron did not prevent Baudin from undertaking further excursions, during which the naturalists collected important scientific data and the crew worked to replenish the ship with vital supplies of food and wood. There was even time to indulge the crew's taste for hunting.

### 6 JULY 1801

The pleasure-lovers, and I have plenty of those, went kangaroo hunting and killed about 20 of them. Some of them were sent aboard the ship and the rest were kept for our consumption on shore.

We put the drag-net out several times in the afternoon but with no luck, for we caught nothing at all. Catching shell-fish was more successful. We collected plenty of rather tasty crabs, nerite* shell-fish of various kinds and, above all, large numbers of oysters, but they were small and hard to open. They had more or less the shape and flavour of those that are eaten in the colonies, either in America or in Ile de France [Mauritius] and Bourbon [Reunion Island].

Amongst the sea-birds that were killed on this first day were some that belonged to a lovely species. Some are known by the name of 'pie de mer' [oyster-catcher – literally: 'sea-magpie'] and have a body half white and half black, with a beautiful red beak and red feet.

Maugé found that two eagles that were killed must belong to a new species, for they appeared to live only on fish and shell-fish, plenty of which we found in their stomachs. For this reason we called the bird the 'aigle pêcheur' [sea-eagle – literally: 'fishing-eagle'].

The sailors and the naturalists appear to have enjoyed their stay in Shark Bay, as indeed did their captain. Such was the enthusiasm of the crew that Baudin was led to wonder on one occasion at their surprising reserves of energy.

### 10 JULY 1801

In the first boat to reach us were a number of hunters and several of those who are sick when it comes to performing duties on board, but who found the strength to run around all day hunting with the sun at its hottest. Amongst them was young Bougainville, who will soon end up completely exhausted.

Hyacinthe de Bougainville, the son of the celebrated French Pacific explorer who owed his place as a midshipman second-class in this expedition to his father's influence, was indeed, at 18, young and inexperienced. Baudin's patience was further tested by a number of other incidents. One of these

---

* Denotes various species of gastropod molluscs found principally in warm shallow coastal waters and characterised by brightly streaked shells.

concerned Henri Freycinet, who was given the fairly straightforward mission of 'going to the southern point of the second and larger one of the Barren Islands [Dorre Island] to determine precisely its latitude and to take various hour-angles there, in order to calculate the longitude'. The first source of annoyance was the needless loss of a day because insufficient supplies had been packed. And Freycinet further upset his captain by defying his orders and failing to fulfil his mission.

## 7 JULY 1801

From the shore we saw the large dinghy leave on its designated mission. I had sent with M. Freycinet the chief yeoman of signals, an educated man who was very dependable. It seemed to me that he was not very pleased to have this companion on his expedition. He would have much preferred to have on board his protégé, midshipman Breton, who was pretty well useless.

## 10 JULY 1801

M. Freycinet came to make his report on his expedition which, as I had gathered from his hasty return, contained almost nothing of interest. Instead of bringing us back some useful observations, he brought back a large number of kangaroos for his personal consumption. In spite of the fact that I had given him no instruction to take his protégé Breton with him, he had done so, not so much for the help Breton could give him as to ensure he had an enjoyable time hunting, at which Breton is most proficient.

The other incidents, one of which has been noted above, inevitably involved François Péron.

## 7 JULY 1801

Citizen Péron, whose extreme enthusiasm prompts him to tackle anything and everything without giving a thought to the dangers to which he is exposing himself, went to explore the western part of the island and, as usual, went alone. He found nothing of interest on his excursion, so to make it worthwhile he went down to the shore to collect some shells.

At first he whiled away his time at the expense of the crabs; as he had taken off his shirt, he wrapped up about fifty of them in it. His zeal should have been better rewarded than it was, for, after he tried to climb on to some rocks, where only small waves appeared to break, he was knocked head over heels by a wave which carried off most of the beautiful shells that he claims to have found. The fall gave him wounds to several different parts of the body, which convinced him to come back, but, instead of heading from west to east, he took a north–south course, so that for the second time he became completely lost. He did not rejoin us until nine o'clock at night, utterly overwhelmed by exhaustion, and having had to abandon his tin box, his shirt and his crabs on the way.

Baudin was more positive, however, in his appraisal of the work undertaken by some of the other naturalists, with Riédlé and Maugé in particular earning his admiration.

## 14 JULY 1801

Furthermore, our head gardener, Riédlé, for whom every moment is precious, found on this small island 70 varieties of plants, most of which will no doubt be unknown to botanists. Maugé the zoologist, who devotes himself to nothing but Natural History and who is anxious to fulfil all his duties, collected ten species of birds which he believes to be new. The others caught some kangaroos and a few lizards. Amongst the latter we found two which are undoubtedly the same as the ones Dampier refers to as guana and they are truly quite hideous. But we caught two of another species whose colouring was extremely beautiful and which were very large. See the drawing from life in the edited journal.

An observation that I have made, which is not perhaps without interest, is that none of the animals that we encountered seemed vicious. The lizards, hideous as they were, allowed themselves to be picked up without trying to run away or defend themselves. Two black snakes, which we did not pick up because of our fear of them, allowed the men observing them all the time that they needed to do so and only hid when they came too close. The wounded kangaroos that were caught still alive did not make any attempt to bite and a little one that was caught unharmed immediately began to lick the hand of his captor.

Amongst the shell-fish, we found no more than four or five species; they were quite beautiful and only two of them seemed unknown to us. Citizen Maugé collected ten kinds of insect, most of which belong to the dung-beetle class. We found only two types of butterfly, one of which was a moth. We collected several caterpillars of the butterfly, which has a rather lovely underside, very similar to that of a European cabbage moth.

The fish that were caught on the line were generally of the perch family, and the only kind that we caught in any quantity were those that the sailors call the captain and which they say is similar to the one commonly found in the colonies. The fish known by the name of parrot are exactly the same as those found in the tropics. However, I have had coloured drawings made of the ones which seemed to me the rarest and most curious.

During our stay ashore, our staple diet consisted of crabs, oysters, nerites, spiny lobsters, fish and kangaroos. I found the dog-fish excellent when it was young and small and preferred it to the kangaroo, which was everyone else's favourite.

On 14 July, with the fine weather apparently coming to an end and the seas 'growing rough', Baudin decided he could no longer wait for Hamelin and the *Naturaliste* and set sail for North-West Cape, whose exact position he was keen to fix. The journey along this vast coastline lasted 38 days and took Baudin as far as the Bonaparte Archipelago. To his frustration, contrary winds and strong currents prevented him from making an accurate survey of the coast. Incomplete though it was, his reconnaissance did allow him to identify and chart a great number of islands and islets, which to this day bear the names the French gave them: the Rivoli Islands, L'Hermite Island, the Forestier Islands, the Lacepede Islands and most of those of the Bonaparte Archipelago, to name a few. During this part of the journey, some of the earlier tensions re-surfaced, as Baudin became increasingly frustrated with the work of his officers. Sub-Lieutenant Picquet was one to incur the captain's displeasure.

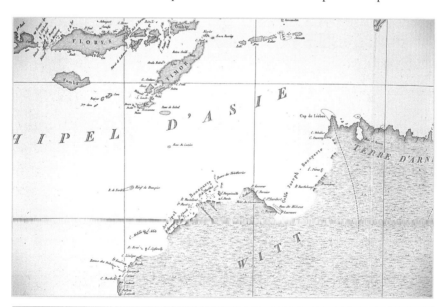

Detail of the French map of New Holland (1804) showing the north-west of Australia and the adjacent islands, including Timor. Published in the *Atlas* of the *Voyage de découvertes aux Terres Australes* (1811)

## 5 AUGUST 1801

At half past seven in the morning I had cause to be particularly annoyed with M. Picquet, who was on duty and making it his sole business to torment the signalmen because he found that the clock was not moving fast enough to suit his impatience: the racket he was causing made it difficult for me to work in my cabin, where I was busy at the time. When we were standing in for land, lead in hand, the signalman in charge of the sounding said to him several times over: '9½ fathoms, M. Picquet . . . 9½ fathoms, M. Picquet . . . M. Picquet, 9½ fathoms', with Picquet taking not the slightest notice. I took my turn to speak up, saying: 'M. Picquet, you must pay attention to the lead and not the clock!' His pride was wounded no doubt by my comments, and his impulsive reaction, which was perfectly reprehensible, was to come to the door of my cabin, which I am always careful to keep open, day or night, when he is on duty. He said in so many words: 'Confound it sir! It's quite ridiculous of you to find fault with me for watching the clock!' I replied that I considered *him* to be the only rude and ridiculous person aboard, and, so that he had no further opportunity to oblige me to punish him as he deserved, I relieved him of the command of a watch until I could get rid of him altogether.

The naturalists, for their part, were growing increasingly frustrated because of the lack of opportunity to study New Holland's natural resources. Unfavourable conditions and the previous loss of the longboat at Geographe Bay meant that any attempt to land would be imprudent.

## 12 AUGUST 1801

Dampier points out, and I agree, that one could land on some parts of these islands at high tide and beach one's boat, then wait for the tide to return before setting off again. That is just what the naturalists would have liked me to do, but, apart from the fact that I no longer have a boat I can risk, this island, like all those that we have sailed past in the last few days, did not look suitable to me for research in Natural History and especially not in the field of botany, for trees were few and far between and these were neither particularly tall nor leafy.

Baudin, meanwhile, had become most unhappy with the bearings taken by his officers. In a move that was sure to irritate them, he decided to entrust this work to someone else.

## 13 AUGUST 1801

It will no doubt be difficult for those who see the ship's log-book to understand fully all the bearings recorded in it. From the very beginning, I have tried every method and argument to get the officers to pay due attention to this work, but all that I have tried to say has been in vain. And as they consider themselves very knowledgeable, it has been impossible for me to persuade them to take the bearings the way I wanted. So, for this reason, I have trained one of the chief yeomen of signals, in whom I recognised considerable intelligence, to take them specially for me, according to my own method, and I hope that no one will find in them the confusion that exists in all the bearings the others have taken.

The final nail in the coffin was the news that their supplies of wood and water were running dangerously low. When Le Bas de Sainte Croix brought this to his attention, Baudin felt he had no alternative but to make for Timor.

## 19 AUGUST 1801

In the morning, the commander informed me, or rather he told me again, that we had only three or four days' wood left and, at the most, 20 days' supply of water at the ordinary rate of rations. For their part, the naturalists, who had not had fresh food for more than a month, were longing to call in at Timor, and although they said nothing to me about it, they discussed it among themselves so as to ensure that their conversations reached me. Given my own state, I myself did not see the need to persist with the survey of the northern part of Van Diemen's Land [the coast near Cape Van Diemen on Melville Island, off present-day Darwin]. A longboat, or any other boat capable of going on ahead of the ship, was growing more and more indispensable, as I needed one both for reconnoitring close in along the shore and for sending in to inspect it. Seeing, therefore, that I could do nothing, I decided to head north to the anchorage that everybody desired with such impatience.

This news had such an effect upon some of the sick on board that several of them found strength enough to come up on deck in order to make sure that it [was] really true.

With supplies low and the atmosphere on board the *Géographe* tense, it was with great relief that, on 22 August 1801, the expedition finally arrived in the idyllic setting of Kupang Bay, where it was also reunited a month later with the *Naturaliste*.

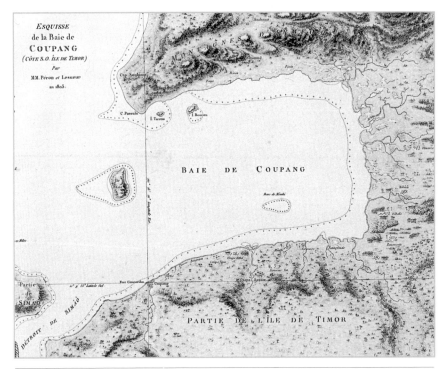

*Sketch of Kupang Bay (south-west coast of Timor Island)*, Péron and Lesueur (1803). Published in the *Atlas* of the
*Voyage de découvertes aux Terres Australes* (1811)

Baudin spent an eventful 11 weeks in Timor. Illnesses caused delays in
building a new longboat; fever and dysentery tragically claimed the lives of a
number of men, including the gardener Riédlé, whose loss was both a great
personal blow and a cause of scientific concern to Baudin; Le Bas de Sainte
Croix was persuaded to leave the expedition, after provoking a duel with one
of Baudin's most loyal officers, Ronsard; and, in a decision that was to divide
the officers, Sub-Lieutenant Picquet was sent home after brandishing a sword
against his captain in reaction to an order to find lodgings on shore. As
dramatic as these events were, they did not deter Baudin from pursuing his
mission. On 13 November 1801, the *Géographe* and the *Naturaliste* sailed out of
Kupang Bay bound for 'la Terre de Diémen' (Tasmania).

# chapter three

# SURVEYING THE SOUTH-WEST

*Flinders from Cape Leeuwin to Nuyts Archipelago, 7 December 1801 to 28 January 1802*

While the French were en route from Timor to Tasmania, the rival British expedition entered Australian waters to begin its work. By making good time on the voyage out, and without protracted stays along the way, Flinders had cut back Baudin's advantage of an earlier departure from Europe. The *Investigator*'s crew sighted land on 7 December 1801, just over six months after the French made landfall. There were other reasons not to dawdle: Flinders had already entered the season best suited to charting the waters of the continent's south, and he was aware that, after the run across the Indian Ocean, the *Investigator* was in need of a refit. His priority, then, was to follow the coast around to the south and east to where shelter could be found.

### 7 DECEMBER 1801

At two in the morning, we had 80 fathoms, and veered towards the land. It was seen from the mast head at five; and the highest part, the same which had been set in the evening, bore N 12° W. This is the largest of the before-mentioned Isles of St Allouarn; but at half past seven, we saw hills extending from behind, and, to all appearance, joining it to the main land. This supposed isle is, therefore, what I denominate Cape Leeuwin, as being the south-western, and most projecting part of Leeuwin's Land. The highest hill lies nearly in latitude 34° 19' south, and longitude 115° 6' east; it is a sloping piece of land of about six hundred feet in elevation, and appeared to be rocky, with a slight covering of trees and shrubs; but this cape will be best known from Mr Westall's sketch.

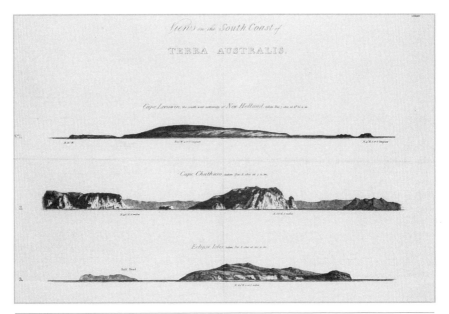

Coastal profiles of Cape Leeuwin, Cape Chatham and the Eclipse Isles, William Westall. Published in *A Voyage to Terra Australis* (1814)

Flinders followed the coast down to Point D'Entrecasteaux, noting as he went his impressions of the land.

> The shore abreast was seven or eight miles distant; and behind it ran a continuation of the same ridge of sandy hillocks which surrounds the bight, and it extended to the southern extreme. Over this ridge were perceived, here and there, the tops of some higher, and less sandy hills, standing a few miles inland; but the general aspect of the country was that of great sterility; nor was there, as yet, any appearance of its being inhabited.

## 8 DECEMBER 1801

> At day light, the ship was found to have been carried to the eastward, and neither Point D'Entrecasteaux nor the two white rocks were in sight; but in the N 19° E, about eight miles, was a head not far from the extreme set in the evening. It afterwards proved to be a smooth, steep rock, lying one mile from the main, and is the land first made upon this coast by captain Vancouver, who called it Cape Chatham . . .
>
> On the east side of Cape Chatham, the shore falls back to the northward, and makes a bight in which is a small reef of rocks. It then projects in a cliffy

head, which lies S 75° E seven miles from the cape, and is called Point Nuyts
in the French chart, upon the supposition, probably, that this was the first land
seen by Nuyts, in 1627. Beyond this point, the coast trends very nearly east,
but forms several projections, some of which are steep and others low; and
between them are sandy bights where small vessels might obtain shelter from
all northern winds. The hills lying at the back of the shore seemed to be
barren, though trees grew thickly on their eastern sides; they are not high,
but it was rare to perceive anything of the interior country above them.

By late in the day on 8 December, Flinders knew from his charts that he
would soon be entering the shelter of King George Sound. In particular, he put
his faith in the charts of George Vancouver, who had sailed those waters in the
*Discovery* in 1791. It was Vancouver who had given it the name of 'King
George III Sound' (it was also known at the time as 'King George's Sound')
and who had named its extensions, Princess Royal Harbour and Oyster
Harbour. Flinders' faith in Vancouver's chart of the Sound and his eagerness
to avoid delays were such that he entered after nightfall.

> The wind blew fresh at this time, and a current of more than one mile an hour
> ran with us, so that, by carrying all sail, I hoped to get sight of King George's
> Sound before dark. At seven, we passed close on the south side of the Eclipse
> Isles; but Bald Head at the entrance of the sound had so different an
> appearance from what I had been led to expect, being a slope in this point of
> view, that the steep east end of Break-sea Island was at first taken for it.
> The error was fortunately perceived in time, and at eight o'clock we hauled up
> round the head, with the wind at west, and made a stretch into the sound.
> It was then dark, but, the night being fine, I did not hesitate to work up by the
> guidance of captain Vaucouver's chart; and having reached nearly into a line
> between Seal Island and the first beach round Bald Head, we anchored at
> eleven o'clock, in 8 fathoms, sandy bottom.

Having found shelter, Flinders could safely undertake the tasks of refitting the
ship and replenishing supplies, while also indulging in some exploration and
scientific work.

## 9 DECEMBER 1801

> King George's Sound had been chosen as the proper place in which to prepare
> ourselves for the examination of the south coast of Terra Australis, and I

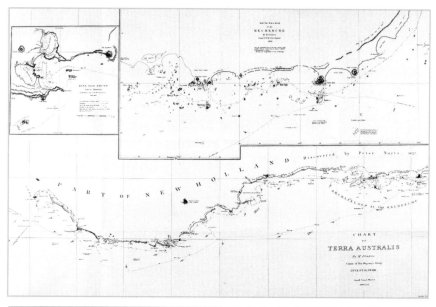

Flinders' charts of the south coast of Terra Australis, showing King George Sound and the Recherche Archipelago (1802). Published in *A Voyage to Terra Australis* (1814)

sought to make the best use of the advantages it might furnish. The first essential requisite was a place of secure shelter, where the masts could be stripped, the rigging and sails put into order, and communication had with the shore, without interruption from the elements; but this, from captain Vancouver's chart and description, I did not expect the outer sound to afford. The facility of quitting Princess Royal Harbour, with such a wind as would be favourable for prosecuting the investigation of the coast, induced me so far to prefer it to Oyster Harbour as to make it the first object of examination; and in the morning, after we had sounded round the ship and found her so placed as to require no immediate movement, I went in a boat for the purpose, accompanied by the master and landscape painter, the naturalist, and some other gentlemen landing at the same time, to botanise in the vicinity of Bald Head.

Seal Island, where we stopped in passing, is a mass of granite, which is accessible only at its western end, as represented in Mr Westall's sketch. After killing a few seals upon the shore, we ascended the hill to search for the bottle and parchment left by captain Vancouver in 1791, but could find no vestiges either of it or of the staff or pile of stones, and since there was no appearance of the natives having crossed over from the main, I was led to suspect that a second ship had been here before us.

With the mystery of Vancouver's missing bottle and parchment in mind, the scientific work of the expedition began. This was the responsibility of those whom Flinders labelled 'the scientific gentlemen'. For men like the naturalist Robert Brown or the artist Ferdinand Bauer, and indeed Flinders himself, 'botanising' and other forms of scientific activity were not enlisted solely in the cause of a disengaged quest for higher knowledge. Close to the surface in their observations and deliberations, as for the French, were always practical issues concerning the availability of shelter, water, wood and so on. Weighing on their minds also was the question of whether the local Aborigines might make their presence felt.

> At Point Possession, on the south side of the entrance to Princess Royal Harbour, we had a good view of that extensive piece of water. Wood seemed not to be abundant near the shores, and therefore a projection two or three miles to the south-west, which was covered with trees, first attracted my notice. The depth of water in going to it was, however, too little for the ship; nor was there any fresh stream in the neighbourhood. Some person, but not captain Vancouver, had nevertheless been cutting wood there, for several trees had been felled with axe and saw. Not far from thence stood a number of bark sheds, like the huts of the natives who live in the forests behind Port Jackson, and forming what might be called a small village; but it had been long deserted.

As he carried out his survey, Flinders continued to look in vain for traces of Vancouver's visit. Instead, he stumbled across evidence of a much more recent visitor.

## 10 DECEMBER 1801

> On the south-west side there were two small streams, in one of which the water was fresh, though high coloured. Returning to the entrance, we landed on the east side, and found a spot of ground six or eight feet square, dug up and trimmed like a garden; and upon it was lying a piece of sheet copper, bearing this inscription: 'August 27, 1800. Chr. Dixson — ship *Elligood*', which solved the difficulty of the felled trees, and the disappearance of captain Vancouver's bottle.

The discovery that a whaler had recently visited these shores solved this particular mystery; but there was evidence of a different kind of human presence that Flinders was now keen to investigate. It was not until 14 December, however, that some of the expedition members made their first contact with Aborigines, whom Flinders refers to variously in his account as 'natives', 'Indians' or 'Australians'. In King George Sound, he appears to have encountered members of the local Minang tribe.

## 14 DECEMBER 1801

Some smokes being perceived at the head of the harbour, Mr Brown and other gentlemen directed their excursion that way, and met with several of the natives, who were shy but not afraid. One man with whom they had communication was admired for his manly behaviour, and they gave him a bird which had been shot, and a pocket-handkerchief; but like the generality of people hitherto seen in this country, these men did not seem to be desirous of communication with strangers, and they very early made signs to our gentlemen to return from whence they came. Next morning, however, we were agreeably surprised by the appearance of two Indians, and afterwards of others, upon the side of the hill behind our tents. They approached with much caution, one coming first with poised spear, and making many gestures, accompanied with much vociferous parleying, in which he sometimes seemed to threaten us if we did not be gone, and at others to admit of our stay. On Mr Purdie, the assistant-surgeon, going up to him unarmed, a communication was brought about, and they received some articles of iron and toys, giving in exchange some of their implements, and after a short stay, left us, apparently on very good terms ···

On the 17th, one of our former visitors brought two strangers with him; and after this time, they and others came almost every day, and frequently stopped a whole morning at the tents. We always made them presents of such things as seemed to be most agreeable, but they very rarely brought us any thing in return; nor was it uncommon to find small mirrors, and other things left about the shore, so that at length our presents were discontinued.

If he was disappointed that his gesture of issuing token gifts was not greeted with displays of boundless appreciation, an expedition inland was to test further Flinders' relations with the local inhabitants. On this occasion, as on many others later during his voyage, Flinders took steps to avoid open confrontation – as, apparently, did the Aborigines. But it is also apparent from Flinders' own account that his willingness to accommodate their wishes had its limitations.

## 23 DECEMBER 1801

I formed a party on the 23rd, consisting of the officers of the ship, the scientific gentlemen, and others, amounting to 13, well armed and provided for two days, in order to visit the lakes behind West Cape Howe. We walked along the shore to the north-western extremity of Princess Royal Harbour, where several small runs of fresh water were found to drain in, from peaty swamps. Striking from thence into the country in a western direction, we had not advanced far when a native was seen running before us; and soon afterward an old man, who had been several times at the tents, came up, unarmed as usual. He was very anxious that we should not go further, and acted with a good deal of resolution in first stopping one, and then another of those who were foremost. He was not able to prevail, but we accommodated him so far as to make a circuit round the wood, where it seemed probable his family and female friends were placed. The old man followed us, hallooing frequently to give information of our movements; and when a paroquet was shot, he expressed neither fear nor surprise, but received the bird with gladness, and attended with some curiosity to the reloading of the gun.

A week later, the contact was renewed. Flinders, for his part, felt it appropriate on this occasion to put his marines on display in full regalia. How this spectacle might have been received by its viewers is of course purely a matter of speculation, but Flinders' account suggests that their response took the form of an excited engagement leading to mimicry, as if the Aborigines might have identified some sense of the ridiculous in the strange rituals of their exotic visitors.

On the 30th, our wooding and the watering of the ship were completed, the rigging was refitted, the sails repaired and bent, and the ship unmoored. Our friends, the natives, continued to visit us; and the old man, with several others, being at the tents this morning, I ordered the party of marines on shore, to be exercised in their presence. The red coats and white crossed belts were greatly admired, having some resemblance to their own manner of ornamenting themselves; and the drum, but particularly the fife, excited their astonishment; but when they saw these beautiful red-and-white men, with their bright muskets, drawn up in a line, they absolutely screamed with delight; nor were their wild gestures and vociferation to be silenced, but by commencing the exercise, to which they paid the most earnest and silent attention. Several of them moved their hands, involuntarily, according to the motions; and the old man placed himself at the end of the rank, with a short staff in his hand, which he shouldered, presented, grounded, as did the marines their muskets, without, I believe, knowing what he did. Before firing, the Indians were made acquainted with what was going to take place, so that the vollies did not excite much terror.

When conditions finally allowed it, Flinders sailed out of King George Sound on the fifth day of the new year. At this point, he was still in charted waters, since Nuyts, Vancouver and d'Entrecasteaux had been there before, not to mention the whaler *Elligood*, but the survey he now began was to be much more thorough than any completed before, allowing him to confer names upon many features that were previously unnamed. Flinders' attitude towards hydrography – the measurement and charting of coastlines and bodies of water – was very much that of the perfectionist. The *Investigator* hugged the shore as closely as possible, so that Flinders might judge distances from ship to shore accurately and determine features on the land beyond doubt. All bearings were laid with the land still in sight and then a rough chart plotted each evening. To avoid risks, the ship withdrew a safe distance overnight, but then returned the next morning as closely as possible to where the survey had been discontinued the previous day. At various points, the landscape painter William Westall was asked to draw coastal profiles which future navigators might use in combination with Flinders' charts. It was painstaking and necessarily slow work, especially when, as was the case just three days out of King George Sound, the *Investigator* found itself among 'this labyrinth of islands and rocks' which was the Archipelago of the Recherche.

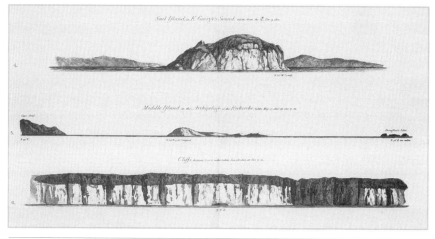

Coastal profiles of Seal Island (King George Sound), Middle Island (Recherche Archipelago), and cliffs in the Great Australian Bight, William Westall. Published in *A Voyage to Terra Australis* (1814)

Though keen to pursue his hydrographic work while the weather was conducive to it, Flinders was also mindful of the scientists' needs to do their own exploration. Having been fortunate in finding a mainland anchorage in a place he named Lucky Bay, he gave them the opportunity to experience the local flora at close hand, an experience they came to regret.

## 10 JANUARY 1802

I went on shore also, to make observations upon the rates of the time keepers; and afterwards ascended a hill at the back of the bay, to take angles with a theodolite. A party of the gentlemen were upon the top, eating a fruit not much unlike green walnuts in external appearance, and invited me to partake; but having breakfasted, and not much liking their flavour, I did but taste them. Mr Thistle and some others who had eaten liberally, were taken sick, and remained unwell all the day afterward. The plant which produced these nuts was a species of zamia: a class of plants nearly allied to the third kind of palm found by Captain Cook on the east coast, the fruit of which produced the same deleterious effects on board the *Endeavour*.

Though Flinders explored alongside the scientists, it was clear that he saw the land and its plants through quite different eyes. Where they marvelled at novelty and abundance, the pragmatist Flinders saw only a lack of potential.

Sand and stone, with the slightest covering of vegetation, everywhere presented themselves on the lower lands; and the many shining parts on the sides of the hills showed them to be still more bare. The vegetation, indeed, consisted of an abundant variety of shrubs and small plants, and yielded a delightful harvest to the botanists; but to the herdsman and cultivator it promised nothing; not a blade of grass, nor a square yard of soil from which the seed delivered to it could be delivered back, was perceivable by the eye in its course over these arid plains.

The sea, at least, offered a bountiful harvest from which to feed the *Investigator*'s crew. Off the southern coast, though, the task of catching fish was not without its perils:

## 12 JANUARY 1802

Several seals were procured on this and the preceding day, and some fish were caught alongside the ship; but our success was much impeded by three monstrous sharks [almost certainly Great White Sharks], in whose presence no other fish dared to appear. After some attempts we succeeded in taking one of them; but to get it on board required as much preparation as for hoisting in the launch. The length of it, however, was not more than twelve feet three inches, but the circumference of the body was eight feet. Amongst the vast quantity of substances contained in the stomach, was a tolerably large seal, bitten in two, and swallowed with half of the spear sticking in it with which it had probably been killed by the natives. The stench of this ravenous monster was great, even before it was dead; and when the stomach was opened, it became intolerable.

Thereafter, the *Investigator* beat its way east, its crew for days on end observing interminable, steep cliffs which forbade any thought of landfall. Finally, on 27 January, Flinders arrived at a significant marking point on his journey, namely the head of the Great Australian Bight. That, at least, was the name he would later grant it in his published chart of 1814, thereby for the first time using the word 'Australian' as part of a place name.

## 27 JANUARY 1802

At the termination of the bank and of the second range of cliffs, the coast became sandy, and trended north-eastward about three leagues, after which it turned south-east-by-east, and formed the head of the Great Australian Bight, whose latitude I make to be 31° 29' south, and longitude 131° 10' east . . .

After steering east-north-east, east, and east-south-east, and having seen the beach all round the head of the Great Bight, we hauled up parallel to the new direction of the coast, at the distance of six miles, and at five o'clock were abreast of the furthest part seen by the French admiral [d'Entrecasteaux] when he quitted the examination. The coast is a sandy beach in front, but the land rises gradually from thence, and at three or four miles back is of moderate elevation, but still sandy and barren. According to the chart of Nuyts, an extensive reef lay a little beyond this part. It was not seen by d'Entrecasteaux, but we were anxiously looking out for it when, at six o'clock, breakers were seen from the mast head bearing S 43° E some distance open from the land. We kept on our course for them, with the wind at south-south-west, until eight o'clock, and then tacked to the westward in 27 fathoms; and the ship's way being stopped by a head swell, we did not veer towards the land until three in the morning, at which time it fell calm.

By the following day, Flinders could surmise that he had reached the limits of the continent as it had been charted by the Europeans who had preceded him. He therefore could have little idea of what lay before him. Perhaps he would find the mouth of one or more great rivers flowing down from the plains of a single great continent. Or perhaps he would be able to confirm the theories of some that the New Holland explored by Dutch navigators and others was quite separate from the coastline explored by his compatriot James Cook, and that perhaps a huge strait running south from what we know as the Gulf of Carpentaria separated two great islands. Whatever the outcome might be, Flinders and his crew at that point must have felt a buzz of excitement at the approach of the unknown coast.

# chapter four

# COLONIAL PROSPECTING IN VAN DIEMEN'S LAND

*The French in Tasmania,*
*13 January to 24 March 1802*

The island now called Tasmania was well known to Europeans long before the arrival of Flinders and Baudin. As early as 1642, the Dutch navigator Abel Tasman came across a coast he named after the man who had despatched him on his voyage of discovery, the East Indies Governor-General Anthony van Diemen. Tasman's landfall was on the western coast of the island near Cape Sorell. From there, his two ships rounded South West Cape, then sailed along the south coast before proceeding into Storm Bay. After being blown out to sea they regained contact with the coastline at North Bay or Marion Bay on the Tasmanian east coast.

Tasman's great achievement was to show that there was a route to the Pacific south of the Australian continent. But Tasman did not circumnavigate Van Diemen's Land and thus did not show that it was an island. More than a century later, in the age of Captain Cook, it was assumed that the coasts explored were those of the mainland. A French expedition under the command of Marc Joseph Marion-Dufresne entered Tasmanian waters in March 1772, landing at Blackman Bay. A skirmish with Aborigines took place there, an event that foreshadowed the expedition's fateful encounter with Maoris in the Bay of Islands just three weeks later. Marion-Dufresne himself and twenty-six others were killed.

The expedition of Bruni d'Entrecasteaux followed two decades later. After anchoring in a bay named after the expedition's vessel, *La Recherche*, d'Entrecasteaux spent five weeks carrying out detailed hydrographic work that was later published in the *Atlas du Voyage de Bruny-Dentrecasteaux*. This expedition was responsible for the charting and naming of the Huon River and Port Esperance, as well as the island still today named after its leader – Bruny Island. But like those who went there before him, d'Entrecasteaux was still none the wiser as to whether Van Diemen's Land was an island.

It was not until 1798, when George Bass and Matthew Flinders conducted their famous circumnavigation in the *Norfolk*, that the question of Tasmania's insularity was finally settled. The significance and quality of the work that Flinders accomplished on this voyage played a large part in the decision to commission his major circumnavigation of Terra Australis. However, it cannot be said that his Tasmanian experience in 1798 was as plagued by human drama as were to be the encounters of the Baudin expedition with the land of Tasmania and its surrounding islands and straits in 1802 and 1803. In fact, during the time that they spent in Van Diemen's Land, Baudin and his company would display all of the qualities and all of the imperfections that gave the rich and troubled character to their voyage of discovery as a whole.

---

On 13 January 1802 the *Géographe* and the *Naturaliste* anchored in D'Entrecasteaux Channel after making rapid progress in their passage from Timor and round the south-western tip of New Holland. This is not to say that their progress had been easy: eleven burials at sea had taken place and Baudin himself had been ill for three weeks of the voyage. Although the initial signs did not appear good – the day before reaching land, Baudin remarked that this was the worst night at sea that they had experienced – the two months spent in Tasmanian waters from January to March 1802 helped to restore better health and spirits to the weary crew and provided formidable results to scientists and navigators alike.

Unlike parts of the continent, which had hitherto impressed them only by their monotony, Tasmania appeared to offer a more picturesque landscape. After an initial decision to anchor in Recherche Bay, conditions forced the two vessels to head past Bruny Island, where the crews sighted a group of Aborigines signalling to them from the shore. They eventually anchored in the bay marked on their charts as 'Great Cove', now called Great Taylor Bay, and,

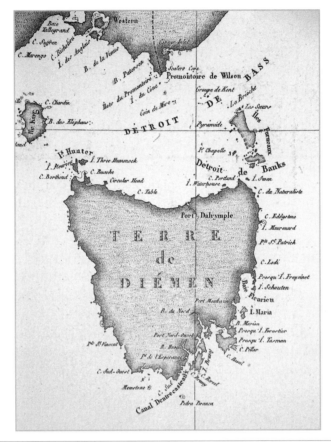

*Terre de Diémen* (Van Diemen's Land), detail of the French map of New Holland (1804). Published in the *Atlas* of the *Voyage de découvertes aux Terres Australes* (1811)

with manoeuvres through D'Entrecasteaux Channel completed, Baudin was able to exclaim with satisfaction how well they had been served by the chart that Beautemps-Beaupré had drawn up while on the earlier voyage of d'Entrecasteaux. Baudin immediately made plans with Hamelin for the following day's activities, plans which seemed to indicate clearly the main objectives of their mission in Van Diemen's Land – the need to renew supplies, the scientific duty to observe the native populations, and, undoubtedly, the political duty to advise on the opportunity for future settlement.

## 13 JANUARY 1802

We both agreed that on the following day [Hamelin's] longboat should go and inspect Port Esperance to make sure that the English had not established a

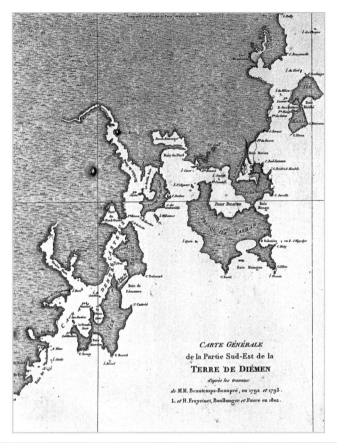

Map showing the complex coastline of south-eastern Tasmania, as charted by the French, L. & H. Freycinet, Boullanger and Faure (1802). Published in the *Atlas* of the *Voyage de découvertes aux Terres Australes* (1811)

settlement there and to see whether there were any convenient places for collecting water. My longboat was assigned the task of reconnoitring the Huon River and Port Cygnet.

At dusk we saw several fires in various parts of this large cove, where we felt as if we were in a pond. Although there was a gale blowing in from south to south-west, the sea was calm; it must never be rough no matter what direction the winds blow from. The view from this anchorage is extremely pleasant, as can be seen from the picture I have had made of it.

We also decided, M. Hamelin and I, that on the following day we would go and examine the coast and the natives – as long as they would allow us to approach them.

Coastal profiles of Van Diemen's Land (*Terre de Diémen*). Views: 1. Mewstone and the De Witt Islands; 2. Tasman Island; 3. East coast of Tasman Peninsula, from Cape Pillar to Cape Hauy. Charles-Alexandre Lesueur or Nicolas-Martin Petit. Muséum d'histoire naturelle, Le Havre – n° 18 027

The orders that Baudin transmitted to Freycinet, who was to command the *Naturaliste*'s longboat on the following day, reflected the commander's meticulous respect for the instruction that his expedition was to avoid all bloodshed and that his men should seek by all means to establish a friendly relationship with the native populations.

## 14 JANUARY 1802

> There is no need for me to recommend you to be actively on your guard to ensure the safety of the longboat and all those accompanying you; but should you meet any natives, which is very likely, you are absolutely forbidden to commit any act of hostility against them, unless the safety of anyone in particular, or all in general, depends on it. According to what is known of their character, the people of this country are not regarded as malevolent, unless they are provoked. It is thus by gifts and acts of kindness that you must influence them in our favour.

Baudin's insistence was well justified: the first contacts were made almost immediately the shore parties landed on Partridge Island, and they were as friendly as the commander could have hoped. He himself set out in the *Géographe*'s dinghy with a number of companions, including Bernier the astronomer, and Captain Hamelin of the *Naturaliste*, and soon encountered a group of natives whose appearance impressed him. He comments in detail on the physical traits and the demeanour of the Tasmanians, who approached the members of his crew with confidence and good humour and who readily permitted the sailors to embrace them and to offer them trinkets.

Most of our belongings appeared to capture their fancy, and they would have been delighted if we had given them our clothes. These men were naked from head to foot, except for one of them who was wearing a skin that partly covered his back and shoulders. They are much paler in colour than the African negroes, and perhaps it is because they do not think they are black enough that they smear various parts of their faces with charcoal. Every one of them was tattooed from the shoulders to about 6" further down. The lines were circular and sometimes vertical. And there was nothing unpleasant about their faces.

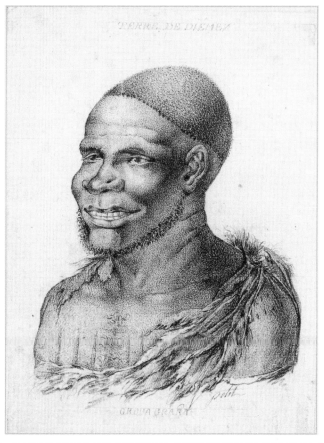

Portrait of 'Grouagrara' (Van Diemen's Land), Nicolas-Martin Petit. Muséum d'histoire naturelle, Le Havre – n° 20 007.2

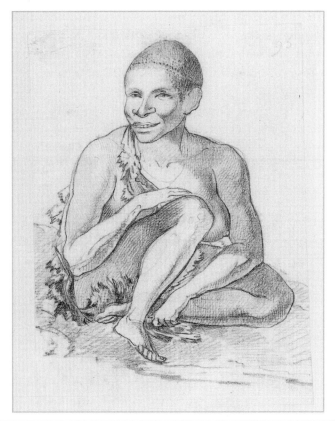

Aboriginal woman in a crouching position (Van Diemen's Land), Nicolas-Martin Petit. Muséum d'histoire naturelle, Le Havre – n° 20 012

Their expression was playful and they had a sharp eye. Their noses were rather flat and they had big mouths. They had beautiful white teeth that were even and perfect – unless one considered them too large. They seemed to us to be between 5'2" and 5'6" in height and were well proportioned, except for their spindly legs and weak calves. They could have been from 25 to 40 years old . . .

We were passed by a second group of six or seven natives who had also communicated with the men guarding the boats and were returning with their presents, which they carried around their necks . . .

Of those who were in this group, two stood out because of the elegance of their dress. One wore a kangaroo skin or the skin of some other animal which covered his shoulders and his chest right down to his navel. His head appeared to be covered by a sort of shapeless wig cap. For quite a while we thought it was made of seaweed, but after examining it more closely we realised that it was his own hair, divided into strips about half an inch wide and one inch long, and held down with grease and reddish-brown dirt. It formed a skull-cap over his head that shook in a different way with every movement he made. The other native who was quite naked simply had his head shaved, with a long rope of hair coiled round it.

In spite of his favourable impression, the commander continued to be attentive to the security of his crew: the next day he advised the officers in charge of a fishing expedition to be on their guard and provided an escort of two armed men. His instinct was again correct, for midshipman Maurouard was hit on the neck by a spear as he was preparing to return to the ship with the rest of the party. Baudin sought to explain the incident rationally and without acrimony.

### 15 JANUARY 1802

While everyone was gathered around the fire waiting for the return of the tide, Citizen Maurouard, being strong and full of energy, decided to test his strength on the native whom he considered the strongest of the group. He started by clasping his wrist in the way young men do in Europe, making signs to his opponent to resist him with all his might, signs which the native understood perfectly. However, his strength was no match for Maurouard's. After this first successful bout, the two athletes wrestled with each other to see which one would bring down his opponent. Maurouard was again the winner and threw the native to the ground. As this scene took place on the sand, the fall was unlikely to cause injury to either party. Besides, it all happened amidst much laughter, and the loser seemed happier with his fall than the victor with his triumph.

Nevertheless, it seems likely to me that, once the natives saw their comrade overcome by superior strength, they would have tried later to let us know that they were not the weaker party when it came to skill and cunning. This is perhaps what prompted the throwing of the spear, for it was the only one they threw. However, it must not be assumed that they wanted us to respond with gunfire, for they are extremely frightened of this weapon – you only have to touch it.

The incident led Baudin to wonder whether some unspecified act of 'treachery' had taken place. Retribution, however, could not be further from his thoughts, as we can see from the measured comments which he made on other events that took place the same day, whether referring to the attempts of Aboriginal women to seduce his crew ('if my men are to be believed') or to a child's clumsy attempt to steal a marlin-spike. His tone was generally that of the bemused observer who sought to understand the unusual spectacle, while retaining his vigilance. He continued to provide an armed escort on the following day and noted that the mood of the Tasmanians had indeed changed since the Maurouard incident. They carried spears and no longer seemed eager for the crew to land. Since the expedition was also in need of water, it was obviously time to move on.

The French left their anchorage the next day and proceeded along D'Entrecasteaux Channel to North West Bay. The sailing was not easy but the wooded shoreline that Baudin sighted was described in glowing terms.

On 19 January the two ships were anchored in a bay on the western side of the tip of Bruny Island, where the search for fresh water supplies began in earnest. Hamelin had established that little water was to be found in the immediate vicinity, so Baudin decided to send a boat, under Breton's command, to investigate the 'North River' (the Derwent). Ronsard was to lead a shore party with the express order of hunting swans. A tent was set up on shore for the astronomer, Bernier, who was to observe the passage of Jupiter across the sun. Ronsard returned the following day, bringing swans and ducks, but also the news that he had found a fresh-water stream. This news became all the more welcome when Baudin discovered that the two days they had spent at their present anchorage had in fact been lost. Not only was the water source indicated on their map virtually non-existent, but the astronomer had failed in his mission to observe the eclipse, because of the inadequacy of his telescopes. After discussing the situation, Baudin and Hamelin decided to move a league or so further on in order to investigate the water source identified by Ronsard. From this anchorage, the dinghies were sent out on various missions: Henri Freycinet was given orders to undertake a detailed reconnaissance of the Derwent and Faure was to determine whether a passage existed between Frederik Hendrik and Marion Bays (Norfolk and Blackman Bays). The crew sent out in the longboat were instructed to fill the water casks.

## 23 JANUARY 1802

Our longboats had also been sent out at daybreak to take our casks ashore and fill them. So, when I left the ship at eight o'clock in my little dinghy, I expected to find everyone at work when I arrived; but in that I was much mistaken, for after rounding a point which had been blocking my view, I sighted my longboat engaged in a swan hunt instead of being where it had orders to be.

It was with some annoyance that I noted its movements, especially as it no longer had time to go in with the high tide as I had calculated.

Baudin did set aside his irritation to make an excursion inland during which he and Guichenot the gardener collected several plants for the herbarium. The party also observed a native camp that appeared to have been only recently deserted. As a result of this excursion, Baudin was able to make an assessment of the entire area surrounding the fresh-water stream from which the expedition was drawing its supplies.

> When I explored the country in the vicinity of this stream, I saw that the low-lying land all around makes up a fairly broad plain criss-crossed by channels into which the sea flows with every tide. The water in them is as salty as in the middle of the bay. If this plain were drained, then cultivated, it would be very fertile, for the soil is excellent. So is the soil on the surrounding hills, which are about a cannon-shot away. This place seemed to me to be a suitable site for a settlement.

However, the prospect of colonisation was distant and it was the captain's disappointment with his crew that was to be the dominant theme of his reports for the next two days. The longboat was just as slow to return as it had been to land, a fact which Baudin attributed to the hunting activities of the crew and the negligence of the officer in charge, who was replaced the following day by the more dependable Ronsard. But Baudin, who saw himself as a man of order and duty, seemed destined to be irritated by the unruly behaviour of his crew. This time it was their appetite for freshly-cooked meat that was responsible for the spectacle that greeted him when he went to visit the observatory on shore.

## 25 JANUARY 1802

> I was sorry, and indeed displeased, to see that the place was becoming like a public tavern for the two ships and that there was constant communication between them; for while I was there, five boats turned up – or rather, the passengers and those transporting them did. On an island that was no more than 25 to 30 feet long by 15 feet wide at its broadest point, there were seven or eight different kitchens and I was told that the day before they had nearly all been burnt alive, along with the tents and instruments, when the fires in two separate kitchens joined up and the grass caught alight. Fortunately, the winds had been off the land or else we would have lost everything.

> Everything I saw made me impatient to leave a place that serves no useful purpose; it can only hold up our operations and prolong our stay in this harbour.

He quickly seized on an indirect means of restoring order. Upon noticing that there was no longer a swan nor a pelican to be found in the area, he concluded that this was a direct result of the hunting that had just taken place and that this was a waste not only of the men's working time but also of precious ammunition. All was now obvious to him: the problem and its solution.

> The men who were supposed to guard the longboats in case of need took example from the conduct of their commanding officer and spread out into the woods as soon as they were ashore, returning only when they were hungry or out of ammunition. As I witnessed what went on during the longboat's second trip, I decided not to give the men on board any firearms in future and to limit their means of defence to a sword, a decision that Captain Hamelin has already made.

Could this be construed as an over-reaction in the face of a natural need for recreation and nourishment after the difficult passage from Timor? Captain Hamelin's prior decision to take exactly the same measure would seem to confirm that the crew had indeed overstepped the mark. In any case, the problem was contained by the precaution taken by both captains, who no doubt understood the reasons behind the crew-members' behaviour.

In fact, these early days ashore had been frustrating for all concerned. The opportunity to collect unique astronomical data had been missed, the collection of water was a slow and boring occupation, the yield in terms of botanical and zoological specimens had been poor, the trees felled by the carpenters did not provide the supply of sound timber they needed, and even the fishing catch was not always plentiful. When Henri Freycinet and Péron returned on 26 January from their reconnaissance in the Derwent, Péron's report that he had likewise found few specimens of interest incurred little in the way of sarcasm from his commander, who was no doubt too preoccupied with transporting water and timber to the ship in high winds and rough weather to dwell on the meagre results obtained by the naturalist.

The return of the Tasmanians distracted the attention of Baudin from the usual labours and their attendant irritations. The crew members who had been sent out on a fishing expedition had encountered on the shores of the northernmost bay of Bruny Island a friendly group of men from the local

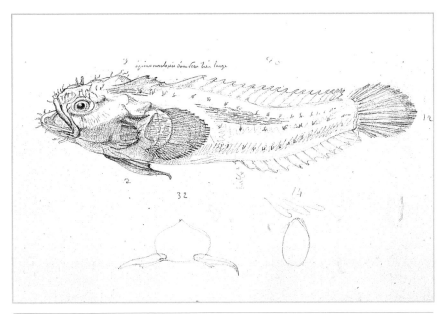

Fish of the Batrachoides family said by the French to inhabit the coasts of Tasmania, but no longer found there, *Batrachoides diemensis* (Lesueur, 1824). Charles-Alexandre Lesueur. Muséum d'histoire naturelle, Le Havre – n° 76 276

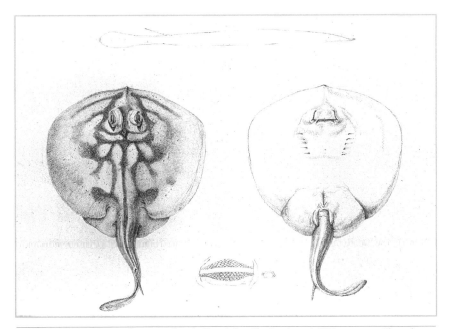

Dorsal and abdominal views of a species of ray the French found in abundance in D'Entrecasteaux Channel. It was a welcome addition to their table because of its 'tender and delicate' flesh. *Urolophus criciatus* (Lacépède, 1804). Charles-Alexandre Lesueur. Muséum d'histoire naturelle, Le Havre – n° 76 751

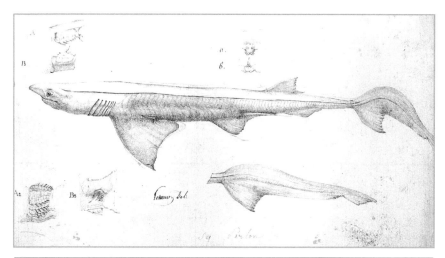

Shark caught by the French in Adventure Bay (Bruny Island), with details of teeth and caudal fin, *Notorynchus cepedianus* (Péron, 1807). Charles-Alexandre Lesueur. Muséum d'histoire naturelle, Le Havre – n° 76 793

Shark caught in North-West Bay (D'Entrecasteaux Channel), designated here as 'Squalus Daubenton', *Emissola antarctica* (Günther, 1870). Charles-Alexandre Lesueur. Muséum d'histoire naturelle, Le Havre – n° 76 828

Nuenonne people, two of whom they thought to have recognised from previous encounters. Not only did this happy meeting seem to augur well for the expedition's future relations with the Aborigines, but it was also part of a successful trip generally: the catch was sufficient to feed the entire crew and contained an unusual specimen of fish whose details were duly recorded. Baudin also noted on that day that he had given instructions to the shore party, led by Bernier the astronomer, that they should take special care to send to the ship any rare birds that were caught, thus expressing once more his concern for the expedition's natural history collection.

No doubt equally anxious to record information on the Aborigines, Baudin went the next day to the same landing-place where his men had met with the group of Tasmanians. He was dismayed to see that the members of what appeared to be the same group – since fires had remained alight in the same spot overnight – had become suspicious and few were now willing to approach the Europeans. This distrust increased when Baudin and his companions headed in the direction of some dense smoke. Not wishing to disturb the already tenuous relations with the Tasmanians, whom they presumed to be concerned for the safety of their women and children, the explorers went about their business of collecting plant specimens. Upon returning to the shore, they were puzzled to see that the distrust of the Aborigines had not abated, since several of their number were now carrying spears. Again the shore party was prudent in its approach and eventually persuaded the natives to sit down with them, where mutual inspection took place. As the Tasmanians examined the clothes and as much of the bodies of their visitors as they were allowed, Petit was sketching them and Baudin memorising the details that he would later record in his journal.

## 30 JANUARY 1802

Of the three natives sitting with us, two had a couple of rather large and freshly inflicted wounds on their legs, and the third had a dislocated finger on his right hand. All three were between 40 and 45 and were rather poorly built, especially in the lower part of the body. Their faces were coated with ground charcoal, over which they had put the red chalk that we had given them. There was nothing unpleasant about their faces; on the contrary, they had strong features and were full of character. Their foreheads were quite prominent, which gave the impression that their eyes were sunken and made them look small from a certain distance. They had very high cheekbones, their mouths were big and their teeth large, white, beautiful and even. Their eyes were sharp, their gaze was anxious and ever watchful. At the slightest move on our part, they were immediately on their feet, especially if somebody touched the gun, whose effect was well known to them and inspired great fear. I have no doubt that some of them must have had an unhappy experience with guns in other circumstances.

During the discussions that we had with these three natives and that lasted almost two hours, we had the time to observe them at our leisure. We pronounced various words for them, which they repeated very distinctly, and I

Aborigine sitting before his fire (Van Diemen's Land), Nicolas-Martin Petit. Muséum d'histoire naturelle, Le Havre – n° 20 005

was even very surprised by how few difficulties they experienced. However, any words in which there were R's and S's were not so easy for them.

Relations improved sufficiently over this time of mutual examination for trade to commence between the parties.

As Captain Hamelin wanted to exchange something for one of their spears, he proposed this to them by signs that were well understood, and it was agreed that they would give us a spear in return for a uniform button. Once the deal was struck, one of them went to fetch a weapon and handed it over upon receiving the agreed price. The two others did the same, handing them over on the same conditions and taking care not to let go of their spears until they had been paid in advance. As one of them had brought two, we tried to see if he

Portrait of 'Parabéri' (Van Diemen's Land), Nicolas-Martin Petit. Muséum d'histoire naturelle, Le Havre –
n° 20 018.1

would agree to give one up if we did not pay him until after we had received it, but he was very careful not to and did not want to hand it over even after he was paid for it. According to the practice we had established, we held on to one end of the spear as we handed over the button, so he was obliged to let it go and he did not seem to like it.

Insisting on the exchange proved unwise, and was particularly unfortunate for Baudin, who was injured in the resulting skirmish. However, he showed courage and restraint in facing his assailants and keeping them at bay until the crew had safely launched the boats.

Once our deals had been done, the natives stood their distance, as if they were frightened that we would use on them the weapons they had just sold us. However, when they saw that we were heading back to our boats, they followed us again. Citizen Petit, who had done a drawing of one of them, had the paper ripped from his hand, but, being as quick as the fellow who had snatched it from him, he took it back and we continued to make for the shore. We had only just arrived when the three natives, with whom we had been on such friendly terms and whom we had showered with presents, began to pick up stones which they immediately threw at us. Several reached the line of our boats, although they landed a long way away, and luckily did not hurt anyone. I was not so lucky as the others, for a fairly large stone hit me just as I was bending over to examine the valve of a seashell and wounded me slightly on the hip. I immediately took aim at the man who had thrown it, an action which gave him such a fright that he put his head down and ran for his life, although he was well out of range of my gun.

Fearing that they might return to the attack as we were getting into the boats, I decided to go up to them again while everyone embarked. Captain Hamelin followed me. We saw the natives again; they were quite a long way off and calling one other with very high-pitched cries which were answered from a distance. We then went back to get in the boats ourselves, convinced that they would soon turn up in rather large numbers. This in fact happened, for shortly after we saw 12 or 15 appear on the shore. We were so far away that we could not make out what they were carrying. They were heading south-west. Since the wind was favourable, we headed towards them, coming back in close to shore. When they saw that we were approaching them much faster than they were walking – even though they had doubled their pace – they split up into several groups and went into the forest, where we soon lost sight of them.

Baudin immediately surmised that relations had soured because of the Tasmanians' dissatisfaction with the exchange of buttons for spears, although he did not reflect upon the possible effects of having appeared to vary the conditions of exchange or consider the prospect that the exchange itself might have been perceived as inherently unfair. However, he did continue to express measured views on the natives, in spite of the injury he had received. On the one hand, he did not consider them to be so dangerous as to be concerned for the safety of the party that was overdue to return from shore – their large numbers would ensure their protection. On the other hand, he was anxious not to inflame a delicate situation. Consequently, he ordered that contact with the Tasmanians be avoided and urged the fishing-party that went out the following day to keep a safe distance from shore.

In the meantime, events had conspired to bring once more to his attention the failings of his crew. He was already impatient with the anxiety expressed by those on board about the men who had failed to return from shore. He took the opportunity to remind them that if they had not wasted so much ammunition on hunting, they would not have had to worry about their fellows on shore being deprived of the protection of firearms. All this was true enough, although hardly an example of diplomacy in a moment of tension. He justified his ill temper by pointing to the inefficiency and lack of discipline of the crew. Many of these judgments appear quite well founded. In this particular case, his annoyance at being pestered about the safety of the longboat turned to justifiable anger when the longboats finally arrived.

## 31 JANUARY 1802

A matter that I found far more unpleasant than anything I had been told about the fate of the men collecting water was the last straw for me. It darkened the black mood I was already in because my longboat was overdue. I was furious about the quality of the water that had been brought back: it all had to be thrown overboard. The skipper of the longboat declared that it was entirely the fault of midshipman Brue – who was the commanding officer – since he had not wanted to wait until the tide was low enough to fill the casks. To prove his point, he made me taste some from a keg of water that had been collected an hour and a half after the casks had been filled and which was very good. The result of this conduct is that we have just lost two days for nothing. The only excuse offered me by the midshipman was that there was an officer in the *Naturaliste*'s longboat who had done just the same and that he had followed his example. According to that principle, I believe that, if the officer in question had taken it into his head to set fire to his boat, my midshipman would have done the same just to follow his lead.

Baudin's bad humour gave way to satisfaction the next day when the longboats returned 'with their full cargo of good water'. He was also comforted by the news that the natives had been friendly to the fishing party the previous day and invited them to dance with them. In compliance with his orders to keep a safe distance, they had refused the invitation, while promising to return. Baudin

Portrait of 'Arra-Maïda' carrying a child on her back (Van Diemen's Land), Nicolas-Martin Petit. Muséum d'histoire naturelle, Le Havre – n° 20 022.3

now thought it time to see for himself whether it was safe to re-establish contact. What followed was another encounter – this time with women and children.

## 1 FEBRUARY 1802

At nine o'clock we left to go fishing. I wanted to see for myself how the natives behaved, especially after the report I had received the day before. When we set off, the weather was very fine, with a light westerly breeze. When we reached the shore, no one was there to meet us, but we barely had time to throw out the net before the natives appeared amid loud exclamations that showed how happy they were to see us. There were 16 of them, but only four were men. The rest of the party was made up of two women, plus children of various ages – the eldest did not appear to be more than 12 years old and the youngest five, apart from a baby, about three months old, at its mother's breast . . .

As I wanted portraits done of the women and some of the children, I asked them to sit down, which they did most obligingly; but since our men were preparing to haul in the net, it was now impossible to stop them from running over to watch, whether it was because this way of fishing was a novelty for them, or for some other reason, I cannot explain.

The delight of the children and even the grown men was at its height when they saw the fish that were caught in the net. Their cries and their antics sufficed to show us how pleased they were. We offered to share our catch with them, but they would accept nothing, making it clear to us that they did not eat fish, but only shell-fish or crustacea.

We put the net out a third time, and while the boat was taking it out to sea to give it the necessary circumference, we went and sat down again at the foot of the other side of the hill facing us. The natives followed and we all sat down together on the grass. I had two men constantly beside me, watching every movement I made because I was the only one with a firearm. If I happened to transfer it from my right hand to my left, their anxiety immediately began to show, and I only had to change its position to see how much they feared the effect of a gun.

The children were growing more and more friendly and could not have played more happily with our men; they had a sense of fun that was most endearing. Their faces, too, were very attractive, not being disfigured by dirtiness or by the red and black colouring the men and women use as body decoration. We had races with them, did somersaults and played various other games that greatly amused the natives. We took advantage of this fun to finish off the drawings which had been roughly sketched when they first arrived.

When the net was pulled in, they all went to the beach just as they had done the first time, particularly the children, who hauled on the ropes with gusto, imitating our men and repeating very intelligibly everything they said. I was truly amazed that these children, who had at first appeared so fearful and shy, should have become as sociable as they did in such a short time – to the point where, if our men would not dance, play or run with them, they tormented them until they did what they wanted. Another thing that is just as extraordinary and difficult to explain is that the men who were with us were the very same ones who, a day earlier, had attacked us with stones as we left. They recognised us perfectly, making it clear to us that they had seen us before. However, they were in our midst and at our mercy. Somebody wanted to remind them of what they had done to us previously, but I objected to it, not wanting them to think we bore them any ill feeling.

This courtesy was followed up by a second invitation to the Tasmanians to join the crew in a meal of fish, even though the catch had been barely sufficient for a day's supply. This offer was similarly refused, simply because, as Baudin remarked, 'they appeared quite amazed to see people eating fish'. The incident that followed once again made it obvious that they preferred to eat shellfish and crustaceans. However, this is not the principal reason why the incident attracted Baudin's interest. It had begun when three of the ship's company had encountered several women returning from a lobster fishing expedition. The women ran into the woods in fright but were followed by the crew, who tried to reassure them by offering them presents. What followed resembled an act of seduction, but Baudin remains discreet as to the extent to which his men may have responded to the implied sexual advances of one of the women.

The first thing we did was sit down, and the lovely ladies, no doubt wanting to please the new group of people around them, smeared their faces with charcoal moistened with saliva and then were so insistent that their admirers did the same that they gave in, with the result that, when they returned, we no longer recognised them except by their clothes. One of the women had gone off into the woods with M. Heirisson and may perhaps have completely satisfied her curiosity, for they were all extremely curious to see not only the chests of our officers and scientists, but also whether they resembled the native men in bodily form or function.

Portrait of an Aboriginal boy (Van Diemen's Land), Nicolas-Martin Petit. Muséum d'histoire naturelle,
Le Havre – n° 20 021.4

Although the women acted boldly in this situation, they became reserved once they had rejoined the group on the shore, which included their 'husbands'. Yet no suspicion or ill will seemed to have been generated, and when the sailors decided to return to their ships their departure caused little disturbance.

The next two days were less eventful, although Baudin was pleased to note the capture of an interesting specimen of kangaroo and also the return of Faure from his excursion to ascertain the existence of a passage from Frederik Hendrik Bay to Marion Bay (Norfolk and Blackman Bays). Faure reported an important correction to the existing charts that showed the Forestier and Tasman Peninsulas as an island – named after Abel Tasman.

## 2 FEBRUARY 1802

> According to the report of the geographer Faure, whom I sent there for this express purpose, it appears that Abel Tasman Land has wrongly been made an island. It is joined to Van Diemen's Land by an isthmus, which can never be covered by the sea and which is about 90 paces in length and about the same in width. Citizen Faure walked all over it and in every direction. You can see on the chart that he has drawn up not only Frederik Hendrik Bay, but also the isthmus connecting the so-called Tasman Island with Van Diemen's Land – there is definitely no channel separating the two.

With this news to buoy his spirits, as well as the safe return on board of the astronomical instruments and the continuing friendliness of the natives, Baudin was suddenly drawn back into the personnel issues that plagued his expedition at all levels. This time he was asked to intervene in a running dispute between Captain Hamelin and his senior officer Milius, who had requested a transfer. Baudin's sympathies went to his loyal companion Hamelin. He was also wary of taking another disgruntled officer on board the *Géographe* and chose instead to maintain the status quo. It was perhaps even of some cold comfort to the commander that the problems affecting his expedition were not all to be traced back to his own ship. As he discovered the following day, there had been some pilfering on board the *Naturaliste*. Many of the natural history specimens that were intended for the expedition's collections had disappeared following the zoologist Levillain's death. Baudin immediately gave strict instructions to Hamelin that the missing objects must be returned.

## 5 FEBRUARY 1802

I have just been informed that, when we sold the various articles belonging to [Levillain], several of those that he had purchased or been given were included. This disposal is absolutely contrary to regulations, which authorise only the sale of linen or anything that is liable to spoil. If these articles are not in this category, you will be so good as to demand their return from those who bought them, draw up an inventory of them, of which you will send me a signed copy, and hold them for his family to dispose of as they see fit. It is said that there were some gold objects, which were also sold off.

His determination was rewarded and his instructions faithfully carried out.

At nightfall Captain Hamelin sent over to me in his dinghy several small chests and pinewood boxes containing various objects of Natural History that had been sold as M. Levillain's belongings. These articles were government property, for we were in no doubt whatsoever that they had been collected by different people during the shore visits we made right up to the time of the death of this trainee-zoologist. I demanded their return in the name of the government so that they could be duly handed over. All the objects were carefully examined upon their arrival on board, and they are now all arranged in specially made chests bearing a label indicating that he assembled or collected them during the voyage.

With this issue resolved, the commander could focus once more on the scientific purpose of his mission. The journal entries of the following days contain various obsevations relating to the customs of the Tasmanians and the collection of specimens. Baudin's comments on the use of fire by the Aborigines reveal his continued interest, as a correspondent of the 'Society of the Observers of Man', in finding a well-reasoned explanation for local customs that were new to him.

## 6 FEBRUARY 1802

Throughout the day we saw large fires not far from the coast. They spread so much with the violence of the wind that by midday everything to port was ablaze. The fire to starboard, although quite large, was smaller. There is no doubt that the natives are responsible for these huge blazes, for the direction of the wind could not have given it the impetus to go off in the different directions that we saw it take. It is not perhaps for the simple pleasure of destroying that they set fire to their forests in this way, and it is reasonable to suppose that there is some useful purpose behind it. If we follow this line of reasoning, it could perhaps have been started merely to burn off the grass and scrub that make walking painful and difficult, or for hunting quadrupeds sighted in the area.

Baudin likewise encouraged Péron in his efforts to observe the customs and language of the Tasmanians, though he could not resist expressing his scepticism regarding the likelihood of obtaining results in an area which the local inhabitants had manifestly deserted.

## 7 FEBRUARY 1802

As Citizens Depuch and Péron had asked to be sent ashore to go and speak with the natives, so that they could add to the vocabulary they had begun, I gave orders that they be given one of our light craft and they set off. Nevertheless, I observed to them that their hopes would be disappointed and that they would find no one. I was convinced that they had moved camp, as I had not seen any smoke in the area where the natives had settled upon their arrival. Although they were firmly convinced that they knew better, events showed that my remarks were not as ill-advised as they thought, for when they returned they reported that they had found no one there.

The fishing activities on the same day brought more obvious joy to Baudin, who expressed his eagerness to protect the unusual specimens that were brought on board and whose nomenclature was a source of inquiry for his naturalists.

Our boat's catch was fairly good. Among the fish caught were three of the type that Anderson calls elephant fish. No doubt this naturalist gave them that name on account of the trunk that hangs from the tip of their snout. His description of them did not seem very accurate to our naturalists. Attached to the underside of one of these three fish were two things that are most extraordinary and that I shall do my best to preserve. The material that they are made of is solid, which allows us to hope for the best.

Baudin's journal entries at this time contain many observations that demonstrate his keen interest in matters of natural history. Hamelin, the captain of the *Naturaliste*, similarly spent time on shore collecting specimens, though he always deferred to Baudin's judgment when it came to assessing their value. At this point, it appears to have been butterflies that occupied the commander's energies – a fact which later drew criticism when Henri Freycinet attributed part of the failure of the mission to the time wasted in Tasmania collecting shells and butterflies. Whether or not such a comment was justified, it high-lighted the tension surrounding the principal objective of the mission – to further the cause of science or to chart and thus to colonise? In Tasmania, at least, Baudin was pursuing with equal vigour the dual objective: his officers did valuable surveying work and both he and his scientists collected data and specimens in great quantity.

## 9 FEBRUARY 1802

Towards midday I went ashore with Captain Hamelin and we stayed there for about three hours. I had intended to collect some native butterflies, but this

A species of butterfly common to Tasmania and mainland Australia. The artist has drawn the caterpillar and the chrysalis as well as dorsal and ventral views of a female specimen. *Belenois java teutonia* (Fabricius, 1775). Charles-Alexandre Lesueur. Muséum d'histoire naturelle, Le Havre – n° 73 009

expedition was unsuccessful. All the ones that I caught were of the same species and not very nice to look at.

The following day was to compensate for this meagre success by bringing in a collector's item of real significance.

### 10 FEBRUARY 1802

Captain Hamelin's boat returned from its fishing expedition, bringing on board a canoe, the only sign of industry that we had so far observed among the natives of this part of the coast. I think that the term 'raft' or 'floating buoy' would be more appropriate than 'canoe' for the bundles of bark they assemble and lash together, and which they use for crossing from one shore to another. The sticks they use to propel it also bear no relation to the paddles used in canoes. See the drawing that I am providing of it. These buoys, which are pointed at both ends and which can be hollowed out to 2 or 3 inches, have the advantage over canoes of not being able to capsize, for their displacement is considerable. The oarsmen in it stand or squat.

Baudin's strongest expressions of satisfaction frequently seem to be reserved for the scientific finds of the day, however small.

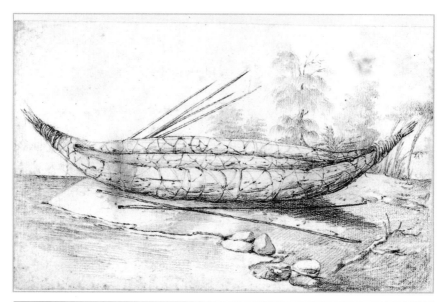

Canoe on a shore; a few spears (Van Diemen's Land), Nicolas-Martin Petit. Muséum d'histoire naturelle, Le Havre – n° 18 004

# 13 FEBRUARY 1802

Although there was only a slim chance of setting sail during the day, I did not want to send out any boat on a fishing expedition; but I did let my longboat go out. It was not on board, as I had planned to tow it astern and use it for dredging. It returned at midday, bringing nothing but a single beautiful shell-fish. Although it was dead, it struck us as being so beautiful and so precious that it helped make up for being kept at anchor. None of us knew what it was nor had we seen anything like it.

Seashell found in North West Bay (D'Entrecasteaux Channel), *Phasianella australis* (Gmelin, 1791).
Charles-Alexandre Lesueur. Muséum d'histoire naturelle, Le Havre – n° 72 059

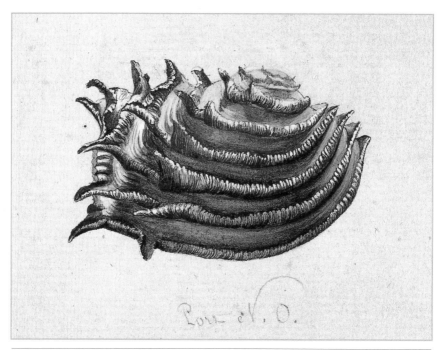

Seashell found in North West Bay (D'Entrecasteaux Channel), *Bassina disjecta* (Perry, 1811). Charles-Alexandre Lesueur. Muséum d'histoire naturelle, Le Havre – n° 72 067

However, given the other sad news that the day was to bring – that the condition of his friend Maugé, the zoologist, was now hopeless – it is not surprising that the commander sought consolation in accomplishing the professional duties that were closest to his heart, nor that these corresponded with the interests that he shared with Maugé, the companion of his previous missions. As unfavourable weather continued to prevent the *Géographe* from leaving D'Entrecasteaux Channel and heading for the next stop at Maria Island, Baudin spent much time with his dying companion and expressed a great sadness that was only punctuated by remarks about the fishing catch or other routine details. It was not until the evening of 16 February that the situation changed and that the French were able to begin their slow progress towards Great Oyster Bay, which they reached two days later, naming many landmarks along the way.

## 18 FEBRUARY 1802

At seven o'clock we rounded Cape Pillar and little Tasman Island, and then set our course for the channel between Hippolyte Rocks and the mainland. As we sailed up the coast, at a distance of 3/4 of a league – sometimes more and often less – we took bearings and views all the way. This part of the coast is sparsely wooded in comparison with D'Entrecasteaux Channel, but on the other hand it presents a great number of highly interesting sites.

As the entire coast between Cape Pillar and Cape Frederik Hendrik is unnamed, we gave a name to each point or cape at which our bearings began and ended.

The highlands forming Cape Pillar are generally arid and sparsely-wooded, but a little to the north of this cape the vegetation has an attractive and varied appearance, with subtle shades of colour. I called the first point to the north of Cape Pillar, abeam of Hippolyte Rocks, Pointe des Organistes [Cape Hauy].

By conferring names upon so many of the coastal features of eastern Tasmania, the expedition left a permanent reminder of its passage in these waters, even though some of the names given by Baudin were later changed by Péron and

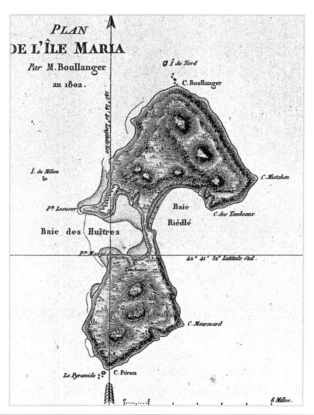

Map of Maria Island showing Great Oyster Bay (*Baie des Huîtres*) and Riédlé Bay, Boullanger (1802). Published in the *Atlas* of the *Voyage de découvertes aux Terres Australes* (1811)

Freycinet. As the surveying continued, the French had further contact with Aborigines, and they were quick to note the similarities and differences between the Tyreddeme people of Maria Island and the Nuenonne group of D'Entrecasteaux Channel.

## 19 FEBRUARY 1802

As we made our way to the north point of Oyster Bay, we saw about 20 natives on the beach, men, women and children. Most of them were armed with a spear of the same construction as the ones in D'Entrecasteaux Channel. They made no hostile signs when we landed. They simply retreated a little further back from the shore. The gestures of friendship that we made after disembarking seemed to reassure them. The presents which soon followed these demonstrations established mutual trust.

After we all sat down together, we examined them closely. They did exactly the same to us. Nevertheless, the women and children stayed a little way off and did not seem to us to be as cheerful as those on Bruny Island, which is no doubt because they have had fewer opportunities to see ships and the strangers in them. The children especially seemed very shy and fearful, despite their fathers' and mothers' invitations to come and get what we were offering them. As they did not dare to come near us, we were obliged to throw the presents over to them and, after picking them up, they quickly retreated.

The grown men, like the women, were completely naked. The latter wore kangaroo skins over their shoulders, as did their sisters of Bruny Channel [sic – D'Entrecasteaux Channel]. The men were better built than those we had already met. Although they were tattooed like the others, these had more stripes on their arms. With the exception of those who seemed to us of smaller build, they had spindly legs and a pot-belly. The women's faces are not attractive and they are not generally well-built nor very tall. One of the men had his face smeared with charcoal. Their customs and lifestyle appeared to us to be similar to those of the channel natives. Before leaving them at sundown, we exchanged some trinkets with them for their spears. The exchange was made very amicably on both sides. We said goodbye to them, giving them to understand that we would return the following day.

Although the encounters of Maria Island led to some rich finds for the artists and scientists, this area also became etched in Baudin's memory for more personal reasons, for it was here that Maugé finally died. He was buried at the point that would later bear his name.

# 21 FEBRUARY 1802

At nine o'clock I set out to attend the burial of a man whose death and whose dying words filled me with grief. A few moments before he died, he said to me: 'I am dying because I was too devoted to you and scorned my friends' advice, but you should at least remember me in return for the sacrifice that I have made for you.'

As we left the ship, all the guns fired a salute. When we were half-way to shore, a second salute was fired and a third as we landed. The body of the naturalist was buried between two casuarinas and two eucalypts; on one of the casuarinas we placed the following inscription, engraved on a lead plaque:

> Here lies Citizen René Maugé, zoologist on the
> expedition of discovery commanded by Captain Baudin
> 3 Ventôse, year 10 of the French Republic.

With the death of Citizen Maugé the expedition has incurred an irreparable loss. This naturalist did not have the title of scientist but, single-handed, he did more than all the scientists put together. Occupied solely with his work, he thought of nothing but his duty, and I never had cause to reproach him on that score.

It is distressing for me to realise that he and Citizen Riédlé, the only two real friends that I had on board, have fallen victim to their friendship for me – their only reason for deciding to embark on a voyage that proved so fatal to them both.

In spite of the commander's intense sorrow, the work of the expedition continued unabated; he proceeded after the ceremony to investigate a source of fresh water, only to encounter the same group of Aborigines as the day before, this time in more difficult circumstances.

Several natives had gathered round our men and had even put the carpenters to flight after making a real nuisance of themselves. They even made several attempts to take away their hatchets. One of our men, the youngest, was forcibly taken off into the woods. They were content to examine him from head to foot, without, I should add, doing him any harm. They did not even take his hatchet when the ceremony was over. When we arrived, the natives withdrew and we had a great deal of trouble gathering them round us. However, we managed to do it by taking our time and making signs of friendship. They all carried a spear and a sort of club, both of which were very

roughly made and unlikely to do much harm when thrown from a short
distance . . .

    The natives of Maria Island were just as familiar with the effects of our
firearms as the natives of D'Entrecasteaux Channel, but they did not hold
them in such fear and the noise of the explosion made little impression on
them. They persuaded M. Ronsard to kill some birds, which they went and
collected themselves and which we gave them. They promptly plucked them,
then lightly grilled them over our fire, before eating them, tripes and all, with a
hearty appetite, letting nothing go to waste.

The strict compliance with orders to avoid violence had again defused a difficult situation and the commander was interested to observe both the eating
habits of the Aborigines and their familiarity with firearms – the latter being
the legacy of their contact with previous French and British visitors to these
parts. By far the outstanding event on Maria Island was the discovery of a
native burial site, the significance of which Baudin recognised, paying due
credit to François Péron.

    Citizen Péron had discovered a tomb and brought back several human bones
and even some pieces of flesh that the fire had not consumed. Citizen
Leschenault also found one, so there seems no doubt that the custom of
burning the dead is practised by the inhabitants of this island and the
mainland. The tomb, of which I am providing a detailed drawing, is, of all the
things that we have seen, the most skilfully and carefully made. These tombs
are infinitely superior to anything else that we have discovered about the
natives, of whom we can say that they are more concerned to preserve and
perpetuate the memory of their dead relatives or friends than they are to think
of their own preservation.

    Citizen Péron, who examined a tomb at some leisure, will give us a more
accurate description than I could from the report I have been given, and
Citizen Petit's drawings will fill in any other missing details.

Baudin returned to this discovery in the lengthy summary that provides a
conclusion to the section in his journal related to the on-shore stay of his expedition in Tasmania. Here he gives more detail and refers to Péron's expertise
in a more positive way than is usually to be found in his references to the
young scientist. He had entrusted to Péron the careful observation of the
Aborigines, no doubt in recognition of the anthropologist's eagerness to make

Aboriginal tombs on Maria Island (front and back views), some carved bark can be seen in the right foreground. The two ships are anchored in the bay. Nicolas-Martin Petit. Muséum d'histoire naturelle, Le Havre – n° 18 020

a significant contribution in this domain. In this, Baudin was indeed to be proven correct, for Péron's report on Maria Island remains a document of interest for historians and anthropologists alike.

> One of the most remarkable things that we have discovered, by a stroke of luck, is the way in which they bury their dead. I am providing a picture of their tombs, but there is no doubt that they burn the dead, keeping only the ashes and the bones that the fire has not destroyed and which they preserve with care. The two tombs that we found and which were dug up presented us with a most surprising sight. We first had to dismantle a kind of hut in the shape of a sugarloaf. The strips of eucalypt bark of which it was made rested on four branches, each curved in a semi-circle and with one end planted in the ground. Under these four hoops, which had roughly the shape of the bottom of a basket, we found two or three thin layers of a type of grass which is very common on this island and which must make good pasture for live-stock. After lifting it off, we found a heap of ashes, among which were several human bones and even some pieces of flesh that the fire had not yet consumed. At one end of the pile of ashes there was a small channel, which is probably where the natives place the body to which they are paying their last respects.

We were all the more delighted with this find since we have learnt nothing on this subject from explorers – at least, not to my knowledge.

Citizen Péron, as an observer of man, will no doubt give a very detailed account of the form of this tomb, as well as his ideas on the origin of this custom among these people – a custom that is very different from those practised in the islands of the Southern Ocean.

Baudin's summary contained many other remarks upon the customs of the different groups of Tasmanians whom the commander and his men had encountered, although these do not include all of the incidents that Péron and others described in their own journals. Péron's encounter with the young and vivacious Ouré-Ouré led him to conclude that her flirtatious behaviour was a reflection of the happiness of the natural state; but in another incident, he evoked the terror and submission of the Bruny Island women whom he assumed, from the scars on their bodies, to be mistreated and brutalised by their jealous and ferocious men-folk.

The question of the crew's sexual encounters is treated with great discretion in all of the accounts of the voyage, and it remains a matter of conjecture as to whether any of the French crew did have intercourse with the native women. The journals, including Baudin's, all refer to the women as unattractive, although Ouré-Ouré seems to have interested more than one of the group of Frenchmen she encountered. We do know, however, that some of the young beardless sailors allowed themselves to be undressed in order to assure the Tasmanians that they were indeed men. Several close inspections are mentioned in the accounts of the expedition. Heirisson's experience on Bruny Island has already been noted; in his summary, Baudin refers to two further incidents of this type.

Having forced the son of the *Naturaliste*'s master-carpenter to go away with them into the wood, they were content to examine him from head to foot without doing him any harm and, once they had satisfied their curiosity, they left him free to rejoin his companions. This young man was carrying a large hatchet which did not tempt them in the least, although they had looked very closely at how he used it.

One of the apprentices from the *Géographe* was also examined by these people, and in Citizen Péron's presence. The natives found him in such a happy state that they expressed great joy and satisfaction.

Naturally, the French seem to have been equally bemused by the appearance and customs of the Tasmanians:

> The men have a rather curious habit that greatly amused our sailors – that is, they almost always hold on to the end of their foreskin, with the result that it is quite long.

Baudin's summary is rich in detail of the daily lives of the inhabitants of Tasmania, a fact which reveals both his inherent interest in the subject and his strict compliance with the scientific objectives of his mission. He took just as great an interest in the natural resources of the island. It is difficult to believe, however, that his scientific observations were totally divorced from considerations of a more pragmatic nature: when assessing the island's suitability for settlement, he notes that it was the French who had first discovered the southern part of the island, before pointing out a possible site for a future colony.

> The channel discovered and explored on the voyage of Rear-Admiral d'Entrecasteaux is unquestionably very useful to navigation, since it provides an infinite number of harbours and resources, whether for ships in need of repair or for those that are simply looking for fresh supplies and a little rest. Its only disadvantage is the difficulty obtaining water to replace what has been consumed by the time you get there. Nevertheless, we have found several streams which could easily be diverted to the sea if one had the wherewithal to make a run-off channel.
>
> The place called Port Cygnet, which I had carefully surveyed, is, of all the places along the channel, the one that seemed most suitable for the establishment of a European colony . . .
>
> Everywhere in this southern part of the large island of Van Diemen's Land, the quality of the soil makes it suitable for cultivation, and its excellence would guarantee the success of any crops if active and hard-working men devoted themselves to the task.

In addition to offering important practical advantages, the south-eastern part of the island was found to be visually attractive, with the commander noting that the scenery to be found on the tip of the Tasman Peninsula, for example, presented a 'very pleasant' aspect and was 'as picturesque as any you could hope to see'.

The expedition headed north to explore the eastern coast of Van Diemen's

TERRE DE DIÉMEN.

1. *Vue du Cap Forestier* (a.) *de la Baie Thouin* (b.) *et du Cap Tourville* (c.)    4. *Suite de l'île Schouten.* (g.) *Détroit du Géographe* (h.)
2. *Vue du Pic d'Arcole* (d.) *et du Pitou Champagny* (e.)    *Cap Degérando.* (i.) *partie Sud de la Presqu'île Freycinet.* (k.)
3. *Vue générale de l'île Schouten : le Cap Sauniérat* (f.) *restant au S ¼ S. O.*

Coastal profiles of the east coast of Tasmania. Views: 1. Wineglass Bay on the east coast of the Freycinet Peninsula, flanked by Cape Forestier (left) and Cape Tourville (right); 2. East coast of Tasmania from about St Patrick's Head to St Helen's Point; 3. Schouten Island from the east; 4. Northern tip of Schouten Island (left) to the southern part of the Freycinet Peninsula (right). (Identifications: F. Horner.) Charles-Alexandre Lesueur or Nicolas-Martin Petit. Published in the *Atlas* of the *Voyage de découvertes aux Terres Australes* (1807)

Land on 27 February 1802. Unfavourable winds prevented the ships from making great headway until 6 March, when Baudin was able to reach the 42nd parallel and take up the hydrographic work at the point where Faure's survey had ceased.

## 6 MARCH 1802

During the morning, the weather was very fine and clear and the breeze was moderate. I had the large dinghy set down and entrusted its command to 1st class midshipman Maurouard. Our geographer, Citizen Boullanger, who is unfortunately so short-sighted that he can only take bearings and angles with his nose to the ground, went on board so that he could get closer to the shore than was possible in a large ship. Before he left, I gave him most explicit instructions to return before nightfall and to position himself with respect to the ship so that he did not leave our sight. All these warnings were in vain. At midday we could no longer see him. He will probably have run so far in to shore that he only stopped when he had no means of getting any closer.

This was a period of great anxiety for Baudin. A collision between the *Géographe* and her consort the day before had already troubled him.

> It would be difficult to explain why the ship [the *Naturaliste*] collided with us
> and broke our spitsail yard. She had passed to leeward with all sails set and
> filled with air. Apparently the officer on duty, in what he thought to be a
> skilful manoeuvre, tried to double us to windward, and wrongly judged the
> distance, so that he caught our head in his foremast rigging. Fortunately we
> bore away in time and avoided being smashed to pieces in the collision.

Indeed, this incident was minor compared with the loss of the dinghy. In
spite of all of the commander's efforts to maintain a landward tack and to
signal to the dinghy with lights and rockets once night fell, it did not return.
By the next day, Baudin's health had taken a turn for the worse. On 8 March
he found himself confined to bed with colic pains that were 'so acute that I got
no relief from any of the remedies that I was made to take.' Worse news was
yet to come:

> Before dark we signalled to the *Naturaliste* to rally but, either because she did
> not see the signal or because she was afraid of colliding with us a second time,
> she headed off in the opposite direction and was soon lost from view. I am not
> too sure how to interpret this manoeuvre.

The *Géographe* was left alone to continue her search to the north of the point
where the dinghy had last been seen. In spite of his misgivings Baudin, who
could not believe that Maurouard or Boullanger would ignore his instructions
to survey to the north, nevertheless complied with the officers' wish to turn
southward. Hopes were raised when a sail was sighted.

## 10 MARCH 1802

> At daybreak on the 19th [Ventôse], we were preparing to stand in for land to
> continue our search for the dinghy. We sighted a sail ahead of us that we first
> took to be the *Naturaliste*, but we soon realised our mistake, for the ship in
> question was rigged out like a schooner. Since I presumed that she must be
> some vessel from Port Jackson and was possibly engaged in the reconnaissance
> of this coast, I bore towards her and, at seven o'clock, after coming to within
> half a pistol shot of her, I hailed her.
>    I was then informed that she was indeed an English schooner on her way

to Maria Island or thereabouts to fish for sea-perch. As I was very glad to take advantage of this opportunity to obtain help for my dinghy, if anyone had happened to sight it, I put a boat down and sent an officer aboard to ask the skipper to be so good as to come and talk to me. He arrived at a quarter past seven, accompanied by someone who was probably his second-in-command. I told him of the mishap that had befallen us and offered to pay him whatever he wanted to stay with me for two or three days so as to omit not even the smallest cove from a thorough search. I could not persuade him to accept my proposal, and he excused himself on the grounds that the fishing season was too far advanced; but he assured me that he himself would not fail to conduct a search in case events had led our men to return to this spot . . .

The *Naturaliste* had also met this vessel and had informed her that we would probably speak to her. Captain Hamelin let me know that he was going to anchor in the strait. It was probably this quite odd idea that led him to part company from us without telling me. At eight o'clock, I had the two men taken back to their schooner, promising them a decent reward if they brought my men to Port Jackson.

Reassured by this news of the *Naturaliste* and of its plans, as conveyed by the captain of the English schooner, Baudin resumed his search for the missing dinghy. Despite finding no trace of it, he continued to believe that its crew would survive and it was perhaps this thought that eventually helped him to overcome his own illness.

## 12 MARCH 1802

The more I thought about this incident, the less I could be persuaded to believe that any unfortunate accident had befallen the dinghy if it had remained close to shore, and I still hope to find it somewhere at the entrance to the strait. It is true that the men in it will have suffered greatly through lack of food and possibly water; but in short, if they have had courage, they will still be alive.

## 15 MARCH 1802

For five days, I had been very unwell with the colic pains that I have mentioned, and it was only from this time onwards that the medicines administered to me began to offer me some relief. The doctors were afraid that I might contract some serious illness and I was of the same opinion myself. But, judging from my state of health today, it looks as if I shall soon be completely recovered.

A collective decision was taken to return north, and by 19 March the *Géographe* had sighted Waterhouse Island, in Banks Strait, where Baudin expected to find the *Naturaliste* waiting.

## 19 MARCH 1802

I coasted along its western side in the hope of finding the *Naturaliste*, to whom I had indicated it as a meeting-place in case we were separated before entering the strait. The more I thought about Captain Hamelin's possible reasons for leaving me on the east coast of Van Diemen's Land, the less I could comprehend them, and I am all the more astonished at not having met him in the designated place. Indeed, I have almost circumnavigated this island and have not seen any sign of him. Perhaps I shall have better luck at Port Dalrymple, for he sent me word by the skipper of the English schooner, to whom I spoke myself, that he was heading into the strait and would anchor wherever he could, which will perhaps make it very difficult to find him.

This assumption was entirely correct, for the *Géographe* remained several days in the area without sighting her consort. At the Furneaux Islands, an eclipse provided an opportunity to reset the chronometers.

## 20 MARCH 1802

The number of islands in this group seemed much larger to us than what is shown in this latitude on the English map, an impression that was probably created by the fact that we were too far off to see the low-lying landmasses linking most of the islands to the others. Moreover, I am giving a very accurate view of the appearance of the land in 40° 21' of latitude and 144° 57' 48" of longitude, according to our chronometers.

Going by the eclipse of the moon observed the day before, we found that our No. 35 differed by only 0° 1' 28" 5''' west from the longitude indicated in the nautical almanac, which gave 11 hours 6' 0" for the time of the middle of the eclipse, while for us it was 1 hour 48' 46" 9'''.

The time was reduced to the Greenwich meridian because, in the nautical almanac published in Paris, somebody inadvertently transcribed the times for the phases of the moon without reducing them to the Paris meridian.

Over the next few days, rough weather prevented Baudin from putting in at Port Dalrymple as he had intended. His reaction was to be relieved that the *Naturaliste* was not with them during the ordeal and had not had to endure the same seas. Of particular concern, as the *Géographe* attempted to stand off the north coast of Tasmania to ride out the storm on the night of 21 March, was the sudden decrease in the depth of the waters. Baudin decided, 'for the sake of everyone's greater peace of mind', to take no further soundings, for if it had been found that the depth was still decreasing, it might have prompted those on board to think they had been 'lost beyond all hope'.

## 23 MARCH 1802

> Judging from the weather that we have just had, the equinox is no less to be feared in these seas than in European waters, and ships that find themselves to the west of the Furneaux Group at such times would do well to keep out to sea until it is past, for if they are not good at holding their course they run the risk of being embayed on these islands by the very rapid currents, and then finding themselves in a lot of trouble, as we ourselves did.

When fine weather returned the next day, minor repairs were made, bedding and clothing aired and the ship disinfected. Baudin was still unaware of what had become of his lost dinghy, but his confidence in the courage and resourcefulness of its crew proved to be well founded. Despite lacking shelter and supplies, they had shown remarkable attention to duty in continuing their survey of the east coast of Tasmania after their accidental separation from the *Géographe*. Having found fresh water and food on a small island, they had headed back to sea to await the return of the mother ship. It was then, on 9 March, that they encountered an English brig, the *Harrington*, which was hunting for seal in the islands of Banks Strait and which offered to take them to Port Jackson.

As luck would have it, the crew of the dinghy were reunited with their compatriots much sooner than expected: while the *Harrington* was lying at anchor near Swan Island, just off the north-eastern tip of Tasmania, the *Naturaliste* hove into view. Hamelin was pleasantly surprised, and understandably relieved, to find the missing men; he also now had in Boullanger some additional geographical expertise with which to conduct his survey of the north coast of Tasmania and some of the off-shore islands. This survey led him to Waterhouse Island, the agreed meeting place in case of separation, but still the *Géographe* did not appear. Hamelin decided to head south to look for her, but the ships seem to have passed one another in the mists of Banks Strait. After sending a party to Port Dalrymple, and realising that there was no further hope of rejoining his commander, Hamelin set sail for the mainland on 7 April.

By this time, Baudin was already long gone. Having weathered the equinoctial storms, he had decided that he must abandon the waters of Tasmania in order to proceed to one of his expedition's most important tasks – the charting of the unknown south coast of New Holland. Separated from the *Naturaliste*, and unaware of the fortuitous sequence of events that had ensured the safe return of his missing dinghy, Baudin set sail for Wilson's Promontory in order to complete his survey before the onset of winter. On 27 March 1802, he sighted land.

# chapter five

# DEFINING BOUNDARIES

*The Race to Chart the Unknown South Coast*

The vast southern coastline of Australia had already begun to yield some of its secrets by the time Flinders and Baudin set out on their quest to 'join the dots' and solve one of the great remaining geographical mysteries. From the west, a succession of navigators had made it as far as Nuyts Archipelago before breaking off to head south – in most cases, in order to round Van Diemen's Land in search of fresh supplies of water. The two largest islands of Nuyts Archipelago, St Peter and St Francis, had taken on great symbolic importance: unsighted since 1627, they marked the beginning of the unknown. At the other end of the continent, the coast of what is now Victoria was beginning to take shape. What remained to be discovered was nevertheless not inconsiderable. More particularly, there was still some speculation in the scientific community as to whether New Holland and 'New South Wales' were separated by a body of water stretching south from the Gulf of Carpentaria, or whether they were indeed connected to form one vast land mass. The race was on to insert the final piece in the puzzle.

Solving this cartographic riddle would not only serve the interests of science, it would also bring considerable honour to the successful explorer and his nation. There was, however, even more at stake than personal glory and national pride. Whether they were explicitly stated or simply implied, geopolitical and commercial concerns were as important during the eighteenth century and into the nineteenth as they had ever been previously. The numerous voyages of discovery that set out from Europe in the second half of the eighteenth century demonstrated clearly that science and empire were

Detail of the *Map of the Great Ocean or South Sea*. Published in the first French edition of the folio *Atlas of the Voyage of La Pérouse Around the World* (Paris: Imprimerie de la République, 1797). This map shows the gaps in European knowledge of Terra Australis before the major discoveries of Bass, Flinders and Baudin.

intimately linked. All of the great colonising nations, and especially the traditional rivals, England and France, were jockeying for position in a quest for strategic and economic advantage. Of particular importance were the Pacific and Indian Oceans. In the age of tall ships, it was vital to have ports of call along the routes to the opulent East. These half-way ports were havens that allowed much-needed rest and the replenishment of supplies. Notwithstanding their scientific objectives, voyages such as those of James Cook to the Pacific were also conceived with geopolitical aims in mind. This was certainly true of the succession of French expeditions to the Pacific and Indian Oceans during the second half of the eighteenth century: Kerguelen, St Allouarn, La Pérouse, d'Entrecasteaux were all seeking, overtly or covertly, to restore the nation's commercial and political pride after losing ground in the North American territories and seeing French influence dwindle in India. England's dominance as a maritime power needed to be challenged.

It is in this context that the charting of the unknown south coast of Australia must be seen. Its location held many strategic advantages and its discovery was consequently held to be of prime importance – in the same way, perhaps, as the race for space ignited the nationalistic passions and scientific energies of the world's superpowers in the twentieth century. The successful establishment of the colony of New South Wales by the British had only intensified French interest in the southern parts of Terra Australis. In addition to their interest in Tasmania, it was the south-west corner of the continent that attracted the attention of the French. Establishing a naval and colonial base there would restore some balance with their rival nation. This would be more readily achieved if it were discovered that a strait separated the western and the eastern parts of Terra Australis. The task of solving this mystery fell, on the French side, to Baudin. But it would be a race: unbeknown to Baudin, Matthew Flinders had been charged by the British authorities with precisely the same mission. While the French were engaged in the exploration of Tasmania, Flinders was already making steady progress along the unknown south coast.

## Sailing From the West
### Flinders from Nuyts Archipelago to Encounter Bay, 28 January to 8 April 1802

Having passed beyond Cape Nuyts on 28 January, the *Investigator* sought shelter in a wide bay offering protection from southerly winds. By naming it Fowler's Bay, after his first lieutenant, Flinders set a trend for the coast-line soon to be encountered; its features in large part were named after the ship's officers, artists and scientists. Other preferred names would be those of prominent Englishmen of the time, the durability of whose names bears little relationship to the contribution they might have made to the expedition. Flinders' account is replete with the new names, which provide a lasting record of his achievement but also an endorsement of claims made for British interests.

### 9 FEBRUARY 1802

At day break in the morning of Feb. 9, when the anchor was weighed from Petrel Bay to prosecute the examination of the unknown coast, we were unexpectedly favoured with a refreshing breeze from the westward, and our course was directed for Cape Bauer.* At noon, the latitude from mean of observations to the north and south, which differed only 1', was 32° 43' 17"; but although our distance from the land could not be more than three leagues, no part of it was distinguishable; the haze was very thick, but it was of a different nature, and had none of that extraordinary refractive power which the atmosphere possessed during the prevalence of the eastern winds. At one o'clock, Olive's Island was indistinctly perceived; and at two we came in with Point Westall, and then steered south-south-eastward along the coast at the distance of four or five miles. At six, a bold cliffy head, which I named Cape Radstock, in honour of admiral Lord Radstock, bore N 75° E, six or seven miles; and the land seemed there to take another direction, for nothing beyond it could be perceived. The wind was at west-south-west, and we kept on the starboard tack till eight o'clock, and then stood off for the night . . .

## 13 FEBRUARY 1802

In the morning, we were surprised to see breaking water about one mile from the ship, and as much from the shore. It was not far from the place where the last tack had been made in the evening, and the master found no more than six feet of water close to it; so that we were fortunate in having escaped. The botanical gentlemen landed early, and I followed them to make the usual observations for the survey.

From my first station, at the north-east end of the island, the largest of the Top-gallant Isles bore S 67° E, four or five miles. It is of little extent, but high and cliffy, and there are three rocks on its south side resembling ships under sail, from which circumstance this small cluster obtained its present name. To the south-west, I distinguished several small islands, of which the northernmost and largest is remarkable from two high and sharp-pointed peaks upon it, lying in latitude 33° 57' and longitude 134° 13'. This cluster, as it appeared to be, received the name of Pearson's Isles; but it is possible that what seemed at a distance to be divided into several, may form two or three larger islands, or even be one connected land. Another island, about one mile long and of moderate height, was discovered bearing S 72° W, about four leagues. It was surrounded with high breakers, as was a smaller isle near it; and the two were called Ward's Isles. These three small clusters, with Waldegrave's Isles, and this larger island, which was named Flinders', after the second lieutenant, form a group distinct from Nuyts' Archipelago, and I gave it the name of the Investigator's Group.

---

\* Patriotic fervour in the First World War caused Cape Bauer to be renamed Wondoma, and an officially sanctioned reversion to the original name is not always observed.

The island named after Flinders' younger brother offered an opportunity for Flinders and some of his companions to submit the newly discovered coast to a scientific gaze. Among the fauna observed were seals whose docility confirmed their unfamiliarity with European ways. Flinders, mercifully, chose to leave them to their blissful ignorance.

> The form of Flinders' Island is nearly a square, of which each side is from three to five miles in length. Bights are formed in the four sides, but that to the north seems alone to afford good anchorage. In its composition, this island is nearly the same as that of Waldegrave's largest isle; but between the granitic basis and the calcareous top, there is a stratum of sandstone, in some places twenty feet thick. The vegetation differed from that of other islands before visited, in that the lower lands were covered with large bushes; and there was very little, either of the white, velvety shrub [atriplex], or of the tufted, wiry grass. A small species of kangaroo, not bigger than a cat, was rather numerous. I shot five of them, and some others were killed by the botanists and their attendants, and found to be in tolerably good condition. We were now beginning to want a supply of water, and the northern part of the island was sought over carefully for it; but the nearest approach to success was in finding dried-up swamps, in which the growing plants were tinged red, as if the water had been brackish. No other trees than a few small casuarinas at a distance from the anchorage, were seen upon the island; but wood for fuel might with some difficulty be picked out from the larger bushes growing near the shore. The beaches were frequented by seals of the hair kind. A family of them consisting of a male, four or five females, and as many cubs, was lying asleep at every two or three hundred yards. Their security was such, that I approached several of these families very closely, and retired without disturbing their domestic tranquillity, or being perceived by them.

The *Investigator* proceeded to Coffin Bay on the south-western coast of the Eyre Peninsula. As Flinders explains in his journal, the origins of the name are much less sinister than might be assumed. It was in the vicinity of Coffin Bay that he made his first encounter of the human kind on the unknown coast. Flinders managed to get close enough to observe the skin colour of the local people but not much more. There were also early signs that the human inhabitants of the unknown coast would treat the European interlopers with caution.

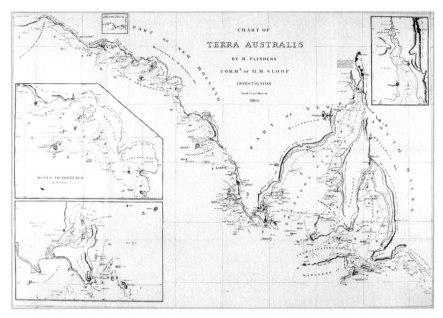

Flinders' chart of the previously unknown south coast of Terra Australis, with insets showing Nuyts Archipelago, Port Lincoln and the head of Spencer Gulf (1802). Published in *A Voyage to Terra Australis* (1814)

## 16 FEBRUARY 1802

The basis of the point [Point Sir Isaac] seemed to be granitic, with an upper stratum of calcareous rock, much similar to the neighbouring isles of the Investigator's Group. Its elevation is inconsiderable, and the surface is sandy and barren, as is all the land near it on the same side. The large piece of water which it shelters from western winds, I named Coffin's Bay, in compliment to the present vice-admiral Sir Isaac Coffin, Bart., who, when resident commissioner at Sheerness, had taken so zealous a part in the outfit of the *Investigator*. Coffin's Bay extends four or five leagues to the south-eastward from Point Sir Isaac; but I do not think that any stream, more considerable than perhaps a small rill from the back land, falls into it, since sandy cliffs and beach were seen nearly all round. On the east side of the entrance, the shore rises quickly from the beach to hills of considerable height, well covered with wood. The highest of these hills I call Mount Greenly: its elevation is between six and eight hundred feet, and it stands very near the water side.

Many smokes were seen round Coffin's Bay, and also two parties of natives, one on each side; these shores were therefore better inhabited than the more western parts of the South Coast; indeed it has usually been found in this country, that the borders of shallow bays and lagoons, and at the entrances of rivers, are by far the most numerously peopled. These natives were black and naked, differing in nothing that we could perceive from those of King George's Sound before described.

Flinders' account reveals that, by the second part of February, hopes were daily growing that the work of discovery would extend beyond the by now almost mundane task of observing land forms. It seemed to him and his men that the line of the coast might at any day turn to the north, signalling that they had reached the south-eastern corner of New Holland and opening up an expanse of water which, if pursued northwards, would lead the *Investigator* to the Gulf of Carpentaria. On the other hand, if Terra Australis were indeed a single land mass, then one would expect to encounter at some point the mouth of a large river draining the continent. The next discovery did nothing to quell speculation on board. Thistle Island was a modest find, though one that would have tragic consequences for the crew of the *Investigator* and the eponymous Mr Thistle.

## 20 FEBRUARY 1802

A tide from the north-eastward, apparently the ebb, ran more than one mile an hour; which was the more remarkable from no set of tide, worthy to be noticed, having hitherto been observed upon this coast. No land could be seen in the direction from whence it came, and these circumstances, with the trending of the coast to the north, did not fail to excite many conjectures. Large rivers, deep inlets, inland seas, and passages into the Gulf of Carpentaria, were terms frequently used in our conversations of this evening; and the prospect of making an interesting discovery seemed to have infused new life and vigour into every man in the ship.

## 21 FEBRUARY 1802

Early in the morning, I went on shore to the eastern land, anxious to ascertain its connection with, or separation from the main. There were seals upon the beach, and further on, numberless traces of the kangaroo. Signs of extinguished fire existed everywhere; but they bespoke a conflagration of the woods, of remote date, rather than the habitual presence of men, and might have arisen from lightning, or from the friction of two trees in a strong wind. Upon the whole, I satisfied myself of the insularity of this land, and gave to it, shortly after, the name of Thistle's Island, from the master who accompanied me. In our way up the hills, to take a commanding station for the survey, a speckled, yellow snake lay asleep before us. By pressing the butt end of a musket upon his neck, I kept him down whilst Mr Thistle, with a sail needle and twine, sewed up his mouth; and he was taken on board alive, for the naturalist to examine; but two others of the same species had already been killed, and one of them was seven feet nine inches in length. We were proceeding onward with our prize, when a white eagle, with fierce aspect and outspread wing, was seen bounding towards us; but stopping short, at twenty yards off, he flew up into a tree. Another bird of the same kind discovered himself by making a motion to pounce down upon us as we passed underneath; and it seemed evident that they took us for kangaroos, having probably never before seen an upright animal in the island, of any other species. These birds sit watching in the trees, and should a kangaroo come out to feed in the daytime, it is seized and torn to pieces by these voracious creatures. This accounted for why so few kangaroos were seen, when traces of them were met with at every step; and for their keeping so much under thick bushes that it was impossible to shoot them. Their size was superior to any of those found upon the more western islands, but much inferior to the forest kangaroo of the continent . . .

No water could be found; and as the ship's hold was becoming very empty, I returned on board, after observing the latitude, with the intention of running over to the main in search of it. But on comparing the longitude observed by Lieutenant Flinders with that resulting from my bearings, a difference was found which made it necessary to repeat the observation on shore; and as this would prolong the time too near dusk for moving the ship, Mr Thistle was sent over with a cutter to the main land, in search of an anchoring place where water might be procured . . .

At dusk in the evening, the cutter was seen under sail; returning from the mainland; but not arriving in half an hour, and the sight of it having been lost rather suddenly, a light was shown and Lieutenant Fowler went in a boat, with a lanthorn [lantern], to see what might have happened. Two hours passed without receiving any tidings. A gun was then fired, and Mr Fowler returned soon afterward, but alone. Near the situation where the cutter had been last seen, he met with so strong a rippling of tide that he himself narrowly escaped being upset; and there was reason to fear that it had actually happened to Mr Thistle. Had there been daylight, it is probable that some or all of the people might have been picked up; but it was too dark to see anything, and no answer could be heard to the hallooing, or to the firing of muskets. The tide was setting to the southward and ran an hour and a half after the missing boat had been last seen, so that it would be carried to seaward in the first instance; and no more than two out of the eight people being at all expert in swimming, it was much to be feared that most of them would be lost.

Over the following days, the *Investigator*'s crew expended much energy in trying to locate the missing crew, but to no avail. It was the first loss of life incurred by the *Investigator* and must have cast a terrible pall over Flinders and the surviving crew. This is barely evident in the Flinders account written many years later, which adopts the matter-of-fact tone pervading the entire work. But it is interesting that Flinders, very much the man of the Enlightenment, whose language is redolent of the scientific and rationalist spirit of his age, saw fit to make mention of an uncanny event preceding the departure from England which seemed to foreshadow, among other things, the deaths of Thistle and his crew.

> This evening, Mr Fowler told me a circumstance which I thought
> extraordinary; and it afterwards proved to be more so. Whilst we were lying
> at Spithead, Mr Thistle was one day waiting on shore, and having nothing
> else to do he went to a certain old man, named Pine, to have his fortune told.
> The cunning man informed him that he was going out on a long voyage, and
> that the ship, on arriving at her destination, would be joined by another vessel.
> That such was intended, he might have learned privately; but he added, that
> Mr Thistle would be lost before the other vessel joined. As to the manner of
> his loss the magician refused to give any information. My boat's crew, hearing
> what Mr Thistle said, went also to consult the wise man; and after the
> prefatory information of a long voyage, were told that they would be
> shipwrecked, but not in the ship they were going out in: whether they would
> escape and return to England, he was not permitted to reveal.
>
> This tale Mr Thistle had often told at the mess table; and I remarked with
> some pain in a future part of the voyage, that every time my boat's crew went
> to embark with me in the *Lady Nelson*, there was some degree of apprehension
> amongst them that the time of the predicted shipwreck was arrived. I make no
> comment upon this story, but recommend a commander, if possible, to prevent
> any of his crew from consulting fortune tellers.

Pine might well have served Samuel Coleridge as a model for the ancient mariner, who cursed his ship when he 'killed the bird That made the breeze to blow'. It seems that Pine was triply prescient, since not only did Thistle come to grief off Thistle Island, but 'the other vessel' – if by this was meant Baudin's *Géographe* – was indeed soon to be joined. Moreover, as Flinders himself could well judge with the benefit of hindsight, Pine's utterances predicted the fate of the *Porpoise*, the ship in which Flinders sought to return to England and which was wrecked off the coast of Queensland.

The next day, 22 February, brought the sad and certain confirmation of the fate of Thistle and his crew.

At daybreak I got the ship under way, and steered across Thorny Passage, over to the main land, in the direction where the cutter had been seen; keeping an officer at the mast head, with a glass, to look out for her. There were many strong ripplings, and some uncommonly smooth places where a boat, which was sent to sound, had 12 fathoms. We passed to the northward of all these; and seeing a small cove with a sandy beach, steered in and anchored in 10 fathoms, sandy bottom; the main land extending from north-half-west, round by the west and south to east-south-east, and the open space being partly sheltered by the northern islands of the passage.

A boat was despatched in search of the lost cutter, and presently returned towing in the wreck, bottom upward; it was stove in every part, having to all appearance been dashed against the rocks. One of the oars was afterwards found, but nothing could be seen of our unfortunate shipmates. The boat was again sent away in search; and a midshipman was stationed upon a headland, without-side of the cove, to observe everything which might drift past with the tide. Mr Brown and a party landed to walk along the shore to the northward, whilst I proceeded to the southern extremity of the mainland, which was now named Cape Catastrophe. On landing at the head of the cove, I found several foot marks of our people, made on the preceding afternoon when looking for water; and in my way up the valley I prosecuted the same research, but ineffectually, although there were many huts and other signs that natives had resided there lately.

From the heights near the extremity of Cape Catastrophe, I examined with a glass the islands lying off, and all the neighbouring shores for any appearance of our people, but in vain; I therefore took a set of angles for the survey, and returned on board; and on comparing notes with the different parties, it appeared that no further information had been obtained of our unfortunate companions.

## 24 FEBRUARY 1802

This morning Lieutenant Fowler had been sent to search the southern islands in Thorny Passage for any remains of our people; but he was not able to land, nor in rowing round them, to see any indication of the objects of his pursuit. The recovery of their bodies was now the furthest to which our hopes extended; but the number of sharks seen in the cove and at the last anchorage, rendered even this prospect of melancholy satisfaction extremely doubtful; and our want of water becoming every day more pressing, we prepared to depart for the examination of the new opening to the northward. I caused an inscription to be engraven upon a sheet of copper, and set up on a stout post at the head of the cove, which I named Memory Cove; and further to commemorate our loss, I gave to each of the six islands nearest to Cape Catastrophe the name of one of the seamen.

Putting the tragedy behind him as best he could, and pursuing a by now dire need to locate fresh water, Flinders continued to follow the line of the coast until arriving at Port Lincoln, which he named after his native province. A boat was sent to an island Flinders named Boston Island in search of water, but without success. So Flinders anchored off the mainland and resolved to go in search of potable water there, eventually procuring it from a somewhat unusual source.

*Entrance of Port Lincoln taken from behind Memory Cove*, engraving by John Pye from a drawing by William Westall. Published in *A Voyage to Terra Australis* (1814)

## 26 FEBRUARY 1802

Fresh water being at this time the most pressing of our wants, I set off the same afternoon, with a party, to examine the lake or mere discovered from Stamford Hill. The way to it was over low land covered with loose pieces of calcareous rock; the soil was moist in some places, and, though generally barren, was overspread with grass and shrubs, interspersed with a few clumps of small trees. After walking two miles we reached the lake, but to our mortification, the water was brackish, and not drinkable: the distance, besides, from Port Lincoln was too great to roll casks over a stony road. This piece of water was named Sleaford Mere. It is one mile broad, and appeared to be three or four in length. The shore was a whitish, hardened clay, covered at this time with a thin crust, in which salt was a component part. The sun being too near the horizon to admit of going round the mere, our way was bent towards the ship; and finding a moist place within a hundred yards of the head of the port, I caused a hole to be dug there. A stratum of whitish clay was found at three feet below the surface, and on penetrating this, water drained in, which was perfectly sweet, though discoloured; and we had the satisfaction to return on board with the certainty of being able to procure water, although it would probably require some time to fill all our empty casks.

## 27 FEBRUARY 1802

Early in the morning a party of men was sent with spades to dig pits; and the time keepers and astronomical instruments, with two tents, followed under the charge of Mr Flinders. I went to attend the digging, leaving orders with Mr Fowler to moor the ship and send on shore empty casks. The water flowed in pretty freely, and though of a whitish colour, and at first somewhat thick, it was well tasted.

Here, too, Flinders found the local inhabitants reluctant to take up contact with the Europeans. He thought their reticence entirely understandable, and decided not to pursue actively an encounter but rather to prepare the groundwork for cordial relations in the future.

## 4 MARCH 1802

Many straggling bark huts, similar to those on other parts of the coast, were seen upon the shores of Port Lincoln, and the paths near our tents had been long and deeply trodden; but neither in my excursions nor in those of the botanists had any of the natives been discovered. This morning, however, three or four were heard calling to a boat, as was supposed, which had just landed; but they presently walked away, or perhaps retired into the wood to observe our movements. No attempt was made to follow them, for I had always found the natives of this country to avoid those who seemed anxious for communication; whereas, when left entirely alone, they would usually come down after having watched us for a few days. Nor does this conduct seem to be unnatural, for what, in such case, would be the conduct of any people, ourselves for instance, were we living in a state of nature, frequently at war with our neighbours, and ignorant of the existence of any other nation? On the arrival of strangers, so different in complexion and appearance to ourselves, having power to transport themselves over, and even living upon an element which to us was impassable; the first sensation would probably be terror, and the first movement flight.

It was this concerted effort to see events from the point of view of the Aborigines that led Flinders to keep a respectful distance and to exercise patience in his interactions with them.

We should watch these extraordinary people from our retreats in the woods and rocks, and if we found ourselves sought and pursued by them, should conclude their designs to be inimical; but if, on the contrary, we saw them quietly employed in occupations which had no reference to us, curiosity would get the better of fear; and after observing them more closely, we should ourselves seek a communication. Such seemed to have been the conduct of these Australians; and I am persuaded that their appearance on the morning when the tents were struck, was a prelude to their coming down; and that had we remained a few days longer, a friendly communication would have ensued. The way was, however, prepared for the next ship which may enter this port, as it was to us in King George's Sound by captain Vancouver and the ship *Elligood*; to whose previous visits and peaceable conduct we were most probably indebted for our early intercourse with the inhabitants of that place. So far as could be perceived with a glass, the natives of this port were the same in personal appearance as those of King George's Sound and Port Jackson. In the hope of conciliating their goodwill to succeeding visitors, some hatchets and various other articles were left in their paths, or fastened to stumps of the trees which had been cut down near our watering pits.

The *Investigator* left Port Lincoln with its water supplies replenished; but, despite the expansive harbour, Flinders was not convinced that it had the makings of a colonial settlement.

> Port Lincoln is certainly a fine harbour; and it is much to be regretted that it possesses no constant run of fresh water, unless it should be in Spalding Cove, which we did not examine. Our pits at the head of the port will, however, supply ships at all times; and though discoloured by whitish clay, the water has no pernicious quality, nor is it ill tasted. This and wood, which was easily procured, were all that we found of use to ships; and for the establishment of a colony, which the excellence of the port might seem to invite, the little fertility of the soil offers no inducement.

The eventual establishment of a township at Port Lincoln would, of course, later prove this assessment to be erroneous. However, in the absence of an obvious water supply, it was not easy to judge the site's potential for settlement.

Although the *Investigator* at this time was sailing to the north, Flinders had already abandoned speculation that the coast's direction signalled a strait dividing New Holland from New South Wales. It did appear likely, though, that the head of the gulf might be the point at which a significant river flowed into the sea; but in this regard, too, Flinders would be disappointed.

## 9 MARCH 1802

> Our prospect of a channel or strait, cutting off some considerable portion of Terra Australis, was lost, for it now appeared that the ship was entered into a gulf; but the width of the opening round Point Lowly left us a consolatory hope that it would terminate in a river of some importance. In steering for the point we came into 4 fathoms, but on hauling to the eastward found 8, although a dry sandbank was seen in that direction. The depth afterwards diminished to 6, on which the course for Point Lowly was resumed; and we passed it at the distance of a mile and a half, in 9 fathoms of water. Here the gulf was found to take a river-like form, but the eastern half of it was occupied by a dry, sandy spit and shoal water. We continued to steer upwards, before the wind; but as the width contracted rapidly, and there was much shoal water, it was under very easy sail, and with an anchor ready to be let go. At four o'clock, in attempting to steer close over to the western side, we came suddenly into 2¹/₂ fathoms; the ship was instantly veered to the eastward, and on the water deepening to 7, we let go the anchor and veered out a whole cable; for the wind

blew a fresh gale right up the gulf, and between S 4° W and 30° E there was no shelter from the land. At sunset, a second anchor was dropped under foot.

We had reached near five leagues above Point Lowly, at the entrance of the narrow part of the gulf; but the shores were low on both sides, and abreast of the ship not so much as four miles asunder. At the back of the eastern shore was the ridge of mountains before mentioned, of which Mr Westall made the sketch given in the Atlas; and the highest peak toward their northern extremity, afterwards called Mount Brown, bore N 32° E. On the western side, upwards, there was moderately high, flat-topped land, whose eastern bluff bore N 36° W, about three leagues, and there the head of the gulf had the appearance of terminating; but as the tide ran one mile an hour past the ship, we still flattered ourselves with the prospect of a longer course, and that it would end in a fresh-water river.

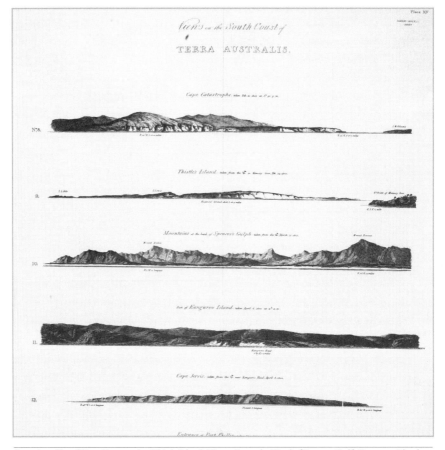

Coastal profiles of Cape Catastrophe, Thistle Island, Mountains at the Head of Spencer Gulf, Kangaroo Island and Cape Jervis, William Westall. Published in *A Voyage to Terra Australis* (1814)

Flinders set out to explore the head of the gulf thoroughly, while Brown, Bauer, Westall and some crew members set off in the hope of scaling Mount Brown.

## 11 MARCH 1802

It seemed remarkable, and was very mortifying, to find the water at the head of the gulf as salt nearly as at the ship; nevertheless it was evident, that much fresh water was thrown into it in wet seasons, especially from the eastern mountains. The summits of the ridge lie from three to four leagues back from the water side, but the greater part of that space seemed to be low, marshy land. To the northward no hill was visible, and to the westward but one small elevation of flat-topped land; all else in those directions was mangroves and salt swamps, and they seemed to be very extensive . . .

Our return to the ship was a good deal retarded by going after the black swans and ducks amongst the flats. The swans were all able to fly, and would not allow themselves to be approached; but some ducks of two or three different species were shot, and also several sea pies or red bills. Another set of bearings was taken on the western shore, and at ten in the evening we reached the ship, where Mr Brown and his party had not been long arrived. The ascent to Mount Brown had proved to be very difficult, besides having to walk fifteen miles on a winding course, before reaching the foot; by perseverance, however, they gained the top at five on the first evening, but were reduced to passing the night without water; nor was any found until they had descended some distance on the following day. The view from the top of Mount Brown was very extensive, its elevation being not less than three thousand feet; but neither rivers nor lakes could be perceived, nor any thing of the sea to the south-eastward. In almost every direction the eye traversed over an uninterruptedly flat, woody country; the sole exceptions being the ridge of mountains extending north and south, and the water of the gulf to the south-westward.

From the head of the gulf, Flinders sailed south, this time following the western coast of Yorke peninsula, and past places on which he would later confer the names of Point Pearce, Corny Point and Hardwicke Bay.

By 20 March the *Investigator* had reached the furthest southerly point of the gulf. Both the gulf itself and the cape at which it terminated Flinders named after the Earl of Spencer, 'who presided at the Board of the Admiralty when the voyage was planned and the [*Investigator*] commissioned'. Beyond Cape Spencer, further land could be seen to the south and, expecting a gale to blow up, Flinders chose to seek its shelter. The land in question was Kangaroo Island.

It is curious to think that, despite the considerable amount of activity in Australia's southern waters from the early seventeenth century right to the end of the eighteenth century – including the visits of Nuyts, Vancouver and d'Entrecasteaux, not to mention the possible unrecorded visits of sealers and whalers – Kangaroo Island and the surrounding mainland should have remained uncharted. Flinders, in pursuing his survey east from Nuyts Archipelago, could hardly miss it.

On the morning following his first sighting of Kangaroo Island, Flinders brought his ship closer, but the high cliffs and a fresh south-west wind prohibited a landing. Instead, he steered an eastward course along the island's northern coast until, about midday, he sighted a point he would later name Point Marsden. Beyond that, the coast curved gently southward into a large bay containing three coves, any of which would offer satisfactory shelter and the opportunity to land. Flinders named it Nepean Bay after the first secretary of the Royal Navy. The strong wind drove the *Investigator* toward the bay's eastern headland where, by evening, it was finally able to lay anchor.

Certainly Flinders and his crew were not the first men to set foot on the island. Centuries earlier, Kangaroo Island had been inhabited by an indigenous population, possibly related to the Aborigines of Tasmania. But they had long since disappeared for reasons which remain unclear, and the mainland Aborigines of Flinders' time did not venture on to the island. The absence of smoke had already suggested that the crew would encounter no human population there, but this theory could only be confirmed or denied by undertaking a landing.

Whatever the history of human occupation might have been, for Flinders the most striking of the island's living creatures were its kangaroos, which he soon encountered in great abundance and exhibiting a tameness which seemed to confirm the absence of humans. On the initiative of Flinders, it was these kangaroos which were to give the island its name.

## 22 MARCH 1802

Neither smokes, nor other marks of inhabitants had as yet been perceived upon the southern land, although we had passed along seventy miles of its coast. It was too late to go on shore this evening; but every glass in the ship was pointed there, to see what could be discovered. Several black lumps, like rocks, were pretended to have been seen in motion by some of the young gentlemen, which caused the force of their imaginations to be much admired; next morning, however, on going toward the shore, a number of dark-brown kangaroos were seen feeding upon a grass plat by the side of the wood; and our landing gave them no disturbance. I had with me a double-barrelled gun, fitted with a bayonet, and the gentlemen my companions had muskets. It would be difficult to guess how many kangaroos were seen; but I killed ten, and the rest of the party made up the number to 31, taken on board in the course of the day; the least of them weighing 69, and the largest 125 pounds. These kangaroos had much resemblance to the large species found in the forest lands of New South Wales; except that their colour was darker, and they were not wholly destitute of fat.

After this butchery, for the poor animals suffered themselves to be shot in the eyes with small shot, and in some cases to be knocked on the head with sticks, I scrambled with difficulty through the brushwood, and over fallen trees, to reach the higher land with the surveying instruments; but the thickness and height of the wood prevented anything else from being distinguished. There was little doubt, however, that this extensive piece of land was separated from the continent; for the extraordinary tameness of the kangaroos and the presence of seals upon the shore, concurred with the absence of all traces of men to show that it was not inhabited.

The whole ship's company was employed this afternoon, in skinning and cleaning the kangaroos; and a delightful regale they afforded, after four months privation from almost any fresh provisions. Half a hundred weight of heads, forequarters, and tails were stewed down into soup for dinner on this and the succeeding days; and as much steaks given, moreover, to both officers and men, as they could consume by day and by night. In gratitude for so seasonable a supply, I named this southern land Kangaroo Island.

After this feast, it was time for the 'scientific gentlemen' to do their work. For his part, even with the *Investigator* at anchor, Flinders devoted some of his energies to his cartographic mission, as he bestowed enduring names on prominent features of the island and of what he could recognise of the mainland.

## 23 MARCH 1802

Next day was employed in shifting the top masts, on account of some rents found in the heels. The scientific gentlemen landed again to examine the natural productions of the island, and in the evening 11 more kangaroos were brought on board; but most of these were smaller, and seemed to be of a different species to those of the preceding day. Some of the party saw several large running birds, which, according to their description, seemed to have been the emu or cassowary.

Not being able to obtain a distinct view from any elevated situation, I took a set of angles from a small projection near the ship, named Kangaroo Head; but nothing could be seen to the north; and the sole bearing of importance, more than had been taken on board, was that of a high hill at the extremity of the apparently unconnected land to the eastward: it bore N 29° 10' E, and was named Mount Lofty. The nearest part of that land was a low point, bearing N 60° E nine or ten miles; but the land immediately at the back was high, and its northern and southern extremes were cliffy. I named it Cape Jervis, and it was afterwards sketched by Mr Westall.

While it has been established that Kangaroo Island had once been inhabited, it is a matter of some speculation whether Flinders and his men were the first Europeans to set foot upon its shores. It is conceivable that American sealers had already landed there. Moreover, the British whaler *Elligood* might well have spent time anchored at Kangaroo Island in 1800, shortly before it came to grief on King Island to the east. That at least would help to explain the marks of fire, of a kind that Flinders had encountered on several occasions previously, and which were found on some of the trees. He toyed with the discomforting idea that the French might have beaten him to the island, not in the person of Baudin, but in that of the ill-fated Count La Pérouse.

A thick wood covered almost all that part of the island visible from the ship; but the trees in a vegetating state were not equal in size to the generality of those lying on the ground, nor to the dead trees standing upright. Those on the ground were so abundant, that in ascending the higher land, a considerable part of the walk was made upon them. They lay in all directions, and were nearly of the same size and in the same progress towards decay; from whence it would seem that they had not fallen from age, nor yet been thrown down in a gale of wind. Some general conflagration, and there were marks apparently of fire on many of them, is perhaps the sole cause which can be reasonably assigned; but whence came the woods on fire? That there were no inhabitants upon the island, and that the natives of the continent did not visit it, was demonstrated, if not by the want of all signs of such visit, yet by the tameness of the kangaroo, an animal which, on the continent, resembles the wild deer in timidity. Perhaps lightning might have been the cause, or possibly the friction of two dead trees in a strong wind; but it would be somewhat extraordinary that the same thing should have happened at Thistle's Island, Boston Island, and at this place, and apparently about the same time. Can this part of Terra Australis have been visited before, unknown to the world? The French navigator, La Pérouse, was ordered to explore it, but there seems little probability that he ever passed Torres' Strait.

*View on the north side of Kangaroo Island*, engraving by William Woolmoth from a drawing by William Westall. Published in *A Voyage to Terra Australis* (1814)

Some judgment may be formed of the epoch when these conflagrations happened, from the magnitude of the growing trees; for they must have sprung up since that period. They were a species of eucalyptus, and being less than the fallen trees, had most probably not arrived at maturity; but the wood is hard and solid, and it may thence be supposed to grow slowly. With these considerations, I should be inclined to fix the period at not less than ten, nor more than twenty years before our arrival. This brings us back to La Pérouse. He was in Botany Bay in the beginning of 1788; and if he did pass through Torres' Strait, and come round to this coast, as was his intention, it would probably be about the middle or latter end of that year, or between thirteen and fourteen years before the *Investigator*. My opinion is not favourable to this conjecture; but I have furnished all the data to enable the reader to form his own judgment upon the cause which might have prostrated the woods of these islands.

On 24 March the *Investigator* weighed anchor in order to continue its examination of the unknown coast which lay to the north of Kangaroo Island, entering the inlet that Flinders would name Gulf St Vincent by 28 March and spending several days exploring it.

> March 24 the morning, we got under way from Kangaroo Island, in order to take up the examination of the main coast at Cape Spencer, where it had been quitted in the evening of the 20th, when the late gale commenced. The wind had continued to blow fresh from the southward; but had now moderated, and was at south-west. We steered north-westward from ten o'clock till six in the evening; and then had sight of land extending from N 62° W to a low part terminating at N 17° E distant three leagues. A hummock upon this low part was named Troubridge Hill, and at first it makes like an island. Nothing was visible to the eastward of the low land; whence I judged there to be another inlet or a strait between it and Cape Jervis. Soon after dusk the wind veered to south-by-east, on which we steered south-westward, and continued the same course until four in the morning; when the largest Althorpe Isle being seen to the north-west, the ship was hove to, with her head eastward . . .

### 27 MARCH 1802

> The wind fixed itself at south-east, and it took us two days to work back against it as far as Troubridge Hill. The shore is generally low and sandy; but with the exception of one very low point, it may be approached within two miles. Many tacks were made in these two days, from the northern land across to Kangaroo Island, and gave opportunities of sounding the intermediate strait . . . Of the two sides, that of Kangaroo Island is much the deepest; but there is no danger in any part to prevent a ship passing through the strait with perfect confidence; and the average width is twenty-three miles. It was named Investigator's Strait, after the ship.

The first land to be seen to the east was Mount Lofty. It could conceivably have been part of a separate land mass, but the sighting of fires in its vicinity led Flinders to speculate quite correctly that it was not on an island. Soon the voyage up the gulf was to confirm that it was on part of the very same land mass as the rest of the unknown coast.

## 28 MARCH 1802

At daylight I recognised Mount Lofty, upon the highest part of the ridge of mountains which, from Cape Jervis, extends northward behind the eastern shore of the inlet. The nearest part of the coast was distant three leagues, mostly low, and composed of sand and rock, with a few small trees scattered over it; but at a few miles inland, where the back mountains rise, the country was well clothed with forest timber, and had a fertile appearance. The fires bespoke this to be a part of the continent ...

No land was visible so far to the north as where the trees appeared above the horizon, which showed the coast to be very low, and our soundings were fast decreasing. From noon to six o'clock we ran thirty miles to the northward, skirting a sandy shore at the distance of five, and thence to eight miles ...

On 30 March Flinders set out with Robert Brown to explore more closely the head of Gulf St Vincent. Here too no fresh water was to be found flowing from some mighty river. The surrounding mud and sand flats at least offered plentiful signs of life as well as landscapes which were more pleasing to the English eye than much of what the coast had hitherto offered.

## 30 MARCH 1802

Microscopic shells of various kinds, not larger than grains of wheat, were heaped up in ridges at highwater mark; further back the shore was sandy, but soon rose, in an undulating manner, to hills covered with grass; and the several clumps of trees scattered over them gave the land a pleasing appearance from the water side. We set off in the afternoon for the Hummock Mount, which stands upon a northern prolongation of the hills on the west side of the inlet, and about eight miles from the water; but finding it could not be reached in time to admit of returning on board the same evening, I ascended a nearer part of the range, to inspect the head of the inlet. It was almost wholly occupied by flats, which seemed to be sandy in the eastern part and muddy to the westward. These flats abounded with rays; and had we been provided with a harpoon, a boat load might have been caught. One black swan and several shags and gulls were seen.

I found the grass upon these pleasant-looking hills to be thinly set, the trees small, and the land poor in vegetable soil. The mountainous ridge on the east side of the inlet passes within a few miles of Hummock Mount, and appeared to be more sandy; but the wood upon it was abundant, and of a larger growth. Between the two ranges is a broad valley, swampy at the bottom; and into it the water runs down from both sides in rainy weather, and is discharged into the gulf, which may be considered as the lower and wider part of the valley.

In choosing a name for the gulf and for the peninsula to its west, Flinders followed a convention which was by that time well-rehearsed.

> In honour of the noble admiral who presided at the Board of Admiralty when I sailed from England, and had continued to the voyage that countenance and protection of which Earl Spencer had set the example, I named this new inlet, the Gulf of St Vincent. To the peninsula which separates it from Spencer's Gulf, I have affixed the name of Yorke's Peninsula, in honour of the Right Honourable Charles Philip Yorke, who followed the steps of his above mentioned predecessors at the Admiralty.

Flinders then proceeded south down the gulf, returning to Kangaroo Island because it offered a familiar shelter, but also to replenish the food supplies and to check on the rates of the ship's time-keepers. On this occasion, the kangaroos were much less plentiful than at the first anchorage, and the ship departed the following day with not much to show for its brief sojourn.

There soon proved to be further reason for disappointment. Having weighed anchor early on the morning of 3 April to proceed with the examination of the coast to the east, Flinders soon discovered that his time-keepers had run down altogether, having not been wound up the previous day. He returned once more to the island and determined to explore it further. Fortuitously, the unplanned return presented the opportunity for an inland expedition which led him to a high sandhill he named Prospect Hill. From its summit he expected to see much of the island's interior, but a pleasant surprise awaited him.

## 4 APRIL 1802

> On the 4th, I was accompanied by the naturalist in a boat expedition to the head of the large eastern cove of Nepean Bay; intending if possible to ascend a sandy eminence behind it, from which alone there was any hope of obtaining a view into the interior of the island, all the other hills being thickly covered with wood. On approaching the south-west corner of the cove, a small opening was found leading into a considerable piece of water; and by one of its branches we reached within little more than a mile of the desired sandy eminence. After I had observed the latitude 35° 50' 2" from an artificial horizon, we got through the wood without much difficulty; and at one o'clock

reached the top of the eminence, to which was given the name of Prospect Hill. Instead of a view into the interior of the island, I was surprised to find the sea at not more than one and a half, or two miles to the southward. Two points of the coast towards the east end of the island, bore S 77° E and the furthest part on the other side, a low point with breakers round it, bore S 33° W, at the supposed distance of four or five leagues. Between these extremes a large bight in the south coast was formed; but it is entirely exposed to southern winds, and the shores are mostly cliffy.

This would be Flinders' only view of the other side of the island, since he was not to chart its southern coast. Of as much interest for Flinders as the topography of the island was its wildlife. He and his exploratory group came upon what he described as a lagoon – now known as American River – in the vicinity of Nepean Bay. It appeared to Flinders to function as both nursery and graveyard for pelicans. His reflections on the idyllic nature of the setting and its wildlife were soon to receive a corrective, however, for on the following day he received word that one of his sailors on a hunting expedition had been bitten by a large and pugnacious seal.

> The entrance of the piece of water at the head of Nepean Bay, is less than half a mile in width, and mostly shallow; but there is a channel sufficiently deep for all boats near the western shore. After turning two low islets near the east point, the water opens out, becomes deeper, and divides into two branches, each of two or three miles long. Boats can go to the head of the southern branch only at high water; the east branch appeared to be accessible at all times; but as a lead and line were neglected to be put into the boat, I had no opportunity of sounding. There are four small islands in the eastern branch; one of them is moderately high and woody, the others are grassy and lower; and upon two of these we found many young pelicans, unable to fly. Flocks of the old birds were sitting upon the beaches of the lagoon, and it appeared that the islands were their breeding places; not only so, but from the number of skeletons and bones there scattered, it should seem that they had for ages been selected for the closing scene of their existence. Certainly none more likely to be free from disturbance of every kind could have been chosen, than these islets in a hidden lagoon of an uninhabited island, situated upon an unknown coast near the antipodes of Europe; nor can anything be more consonant to the feelings, if pelicans have any, than quietly to resign their breath, whilst surrounded by their progeny, and in the same spot where they first drew it.

Alas, for the pelicans! Their golden age is past; but it has much exceeded in duration that of man. I named this piece of water Pelican Lagoon. It is also frequented by flocks of the pied shag, and by some ducks and gulls; and the shoals supplied us with a few oysters . . .

## 5 APRIL 1802

Not being able to return on board the same night, we slept near the entrance of the lagoon. It was high water by the shore, on the morning of the 5th, at six o'clock; but on comparing this with the swinging of the ship, it appeared that the tide had then been running more than an hour from the westward. The rise in the lagoon seemed to be from four to eight feet.

Australian sea lions, *Neophoca cinerea* (Péron, 1816), Ferdinand Bauer. Naturhistorisches Museum, Vienna

A few kangaroos had been obtained during my absence, as also some seal skins; but one of the sailors having attacked a large seal incautiously, received a very severe bite in the leg, and was laid up. After all the researches now made in the island, it appeared that the kangaroos were much more numerous at our first landing place near Kangaroo Head, than elsewhere in the neighbourhood. That part of the island was clearer of wood than most others; and there were some small grass plats which seemed to be particularly attractive, and were kept very bare. Not less than thirty or forty cassowaries were seen at different times; but it so happened that they were fired at only once, and that ineffectually. They were most commonly found near the longest of the small beaches to the eastward of Kangaroo Head, at the place represented in the annexed plate; where some little drainings of water oozed from the rocks. It is possible, that with much time and labour employed in digging, water might be procured there to supply a ship; and I am sorry to say, that it was the sole place found by us where the hope of procuring fresh water could be entertained.

On 6 April, his time-keepers wound and his last set of observations carefully completed, Flinders weighed anchor and steered out of Nepean Bay with the assistance of a light south-west breeze. At about noon he anchored, giving William Westall the opportunity to make a sketch of the island off Kangaroo Head. With winter approaching, and eager to complete his charting of the unknown coast before a lack of provisions forced a return to Port Jackson, Flinders determined to push further east. At the same time, winds and tide conspired to make his task a difficult one, so that a prolonged struggle ensued as he attempted to negotiate the passage between the eastern end of Kangaroo Island and the mainland. Not until April 8, and after taking advantage of the shelter offered by Antechamber Bay, did the *Investigator* finally manage to tack its way eastwards past The Pages and out of the strait. Flinders left the eastern shores of Kangaroo Island behind, quite unsuspecting that a much more unusual encounter awaited him just a few hours later.

### Sailing From the East
### Baudin from Wilson's Promontory to Encounter Bay, 30 March to 8 April 1802

While Flinders was exploring Kangaroo Island, the *Géographe*, now separated from its consort the *Naturaliste*, was sailing from the other direction, its crew excited by the prospect of discovery but unaware that a rival expedition had already begun the task of charting the unknown south coast. After spending nearly two and a half months in Van Diemen's Land, Baudin crossed Bass Strait in the direction of Wilson's Promontory, whose exact position he was keen to determine. The contours of the southern coast of what is now Victoria had, of course, been sketched thanks to the combined efforts of George Bass in 1798 and Lieutenant James Grant in 1800. Bass had famously sailed south from Sydney in a whaleboat, past Cape Howe and Point Hicks and thereafter along a hitherto uncharted coast round Wilson's Promontory and as far as Western Port. From the other direction, Grant, sailing in the *Lady*

*Nelson*, had journeyed round the Cape of Good Hope with instructions to head through the newly discovered Bass Strait. Having sighted land somewhere near Mount Gambier, he had completed a first reconnaissance of the coast eastwards to Wilson's Promontory. Grant's brief, however, was not to conduct a thorough survey, and his representation of the Victorian coastline was therefore sketchy. Likewise, the English chart drawn up by Flinders from the indications of Bass was necessarily rough, and Baudin, having verified the position of Wilson's Promontory, was critical of it.

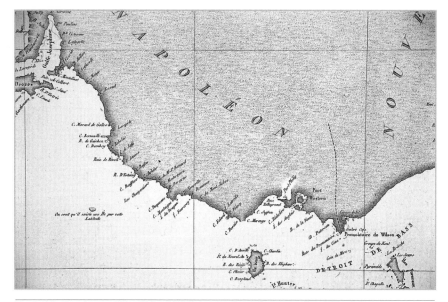

Detail of the French map of New Holland (1804) showing the south-east coast from Wilson's Promontory to Encounter Bay. Published in the *Atlas* of the *Voyage de découvertes aux Terres Australes* (1811)

With the benefit of some fine weather and favourable winds, Baudin was able to conduct a much more accurate survey of the coast from Wilson's Promontory right round to Mount Schanck (Grant's landfall on his journey in the opposite direction), although, significantly, the French captain was to miss the entrance to Port Phillip. On 30 March, Baudin found his way to Western Port. He was struck by the pleasant aspect of the land here, though there were signs that the atmosphere on board the ship was less agreeable.

### 30 MARCH 1802

All this part of the coast is high, well-wooded and of pleasant appearance.
There are small, insignificant coves with beaches of white sand where the sea

sometimes breaks, but always on the shore. I named the cape, which seemed to me the furthest south since Wilson's Promontory, 'Cap des Représentations' ['Protest Cape' – now Cape Patten] for the various protests that the staff made to me at that particular time.

Whatever these protests were, they did not prevent Baudin from enjoying the aspect of the coast as he followed it round to a point near Warrnambool – all the time, however, with an eye to possible landing points or safe harbours.

## 31 MARCH 1802

The shoreline along which we coasted from seven to midday is high and hilly; it is just as varied and pleasant to the eye as the coast of the day before, being almost completely wooded right down to the shore, except, however, for some large white patches which could be seen in various places and which could serve as landmarks . . .

During the afternoon we continued to follow the coast, which was now different in nature and appearance. Although the land along the seashore is high with steep cliffs, it seems arid as far back as a line of mountains which can be seen in the interior and which are well-wooded. In the morning we had sighted some smoke to the west of this point, which indicated that this area was inhabited. Indeed, it was the first smoke that we had seen since leaving the promontory. We saw the same fire again in the afternoon, on top of a knoll along the shoreline, but it was not very big.

All the coast we sailed past struck me as inaccessible and unable to offer any shelter for a small boat, even though it is broken up into several fairly large coves, which would seem to indicate an easy landing. The sea breaks along the entire stretch of shore. Being very close in, we established this as an incontrovertible fact.

Next day, the *Géographe* entered Portland Bay, where an encounter with Lady Julia Percy Island caused some concern.

## 1 APRIL 1802

After identifying the point at which we had stopped the previous day, we sailed along the coast to examine some fairly high land that lay a little to leeward of us and seemed to jut out a long way . . . As there was a good breeze, we drew quickly and easily alongside this stretch of land, which we identified as an island. We saw that it lay a good league or so from the mainland and that the channel in-between was easy to pass through . . . As this was my intention, we hugged the wind as closely as we needed to run in for the channel. But just as we were about to double the island, the wind suddenly dropped and we were carried much closer than I would have liked towards a long line of rocks running along its entire eastern coast . . . Soon after, we felt a slight catspaw from the south-east and we were very quick to take advantage of it to move away from this island, which we rounded to the south at a distance of one league. This island is completely bare of trees and seems to be covered only with a type of very low-growing heath; it did not appear to offer anything in the way of resources . . . Before leaving this island, I named it 'Ile aux Alouettes' [Lark Island] because we caught a lark that alighted on the ship while we were abeam of it.

Further anxiety was caused as they crossed Discovery Bay, where a low-lying rock suddenly loomed ahead of them.

## 2 APRIL 1802

Throughout the afternoon, we continued to coast along the shore, which is quite uniform in height, except for a few mountain peaks that can be seen in the hinterland of this region. The seashore is made up of a continuous line of dunes, at the foot of which the sea breaks with such force that it would be impossible to land there. At about half past three, as we were heading north-west with a fresh south-easterly breeze, we entered a bay that was just as large as the one we encountered the day before, but with a smaller entrance. Just when we were sailing along without the slightest fear for our safety, we saw, directly ahead of us, a rock that we had been unable to see in the sun's glare. We were then no more than two miles from it, which meant that we only just had time to go on the port tack and head south-south-west and south-west in order to double it . . . I took no sounding abeam of the hazard I have just mentioned so as not to demoralise anyone, in the event that the water was shallow. A bonus of one louis was given to Céré, the topman, who sighted it first and gave us the warning.

From Mount Schanck, Baudin found himself charting a coast that had not previously been seen by European eyes. For the next six days, however, the hopes of some exciting discoveries were to be disappointed: this low-lying sandy stretch of coast culminating in the long and uninterrupted strip now known as the Coorong revealed very few distinguishing features and struck the French only by its monotony. There was also no joy in the search for signs of inland waterways, as Baudin, like Flinders shortly after him, failed to notice the narrow outlet of Australia's most significant river system.

## 3 APRIL 1802

Throughout the afternoon, we sailed along a very low and level stretch of coast, where the only rising ground was provided by the sand dunes, which were of varying height . . . We continued our course south of east so as to go and check the last bearing we had taken, our intention being, as far as possible, to leave no gap along this whole coast . . .

During the night, we could hear the roar of the surf along the coast so clearly that, if the lead had not shown us that we were a fair way out to sea, we would have thought we were no more than a league off shore.

## 4 APRIL 1802

Throughout the morning, we could hear the noise that the sea made on the shore or on the reefs lying a little way out. We could make them out perfectly from on deck and could see the huge swell rising over them . . .

At about two o'clock, after making a clear sighting of the positions fixed by the last bearings we had taken, we set off to continue our work, following the coastline and keeping in so close that we were often only in 15 fathoms of water and less than a league off shore. The land in this part was the lowest-lying of any we had yet seen. We could clearly see several medium-sized peaks further inland, but these were few in number. The whole shoreline is made up of a line of sand dunes, most of which are barren and without vegetation. Just a little way out from the beach we could make out a continuous line of rocks over which the waves broke with extraordinary force. This was the cause of the constant noise that we could hear.

Over the next two days, the coastal profile eventually became a little more varied, with a number of capes and small islands coming into view – including the rocks that Flinders would later name in honour of the French captain. Of note here is the meticulous care Baudin takes in describing the shape of these cliffs and rocky islands. It is perhaps a sign of the times that he should have constant recourse to military images in order to paint these verbal pictures.

## 6 APRIL 1802

After determining our position, we continued our course west of north, sailing along the coast and keeping a league off shore at most. In this part, the coastline is entirely made up of barren and unattractive sand dunes. Inland, you can see that the terrain is fairly high and well-wooded.

During the morning, we hugged the coastline of a very large bay [Rivoli Bay] with a rather deep inlet in its north-east section that ends in a cape [Cape Martin] jutting out into the sea. At the tip of the cape lies a small island [Penguin Islet] that extends about half a league off shore . . . This island is completely surrounded by rocks and is thus inaccessible. The same applies to the whole coast, which is shielded by a reef and a line of large rocks of varying heights that make landing impossible . . .

Around three o'clock, we sighted a reef lying under water at about half a league off shore. We noticed it quite late, for it was already on our beam when we sighted it from on deck. We immediately went on the port tack, with the winds south-south-east, in order to bear off a little. Nevertheless, we were no more than a mile off when we passed it . . .

After gradually returning to a north-north-westerly course, we went on to sight another cape lying north by north-west of us [Cape Rabelais]. It seemed to mark the endpoint of the section of coast running in that direction. The cape is made up of a point that juts out and drops away steeply into the sea. In front of it there are three small rocks, one of which is particularly remarkable when approached from the east, for it is split in two and forms a crenel much like that of a fortress. The coast forms another large inlet here [Nora Creina Bay], and appears to run north by north-west. The land is not so low-lying nor is it formed by sand dunes like those that we had seen for more than half the day.

## 7 APRIL 1802

Throughout the morning, the sky was dark and overcast and the horizon was misty, which gave us the impression that the visible section of coastline was divided into an infinite number of small islands. However, when the mist cleared the coastline from north-north-west to east appeared in all its entirety. As I remarked yesterday, here the land is high and covered in trees, dropping steeply down to the sea where the shore is not a line of barren, sterile sand dunes, like the coast we had sailed along for most of the day. Roughly in the middle of the inlet that the coast forms at this point lie two islets or rocks, which are longer than they are high and whose form makes them easy to recognise: they are split in such a way that their openings resemble the crenels of a fortress on which cannons have been placed. The waves break over these rocks from every direction, but there is no broken water further out to sea.

At half past nine, while sailing along the coast a league off shore, I took soundings. I thought that we might be in 15 fathoms at that distance, but we found only ten. At that point we would still have held our course, had the depth not decreased to eight and even six fathoms without us receiving any other indication of such a sudden decrease. But as we started to head a little further out to sea, we were very surprised to see a rock at water level which we had not previously sighted and which even the look-out men had not seen . . . This rock, over which the sea breaks with force, is surrounded by reefs and appears to be joined to the mainland by a chain of rocks [the Baudin Rocks or Godfrey Islands] which make it impassable, even though the channel between the rock itself and the mainland is more than a league wide. We passed this hazard at a distance of 1½ leagues in 15 fathoms, rounding it on its western side. It would be wise for future navigators to be on their guard against a hazard that is so far out from the mainland.

At this point, the French entered the broad stretch of coast now known as Lacepede Bay, and which ends in the more well-defined indentation of Encounter Bay. In noting his impressions of this section of coastline, Baudin was unable to hide a growing sense of desolation.

## 8 APRIL 1802

The stretch of coast that we had been following since yesterday consisted entirely of sand dunes which inspired nothing but sadness and regrets. Quite apart from the wretched and unpleasant appearance of this shore, the sea breaks all the way along it with extraordinary force, and the two or three swells that appear before the waves reach the shore indicate that there is a bar which must extend at least half a mile out to sea.

The look-out men at the mast-heads and the interested observers who wished to join them reported that in the hinterland, as far as the eye could see, there was nothing but arid sand with no vegetation.

It was at this point, and in this frame of mind, that Baudin famously 'bumped into' Flinders, thereby discovering that he had a rival in his quest to chart the unknown south coast.

# chapter six

# CROSSED PATHS IN THE SOUTHERN OCEAN

*Baudin and Flinders in Encounter Bay,*
*8 April to 9 April 1802*

Some background to this encounter between the French and English navigators is useful in order to set the scene for the various accounts of it.

When they left Europe, both expeditions were well aware of the possibility of running into a naval vessel sailing under the flag of the other's nation – and that, during a period of war. The conflict between Britain and Revolutionary France was well into its eighth year in 1800, when Baudin set sail. While the Peace of Amiens would put a temporary halt to hostilities in October 1801 (lasting until 1803), neither Baudin nor Flinders could have been aware of this when they crossed paths in April 1802. Their meeting would therefore highlight the importance of the diplomatic precautions that had been taken in preparing the two voyages: recognising the scientific nature of the two expeditions, each nation had issued its rival with a passport guaranteeing safe passage for the captains in the event of such an encounter with the 'enemy'.

Notwithstanding these precautions, the surprise factor would still have been significant – though not in equal proportions. The French expedition had left well before that of Flinders and, in applying for a British passport, the French authorities had provided full details concerning the nature and purpose of their voyage. Flinders was therefore well aware of the possibility – albeit remote – of coming across a vessel under the command of Nicolas Baudin. The same could not be said of the French captain, who was already a good month out of Mauritius by the time France issued its passport for the Flinders expedition. Baudin would certainly have known of Flinders and his earlier hydrographic work on the Australian coast. Furthermore, encounters with ships flying English colours were to be expected, as the recent meeting with the *Harrington* had confirmed. Nevertheless, while he might not have shown it when it happened, Baudin had more reason to be surprised at the encounter than his English counterpart.

The discussions between the two captains took place in English, which Baudin spoke rather poorly. This would certainly have had an influence both on the nature of the exchanges and on the impressions formed on both sides. The two meetings were also rather intimate affairs: the *Investigator*'s botanist, Robert Brown, was the only other direct participant.

## Flinders on Baudin

The *Investigator* had just emerged from Backstairs Passage, a sojourn on Kangaroo Island and a thorough charting of a large portion of the unknown coast behind it. Baudin was sailing from the east, with a prolonged and successful exploration of Van Diemen's Land behind him. He had made his way north toward mainland Australia, joining it near Wilson's Promontory and following it to the west. At this point, the *Géographe* was sailing solo, having lost contact with its consort, the *Naturaliste*, off the north-eastern tip of Van Diemen's Land. Thus it was just a single set of sails that presented itself to the *Investigator*'s watch on the afternoon of 8 April 1802.

### 8 APRIL 1802

Before two in the afternoon we stretched eastward again; and at four, a white rock was reported from aloft to be seen ahead. On approaching nearer, it proved to be a ship standing towards us; and we cleared for action, in case of being attacked. The stranger was a heavy-looking ship, without any top-gallant masts up; and our colours being hoisted, she showed a French ensign, and afterwards an English jack forward, as we did a white flag. At half past five, the land being then five miles distant to the north-eastward, I hove to; and learned, as the stranger passed to leeward with a free wind, that it was the French national ship *Le Géographe*, under the command of Captain Nicolas

Baudin. We veered round as *Le Géographe* was passing, so as to keep our broadside to her, lest the flag of truce should be a deception; and having come to the wind on the other tack, a boat was hoisted out, and I went on board the French ship, which had also hove to.

As I did not understand French, Mr Brown, the naturalist, went with me in the boat. We were received by an officer who pointed out the commander, and by him were conducted into the cabin. I requested Captain Baudin to show me his passport from the Admiralty; and when it was found and I had perused it, offered mine from the French marine minister, but he put it back without inspection. He then informed me that he had spent some time in examining the south and east parts of Van Diemen's Land, where his geographical engineer, with the largest boat and a boat's crew, had been left, and probably lost. In Bass' Strait Captain Baudin had encountered a heavy gale, the same we had experienced in a less degree on March 21, in the Investigator's Strait. He was then separated from his consort, *Le Naturaliste*; but having since had fair winds and fine weather, he had explored the south coast from Western Port to the place of our meeting, without finding any river, inlet, or other shelter which afforded anchorage. I inquired concerning a large island, said to lie in the western entrance of Bass' Strait [King Island – Flinders knew of it through the account of a Captain Reid, who had come upon it in a sealing vessel in 1799]; but he had not seen it, and seemed to doubt much of its existence.

Captain Baudin was communicative of his discoveries about Van Diemen's Land; as also of his criticisms upon an English chart of Bass' Strait, published in 1800. He found great fault with the north side of the strait, but commended the form given to the south side and to the islands near it. On my pointing out a note upon the chart, explaining that the north side of the strait was seen only in an open boat by Mr Bass, who had no good means of fixing either latitude or longitude, he appeared surprised, not having before paid attention to it.

I told him that some other, and more particular charts of the Strait and its neighbourhood had been since published; and that if he would keep company until next morning, I would bring him a copy, with a small memoir belonging to them. This was agreed to, and I returned with Mr Brown to the *Investigator*.

The amiability and civility of the occasion must be taken as an indication of the natural respect in which each held the other, and of the mutually held view that work conducted in the name of exploration and scientific endeavour for the greater good of the international community of scholars transcended national boundaries and the vagaries of international politics.

At the same time, it was apparent to Flinders that, after this initial gathering, his interlocutor was not yet clear about whom he was dealing with; he had shown a remarkable lack of curiosity concerning the motives and goals that had brought the British expedition to the other side of the globe. Baudin's tone seemed to change, however, the following day at the agreed second meeting, for which the French again played the role of hosts. Despite the evident language problems, and allowing for the likelihood that much information went astray or was misinterpreted, this second meeting seems to have proved highly informative for both parties. According to Flinders' account, however, it was not until near the end that the penny finally dropped for Baudin: his helpful counterpart was none other than the man whose charts he had been using.

## 9 APRIL 1802

It somewhat surprised me, that Captain Baudin made no enquiries concerning my business upon this unknown coast, but as he seemed more desirous of communicating information, I was happy to receive it; next morning, however, he had become inquisitive, some of his officers having learned from my boat's crew that our object was also discovery. I then told him, generally, what our operations had been, particularly in the two gulfs, and the latitude to which I had ascended in the largest; explained the situation of Port Lincoln, where fresh water might be procured; showed him Cape Jervis, which was still in sight; and as a proof of the refreshments to be obtained at the large island opposite to it, pointed out the kangaroo skin caps worn by my boat's crew; and told him the name I had affixed to the island in consequence. At parting, the captain requested me to take care of his boat and people, in case of meeting with them; and to say to *Le Naturaliste*, that he should go to Port Jackson so soon as the bad weather set in. On my asking the name of the captain of *Le Naturaliste*, he bethought himself to ask mine; and finding it to be the same as the author of the chart which he had been criticising, expressed not a little surprise; but had the politeness to congratulate himself on meeting me.

The situation of the *Investigator*, when I hove to for the purpose of speaking to Captain Baudin, was 35° 40' south, and 138° 58' east. No person was present at our conversations except Mr Brown; and they were mostly carried on in English, which the captain spoke so as to be understood. He gave me, besides what is related above, some information of his losses in men, separations from his consort, and of the improper season at which he was directed to explore this coast; as also a memorandum of some rocks he had met

with, lying two leagues from the shore, in latitude 37° 1', and he spoke of them
as being very dangerous.

Neither at this time nor at any later point did Flinders reveal any sign of
resentment toward Baudin. Indeed, he was careful to acknowledge the
Frenchman's prior exploration of the coast to the east of Encounter Bay.
Moreover, it was Flinders, as we have noted, who gave the name Baudin's
Rocks to the dangerous rocks of which Baudin had warned him. These rocks
in Guichen Bay were later renamed the Godfrey Islands, though locals still
refer to them by their original name. The encounter seems to have concluded
in the spirit of amiability with which it began, as Baudin's account confirms.

## Baudin on Flinders

The sight of another sail in Encounter Bay immediately raised hopes that the
*Géographe*'s lost consort, the *Naturaliste*, had somehow found its way there.
Hope soon gave way to surprise, however, as the French came to the realisation
that there was another European ship in these waters. Furthermore, the men
on board this ship seemed to be well informed about the French expedition –
a fact which only heightened the astonishment of Baudin and his crew.

### 8 APRIL 1802

In the afternoon, we continued to coast along a sandy shoreline made up
entirely of dunes the same as before. But towards three o'clock we began to see
some higher ground which did seem pleasant in appearance. A little later we
saw a ship which we first took to be the *Naturaliste*, for nothing could be
further from our thoughts than to imagine there were any other Europeans in
these parts at this time of the year. Nevertheless, we were greatly mistaken, for
as we drew near we realised from her masts and her size that she was not the
*Naturaliste*. Finally, at five o'clock, when we were both able to make one
another out perfectly, the other ship gave us a signal which we did not
understand and consequently did not answer. She then ran up the English flag
and shortened sail. In turn we hoisted the national flag and I braced sharp up
to draw alongside her. As she hailed us first, we were asked about our colours.
I replied that they were French. Next we were asked if Captain Baudin was in
command. I was very surprised, not only at the question, but also at hearing
myself named. Once I said yes, the English ship hove to.

What happened next set the scene for the meeting that was about to take place between these explorers from two rival nations: upon receiving confirmation that it was indeed Captain Baudin to whom he was speaking, Flinders and his officers saluted him by removing their hats. Baudin, no doubt surprised and flattered by this gesture of respect, immediately responded with his own salute and prepared to welcome the English captain on board the *Géographe*. During their meeting, which took place in his cabin, Baudin spoke at great length of the surveying work he had carried out to this point.

> Since I saw she was preparing to send a dinghy across, I also brought to so as to wait for it. The English captain, Mr Flinders – the self-same Flinders who discovered the Strait which ought to bear his name, but which has most inappropriately been called Banks Strait [between the north-east tip of Tasmania and the Furneaux Group] – came aboard, expressing his delight at making such a pleasant encounter, though he was extremely reserved about everything else. As soon as I learnt his name, I paid him my compliments, informing him of the great pleasure it gave me to make his acquaintance and of all that we had done systematically up till then in terms of geographical work. As it was already late, Mr Flinders told me that, if I were willing to tack out to sea during the night, then head back to shore and wait till dawn, he would come back on board the following day and give me various particulars about the coast that he had examined from Cape Leeuwin up to here. I was delighted with his proposal, and we agreed to remain together throughout the night – a night which turned out to be very fine.

The next day, Flinders in turn provided his counterpart with valuable geographical information and charts. Of particular interest to Baudin was the indication that a safe port could be found on a large island nearby, which Flinders had named after its resident marsupials.

## 9 APRIL 1802

> On morning of the 19th [Germinal], when Mr Flinders was preparing to come aboard again as he had told me he would the previous day, I again hove to in order to wait for him. He arrived at half past six, accompanied by the same person who had been with him the day before. As he was much less reserved on this second visit than he had been previously, he told me that his ship was called the *Investigator* and that he had left Europe about eight months after I had. He also told me that he had begun his reconnaissance of the coast of

New Holland at Cape Leeuwin, after which he had visited the Isles of St Peter and St Francis, as well as the entire coast up to our meeting place. He further gave me the map of a harbour that he had discovered on an island only 15 or 20 leagues away and that he had named Kangaroo Island because of the great numbers of kangaroos to be found there. According to his report, the island is long, high and covers a large area, and the channel separating it from the mainland is easy to navigate. He stayed six weeks there and consequently had time to explore it.

Before we separated, Mr Flinders gave me several charts published by Arrowsmith since our departure. As I told him of the accident that had befallen my dinghy and asked him to give it all the help he could, if by any chance he came across it, he told me that he had met with a similar misfortune on his Kangaroo Island, where he had lost eight men and a boat. His companion ship had also been separated from him during the equinoctial gale which I had weathered partly in Bass Strait and then outside. As he left, Mr Flinders told me that he was going to head for the strait to try to reconnoitre a land mass that is said to exist between the Hunter Group and the harbour that they have named Western Port. At eight o'clock we parted, each wishing the other a safe voyage.

In addition to the discrepancies that point to communication difficulties, these journal entries clearly contradict Flinders' suggestion that it was not until their second meeting that the French captain became aware of his English counterpart's identity. Indeed, Baudin's account reveals from the outset his great respect for Flinders and his pleasure at their meeting. Its matter-of-fact tone, however, masks any other sentiments he might have felt. It also says nothing of the atmosphere on board ship during this encounter. The *Géographe* would surely have been abuzz with speculation on the nature and purpose of this British expedition. The same could also be said of the crew on the *Investigator*. Some indication of the mixed emotions felt by the French, particularly their disappointment at learning of Flinders' discoveries on the unknown coast, can be detected in a letter Baudin sent from Port Jackson to the Minister of Marine in Paris on 11 November 1802, some months after the encounter:

The weariness which we had been feeling for some time at seeing nothing but coasts, for the most part arid and offering nothing by way of resources, was dispelled by the expectation that we would have more luck from then on; another distraction, that was pleasanter still, was provided by the object that suddenly came into view; we saw a ship with square sails and not one of us doubted that it was and could only be the *Naturaliste*. As this ship was tacking south and we were tacking north, we did not take long to approach one another, but imagine our astonishment when we saw it fly a white flag from the mainmast. It was no doubt a recognition signal, to which we were unable to reply. A little later, this signal was lowered and the English flag and pennant replaced it. We responded by hoisting our own and we continued to advance towards each other. As the manoeuvre performed by the English ship showed that she wished to speak with us, we stood towards her. When we were within speaking distance I was asked: 'What's your ship?' I replied simply that it was French. 'Is it Captain Baudin's ship?' 'Yes, the same.'

The English captain then saluted me graciously, saying: 'I am indeed delighted to make this encounter.' I then responded in the same way, without knowing to whom I was replying. But since they were preparing to come on board, I hove to.

Mr Flinders, the commander of the ship, came on board himself. As soon as I learnt his name, I no longer doubted that he was, like us, engaged in the exploration of the south-west coast of New Holland, and, in spite of the reserve which he showed on this first visit, it was easy for me to see that he had already surveyed part of it. After I had invited him to come into my cabin, where we were alone, the conversation became freer. He informed me that he had left Europe eight months after us and that he was going to Port Jackson, having called in at the Cape of Good Hope.

I had no hesitation about acquainting him with the work we had done on the coast so far; I even told him of the errors which I had noticed in the chart he had given us of the straits which separate New Holland from Van Diemen's Land.

Mr Flinders remarked to me that he was not unaware that this work was still in need of verification, inasmuch as the chart had been drawn from somewhat uncertain data and the boats that had been used for the purpose were not suitable for obtaining very precise results. At last, becoming less circumspect than he had been so far, he told me that he had located Cape Leeuwin and followed the coast up to the present spot; he then proposed that our ships should remain together during the night; that tomorrow at daylight he would come back on board, to give me some details which might be useful to me. I accepted his proposal with pleasure and we tacked to windward at a short distance from each other. It was seven in the evening when he returned to his ship.

On the 19th [Germinal – 9 April], Mr Flinders was on board at half past six in the morning; we breakfasted together and we both discussed our work; he appeared to me to have been more fortunate in his discoveries than I was; he had explored a large island that was only 12 to 15 leagues away when we met him. According to his account, he stayed there six weeks in order to make a map of it and, with the assistance of a sloop which followed him, he explored two deep gulfs that form part of the main coast whose position he sketched for me, as well as the position of his island to which he had given the name of Kangaroo Island because of the large number of these quadrupeds which he found there. This island, although only a short distance from the continent, did not appear to him to be inhabited.

A misfortune similar to one we had experienced on the eastern coast of Van Diemen's Land had happened to Mr Flinders; on this coast he lost a boat and eight men. His sloop was also missing and he was not a little anxious about its fate.

Before we took leave of one another, the Captain asked me if I had noticed land, said to exist to the north of the [Hunter] islands. I replied that I had not; since I had followed the coast very closely from the promontory to Western Port, I could not have come across it, if it was situated in the position he indicated; he appeared extremely satisfied with my reply, no doubt in the hope of being the first to discover it. Perhaps the *Naturaliste*, which has been looking for us in this strait, will have done so.

At the moment of his departure, Mr Flinders presented me with several new maps published by Arrowsmith and with a printed memoir by himself on his discoveries in the strait, the north coast of the island of Diemen and its eastern portion. He also invited me to put in at Port Jackson – whose resources he praised too highly perhaps – if I should be making a long stay in these seas.

---

## Péron on Flinders

François Péron, in writing up the official account of the French expedition, is, typically, much less circumspect in describing the encounter with Flinders. In the first volume of his *Voyage de découvertes aux Terres Australes* (Paris, 1807), his rendering of the meeting, while it concurs in most respects with those of the two captains, nevertheless contains some embellishments, as Flinders was prompt to point out.

The fishing was only just over when a signal was made from the mast-head that there was a sail on the horizon. At first everyone thought it was the *Naturaliste*, and we were all overjoyed, but we were soon close enough to the other ship to realise that it was not our consort. As she was heading towards us on a parallel course and in full sail, it was not long before she was abeam of us: she then hoisted the English flag; we in turn hoisted French colours and, following her lead, hove to. At this point, the English captain hailed us and asked if we were not one of the two ships which had left France on a voyage of discovery to the Southern Hemisphere. On our answering in the affirmative, he immediately sent out a boat and a little later we welcomed him on board. We learnt that he was Captain Flinders, the very same person who had already circumnavigated Van Diemen's Land; the name of his ship was the *Investigator* and it was eight months since he had sailed from Europe with the intention of reconnoitring the whole coast of New Holland and the archipelagos of the South Seas; he had been off the coast of Nuyts' Land for about three months; he had been held back by contrary winds and had not been able to sail behind the St Peter and St Francis Islands as he had intended; at the time of his departure from England he had another ship with him, from which he had been separated by a violent storm; a few days earlier, the same equinoctial gale which had put us in such terrible danger in Bass Strait had caused the loss of his longboat, along with eight of his best seamen and his First Officer. This curious similarity between the disasters we have both experienced may serve as further proof of the extent of the perils in store for expeditions of this sort.

Even while providing us with all these details, Mr Flinders was very reserved on the subject of his own particular operations. Yet we learnt from some of his seamen that he had suffered greatly from those south winds which had been so favourable to us – which was when we came to appreciate all the more the wisdom that had dictated our own instructions. After conversing with us for over an hour, Captain Flinders returned on board his own ship, promising to come back the next day and bring us a particular chart of the River Dalrymple, which he had just published in England.

On 9 April, Captain Flinders did indeed return to give us the chart and soon after we left him in order to continue our geographical work.

When Flinders eventually read this account of the meeting, years after the encounter, he was surprised, to say the least, at the implicit claim that Péron had participated in the discussions. When writing up the official account of his voyage, published in 1814, Flinders highlighted Péron's 'with us', commenting that 'no person except Mr Brown was present at my conversation with Captain Baudin, as I have already said.' Even more scandalous, for Flinders, was the following claim laid by Péron on the whole portion of the south coast he and Freycinet called 'Terre Napoléon':

> Of this great expanse [the south coast of Terra Australis], only that part which stretches from Cape Leeuwin to the Isles of St Peter and St Francis was known at the time of our departure from Europe. Discovered by the Dutch in 1627, it had more recently been visited by Vancouver and above all d'Entrecasteaux; but the latter navigator having himself been unable to go further than the Isles of St Peter and St Francis, which form the eastern extremity of Nuyts' Land, and the English not having explored further south than Western Port, the whole section of coast between this latter point and Nuyts' Land was consequently still unknown at the time we arrived on these shores.

These extravagant claims made by the French in their official account understandably angered Flinders. He found them personally offensive, because they quite brazenly down-played and distorted his own achievements in charting the unknown coast to the west of Encounter Bay; but they also rode roughshod over the exploratory work of James Grant. Flinders and Baudin could not have learned of it until they reached Port Jackson, but Grant had already

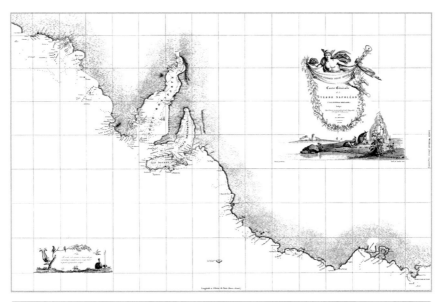

*Carte Générale de la Terre Napoléon*, L. Freycinet (1808). Published in the *Atlas* of the *Voyage de découvertes aux Terres Australes* (1811)

charted a lengthy stretch of the Victorian coast in the *Lady Nelson*. As Flinders pointed out, the French claims of original European discovery must in reality be confined to the section of coast stretching from Encounter Bay south-east-wards to a position close to the current border between South Australia and Victoria:

> M. Péron should have said, not that the south coast from Western Port to Nuyts' Land was then unknown; but that it was unknown to them; for Captain Grant of the *Lady Nelson* had discovered the eastern part, from Western Port to the longitude 140°, in the year 1800, before the French ships sailed from Europe; and on the west I had explored the coast and islands from Nuyts' Land to Cape Jervis in 138° 10', and was, on the day specified, at the head of the Gulf of St Vincent.'

Flinders was very careful to state his claim and to set precise limits on the extent of the French achievement. He seemed particularly offended at the use of Napoleonic references to designate features he himself had named.

> At the above situation of 35° 40' south, and 138° 58' east, the discoveries made by Captain Baudin upon the south coast have their termination to the west; as mine in the *Investigator* have to the eastward. Yet Monsieur Péron, naturalist in the French expedition, has laid a claim for his nation to the discovery of all the parts between Western Port in Bass' Strait, and Nuyts' Archipelago; and this part of New South Wales is called Terre Napoléon. My Kangaroo Island, a name which they openly adopted in the expedition, has been converted at Paris into L'Isle Decrès [after the Minister of Marine]; Spencer's Gulf is named Golfe Bonaparte; the Gulf of St Vincent, Golfe Joséphine; and so on, along the whole coast to Cape Nuyts, not even the smallest island being left without some similar stamp of French discovery.

Flinders gave short shrift to the idea that Péron could not have known of the prior British claims when he and Freycinet came to write up the official French account.

> It is said by M. Péron, and upon my authority too, that the *Investigator* had not been able to penetrate behind the Isles of St Peter and St Francis; and though he doth not say directly, that no part of the before unknown coast was discovered by me, yet the whole tenor of his Chap. XV induces the reader to

believe that I had done nothing which could interfere with the prior claim of the French.

Yet M. Péron was present afterwards at Port Jackson, when I showed one of my charts of this coast to Captain Baudin, and pointed out the limits of his discovery; and so far from any prior title being set up at that time to Kangaroo Island and the parts westward, the officers of the *Géographe* always spoke of them as belonging to the *Investigator*. The first lieutenant, Mons. Freycinet, even made use of the following odd expression, addressing himself to me in the house of Governor King, and in the presence of one of his companions, I think Mons. Bonnefoy, 'Captain, if we had not been kept so long picking up shells and catching butterflies at Van Diemen's Land, you would not have discovered the south coast before us.'

The English officers and respectable inhabitants then at Port Jackson, can say if the prior discovery of these parts were not generally acknowledged; nay, I appeal to the French officers themselves, generally and individually, if such were not the case. How then came M. Péron to advance what was so contrary to truth? Was he a man destitute of all principle? My answer is, that I believe his candour to have been equal to his acknowledged abilities; and that what he wrote was from over-ruling authority, and smote him to the heart: he did not live to finish the second volume.

The motive for this aggression I do not pretend to explain. It may have originated in the desire to rival the British nation in the honour of completing the discovery of the globe; or be intended as the forerunner of a claim to the possession of the countries so said to have been first discovered by French navigators. Whatever may have been the object in view, the question, so far as I am concerned, must be left to the judgment of the world; and if succeeding French writers can see and admit the claims of other navigators, as clearly and readily as a late most able man of that nation [M. de Fleurieu] has pointed out their own in some other instances, I shall not fear to leave it even to their decision.

It is a measure of Flinders' generosity, or perhaps a sign of his belief and trust in the explorers' unwritten code of honour, that he should have sought an alternative, political explanation for the deceit perpetrated by Péron and, to a lesser extent, Freycinet.

In their journal entries, Flinders and Baudin do not reveal many of their feelings, so that we can only speculate as to their respective moods on the afternoon of 9 April as they left each other in their wakes. Baudin may have been lamenting the time lost at various points during his voyage, so that the fame and recognition to be derived from the first charting of the previously unknown coast to the west was denied him. This, at least, was the impression he made on Flinders, who was to write in his account: 'I did not apprehend that my being here at this time, so far along the unknown coast, gave him any great pleasure.' Flinders similarly may have wondered whether, with hindsight, he himself should have spent so much time charting the coastline to the west of the 'unknown' coast, of which d'Entrecasteaux in particular had already compiled competent charts. If he had made directly to the unknown coast, as indeed his orders from the Admiralty demanded, he would probably have been able to deny the French any claims of original discovery at all.

Both captains might well have felt a tinge of disappointment at the unexpectedly sudden resolution of the mystery of the southern coast. The accounts which each gave the other on April 8 and 9 confirmed that there was no great strait separating New Holland in the west from New South Wales in the east. Patches on the northern coasts aside, the biggest pieces on the jigsaw of Terra Australis were set in place; its shape was known. Baudin and Flinders now realised that they were dealing with just one massive continent.

That being indubitably the case, there was one more mystery to solve: how could it be that a continent so large had such a dearth of rivers carrying the rain which fell on its huge surface to the sea? Perhaps they had inadvertently distracted each other, or perhaps at that time of year the tell-tale signs of the mouth of a river were as good as invisible; in any case, both Flinders and Baudin missed the mouth of the continent's largest river system where it emptied into the sea just a short distance from where they had met.

# chapter seven

# FALSE DISCOVERIES

*Flinders from Encounter Bay to Port Jackson,*
*9 April to 9 May 1802*

After their meeting, the two captains set off in opposite directions, each following the coastline that the other had freshly charted. Concerned that the
winter gales would soon be upon him, Flinders decided not to dwell on the
section of coastline that Baudin had just charted. Of much more interest to
Flinders was the large island that was said to be located on the western side of
Bass Strait. Flinders' belief that such an island existed stemmed from accounts
by sealers, such as Captain Reid, who had landed on the southern part of the
island in 1799. Flinders had seemed pleased to learn from Baudin that the
French did not know of its existence, since this left open the possibility that
Flinders might take on the mantle of its official discoverer. What he did not
know, however, was that this mantle had already been claimed by Lieutenant
John Murray, who had also given King Island its name. Some two weeks
after the meeting in Encounter Bay, a large island indeed came into view.

## 22 APRIL 1802

A boat was immediately hoisted out, and I landed with the botanical
gentlemen. On stepping out of the boat, I shot one of those little bear-like
quadrupeds, called Womat [wombat]; and another was afterwards killed.
A seal, of a species different to any yet seen by us, was also procured; its
phippers [sic] behind were double, when compared to the common kinds of
seal, and those forward were smaller, and placed nearer to the head; the hair
was much shorter, and of a bluish, grey colour; the nose flat and broad; and the

fat upon the animal was at least treble the usual quantity. I never saw the sea elephant, and possibly this might have been a young female; but there was no appearance of any trunk.

So productive was the scientific party's first day on the island that the exercise was repeated the following day. Thereafter, Flinders was anxious that the time had come for him to make his way to Port Jackson. Before that, he wanted to sail toward the high land already sighted on the north side of Bass Strait and to trace it to the east for as long as his provisions would permit.

Captain James Grant had been the first to sail from west to east through the strait, in 1800, but a shortage of water and provisions had prohibited him from making a detailed survey. He soon returned to the strait, however, and conducted a more detailed survey from March to May 1801. Flinders had not yet left England in the *Investigator*, but, like Baudin, he could not have known of Grant's explorations until his arrival in Port Jackson.

Like Grant before him, when Flinders travelled eastward along the Victorian coast he could not afford to dally. To his English eyes, the southern coast of the mainland had thus far proved barren and uninteresting; moreover water had been hard to come by. Port Jackson, with its guaranteed supplies of water and food, beckoned. As he sped along it, however, the coast of what is

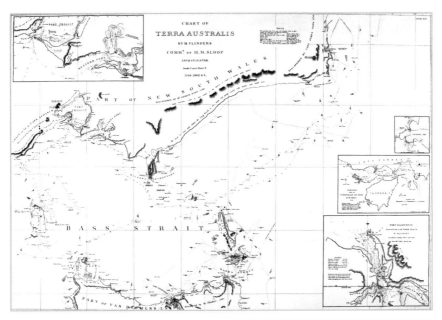

Flinders' chart of Bass Strait with inset showing Port Phillip and Western Port on the Victorian coast (1798, 1802, 1803). Published in *A Voyage to Terra Australis* (1814)

now Victoria appeared altogether more pleasing than that to the west, its prospects for settlement much more promising.

## 24 APRIL 1802

The time was fast approaching when it would be necessary to proceed to Port Jackson; both on account of the winter season, and from the want of some kinds of provisions. Before this took place, I wished to finish as much of the south coast as possible, and would have recommenced at Cape Bridgewater had the wind been favourable; but it still blew fresh from the southward, and all that part remained a lee shore. I determined, however, to run over to the high land we had seen on the north side of Bass' Strait; and to trace as much of the coast from thence eastward, as the state of the weather and our remaining provisions could possibly allow . . .

At three in the afternoon the northern land was in sight, and the highest hills of King's Island were sinking below the horizon, as seen from the deck. Their distance was twenty-five miles; and consequently the elevation of them is between four and five hundred feet above the level of the sea. At five o'clock, a bluff head, the most projecting part of the northern land, was distant three or four leagues; it was Captain Grant's Cape Otway . . . On the west side of Cape Otway the coast falls back somewhat to the north, and projects again at the distance of ten or eleven miles; where it is not, as I think, more than three leagues to the east of the headland seen under the lee at eight in the evening of the 20th. From Cape Otway, eastward, the shore trends east-north-east about three leagues, to a projection called Cape Patton, and according to Captain Grant, a bay is formed between them; but at three leagues off, nothing worthy of being called a bay could be perceived. Beyond Cape Patton the coast took a more northern direction, to a point with a flat-topped hill upon it, and further than this it was not visible.

## 25 APRIL 1802

The whole of this land is high, the elevation of the uppermost parts being not less than two thousand feet. The rising hills were covered with wood of a deep green foliage, and without any vacant spaces of rock or sand; so that I judged this part of the coast to exceed in fertility all that had yet fallen under observation.

Proceeding to the east, Flinders fully expected to approach Western Port, explored by his friend George Bass. Instead he stumbled upon a large mass of water which he naturally assumed to be Western Port, especially as Baudin had told him nothing of any such feature, other than Western Port. But it was an entirely different body of water, and Flinders understandably assumed he had made a significant discovery. His hopes were once again to be dashed: John Murray, who had replaced James Grant as the commander of the *Lady Nelson*, had taken on the task of completing Grant's exploration of this part of the southern coast and had come across Port Phillip in January 1802, naming both the bay itself and its key landmarks. As usual, in writing his narrative Flinders fully respected the nomenclature stemming from a voyage made just weeks before his own passage through those waters.

## 26 APRIL 1802

In the morning we kept close to an east-south-east wind, steering for the land to the north-eastward; and at nine o'clock captain Grant's Cape Schanck, the extreme of the preceding evening, was five leagues distant to the N 88° E, and a rocky point towards the head of the bight, bore N 12° E. On coming within five miles of the shore at eleven o'clock, we found it to be low, and mostly sandy; and that the bluff head which had been taken for the north end of an island, was part of a ridge of hills rising at Cape Schanck. We then bore away westward, in order to trace the land round the head of the deep bight . . .

On the west side of the rocky point there was a small opening, with breaking water across it; however, on advancing a little more westward the opening assumed a more interesting aspect, and I bore away to have a nearer view. A large extent of water presently became visible within side; and although the entrance seemed to be very narrow, and there were in it strong ripplings like breakers, I was induced to steer in at half past one; the ship being close upon a wind and every man ready for tacking at a moment's warning. The soundings were irregular between 6 and 12 fathoms, until we got 4 miles within the entrance, when they shoaled quick to 2³/4. We then tacked; and having a strong tide in our favour, worked to the eastward between the shoal and the rocky point, with 12 fathoms for the deepest water. In making the last stretch from the shoal, the depth diminished from 10 fathoms quickly to 3; and before the ship could come round, the flood tide set her upon a mud bank, and she stuck fast. A boat was lowered down to sound; and finding the deep water lie to the north-west, a kedge anchor was carried out; and having got the ship's head in that direction, the sails were filled and she drew off into 6 and 10 fathoms; and it being then dark, we came to an anchor.

The extensive harbour we had thus unexpectedly found I supposed must be Western Port, although the narrowness of the entrance did by no means correspond with the width given to it by Mr Bass. It was the information of Captain Baudin, who had coasted along from thence with fine weather, and had found no inlet of any kind, which induced this supposition; and the very great extent of the place, agreeing with that of Western Port, was in confirmation of it. This, however, was not Western Port, as we found next morning; and I congratulated myself on having made a new and useful discovery; but here again I was in error. This place, as I afterwards learned at Port Jackson, had been discovered ten weeks before by Lieutenant John Murray, who had succeeded Captain Grant in the command of the *Lady Nelson*. He had given it the name of Port Phillip, and to the rocky point on the east side of the entrance, that of Point Nepean.

## 27 APRIL 1802

Our situation was found in the morning to be near two miles from the south shore, and the extreme towards Point Nepean bore N 83° W, two leagues. About three miles to the north-by-west were some dry rocks, with bushes on them, surrounded with mud flats; and they appeared to form a part of the same shoal from which we had three times tacked in 2½ and 3 fathoms. The mud bank where the ship had grounded, is distinct from the middle shoal, but I am not certain that it is so from the south shore, from which it is one mile distant. The Bluff Mount (named Arthur's Seat by Mr Murray, from a supposed resemblance to the hill of that name near Edinburgh) bore S 76° E; but from thence the shore trended northward so far, that the land at the head of the port could not be seen, even from aloft. Before proceeding any higher with the ship, I wished to gain some knowledge of the form and extent of this great piece of water; and Arthur's Seat being more than a thousand feet high and near the water side, presented a favourable station for that purpose.

After breakfast I went away in a boat, accompanied by Mr Brown and some other gentlemen, for the Seat. It was seven or eight miles from the ship; and in steering nearly a straight course for it, we passed over the northern skirt of the shoal where the ship had touched; but afterwards had from 7 to 5 fathoms nearly to the shore. Having observed the latitude there from an artificial horizon, I ascended the hill; and to my surprise found the port so extensive, that even at this elevation its boundary to the northward could not be distinguished. The western shore extended from the entrance ten or eleven miles in a northern direction, to the extremity of what, from its appearance, I called Indented Head; beyond it was a wide branch of the port leading to the westward, and I suspected might have a communication with the sea; for it was almost incredible, that such a vast piece of water should not have a larger outlet than that through which we had come.

I took an extensive set of bearings from the clearest place to be found on the north-western, bluff part of the hill; and we afterwards walked a little way back upon the ridge. From thence another considerable piece of water was seen, at the distance of three or four leagues; it seemed to be mostly shallow; but as it appeared to have a communication with the sea to the south, I had no doubt of its being Mr Bass' Western Port.

Arthur's Seat and the hills and valleys in its neighbourhood, were generally well covered with wood; and the soil was superior to any upon the borders of the salt water, which I have had an opportunity of examining in Terra Australis. There were many marks of natives, such as deserted fire places and heaps of oyster shells; and upon the peninsula which forms the south side of the port, a smoke was rising, but we did not see any of the people. Quantities of fine oysters were lying upon the beaches, between high and low water marks, and appeared to have been washed up by the surf; a circumstance which I do not recollect to have observed in any other part of this country . . .

Under the illusion that he was the first European to explore the bay, Flinders took a boat and provisions for three days to undertake a thorough survey. He made a landing on the evening of 29 April close to a site which, as it happened, was favoured by the local inhabitants. They proved less circumspect than others along the southern coast, with the result that an amiable exchange could take place.

## 30 APRIL

In the morning, a fire was perceived two hundred yards from the tent; and the Indians appeared to have decamped from thence on our landing. Whilst I was taking angles from a low point at the north-easternmost part of Indented Head, a party of the inhabitants showed themselves about a mile from us, and on landing there we found a hut with a fire in it, but the people had disappeared, and carried off their effects. I left some strips of cloth, of their favourite red colour, hanging about the hut; and proceeded westward along the shore, to examine the arm of the port running in that direction.

Three natives having made their appearance abreast of the boat, we again landed. They came to us without hesitation, received a shag and some trifling presents with pleasure, and parted with such of their arms as we wished to possess, without reluctance. They afterwards followed us along the shore; and when I shot another bird, which hovered over the boat, and held it up to them, they ran down to the water side and received it without expressing either surprise or distrust. Their knowledge of the effect of firearms I then attributed to their having seen me shoot birds when unconscious of being observed; but it had probably been learned from Mr Murray . . .

The apparent tractability of the indigenous population did not pass unnoticed. Flinders completed his explorations the next day before returning to the *Investigator* and giving some thought to the appropriateness of the port for settlement. Next to issues of navigability, adequacy of water supplies and fertility of the land, he also pointed to the likelihood of 'friendly intercourse' with the local population. In retrospect, the locals might well have wished they had displayed a more grudging demeanour to their visitors; as it happened, only concerns about the availability of fresh water delayed the inevitable.

## SUNDAY 2 MAY

I find it very difficult to speak in general terms of Port Phillip. On the one hand it is capable of receiving and sheltering a larger fleet of ships than ever yet went to sea; whilst on the other, the entrance, in its whole width, is scarcely two miles, and nearly half of it is occupied by the rocks lying off Point Nepean, and by shoals on the opposite side. The depth in the remaining part varies from 6 to 12 fathoms; and this irregularity causes the strong tides, especially when running against the wind, to make breakers, in which small vessels should be careful of engaging themselves; and when a ship has passed the entrance, the middle shoals are a great obstacle to a free passage up the port. These shoals are met with at four miles directly from the entrance, and extend about ten miles to the east-south-east, parallel with the south shore; they do not seem, however, to be one connected mass, for I believe there are two or three deep openings in them, though we had not time to make an examination.

No runs of fresh water were seen in my excursions; but Mr Charles Grimes, surveyor-general of New South Wales, afterwards found several, and in particular, a small river falling into the northern head of the port. Mr Grimes was sent by Governor King, in 1803, to walk round, and survey the harbour; and from his plan I have completed my chart of Port Phillip. The parts of the coast left unshaded are borrowed from him, and the soundings written at right angles are those of his companion, Lieutenant Robbins.

The country surrounding Port Phillip has a pleasing, and in many parts a fertile appearance; and the sides of some of the hills and several of the valleys, are fit for agricultural purposes. It is in great measure a grassy country, and capable of supporting much cattle, though better calculated for sheep. To this general description there are probably several exceptions; and the southern peninsula, which is terminated by Point Nepean, forms one, the surface there being mostly sandy, and the vegetation in many places, little better than brush-wood. Indented Head, at the northern part of the western peninsula, had an appearance particularly agreeable; the grass had been burned not long before, and had sprung up green and tender; the wood was so thinly scattered that one might see to a considerable distance; and the hills rose one over the other to a moderate elevation, but so gently, that a plough might everywhere be used. The vegetable soil is a little mixed with sand, but good, though probably not deep, as I judged by the small size of the trees . . .

Were a settlement to be made at Port Phillip, as doubtless there will be some time hereafter, the entrance could be easily defended; and it would not be difficult to establish a friendly intercourse with the natives, for they are acquainted with the effect of firearms, and desirous of possessing many of our conveniences. I thought them more muscular than the men of King George's Sound; but, generally speaking, they differ in no essential particular from the other inhabitants of the south and east coasts, except in language, which is dissimilar, if not altogether different to that of Port Jackson, and seemingly of King George's Sound also. I am not certain whether they have canoes, but none were seen.

In the woods are the kangaroo, the emu or cassowary, paroquets, and a variety of small birds; the mud banks are frequented by ducks and some black swans, and the shores by the usual sea fowl common in New South Wales.

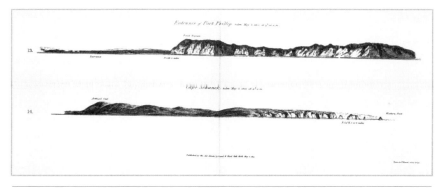

Coastal profiles of Port Phillip and Cape Schanck, William Westall. Published in *A Voyage to Terra Australis* (1814)

The range of the thermometer was between 61° and 67°, and the climate appeared to be as good and as agreeable as could well be desired in the month answering to November. In 1803, Colonel Collins of the marines was sent out from England to make a new settlement in this country; but he quitted Port Phillip for the south end of Van Diemen's Land, probably from not finding fresh water for a colony sufficiently near to the entrance . . .

The *Investigator* departed from Port Phillip with the last half of the ebb on 3 May, Westall taking a view of the entrance when the ship was some five miles distant. As they headed east, Westall also sketched Cape Schanck and the ridge of hills leading to Arthur's Seat. The coast to the east – Western Port and beyond – Flinders knew to be charted territory, so he set sail for Port Jackson.

# PUSHING THE BOUNDARIES

*Baudin from Encounter Bay to Port Jackson,*
*9 April to 20 June 1802*

Baudin would also make his way to Port Jackson following the meeting with Flinders in Encounter Bay, but by a much more indirect route. Despite what he had just learned of the work Flinders had already accomplished, Baudin was determined to pursue his reconnaissance of the south coast. He was particularly keen to explore the mainland behind the St Peter and St Francis Islands – a key task set for him in the instructions he had received for the voyage. In the wake of the meeting of the *Investigator* and the *Géographe* on 9 April, the French therefore continued on their westerly course, sighting Kangaroo Island for the first time later that same day.

Baudin and his ship's company might understandably have been in a sombre mood as they left Encounter Bay behind them. They had learned, during the course of that fateful meeting with Flinders, that their hopes of being the first to explore the entire length of the unknown coast had been dashed. In these circumstances, one would fully expect Baudin's impressions of the area to the west of Encounter Bay to be coloured by a feeling of immense disappointment. This certainly appears to have been the case, judging by the report that he made to his Minister from Port Jackson on 11 November: 'We explored a large portion of the north coast of Kangaroo Island; the various aspects which it offered served to make us regret not being the first to discover it.' However, his feelings on that point are not given prominence in the diary entries relating to his journey through Backstairs Passage on 11 April 1802.

Despite some frustration at not being able to approach Kangaroo Island –

he was soon forced to abandon his quest to land, for the time being at least, and decided instead to proceed to explore the nearby gulfs – he noted that the island and its bays appeared hospitable:

> We sailed along a fairly long stretch of the eastern coast of Kangaroo Island and inspected several bays which were quite deeply indented and where, in the good season – summer, that is – there must be good anchorages and shelter from the north-west through to the south to south-west winds . . . The hinterland looks quite pleasant and, although most of the trees had lost their leaves, there remained enough greenery for the view to be attractive.

Baudin then conducted an initial, very cursory examination of the two gulfs to the north of Kangaroo Island. What he did manage to see, however, led him to think that a return visit to these shores might prove fruitful. Again, the arid appearance of much of the land bordering the gulfs was cause for disappointment, as was the lack of any safe shelter for ships. Nevertheless, the French were struck by the pleasant scenery they found along certain parts of the Fleurieu Peninsula – so called in honour of Count Fleurieu, the celebrated geographer and former Minister of Marine who had drawn up Baudin's instructions. (The French name, proposed by Louis Freycinet when he later came to draw up his atlas, was not used on official maps and naval charts during the nineteenth century, but was restored in 1911 on the occasion of a visit to Australia by one of the Count's descendants and the successor to his title.)

## 12 APRIL 1802

> The small section of coast that we surveyed in the course of the day is high and hilly. We saw no visible sign of any hazard. Most of the mountains were bare of trees; some had trees that had lost their leaves, and on most of them the ground appeared quite arid, being covered with dry, straw-coloured grass . . . The land here bears considerably to the north, which appears to indicate a gulf [Gulf St Vincent] where we hoped to find some harbours, for it is very surprising that we have not yet found a single one along the entire stretch of coast that we have examined.

## 13 APRIL 1802

> As a stiff breeze continued to blow throughout the morning, we made good headway and explored the coast from barely a league offshore and sometimes less. All along the coast the bottom was found to be suitable for anchorage;

it was sandy, although a little hard, with a depth that varied from 16 to 20 fathoms. This section of the coast had very few trees, but nevertheless provided several rather picturesque views. We found no shelter for ships and only one bay of a decent size, with a beach of what appeared to be very white sand. The other bays had cliffs that dropped sharply into the sea and did not appear to offer any places for landing. Although these bays were sheltered from the wind, the waves broke on the shore as if they had passed over a sand bar.

Pursuing this northerly course, Baudin struck shallow water and the crew had to remain on duty all night tacking in order to find safer depths. As the captain noted: 'We were lucky to have fine weather; otherwise we might have found ourselves in a very tricky situation. I gave this gulf the name of Golfe de la Mauvaise [Difficult Gulf] because of the fatigue that it caused the whole crew.' The night-time manoeuvres brought him within sight of Yorke Peninsula, the eastern coast of which he was unable to examine in any detail, however, because of the variable winds and his reluctance to venture into shallower waters. Baudin's survey of Spencer Gulf was equally frustrating.

## 16 APRIL 1802

Since the current was in our favour, we headed across the channel to the mainland which looks particularly depressing in these parts. We had no trouble making out two high headlands formed of brown rocks of a particularly dreary colour; in between were white sand dunes, most of them without any kind of vegetation.

During this brief foray into Spencer Gulf, Baudin took stock of the ship's supplies and decided it would be prudent to reduce the water rations – a decision that caused discontent among the officers and naturalists.

## 17 APRIL 1802

As we still had a great deal to do on the coast of New Holland and had barely two months' water supply left, I thought it appropriate to begin cutting back rations in good time; that is, instead of distributing two and a half bottles of water per person, we now gave out no more than two. There can be no doubt that this was not much of a reduction, for we were still distributing more than the regulations for long voyages prescribed. Nevertheless, the decision caused some dissatisfaction – not amongst the sailors, but in another quarter. Be that as it may, it will in no way alter the decision I have taken on the matter, for I am convinced that we can all do without tea and coffee twice a day. So, like it or not, I was the first to comply – and with good grace.

Baudin's patience with his officers was again tested during the night of 19–20 April. A change in the weather had forced him to abort his exploration of Spencer Gulf and to return to its entrance, where the *Géographe* encountered strong winds and rough seas.

### 19 APRIL 1802

Last night was very tiring for the crew and myself in that we spent it constantly on deck. With the exception of those who changed watch, all the officers had slept every bit as soundly in their beds as if the ship had been in a situation of absolute safety. As it was not the first time that they had done so, in even more critical situations than the one we faced, I was not at all surprised by it and left them in complete peace, a course of action that I have decided to follow whenever such an occasion arises.

The heavy seas and squally winds lasted for three more days, thereby preventing Baudin from conducting any serious survey of the gulf, and also taking quite a toll on the crew. By the time the weather finally calmed down, Baudin had been forced back to the entrance of Spencer Gulf, from where he decided to push on and follow the west coast of the Eyre Peninsula. His plan was to make for the islands of St Peter and St Francis, and to attempt to pass between them and the mainland – something that Flinders had been unable to do. However, the atmosphere on board the *Géographe* was deteriorating. Many of the crew were tired or sick, and this placed great strain on the running of the ship. In the circumstances, there is reason to question the wisdom of pressing on rather than turning back and seeking some much-needed rest and recovery at Port Jackson. Baudin was determined to carry out the task expected by his government and was exasperated that his officers did not share his sense of duty.

### 28 APRIL 1802

During the morning, Citizen [Henri] Freycinet came to inform me that, since most of our helmsmen were sick and unfit to perform their duties, it was absolutely necessary to choose some men from the rest of the crew who could replace them. He also told me that, in order to overcome this difficulty, he was requesting the authorisation to have the master carpenter and the second caulker take the helm. I pointed out to him that in these circumstances it was not so much orders that were needed as a simple request made with good grace, seeing that the two men plied trades that were so different from the ones for which he required their services. It was clear that he did not like my reply, for he answered that taking such a step with regard to men so inferior to him was impossible for an officer like himself etc, etc.

I then decided to give a written order, which is entered in the ship's log kept by the officers, to the effect that all the midshipmen, both 1st and 2nd class, should do an hour and a half [at the helm] during the watch, which was certainly not an arduous task for them and one that could only be good training. However, the result was completely the opposite of what I had expected, for all these gentlemen considered the task beneath them and schemed to get out of it. M. Bougainville, who was on duty first, refused categorically to do it and used the excuse of sickness to cover up his disobedience. M. Brue claimed that regulations entitled him to exemption from it. Midshipman [Charles] Baudin was the only one to do it willingly, which made him the butt of many jokes on the part of his friends. They all expected me to punish them in another way, but they were quite mistaken, for I simply barred them from any kind of duty on board, saying that I would do without them at the helm quite as easily as I had done without them for everything else.

Charles Baudin was rewarded for his co-operation a few days later, when the captain promoted him to the rank of midshipman first class – just reward, no doubt, but this could only have exacerbated the already strained relations between the captain and most of his officers. There was no joy to be had, either, when the ship finally sighted the islands of St Peter and St Francis. On the one hand, the barren aspect of these islands provided no relief from the 'dreary and unpleasant' nature of the coast they had been following since they left Spencer Gulf – prompting the French captain to note laconically: 'I am not at all surprised that they should have been given the names of two saints who had taken vows of poverty.' But more importantly, contrary winds did not allow Baudin to fulfil his ambition of navigating between these islands and the mainland. The fact that he persisted in his efforts despite such unfavourable conditions can certainly be viewed as courageous; but in the context of his growing isolation from his officers, as well as the fatigue and sickness experienced by his crew, a number of whom were now coming down with scurvy, it was becoming increasingly difficult to follow their chosen course.

## 5 MAY 1802

The heavy seas, the wind, the drift and the ship's sails did not favour the course we were obliged to take; however, we doubled them [the islands] during the night, in never any less than 43 to 45 fathoms, bottom of good, fine sand.

As I was more afraid of a sudden change of wind than I was of the land, I spent the whole night on deck. None of the officers on board know what it is like to be in such a situation, where the most competent mariners can often find themselves at a loss. As usual, my only companion was the person who happened to be on duty. The others spent the night very peacefully in their cabins.

## 6 MAY 1802

Everybody was longing to put in to shore and indeed it was a real necessity. There was no more wood; every day we had to resort to all kinds of means to find some; and our water supply would soon run out. I was sorely tried by these hardships, like everyone else, but my desire to carry out the government's plans meant that they were more bearable for me than for the others. The advanced state of scurvy that was beginning to affect several members of the crew was what distressed me most, but I nevertheless persisted in my resolution to pass around the St Peter Islands to the west, a course that was neither long nor difficult if ever the weather turned fine.

## 7 MAY 1802

During the morning I had complaints from the crew about the bad quality of the salted meat which had just been distributed and which indeed was not good. It nevertheless came from a cask that was intact and in good condition. I gave orders for it to be put to one side so that another could be opened, but this one was even worse than the first. We then brought out a third which finally turned out to be very good. As we had only one more of these casks, we put off until the next day the task of locating it.

After several frustrated efforts to round the St Peter group, Baudin finally decided to push a little further westwards, where he sighted land at Cape Adieu. Here again, the weather proved to be his nemesis. Rough seas, squally winds and a falling barometer, combined with the deteriorating conditions on board, convinced him at last that he should interrupt his survey at this point and head for Port Jackson.

## 8 MAY 1802

> All of the following considerations – my serious reflexions about the position I
> was in, the weakened state of my crew, which now consisted of only thirty men
> for the handling of the ship, our pressing need for firewood, the shortness of
> the days, and no end of other private reasons – persuaded me to abandon the
> coast and head first for D'Entrecasteaux Channel, where the anchorage is
> good, and from there to make for Port Jackson, for I have always remained
> hopeful that the dinghy that is presumed lost would manage to get there.
> As the news of the change of course soon spread, everyone expressed his
> satisfaction with it and indeed this was what we all really needed.

The decision to return to Tasmania, rather than taking the more direct route
to Port Jackson through Bass Strait, drew virulent citicism from Péron in the
official account of the voyage. However, given the urgent need for wood and
water, the contrary winds Baudin had encountered along the south coast, the
probability of rough seas in Bass Strait and the lack of knowledge about
resources in these shores, it appeared more prudent to Baudin to make for the
nearest known safe anchorage with a ready and certain source of supplies. At
any rate, no one else on board seems to have been perturbed by this decision;
on the contrary, the officers and crew were pleased at the prospect of some
respite, though they were made to earn it.

The *Géographe* made the south-eastern corner of Tasmania in good time,
but constant rain, heavy seas and the onset of colder temperatures had made
the passage particularly unpleasant. Rough weather also prevented Baudin
from entering the familiar D'Entrecasteaux Channel on 19 May. Luck had not
yet entirely deserted him, for he was able to anchor next day in Adventure Bay,
on the eastern side of Bruny Island, and to find there all of the supplies that
were needed. The return to an hospitable shore brought on a flurry of activity
and enthusiasm for research.

## 20 MAY 1802

> The absolute need for firewood then persuaded me to take the decision to
> make for the anchorage in Adventure Bay, which I was lucky enough to
> manage by sailing from the Iles Borelles [Friar Rocks] to the Bay, keeping
> almost within gun-shot of the shore and occasionally seeing the mountain-tops,
> but not the shoreline. Within the group of the Iles Borelles, I was surprised to
> find the sea as big as it was, which made me suspect that east or south-easterly
> winds had been prevailing for some time on this coast.

At about eight o'clock the weather cleared a little, which then made it easy for me to recognise Adventure Bay from the chart made of it by the geographers on General d'Entrecasteaux's expedition. This meant that we were already very close to it when the weather led me to hope we would be able to anchor there – which in fact occurred at half past eight. I cannot recall having seen a more picturesque sight than the one provided by the aptly named Cap Cannelle [Fluted Cape].

As soon as we were at anchor, the longboat and all the men on board who were fit enough to wield an axe were sent ashore to obtain wood.

Two more boats were also sent out, one to transport the scientists and others and the second to go fishing. Our sick men, who took a great interest in that particular boat, waited with much impatience for its return. Their hope of enjoying a good meal during the day was not realised, for the boat did not come back until very late; but it at least brought back a catch that was plentiful enough for everyone to feel its effects, even though there had been only four men with lines.

Our longboat and the scientists returned with about four cords of wood; the scientists did not bring back many new things, but they had found the names of several people from the *Recherche* [one of d'Entrecasteaux's two frigates] carved into the bark of trees.

Everything was made ready for a second wood-gathering trip during the night if the weather turned fine.

Citizen Péron, who is always making new discoveries – or thinks he is – claimed to have found a river that no one had seen before, since it is mentioned by none of the explorers who have examined this area better than we have. Whatever the case may be, water was everywhere; it could be found in all the ravines. It had apparently already rained heavily along this part of the coast. The vegetation was so vigorous that all the trees were covered in foliage of a beautiful green that looked infinitely more attractive than when we first ran in for the strait in the middle of summer.

The fish that we caught were of the same species as those that were already familiar to us. The gardener, who is not one of the scientists, was nonetheless capable of finding four new plants that we had not encountered anywhere else.

Lharidon, the doctor, thought he had settled the matter of the quadrupeds and brought back some charred bones which in my view belonged to seals or to some other marine animal which had been eaten by the natives. If they do belong to a land animal, which is unlikely, it must be larger than an elephant.

Unfortunately, this euphoria did not last: the unruly behaviour that broke out the next day revealed not only the fragile psychological state of the crew but also Baudin's increasing impatience with his officers, notably Bougainville, whom he blamed for inciting the others to insubordination. Perhaps it was this hostility, combined with the disappointment of having being unable to make the first complete survey of the unknown coast, that caused Baudin to make the decision to survey the remaining section of Tasmania's east coast before heading for Port Jackson. He persisted with this plan – a plan that would delay his arrival at Port Jackson – even though he was informed that the condition of many of the sick had deteriorated.

### 23 MAY 1802

> During the day, the doctor informed me that several of our sick were worse than usual, although the weather was mild and there was no dampness in the air. This was all the more surprising to me in that I thought that the circumstances would have hastened their recovery rather than aggravate their illness. Working on the advice I had just received, I tried to establish why this should be so and managed to discover the reason – which is that they had followed the example of the gluttons and had eaten so much fish that most of them had suffered attacks of indigestion. Those who had not previously been affected by dysentery got off with a few stomach pains, but those who had already suffered from it and had not recovered came down with it again, which makes it extremely doubtful they will survive.
>
> My cook, who was not in the latter category, but who had been sick for three months and was consequently on a diet, ate with such gusto that he had an attack of indigestion that ended his race on the very day of our departure.

Not surprisingly, the atmosphere on board was now infernal. Not only was the weather so bad that Baudin's attempts at surveying the coast came to naught, but the men were so ill that it was difficult to assemble sufficient crew to handle the ship, particularly in such rough conditions. To make matters worse, Baudin became increasingly sensitive to the criticisms openly expressed by his officers.

### 24 MAY 1802

> As the sky was very overcast, it did not look as though we would get to see the sun cross the meridian at midday and indeed we did not. However, everybody, and especially the scientists, claimed to recognise clearly the cape that I had

named Cap Pelé [Bald Cape – now Cape Tourville] and I was the only person
not to recognise either the cape or the aspect of the surrounding land that lay to
north and south of it. This particularly surprised me as I thought and still do
think my memory as good as theirs, although I do not possess their intellect . . .

This mistake of mine was a source of satisfaction to more than one person
on board and only served to convince every one of them that he was more fit to
run the ship than I was.

As I had completely forgotten that I was in my bed sick at the time we
were on this part of the coast, I no longer found it hard to understand why I
did not recognise land that I had never seen.

Some were deeply affected by the mood of recrimination and spitefulness
that reigned on board, to such a point that the commander tried, unsuccess-
fully, to restore order.

## 26 MAY 1802

During the morning one of the helmsmen, who had been suspected of stealing
fish-hooks, was so offended by the suspicion that he made a hell of a row. I was
unable to quieten him down, in spite of my repeated orders for him to do so. As
soon as I returned to my cabin he would start up again. Fed up with the racket,
I gave orders that he be given 12 strokes of the lash – which was about to be
carried out when he jumped overboard in an attempt to avoid it, in spite of the
heavy weather. We instantly backed all our sails and put out the small dinghy.
As he was a good swimmer we had no trouble catching him. My intention was
for him to receive 20 strokes of the cat-o'-nine-tails when he returned, but, as
the doctors found him in no fit state to receive them, it was put off.

In spite of this suffering, Baudin doggedly followed his plan of action.

## 27 MAY 1802

During the morning, someone, but I do not know who, blamed Lharidon, the
doctor, for being the one responsible for me staying so long at sea because he
was not keeping me informed of the condition of our sick nor of their number.
Lharidon thus brought me a long list containing this information –
information of which I was certainly in no need since I was just as aware of the
numbers of the sick as he was. If it had been within my power to lessen their
sufferings, no doubt I would have done so, but I could not be persuaded to
abandon a coast whose bearings had been neglected when we sailed along it in

both directions while searching for our dinghy. So I asked him to tell those who had put him up to making these protests to me that we were out at sea as a result of their negligence and that, if there was a case to answer, they had only themselves to blame.

To the ever-increasing protests of the officers and crew, Baudin could only repeat his determination to complete his charts.

## 28 MAY 1802

As everybody knew that I intended to put in at Port Jackson, although I had not communicated my decision to anyone, the officers, along with the naturalists and scientists, were greatly annoyed that I did not take advantage of the good wind to steer a course for it. It made pretty well no difference to me, since my decision was made and I was determined to wait a little longer before leaving this coast rather than come back to it a third time.

In fact, he was making sacrifices in order to sustain his men, all the while noting the deteriorating conditions on board.

## 30 MAY 1802

Since our supplies of fresh food had almost run out and since, luckily for them, I had saved up the little I had left after my last illness, I instructed that they be given one of my three remaining pigs, which I had gone without so that they could be made available to anyone who fell sick. They were given enough for three meals and the rest was salted for their future use.

Today two more men were confined to sick bay, complaining of great pain without having any apparent signs of illness. Among them was the baker, who was extremely useful to those who were already indisposed. This meant that the sick were suddenly deprived of supplies of fresh bread.

## 31 MAY 1802

In the afternoon, I ordered all hands on deck to clean the ship, and not before time, for we had neglected to do it since leaving Adventure Bay. When we had finished, every part of the vessel was disinfected, including the sick bay.

Most of the sick were complaining openly that I was bent on ensuring they died at sea by not trying to put in at some place where they could find relief. This meant that they made no allowance for the fact that I was depriving myself in order to give them fresh meat, which I could have eaten, and also that they considered me to be the prime cause of their ailments for having stayed too long at sea. The officers and scientists were making the same complaints and were blaming, if not me directly, the doctor at any rate; they were constantly telling him that he was misinforming me about the situation, the number of the sick and the likelihood that they would all die.

As I did not see things the same way as all these gentlemen, I continued to keep out to sea rather than be compelled to return a fourth time to this [coast], which, all because of them, was not surveyed at the time. This was when I was unfortunately sick and unable to take advantage of the opportunity which we had then and which was so favourable, since we sailed along it three times from north to south and from south to north.

It was not until 4 June 1802 that Baudin relented and finally decided to head for Port Jackson. Fittingly enough, the weather was rough to the last, and as constant as Baudin's recriminations. Only with a small piece of luck could the afflicted vessel arrive safely at its destination.

### 4 JUNE 1802

During the night the gusts and squalls were more persistent and even stronger than they had been throughout the day. But luckily we had nothing to alter in the set of our sails, as it would have been impossible to manage with only four men fit enough to remain on deck, including the officer of the watch. That convinced me to run free and make for Port Jackson, for we were no longer in a fit state to remain at sea.

It was certainly against my will that I was forced to give up the idea of completing the charting of the east coast of Van Diemen's Land; but the truth of the matter is that it is entirely the fault of the officers who, in their ignorance of the fact that one should never waste a moment at sea, neglected to do the work when we were searching for our dinghy, on the grounds that Citizen Boullanger was doing it and that they did not want to compete with him on that score. None of this would have happened if, during that unhappy time, I had not been most unwell, for we would be in a very different position from the one we are in now.

While there were good reasons for Baudin to call in at Tasmania on his way from the unknown coast to Port Jackson, it is much more difficult, given the circumstances on board, to justify the delays caused by his renewed survey of its east coast. It may well be that he, too, was in urgent need of some respite from the rigours of the voyage. But the obstinate determination with which

Baudin set about improving on the pre-existing charts of Tasmania, particularly those of his compatriots, may also be an indication that this work was a matter of great pride for Baudin and the French authorities. The hydrographic work carried out by both the *Géographe* and the *Naturaliste* allowed them to produce detailed and accurate charts of the complex maze of coves and islands along the eastern sea-board of 'Van Diemen's Land' – thereby building on the already excellent work done by d'Entrecasteaux's expedition ten years earlier. This sense of continuity, in navigational and cartographic terms, highlights the symbolic importance of Tasmania for the French: it formed an important part of their legacy as explorers. Although Baudin and his men had encountered misadventures in its waters, they had largely enjoyed the time spent on the island. It is all the more regrettable, then, that their final impressions as they left Tasmania in their wake, bound for Port Jackson, should have been soured by the fatigue, illness and low morale that reigned on board.

# chapter nine

# THE ENCOUNTERS OF PORT JACKSON

*Respite in Sydney Town*

Sydney Town was to provide much needed respite for the two expeditions in the late autumn and winter of 1802, once they had finally arrived safely in port after the discoveries, dramas and disappointments of previous months. If the momentous encounter of the two rival expeditions off the southern coast could hardly have been foreseen when the French and British governments delivered their original instructions to Baudin and Flinders, the shared experience of colonial life in Terra Australis was likewise an unexpected moment in their voyages – particularly for the French, whose instructions had not included a stay in British territory and who, ironically, had a far happier experience of colonial hospitality in Port Jackson than in their own territory of Mauritius. For Flinders, on the other hand, the stopover had been planned, and it offered the opportunity to renew old friendships, as well as – by chance or destiny – to experience even closer encounters with the French.

---

### In His Element: Flinders and Sydney Town

Naturally, Sydney Town was by no means terra incognita to Flinders. He had first sailed there in 1795 aboard the *Reliance*. On board also at that time were the new governor of the colony, John Hunter, as well as the surgeon, George Bass, with whom Flinders had struck up a close, enduring and productive relationship.

By 1802, when he arrived in the *Investigator*, the colony's existence was less tenuous than it had been through its founding years, though it was scarcely thriving. It was still a penal outpost at the farthest reaches of the British Empire, but with every passing year there was a smaller proportion of the colony dependent on the often scanty supplies of the government stores. When Flinders had first arrived in 1795, New South Wales had a British population of just 3211, most of whom – 59 per cent – were convicts. The others were mainly military and administrative personnel, but very few were free migrants. When he returned as captain of the *Investigator*, the colony had a new governor in Philip Gidley King, who had taken office in September 1800. Under King, the colony's capacity not only to support itself but also to export a range of goods had vastly improved. With his support, the whaling and sealing industries in particular made great advances. Despite an acute shortage of labour, King was also able to press on with the construction of the settlement's infrastructure, so that the built environment Flinders found before him in 1802 must have appeared a remarkable advance on the motley collection of buildings and roads which had greeted him in 1795.

King's tenure proved a noteworthy filip in the continued exploration of the continent. He had sent James Grant to complete the exploration of Bass Strait and survey Western Port, and James Murray to explore further to the west, where he beat Flinders to the discovery of Port Phillip and other parts of what was to become the Victorian coast. No achievement in this regard was more important, though, than the invaluable assistance he lent both Flinders and Baudin, whose admiration and friendship he soon won.

Flinders arrived well before Baudin in Port Jackson, but Captain Hamelin in the *Naturaliste* was already there. Separated from his consort in Bass Strait on 8 March, Hamelin had made his way to Port Jackson, arriving at the Heads on 24 April 1802. His vessel was among the handful Flinders and his crew, still apparently glowing with rude health, found at anchor when they entered the harbour in early May.

## 9 MAY 1802

There was not a single individual on board who was not upon deck working the ship into harbour; and it may be averred, that the officers and crew were, generally speaking, in better health than on the day we sailed from Spithead, and not in less good spirits. I have said nothing of the regulations observed after we made Cape Leeuwin; they were little different from those adopted in the commencement of the voyage, and of which a strict attention to cleanliness, and a free circulation of air in the messing and sleeping places formed the most essential parts. Several of the inhabitants of Port Jackson expressed themselves never to have been so strongly reminded of England, as by the fresh colour of many amongst the *Investigator*'s ship's company.

So soon as the anchor was dropped, I went on shore to wait upon His Excellency Philip Gidley King, Esq., governor of New South Wales, and senior naval officer upon the station; to whom I communicated a general account of our discoveries and examinations upon the south coast, and delivered the orders from the Admiralty and Secretary of State. These orders directed the governor to place the brig *Lady Nelson* under my command, and not to employ the *Investigator* on other service than that which was the object of the voyage; and His Excellency was pleased to assure me, that every assistance in the power of the colony to render, should be given to forward a service so interesting to his government, and to himself. The *Lady Nelson* was then lying in Sydney Cove; but her commander, Lieutenant Grant, had requested permission to return to England, and had sailed six months before.

Besides the *Lady Nelson*, there were in the port His Majesty's armed vessel *Porpoise*, the *Speedy*, south-whaler, and the *Margaret*, privateer; also the French national ship *Le Naturaliste*, commanded by Captain Hamelin, to whom I communicated Captain Baudin's intention of coming to Port Jackson so soon as the bad weather should set in. *Le Géographe*'s boat had been picked up in Bass' Strait by Mr Campbell of the brig *Harrington*, and the officers and crew were at this time on board *Le Naturaliste*.

The duties required to fit the ship for prosecuting the voyage with success being various and extensive, Cattle Point, on the east side of Sydney Cove, was assigned to us by the governor for carrying on some of our employments, whilst others were in progress on board the ship and in the dockyard. On the morning after our arrival, we warped to a convenient situation near the point, and sent on shore the tents, the sail-makers and sails, and the cooper with all the empty casks. Next day the observatory was set up, and the time keepers and other astronomical instruments placed there under the care of Lieutenant Flinders; who, with Mr Franklin his assistant, was to make the necessary observations and superintend the various duties

*View of Port Jackson, taken from the South Head*, engraving by John Pye from a drawing by William Westall.
Published in *A Voyage to Terra Australis* (1814)

carrying on at the same place; and a small detachment of marines was landed
for the protection of the tents . . .

To supply the place of the cutter we had lost at the entrance of Spencer's
Gulf, I contracted for a boat to be built after the model of that in which
Mr Bass made his long and adventurous expedition to the strait. It was twenty-
eight feet seven inches in length over all, rather flat floored, head and stern
alike, a keel somewhat curved, and the cut-water and stern post nearly
upright; it was fitted to row eight oars when requisite, but intended for six in
common cases. The timbers were cut from the largest kind of banksia, which
had been found more durable than mangrove, and the planking was of cedar.
This boat was constructed under the superintendance of Mr Thomas Moore,
master builder to the colony; and proved, like her prototype, to be excellent in
a sea, as well as for rowing and sailing in smooth water. The cost at Port
Jackson was no more than £30; but this was owing to some of the materials
being supplied from the public magazines.

*Sydney: Government House* (1802), William Westall. National Library of Australia

Apart from replacing the lost cutter, there was much work to be done in port. The *Investigator*'s stores were surveyed and items replaced as far as possible, fresh provisions and water taken on board, the masts stripped and re-rigged. While this was going on, Brown, Bauer and Westall with their assistants made excursions into the interior of the country to continue their botanising and drawing. Flinders, for his part, devoted his attention to completing fair charts of the south coast, which would be sent back to the Admiralty.

It was not all work, though. Flinders soon had opportunity to interrupt his labours on 4 June, when the King's birthday was celebrated. In the company of his principal officers, Flinders made his way to visit Governor King, who regaled them with a 'splendid dinner' attended by no fewer than forty ladies as well as civil, military and other naval officers.

A couple of weeks later, on 20 June, Captain Baudin finally arrived in the *Géographe*. The condition of his ship and its crew offered a most striking contrast to that of the *Investigator* more than a month earlier, although in just what state the *Géographe* entered Sydney Harbour still offers cause for debate. As historian Frank Horner has demonstrated, Flinders' account dramatises the situation of the French somewhat, in that the figures it contains for the proportion of the sick to the able-bodied on the *Géographe*'s crew are incorrect. Flinders' version of events, alongside the French account written by Péron and Freycinet, in which

Baudin's competence is called into question, has also given rise to the story of the *Géographe*'s completely crippled state – another detail that Horner questions, by referring to the eye-witness account provided by the journal of Ronsard of the *Géographe*. Sickness had certainly caused the ship to be seriously undermanned. Even if the crew had been able to manage the manoeuvres required to enter the harbour, they were unquestionably in a poor state. They were in dire need of fresh food supplies and urgent medical attention, which were generously and unstintingly provided by Governor King, just as he had done for the *Naturaliste* when she arrived in April, and indeed for the *Investigator*. Flinders justifiably insists on the kind and unprejudiced attentions paid to the French, a debt which all the French accounts gratefully and warmly acknowledge.

## 20 JUNE 1802

> Captain Baudin arrived in *Le Géographe* on the 20th, and a boat was sent from the *Investigator* to assist in towing the ship up to the cove. It was grievous to see the miserable condition, to which both officers and crew were reduced by scurvy; there being not more out of one hundred and seventy, according to the commander's account, than twelve men capable of doing their duty. The sick were received into the colonial hospital, and both French ships furnished with everything in the power of the colony to supply. Before their arrival, the necessity of augmenting the number of cattle in the country had prevented the governor from allowing us any fresh meat; but some oxen belonging to government were now killed for the distressed strangers; and by returning an equal quantity of salt meat, which was exceedingly scarce at this time, I obtained a quarter of beef for my people. The distress of the French navigators had indeed been great; but every means were used by the governor and the principal inhabitants of the colony, to make them forget both their sufferings and the war which existed between the two nations.

As chance would have it, a fragile peace had broken out in Europe, which helped to ease any tensions that might have arisen between the hosts and their new guests. Yet for Baudin, a convivial gathering aboard the *Investigator* quickly became a somewhat deflating experience. Flinders not only showed him the extent of his own explorations of the south coast, as he had done during their meeting in Encounter Bay, but also pointed out that Captain Grant could claim prior discovery of parts of the Victorian coast that Baudin thought he had been the first to chart. Baudin, for his part, did not produce any charts of his own at the gathering, perhaps for technical reasons, as Flinders speculated.

His Excellency, Governor King, had done me the honour to visit the
*Investigator*, and to accept of a dinner on board; on which occasion he had been
received with the marks of respect due to his rank of captain-general; and
shortly afterward, the Captains Baudin and Hamelin, with Monsieur Péron
and some other French officers, as also Colonel Paterson, the lieutenant
governor, did me the same favour; when they were received under a salute of
eleven guns. The intelligence of peace, which had just been received,
contributed to enliven the party, and rendered our meeting more particularly
agreeable. I showed to Captain Baudin one of my charts of the south coast,
containing the part first explored by him, and distinctly marked as his
discovery. He made no objection to the justice of the limits therein pointed out;
but found his portion to be smaller than he had supposed, not having before
been aware of the extent of the discoveries previously made by Captain Grant.
After examining the chart, he said, apparently as a reason for not producing
any of his own, that his charts were not constructed on board the ship; but that
he transmitted to Paris all his bearings and observations, with a regular series
of views of the land, and from them the charts were to be made at a future
time. This mode appeared to me extraordinary, and not to be worthy of
imitation; conceiving that a rough chart at least should be made whilst the land
is in sight, when any error in bearing or observation can be corrected; a plan
which was adopted in the commencement, and followed through the voyage.

The hydrographic practice that Flinders attributed to Baudin, and that he
judged greatly inferior to his own, does not, however, correspond to the reality:
while the final charts were indeed completed in Paris after the expedition,
working charts were also drawn up during the course of the voyage, and
were integral to French hydrographic practice. Since there could be no
suggestion that Flinders would seek deliberately to misrepresent Baudin,
could there have been difficulties of communication between the two captains,
as indeed there had been during their south coast encounter? The development of Baudin's close relationship with King was assisted by the fact that the
governor could speak French. With Flinders there was not perhaps the
linguistic means of achieving greater understanding, even though his discussions with Baudin were perfectly friendly and courteous. In any case, Flinders
understandably chose to highlight his own and his countrymen's achievements at the expense of the French in recording his conversation with Baudin.
The cordiality of the behaviour of both seamen could not mask their rivalry.
As history has shown, the good reputation of the one was tightly bound up

with the poor reputation of the other. If Flinders' attitude was understandable, so too was Baudin's reaction, as reported by Flinders. No doubt the commander's mood had darkened with the sudden recognition of the limits of his hydrographic achievement on the unknown south coast.

Other meetings must have taken place between the French and British sailors, who worked side by side refitting their ships at Bennelong Point and whose officers were regularly entertained by the governor; but there is only slight reference to any further conversations recorded between the captains. Flinders noted before his departure his scepticism about the timetable that Baudin proposed to follow in his future survey of the north-west coast. Still, it is of interest to know that friendly confidences continued to take place; Flinders naturally reported on them to his own advantage, as Baudin would certainly have done had he recorded them. During the entire period, in any case, the two navigators had other duties to preoccupy them, since they were busily engaged in supervising repairs to their vessels.

By the middle of July, the rejigging and provisioning of the *Investigator* were complete and Flinders was ready to continue his voyage. The *Investigator* was now to be accompanied by the sixty-ton brig *Lady Nelson*, commanded by acting-Lieutenant John Murray, but placed under the orders of Flinders. With its sliding keels, the *Lady Nelson* was ideally suited to the charting of shallow waters, including rivers.

Before he sailed, however, Flinders needed to supplement his own crew aboard the *Investigator*. Apart from being short the eight men who had gone missing presumed drowned at the entrance to Spencer Gulf, he had to discharge an invalided marine and the man bitten by a cantankerous Kangaroo Island seal. Requiring fourteen to complete the company, and able to draw only on the population of a colony suffering chronic labour shortages, Flinders had to cast his net broadly.

## JULY 1802

Mr John Aken, chief mate of the ship *Hercules*, was engaged to fill the situation of master, and five men, mostly seamen, were entered; but finding it impossible to fill up the complement with free people, I applied to the governor for his permission to enter such convicts as should present themselves, and could bring respectable recommendations. This request, as every other I had occasion to make to His Excellency, was complied with; and when the requisite number was selected, he gave me an official document, containing clauses relative to these men, well calculated to ensure their good conduct. As this document may be thought curious by many readers, it is here inserted; premising, that the men therein mentioned, with the exception of two, were convicts for life.

'By His Excellency Philip Gidley King, Esq., captain-general and governor in chief, in and over His Majesty's territory of New South Wales and its dependencies, &c., &c., &c.

'Whereas Captain Matthew Flinders, commander of His Majesty's ship *Investigator*, has requested permission to receive on board that ship the undermentioned convicts as seamen, to make up the number he is deficient. I do hereby grant

| | | |
|---|---|---|
| Thomas Toney | Thomas Martin | Joseph Marlow |
| Thomas Shirley | Joseph Tuzo | Richard Stephenson |
| Thomas Smith | Francis Smith | Charles Brown |

permission to ship themselves on board His Majesty's ship *Investigator*; and on the return of that ship to this port, according to Captain Flinders' recommendation of them, severally and individually, they will receive conditional emancipations or absolute pardons, as that officer may request.

'And in the interim I do, by virtue of the power and authority in me vested, grant a provisional-conditional emancipation to the said Thomas Toney, &c., for the purpose of their being enabled to serve on board His Majesty's said ship *Investigator*, whilst in the neighbourhood of this territory; which conditional emancipation will be of no effect, in case any of those named herein do individually conduct themselves so ill, as to put it out of Captain Flinders' power to recommend them for a conditional or absolute pardon on his return to this port.

'Given under my hand and seal at government house Sydney, in New South Wales, this 15th day of July, in the year of our Lord 1802. ( Signed) Philip Gidley King, (L. S.)'

Several of these men were seamen, and all were able and healthy; so that I considered them a great acquisition to our strength. With respect to themselves, the situation to which they were admitted was most desirable; since they had thereby a prospect of returning to their country, and that society from which they had been banished; and judging from the number of candidates for the vacancies, such was the light in which a reception on board the *Investigator* was considered in the colony. When the master was entered, one of the men, being over the complement, was sent to the *Lady Nelson*, with a reserve of the privilege above granted.

As his instructions from the Admiralty required, Flinders consulted with Governor King on the continuation of his voyage. They decided that there was little to be gained from returning to the south coast at that time, especially given the likelihood of inclement winter weather there. Instead it was resolved that the *Investigator* should sail north to Torres Strait and the east side of the Gulf of Carpentaria before the expected onset of the monsoon season in November. Then Flinders would embark on an exploration of the north and north-west coasts.

Later in his account of his adventures, Flinders offered his English readers an overview of the state of their fledgling colony in a far-flung part of the globe. He restricted himself to some general comments, being well aware that by the time of publication – not until 1814 – many of his observations from more than a decade earlier would have been superseded. The report was sober enough, pointing to some of the serious difficulties faced, but was over-whelmingly sanguine about the colony's future.

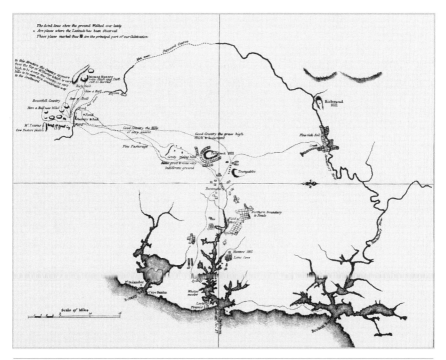

Map showing the extent of the settlement in 'New South Wales' in May 1798. Reproduced from David Collins, *An Account of the English Colony of New South Wales* (London: Cadell & Davies, 1798)

## JULY 1803

In 1803 it [the colony] was progressively advancing towards a state of independence on the mother country for food and clothing; both the wild and tame cattle had augmented in a proportion to make it probable that they would, before many years, be very abundant; and manufactures of woollen, linen, cordage, and leather, with breweries and a pottery, were commenced. The number of inhabitants was increasing rapidly; and that energetic spirit of enterprise which characterises Britain's children, seemed to be throwing out vigorous shoots in this new world. The seal fishery in Bass' Strait was carried on with ardour; many boats were employed in catching and preparing fish along the coast; sloops and schooners were upon the stocks; various detached settlements were in a course of establishment, and more in project. And all this, with the commerce carried on from Sydney to Parramatta and the villages at the head of the port, and to those on the rivers falling into Broken and Botany Bays, made the fine harbour of Port Jackson a lively scene of business, highly interesting to the contemplator of the rise of nations.

In Sydney and Parramatta, houses of stone or brick were taking place of wood and plaster; a neat church was built in the latter, and one commenced in the former place; wharfs were constructing or repairing; a stone bridge over the stream which runs through the town of Sydney was nearly finished; and the whiskey, chariot, and heavy-laden waggon were seen moving on commodious roads to different parts of the colony. In the interior the forests were giving way before the axe, and their places becoming every year more extensively occupied by wheat, barley, oats, maize, and the vegetables and fruits of southern Europe . . .

Amongst the obstacles which opposed themselves to the more rapid advancement of the colony, the principal were, the vicious propensities of a large portion of the convicts, a want of more frequent communication with England, and the prohibition to trading with India and the western coasts of South America, in consequence of the East-India-Company's charter. As these difficulties become obviated and capital increases, the progress of the colonists will be more rapid; and if the resources from government be not withdrawn too early, there is little doubt of New South Wales being one day a flourishing country, and of considerable benefit to the commerce and navigation of the parent state.

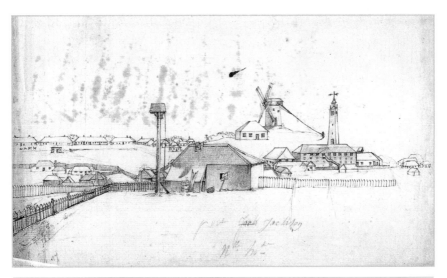

*Port Jackson*, view of Sydney in 1802 showing various military buildings (barracks, officers' quarters, powder magazine) as well as a windmill, a church, and grain and vegetable stores. The tall structure in the foreground is a bell from a chapel that burned down in 1798. Charles-Alexandre Lesueur. Muséum d'histoire naturelle, Le Havre – n° 16 068

## *Among Friends: Baudin and the Governor*

Baudin's opinions on the colony in which he arrived in June 1802 are not as well known as those of Flinders, or indeed as those of Péron, who gave enthusiastic descriptions of the site and its flourishing industries in the official account of the voyage. Péron would later claim, in a controversial report he wrote for the Governor of Mauritius, that one of the expedition's secret objectives was to spy on the British. Perusal of Baudin's own documents pertaining to the stay at Port Jackson does not offer much support for the view that the French were on a mission of espionage, although his report to the Minister from Timor in 1803 does indicate how impressed he was by the size and prosperity the colony had attained in such a short time. Unfortunately, his journal can throw no light on the question, since it breaks off at the moment preceding his arrival at Port Jackson.

However, some of his opinions can be gleaned from the correspondence he exchanged with his superiors and with the governor of the colony, Philip Gidley King. While this latter correspondence naturally does not relate to the expedition's supposed secret objectives, it does give true insight into the character of the French commander and captures the spirit that animated him, in a way that few of the official records of his voyage could do. The task master who was determined to complete the survey of the east coast of

Tasmania is no longer in evidence here; the warm friendship which he struck with Governor King seems to have relieved him of the loneliness he had suffered upon losing his closest friends in the course of the voyage and of the daily irritation he experienced in dealing with his officers and scientists, whom he found to be uncooperative and overly susceptible to criticism. Baudin's esteem must also have been a welcome relief for the governor in the midst of the daily intrigues that marked life in the colony. In this respect, their situations were remarkably similar and their friendship was obviously a reminder of the civilities they both cherished as part of a more genteel society than that to which they were presently confined. That they planned to have dinner upon their return to Europe is testimony to this nostalgia.

Panorama of Port Jackson, the French camp is in the foreground, on the eastern side of Sydney Cove. Engraving by Pillement and Duparc from a drawing by Charles-Alexandre Lesueur, Barr Smith Library

The aspect of King's character that struck Baudin and his compatriots most forcefully was his great humanity. This was displayed immediately upon the arrival of the *Géographe*. When Baudin wrote his first request for assistance to the governor, he must already have been aware that it would be met. The kindly reception that awaited his lieutenant, Ronsard, like that afforded his companion Hamelin in April, would have reassured him as much as did King's first letter to him. On 22 June 1802 Baudin wrote to King that:

> The situation of 23 members of my crew, who are affected by scurvy to a greater or lesser degree as a result of a long period at sea, leads me to hope that you will kindly allow them to be transported to your military hospitals in order for them to recuperate.
>
> This illness, as you know, requires only medical attention, peace and quiet and a change of diet, and I am convinced that they will recover if you consent to their admission.

If you consider it a good idea, I would also like to set up several tents on
shore in order to facilitate the work of our astronomers, whose observations
will be conveyed to you. The place where Mr Flinders has set up seems to me
the most suitable, provided that you have no objection.

As I shall be obliged to replace some food supplies, such as biscuit, flour,
salt meat, spirits, fresh meat, vegetables, etc, etc, I shall, with your kind
permission, send you a note setting out the quantities required, with the
request that they be supplied to me from Government or private stores,
if these exist.

King's favourable reply, coupled with a generosity that went well beyond the
services requested, was responsible for the rapid improvement in the expedition's health and fortunes. When the *Naturaliste* came back into port a few
days later, its crew was also treated to the same hospitality and was warmly
welcomed, in spite of the fact that they had been farewelled only the previous
month. Although it had been Captain Hamelin's intention to return to
Mauritius, lack of supplies had forced him back to Port Jackson. This gave
him the opportunity to explain to his commander what had occupied him since
the two ships had been separated three months earlier. Baudin was no doubt
pleased with the surveying work that had been done in Tasmania and Bass
Strait, and he appears to have made no objection to Hamelin's plan to return
to France. Indeed, it seemed to restore some of his energy. He and Hamelin
made preparations for repairing their ships and reorganising their affairs so
that the *Naturaliste* could return to France, not only with the scientific collections, but also with the crew and scientists whom Baudin considered least
useful to the success of the expedition. At this point, Baudin purchased a
schooner, the *Casuarina*, which would replace the *Naturaliste* and compensate
for some of her shortcomings by performing better when it came to close
surveys of the coastline.

It is easy to see why Baudin did not treat Hamelin to the harsh recriminations that were the lot of his junior officers. Hamelin's unilateral decision to
return to France may well have surprised the commander, but their relationship does not appear to have been affected by it. Baudin seems genuinely to
have liked Hamelin, and certainly appreciated a loyalty that had otherwise
been in short supply amongst his companions. If Hamelin was occasionally
exasperated by his commander, he was too much of a professional to let it
show, and he continued to provide Baudin with his discreet support until
they were finally to go their separate ways.

View of Sydney Cove, the French camp on Bennelong Point can be seen on the right. The ship may be the *Géographe*. Charles-Alexandre Lesueur. Muséum d'histoire naturelle, Le Havre – n° 16 070

Much work was to be done on the ships before their departure; the *Naturaliste* received new rigging and was treated for its infestation of rats, while the *Géographe* had its copper sheathing replaced. The *Casuarina* was equipped for her new role, and the scientific collections were carefully stowed on the *Naturaliste*. These collections received an unexpected boost with the gift of Pacific Island artefacts from George Bass, by whom the French were most favourably impressed. His arrival in port from the Pacific with a cargo of salt pork also assisted them greatly in replenishing much needed supplies. Given the intensity of preparations, Baudin was far too busy during this time to take much advantage of the possibilities offered to the scientists to wander further afield, although we do know that he journeyed up the Hawkesbury River on one occasion. His scientists had more opportunities than their commander to collect specimens and to observe the Aborigines of Port Jackson, and generally to add to the already rich collections of drawings and specimens.

In spite of these activities, relations between Baudin and the rest of his men did not improve greatly during the stay at Port Jackson. The respite from the cramped quarters of the ship had obviously helped to ease the friction, but Baudin is still recorded as having difficulties with his officers, namely Ronsard, who was angered at not receiving promotion, and Milius, who, over some unknown slight, wrote on 9 July 1802 an emotional letter to Governor King.

*Caves, hunting and fishing of the natives of Port Jackson*, engraving by A. Delvaux and J. Devilliers from a drawing by Charles-Alexandre Lesueur. Published in the *Atlas* of the *Voyage de découvertes aux Terres Australes* (2nd edition, 1824)

Canoes used by Aborigines (New South Wales). The birds moving across the surface of the water are black swans. The tree at the foot of which two natives can be seen is a casuarina, all the others are eucalyptus trees. Engraving by Milbert and Fortier from a drawing by Charles-Alexandre Lesueur. Published in the *Atlas* of the *Voyage de découvertes aux Terres Australes* (1807)

Whatever repugnance a man of sensibility may feel about speaking of himself, circumstances often oblige him to break his silence. I find myself in that position today and I value your esteem too highly to remain silent any longer. I shall not repeat to you all of the false rumours that have been spread about me; I despise calumny too much to respond to it. I shall not therefore touch a chord that must be foreign to you and which can only produce sounds that are painful to my own ears. It will probably suffice, Your Excellency, that you have the word of an officer who did everything honour required so that no further advantage should be taken of your kindness. I would like to think that this should be sufficient to convince you of my innocence.

I shall not remind you, Your Excellency, of the little scene that occurred at your residence and which arose because I took leave of my senses, although my heart was not in it. I made my apologies to you several days later and you had the generosity to forgive my rash behaviour. This is the only fault I have committed and all the rest is mere imposture.

Although my pen is loath to write of M. Baudin, I shall never be able to forget that it is by his doing that I have been suddenly deprived of your company. I was able to pardon his injustice when he accused me daily of committing new faults that existed only in the imagination of those who turned him against me; however, drawing strength from my innocence, I do not make the least effort to avoid the blows he inflicts on me; I confine myself to expressing my pain and to pitying him.

Forgive me, Your Excellency, for bothering you, but upon leaving your colony, I thought I should clear my name and reclaim your good opinion which is very dear to me.

Relations between Baudin and his junior officers had gone beyond the point of no return, but this does not seem to have altered the affection in which the French commander was held by Governor King, who handled this matter tactfully and continued to see Baudin on a regular basis. King's diplomacy also helped to smooth over some potentially damaging situations, such as the incident which occurred during the French commemoration of the tenth anniversary of the Republic on 22 September. The day had begun in an inauspicious fashion, according to Henri Freycinet, who, as an ardent republican, found the celebrations rather paltry. To make matters worse, the French officers were wrongfully accused of slighting the English government by hoisting its flag in a position considered inappropriate. Baudin wrote to King the next day, explaining their actions were due to a simple misunderstanding.

NOUVELLE-HOLLANDE : *TERRE NAPOLÉON*.

1. *Cap Marengo,* (a.) *Cap Suffren,* (b.)
2. *Vue des Terres de la Baie Descartes : Cap Duquène,* (c.) *Cap Montesquieu,* (d.)
3. *Vue d'une partie des côtes de la Baie Lacépède : Cap Bernouilli,* (e.) *Pointe de Nazareth,* (f.)
4. *Vue d'une partie des côtes de la Presqu'île Fleurieu : Cap Lacsignan,* (g.) *Cap Volney,* (h.)

5. { *Î. Eugène l'une des Îles* JOSÉPHINE, (i.) *Î. de l'Archipel S. François,* (k.l.)
{ *Î. Turenne,* (k.) *Î. Lagrange,* (l.)
6. { *suite de l'Archipel* } { *Î. Fénélon,* (m.) *Î. Talleyrand,* (n.)
7. { *S. François.* { *suite de l'Î. Talleyrand,* (o.) *Î. Malesherbes,* (p.) *Î. Cuvier,* (q.)

Coastal profiles of *Terre Napoléon* (south coast of New Holland). Views: 1. *Cap Marengo et Cap Suffren* (Cape Otway to Cape Patten, south coast of Victoria); 2. *Baie Descartes* (Bridgewater Bay, south coast of Victoria); 3. *Baie Lacépède* (south-east coast of South Australia, from Cape Jaffa); 4. *Péninsule Fleurieu*; 5–7. Nuyts Archipelago. Charles-Alexandre Lesueur or Nicolas-Martin Petit. Published in the *Atlas* of the *Voyage de découvertes aux Terres Australes* (1807)

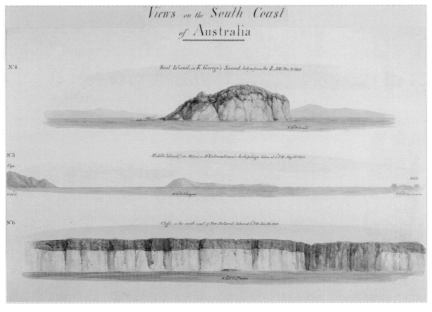

*Views on the south coast of Australia*: 1. Cape Leeuwin (WA); 2. Cape Chatham (WA); 3. Eclipse Island (WA); 4. Seal Island (King George Sound, WA); 5. Middle Island (Recherche Archipelago, WA); 6. Cliffs in the Great Australian Bight (SA). William Westall. National Library of Australia

Green rosella (North-West Port, Tasmania), *Platycercus caledonicus* (Gmelin, 1788), Charles-Alexandre Lesueur.
Muséum d'histoire naturelle, Le Havre – n° 79 030

Port Lincoln parrot or Australian ringneck, *Barnardius zonarius zonarius* (Shaw, 1805), Ferdinand Bauer.
Natural History Museum, London

Crab, *Charybdis (Charybdis) feriata* (Linnaeus, 1758), Charles-Alexandre Lesueur. Muséum d'histoire naturelle, Le Havre – n° 73 076

Blue swimmer crab, *Portunus pelagicus* (Linnaeus, 1760), Ferdinand Bauer. Natural History Museum, London

Bridled, golden-eyed or small brown leatherjacket (southern coast of Australia), *Acanthaluteres spilomelanurus* (Quoy and Gaimard, 1814), Charles-Alexandre Lesueur. Muséum d'histoire naturelle, Le Havre – n° 76 131

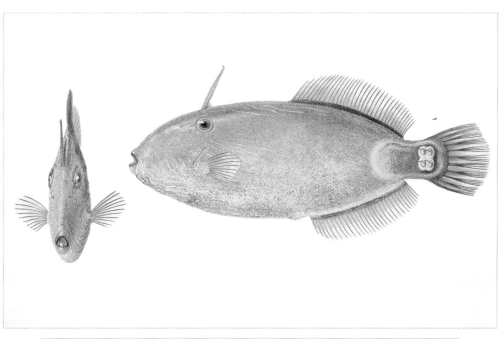

Spiny-tailed or Brown's leatherjacket (southern Australian waters – this specimen caught at King George Sound, Western Australia), *Acanthaluteres brownii* (Richardson, 1846), Ferdinand Bauer. Natural History Museum, London

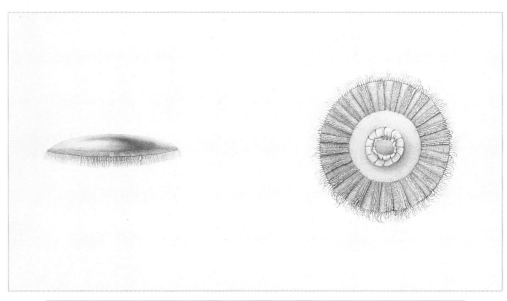

Jellyfish (Shark Bay area of Western Australia), *Zygocanna purpurea* (Péron and Lesueur, 1810),
Charles-Alexandre Lesueur. Muséum d'histoire naturelle, Le Havre – n° 70 031

Weedy or common seadragon (southern Australia – these specimens caught at King George Sound, Western Australia), *Phyllopteryx taeniolatus* (Lacépède, 1804), Ferdinand Bauer. Natural History Museum, London

Fish common to the entire Indo-Pacific, from southern Africa to Japan, *Dactyloptena orientalis* (Cuvier, 1829), Charles-Alexandre Lesueur. Muséum d'histoire naturelle, Le Havre – n° 76 858

Butterfly cod (specimen caught at Strong Tide Passage, Queensland), *Pterois* sp., Ferdinand Bauer. Natural History Museum, London

Display of eight frogs from Port Jackson, *Litoria* sp., Charles-Alexandre Lesueur. Muséum d'histoire naturelle, Le Havre – n° 77 001

Southern bell frog (south-eastern Australia – this specimen may have been collected on Kangaroo Island, South Australia), *Litoria raniformis* (Keferstein, 1867). Ferdinand Bauer. Natural History Museum, London

Several platypuses by the edge of a pond, *Ornithorhynchus anatinus* (Shaw, 1799), Charles-Alexandre Lesueur. Muséum d'histoire naturelle, Le Havre – n° 80 034.1

Common wombat, *Vombatus ursinus* (Shaw, 1800), Charles-Alexandre Lesueur. Muséum d'histoire naturelle, Le Havre – n° 80 069.1

Platypuses (specimens collected at Port Jackson), *Ornithorhynchus anatinus* (Shaw, 1799), Ferdinand Bauer. Natural History Museum, London

Common wombat, *Vombatus ursinus* (Shaw, 1800), Ferdinand Bauer. Natural History Museum, London

Two kangaroos, *Thylogale thetis* (Lesson, 1827), Charles-Alexandre Lesueur. Muséum d'histoire naturelle, Le Havre – n° 80 061

Black-footed rock wallaby (Recherche Archipelago, Western Australia), *Petrogale lateralis hacketti* (Gould, 1842), Ferdinand Bauer. Natural History Museum, London

Two phalangers in a tree, *Trichosurus vulpecula* (Kerr, 1792), Charles-Alexandre Lesueur. Muséum d'histoire naturelle, Le Havre – n° 80 092

Koala (animals captured at Hat Hill, south of Botany Bay, New South Wales), *Phascolarctos cinereus* (Goldfuss, 1817), Ferdinand Bauer. Natural History Museum, London

Jellyfish (specimen collected off the north-west coast of Western Australia), *Cassiopea andromeda* (Forsskål, 1775),
Charles-Alexandre Lesueur. Muséum d'histoire naturelle, Le Havre – n° 70 049

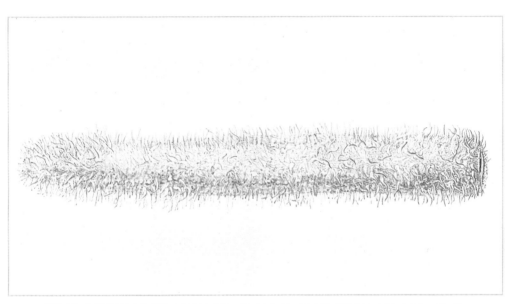

Pyrosome (observed during the outward journey from France to Mauritius), *Pyrosoma atlanticum* (Péron, 1804), Charles-Alexandre Lesueur. Muséum d'histoire naturelle, Le Havre – n° 75 011

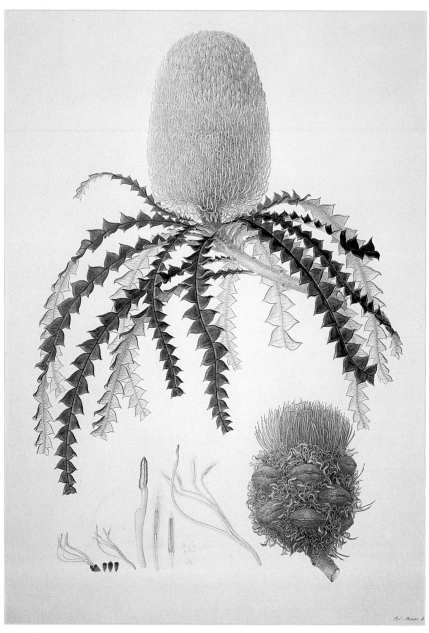

Showy banksia (specimen collected at Lucky Bay, Western Australia), *Banksia speciosa*, Ferdinand Bauer.
Natural History Museum, London

Cabbage palm (collected on islands in the Gulf of Carpentaria, Northern Territory), *Livistona humilis*, Ferdinand Bauer. Natural History Museum, London

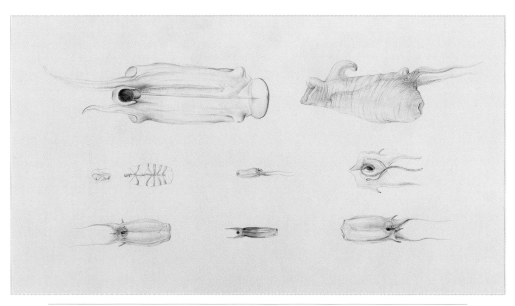

Salps (gelatinous plankton), *Pegea confoederata* (Forsskål, 1775), *Cyclosalpa bakeri* (Ritter, 1905), *Thalia democratica* (Forsskål, 1775), Charles-Alexandre Lesueur. Muséum d'histoire naturelle, Le Havre – n° 75 006

Sea squirts, *Polycarpa* sp., *Pyura* sp. and *Polycarpa aurata clavata* (Hartmeyer, 1919), Charles-Alexandre Lesueur.
Muséum d'histoire naturelle, Le Havre – n° 75 020

Bitter bark (plant material collected on the east coast of Queensland and on islands in the Gulf of Carpentaria), *Petalostigma pubescens*, Ferdinand Bauer. Natural History Museum, London

Crows ash, *Flindersia australis*, Ferdinand Bauer. Natural History Museum, London

'Ouriaga' (Bruny Island, south-east Tasmania), Nicolas-Martin Petit. Muséum d'histoire naturelle, Le Havre – n° 20 015.2

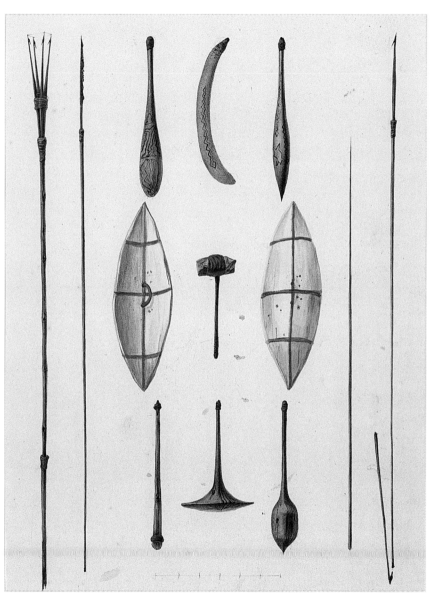

Weapons used by the Aborigines of 'New Holland', Charles-Alexandre Lesueur. Muséum d'histoire naturelle, Le Havre – n° 16 035.1

*Chasm Island, Native Cave Painting* (1803) (Gulf of Carpentaria), William Westall. National Library of Australia

*Part of King George III Sound on the South Coast of New Holland, December 1801*, William Westall. National Maritime Museum, Greenwich, London

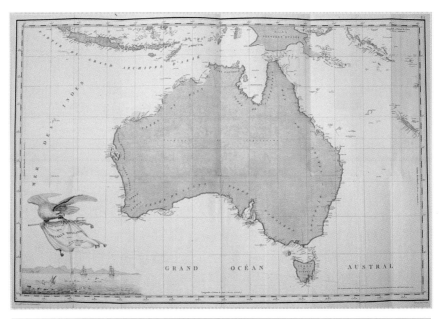

*Carte Générale de la Nouvelle Hollande*, Louis Freycinet. Published in the *Atlas* of the *Voyage de découvertes aux Terres Australes* (1811)

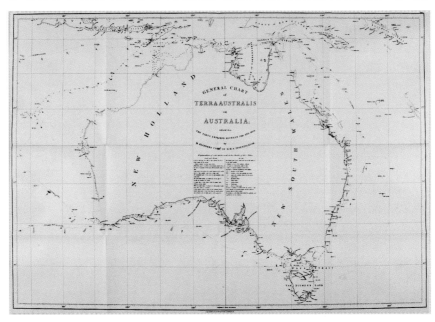

*General chart of Terra Australis or Australia*, Matthew Flinders. Published in *A Voyage to Terra Australis* (1814)

I sent to you yesterday the report of the officer on duty on board the *Géographe* when the ship was dressed and today I am sending you the report from the officers who were also present at that time. These should convince you that there is no one among us who is unacquainted with the respect that is due not only to His Britannic Majesty's flag but also to the flag of any nation whatever its standing within the political system of Europe.

The letter that I sent to Mr Harris [the harbour-master], a copy of which is enclosed, will enable you to judge how justified I was to complain of the careless and thoughtless conduct that was reflected in the report he [Harris] made to you and that caused me to write a letter of reprimand to officers who by no means deserved it.

(Enclosure), Baudin to John Harris

Sir,

According to what you told me yesterday morning on behalf of His Excellency the Governor, you must certainly have been assured that I would take all of the necessary steps to inform myself on a matter that appeared to me all the more extraordinary in that, among all the French officers who serve in the division under my command, there is not a single one who is not convinced, as I am myself, that it is impossible to repay the debt of gratitude that we owe to Governor King, Colonel Paterson and the principal inhabitants of this colony for the courteous, affectionate and distinguished manner with which they have received us.

The response that I received from each of my officers individually, the original of which I am sending to the Governor, is so authentic and so detailed that, to my sorrow, I realised that you made your complaint on the basis of dubious and thoughtless reports. Indeed, your complaint was so ill-founded that it led to a show of disrespect for which I would have grounds for an official complaint were I not aware of the reasons behind it.

Whatever the case may be, it is nevertheless true that by placing too much trust in what you told me I sent a letter full of bitter reproaches to all of my officers, whereas, in their response, whose veracity cannot be questioned, they have scrupulously adhered to the laws of honour, loyalty and courtesy that dictate their conduct.

If you would be good enough to glance over the laws of honour of the French Navy, laws that we have always respected, you will see at *article 11, chapter 17, page 268, that the place of honour for the flag of a foreign nation which we intend to distinguish must be on the starboard of the main yard arm*. The same law adds: *when it is unnecessary to make this distinction this place shall only be occupied by a French flag*.

Consider then, sir, whether, having strictly respected this formality, I am not entitled to complain bitterly about the way in which you, and those who accompanied you, have proceeded in this matter, and about the indiscreet talk that has circulated on this subject. Given your ignorance of our customs, such talk should have been deferred, at least until you were better informed. You could perhaps tell me, by way of excusing yourself and those who complained, that your way of dressing English ships is different from ours; but, in that case, I would have replied that, since I was unacquainted with it, I would never have permitted myself to make the slightest remark, and that I could not have imagined that it was out of contempt or for any other trivial reason that you would not have hoisted the French flag in the place determined by our regulations for the flag of any nation to which respect is due.

I trust, sir, that you will kindly take a courteous approach towards the French officers, who have conducted themselves with honour and loyalty, to apprise them that it is in error and on false reports that you came to doubt for a single moment their intentions, especially since they are all aware of the respect and consideration that are due to His Britannnic Majesty's flag, which is precisely the reason why it was hoisted to the privileged place that it occupied on board the corvette under my command.

What happened to the *Casuarina* which, like me, flew the English flag on the starboard of her main yard arm, and not in the place you thought it should be placed, has been made too public to be doubted. Moreover, I am sending a copy of this letter to the Governor, since your conduct in this matter has stirred up too much fuss and been too thoughtless for him not to be informed.

Baudin's defence of his officers is as forceful as it is unquestionable. His sense of honour extends to them and he is clearly acting out his role as commander. What is unfortunate is that this sentiment did not emerge the instant that the matter was brought to his attention, and that his first instinct was to reproach his officers with improper or thoughtless conduct. In other words, this incident reveals both sides of this decent, yet irascible man, who was estranged from those whom his first duty was to protect. Nonetheless, the tone of this letter is as proper and dignified as the circumstances could require. Part of his loyalty is also directed explicitly to his friend Governor King, to whom he demonstrates his abhorrence of disrespectful conduct. In his handling of the matter,

King was to respond with characteristic tact and courtesy, and the incident had no immediate repercussions on relations between the French and British in the colony. In the following days, perhaps even by way of thanks, Baudin announced his intention to donate a not inconsiderable sum to the charitable works of Mrs King, to whom he wrote on 1 October 1802.

> Madam,
> On the eve of my departure I take the liberty of sending fifty pounds sterling of which I beg your acceptance to be employed for the benefit of the Orphan Institution. Although a stranger in this colony, I hope you will not deprive me of the pleasure which I receive on this occasion of proving to you the esteem in which I hold that and similar institutions, particularly while they are watched over by persons who, like you, know how to put a just value on the present utility and future advantages of them.

Yet it seemed that troublemakers were determined to cause difficulties for Baudin and his men, and new accusations of impropriety were made – this time concerning the illegal resale of spirits that the French had purchased from the cargo of the *Atlas*. These supplies had been intended purely for the crew's consumption. On this occasion, Baudin was more cautious than before, and his prompt investigation of the charge that his officers had sold spirits to inhabitants of the colony did not include hasty accusations of his own. His defence of his officers in his letter to King on 4 October could not be faulted.

> The complaint that was made to you in recent days and which you kindly brought to my attention was such as to leave you in doubt that I would do my utmost to discover whether it had any foundation and whether any of the officers serving in the expedition under my command could be those who had the temerity to disobey your orders and mine in a manner so contrary to the laws of honour prevailing in our Navy – laws with which you are fully acquainted.
>
> The information of every type that I have obtained has convinced me that no French officer, on board the *Géographe*, the *Naturaliste* or the *Casuarina*, is guilty of the offence as charged; however, since any information that I personally acquired did not satisfy the person who accused my officers, I have ordered Messrs St Cricq and Freycinet to report to you immediately to answer for their conduct, as they are the two officers who have been singled out. What they have to say will permit you to judge whether they deserved to be publicly accused.

I hope that you will be so kind as to inform me whether they have indeed been guilty of insubordination; and, if it has been proven that they sold rum for money, I shall make an example of them so that the public will know just how scrupulous we are about such matters; but, on the other hand, if the case is not proven, I shall demand justice from you so that he who has slandered them to Colonel Paterson and yourself will be compelled to make such amends as would be expected of the French military officers, once it has been demonstrated that, after public criticism of their conduct, they were unjustly accused or maliciously compromised. Any affair in which an attack is made on an officer's honour is a delicate matter. You know that suspicion, even when it is unfounded, is a slur that is hard to forgive, and I shall not keep from you the fact that I was obliged to use my authority to avoid a scene whose consequences would be extremely unpleasant, whatever was to transpire. Whether by indiscretion or by spite, one thing is nonetheless true: that my officers and myself have been compromised in this affair. I have attached no great importance to it as far as I am concerned, and you are aware that, instead of exchanging rum at its real value in this country, I have set its price at 10 shillings so that those who have obtained natural history specimens or supplies for me made a profit that bound them to serve us well.

I can also assure you, on my word of honour, that not a single pint of the 800 gallons of brandy that you allowed me to take from the *Atlas* was taken ashore. The whole quantity has been set aside solely for our own consumption when at sea.

If he or they who have made the complaint had reflected on the consequences of the steps they have taken, I do believe that they would have been more cautious in their conduct and more guarded in their talk; but, since this was not the case, I expect to obtain the redress that is due to outraged honour, for you can have no doubt that were one of my officers to depart from the mutual respect that all men owe one another I would subject them to all that one would expect in such circumstances.

Honour was indeed avenged, for Governor King was quick to absolve the officers of blame and to secure a formal apology from their principal accuser, one Captain Kemp. Baudin was again quick to respond.

The letter that was sent to me by Mr Kemp, Captain in the New South Wales Corps, having been communicated to an assembly of all the officers, I am writing to send you [King] a copy of the response they thought it appropriate to make, and which is as follows:

On board the *Géographe*
7 October 1802

Citizen Commandant,

In compliance with your orders, I have called on board by cannon signal all the officers of the division. I communicated to them the letter written to you by Mr Kemp, Captain in the New South Wales Corps.

All the French officers, convinced that Mr Kemp was the first to have voiced the false accusation brought against them and had used every means to substantiate it, had resented all the more keenly the disloyalty of this conduct in that they least expected it from an English officer. They noted with pleasure that Mr Kemp had never intended to attack their honour. They feel assured of this, because it is one of their principles never to doubt the word of an officer. They would have preferred that Mr Kemp, who knew the scrupulous conduct of French officers, had refrained from substantiating the words of a person of no account by repeating the rumours that would never have reached the Governor nor ourselves if they had not been voiced by someone who could give them some plausibility.

The officers of the French expedition are touched by the marks of esteem of the gentlemen and officers of the New South Wales Corps and can assure them that the esteem they have for them could not be altered by the wrongs done by any individual.

Ronsard
Freycinet, the elder
Freycinet, the younger
St Cricq
etc, etc, etc

This was the last major incident to endanger the harmony between the French and their hosts. After five months of respite and refurbishment, the expedition was now in a position to pursue its voyage. The three ships were to leave together, with the *Naturaliste* to separate from the *Géographe* and the *Casuarina* in Bass Strait and set her course for Mauritius. There were also to be some British passengers aboard. Hamelin took with him Surgeon Thomson, accompanied by his wife and a male servant, all of whom were returning home to

England. Thomson would leave an interesting account of this voyage. Baudin was accompanied by a young convict girl whom historian Anthony Brown has identified as Mary Beckwith. Along with her mother, she had been sent to Port Jackson after both were found guilty of stealing some calico from a draper's shop in London. Her status on board the *Géographe* and her ultimate destination remain a mystery. All that Baudin's journal reveals is that her behaviour was of more interest than her looks, which perhaps was meant, ineffectively, to counter the impression on board ship that she was his mistress. What we do know is that her apparently drunken and dissolute behaviour was indeed so interesting that Baudin attempted to have her disembarked at Timor.

*View of a part of the town of Sydney, capital of the English Colonies in the Southern Lands, and of the entrance to Port Jackson in which this town is situated*, engraving by Pillement and Née from a drawing by Charles-Alexandre Lesueur. Published in the *Atlas* of the *Voyage de découvertes aux Terres Australes* (1807)

Of rather more importance to Baudin at this time was his wish to pay due and full respects to his friend the Governor. Before he left, the commander wrote a letter on 2 November 1802 to his old foes, the administrators of Mauritius, informing them of the extreme kindness that King had lavished on him in a so-called enemy port and exhorting them to offer the same assistance should any English sailor be compelled to put into port in Mauritius. It is

only too sad that this letter did not bear Flinders' name or come into the possession of these same administrators when Flinders was later to find himself in
the circumstances that Baudin had foreseen.

I write to inform you of my stopover in this colony by way of the American
ship the *Fanny*, and Captain Smith who is on his way to Batavia. The details I
went into in order to acquaint you with the unhappy situation in which I then
found myself would have enabled you to judge the state of distress to which
we were reduced and how fortunate we were to have chosen this port in
preference to all others.

The assistance we obtained here, the acts of kindness of Governor King
towards us all, the generous care he provided for the recovery of our sick, his
love for the progress of science – in short, everything seemed to have combined
to make us forget the troubles of a long and painful navigation that was
impeded by the elements. And yet the signing of peace was still not known and
we only learnt of it once our sick had recovered, our ships were repaired, our
supplies on board and our departure imminent.

Whatever the duties of hospitality may be, Governor King has given the
whole of Europe the example of an act of charity which should be made
known and which I take great pleasure in making public.

On our arrival in Port Jackson, the stock of wheat was very limited and
future supplies were still uncertain. The arrival of 170 men was not a happy
circumstance at that time; nonetheless, we were well received, and when our
present and future requirements were known, these were supplied by reducing
part of the daily ration allowed to the inhabitants and the garrison of the
colony. The Governor was the first to set the example. By this means, which
does such honour to the humanity of he who practised it, we enjoyed
favourable treatment which we would perhaps have had difficulty
experiencing anywhere else.

In accordance with such conduct, which will probably serve all nations as
an example for the future, I consider it my duty, as much out of gratitude as by
emulation, to recommend particularly to you Mr _____, commander
of H.M.S. _____.

Although his intention is not to go directly to Mauritius, it is possible that
unforeseen circumstances may cause him to put into port in the colony under
your administration. As a witness to the treatment that his compatriots
lavished on us effectively, I hope that he will be persuaded by his own
experience that the French are no less hospitable or charitable; then his nation

will only have over us the advantage of having done in times of war what happier times will enable us to repay her in times of peace.

Apart from the supreme irony of history that was Flinders' later imprisonment on Mauritius, the final word on the Port Jackson encounters must remain with Baudin, who had probably made the most significant encounter of his voyage. His parting words to King are filled with rare emotion and express a sensitivity that he had shown on only few occasions – at the death of Riédlé, Maugé and Levillain, but also when his men's lives were first endangered on the coast of western Australia. Baudin did have a gift for loyal friendship, as we have seen in his dealings with Hamelin and with the Danish consul in Mauritius, but this new friendship was clearly out of the ordinary. The letter Baudin wrote to King on 16 November 1802, two days before his departure from Port Jackson, bears witness to a deep and abiding affection.

> Upon departing this colony, I bequeath to the French nation the duty of offering you the thanks that you deserve, as Governor, for all that you have done, for us as well as for the greater success of our expedition; but it is for me to tell you how precious to me your friendship has been and will remain in the future, if you permit me to send you my regards whenever the opportunity arises.
>
> The candour and fairness of your conduct towards me leave me in no doubt that you will grant me the permission I request, especially since the opportunities for us to meet, after my departure from this port, shall most likely be rare; it will therefore be a satisfaction for me to correspond with you from whatever country to which events may take me. This is, as you know, the only means at the disposal of men who love and esteem one another, and it will be the means that we can both employ if, on my part, I have been able to inspire in you, by my conduct, the same feelings with which your conduct has filled my heart.

Subsequent events in Bass Strait, in which both men were obliged to play out their roles as representatives of their country, did not affect their mutual feelings. Baudin was never to forget the happy moments he had spent in Port Jackson.

For Flinders, the reprovisioning of the *Investigator* at Port Jackson was an enforced interlude which he wanted to put behind him as soon as he could. The Admiralty's instructions and his own ambition demanded now that he sail north to continue his work before the monsoon season set in. If he did not manage that, as indeed he suspected he would not, then his plan was to sail to Fiji to take shelter before completing his task.

The voyage took him further than he had ever been before. On board the *Norfolk* in 1799, he had sailed as far as Hervey Bay. Beyond that, the coast had been surveyed by his countryman James Cook in 1770. Cook's survey was necessarily patchy, however, and performed with relatively unsophisticated equipment, so that the meticulous Flinders saw the need to check and correct his forerunner's charts. In this he was aided by the presence of the *Lady Nelson*, but eventually the latter's slowness persuaded Flinders to send it back to Port Jackson in October 1802 for repairs and a refit.

In sailing north of Port Jackson he entered waters which were to remain unknown to his French counterpart. Other encounters nevertheless awaited Flinders in these waters. There was, more particularly, frequent interaction with the indigenous population, during which Bungaree stepped into the role of intermediary, often with only limited success: apart from some broken English, to which he would occasionally resort, Bungaree spoke only the language of the Eora people from around Port Jackson.

At one point, relations with the Aborigines turned tragically sour. While in the Gulf of Carpentaria the *Investigator* anchored off an island in Blue Mud Bay, and a number of people went ashore. They came across a group of Aborigines, and by their own account sought peaceful contact. For whatever reason, the peace was not maintained. As a result of a skirmish, an Aborigine was shot and killed. Flinders had reason to be angry – the killing had been in direct contravention of his orders – but he chose not to punish any of those responsible.

Well before he had completed his characteristically meticulous survey of the Gulf of Carpentaria, Flinders was alerted once more to the parlous state of the *Investigator* as it leaked relentlessly. In a sheltered location in the gulf he took the opportunity to commission a report on the *Investigator* from the master and the carpenter. The result was deeply unsettling. The report revealed that a good part of the ship's timber was either entirely or partly rotten. If the *Investigator* were to go ashore 'under unfavourable circumstances' they judged that she would fall apart; the best that could be hoped for was that in fine weather she might hold together another six months.

A prolonged continuation of a voyage of the kind Flinders had envisaged was out of the question, and there his dilemma truly began. Less than half of his task was completed, and yet to pursue it further in the *Investigator* would be to risk not only the lives of all on board but also the invaluable charts and scientific collections. Moreover, the monsoon season was approaching; to expose the ship to a severe storm might bring immediate disaster. There was no easy solution; at best, his dream of a thorough examination of the entire continent would have to be deferred. In the short term, he chose to spend the rest of the season carefully surveying the rest of the gulf before returning cautiously to Port Jackson where he might reassess his options.

On 6 March 1803, while in the vicinity of the Wessel islands, the *Investigator* and its crew took their leave of the northern coast and headed for Timor. The state of the ship was the main motive for the departure, yet by now other factors, including the crew's health, were weighing on Flinders' mind. Indeed, his own health had taken a turn for the worse; he reported scorbutic sores – the classic signs of an onset of scurvy – which prevented him from climbing to the masthead or making expeditions in the boat. In him and others, fatigue was setting in and was soon to have fatal consequences.

By the time the ship arrived at the Dutch outpost of Kupang on Timor at the end of March, the situation had deteriorated. The surgeon reported that 22 men were suffering from scurvy; the supplies of fresh fruit and vegetables were in desperate need of replenishment. At the same time, Kupang presented dangers of its own. As if to remind himself of this, Flinders visited the cemetery where Baudin's gardener Anselm Riédlé was buried – next to David Nelson, gardener aboard Bligh's *Bounty*.

The fates of Riédlé and Nelson would be shared by many members of Flinders' crew. The fresh provisions helped to keep the scurvy at bay, having an almost immediate effect in improving the crew's health, but within days of leaving Kupang dysentery began to take its toll. With barely enough hands to crew the ship, Flinders dashed south to the south-western corner of the Australian continent, thus completing its circumnavigation. Then he proceeded as quickly as the elements would allow him to Port Jackson. Even after the arrival, crewmen continued to succumb to illness. Peter Good followed his fellow gardeners Riédlé and Nelson to the grave. He was too sick even to be removed from the ship to the colonial hospital, whose staff did what they could to coax his colleagues back to health.

Flinders too continued to suffer from the scorbutic sores; he felt 'debilitated in health and I fear in constitution'. His mood was worsened by the

confirmation of the already firm suspicion that the *Investigator* was unseaworthy, and by the news from England that his father had died.

In these miserable circumstances, Flinders resolved to return to England
in order to plead with the gentlemen of the Admiralty that they might place
a fresh vessel at his disposal to complete his task. Armed with his charts, the
tangible fruits of his labours to that point, he was sure that his request could
hardly be refused.

# chapter ten

# THE POLITICS OF EXPLORATION AND DISCOVERY

*Baudin on King Island,*
*6 December to 28 December 1802*

While the expeditions of Flinders and Baudin were undoubtedly characterised by the spirit of scientific endeavour, it is clear that national interests and
personal pride were also very much at stake. Nowhere is this more evident
than in Bass Strait. On the mainland side, Hamelin's explorations of Western
Port in the *Naturaliste* and his painstaking survey of the coast between Western
Port and Wilson's Promontory aroused English suspicions about the colonial
designs of the French; and on the other side of the strait, King Island became
the site of some intense political manoeuvring, particularly on the part of its
namesake, Governor King. In both instances, the prior claims of the English
were fairly well established. Western Port had been discovered by Bass in
1798 and an initial survey was subsequently made by Francis Barrallier, an
ensign in the New South Wales Corps who was appointed by Governor King
to accompany James Grant in his voyage of March–May 1801 on the *Lady
Nelson*. King Island was first sighted in 1798 by sealer Captain William Reid
on the *Martha* and named in 1801 by Captain John Black on the *Harbinger*.
(Interestingly, the abundance of seals on the islands of Bass Strait was later to
lead to some violent skirmishes between English and American sealers.) Other
English navigators would also see King Island before the French, and a survey
of it had already been done by Lieutenant John Murray in the *Lady Nelson*.
Nevertheless, the interest taken by the French in these parts, coupled with their

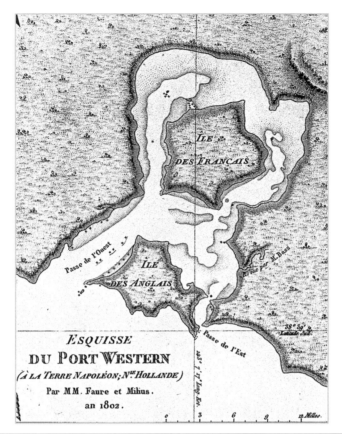

*Sketch of Western Port*, Faure and Milius (1802). Published in the *Atlas* of the *Voyage de découvertes aux Terres Australes* (1811)

apparent fondness for D'Entrecasteaux Channel and the south-east of Tasmania, would be sufficient to cause King some concern and to spur him into action.

When Baudin returned to the waters of Bass Strait following the stay in Port Jackson, it was as the leader of a veritable convoy: in addition to the *Naturaliste*, which was now heading back to France, the *Géographe* was followed by its new consort, the *Casuarina*, under the command of Louis Freycinet, and by an American merchant ship, the *Fanny*, which was en route for Batavia. This was a foretaste of the considerable amount of maritime traffic that would shortly be seen around the islands off Tasmania's northern coastline. Before Baudin could set to work, however, he had one painful duty to perform: to bid farewell to Captain Hamelin on the *Naturaliste*. Not far from King Island, the winds appeared favourable for a westward passage, so Baudin signalled Hamelin to take advantage of the conditions and sail on.

## 6 DECEMBER 1802

After this explanation we wished one another a safe journey and good health and
he bore away. This moment of separation was intensely painful for me and I felt
such a pang of sorrow that I had to take to my cabin. I was truly fond of Captain
Hamelin for his personal qualities; when you have shared the same dangers for
two years it was natural to be as deeply affected by his departure as I was.

As Baudin ran in for King Island, however, he was astonished to see the
*Naturaliste* returning: the winds had turned around and Hamelin had decided
it would be prudent to wait until conditions were more favourable. The two
captains were naturally pleased to have the opportunity for a final farewell
supper at anchorage in Sea Elephant Bay – though Baudin could not find any
kind words for the officers on board.

## 8 DECEMBER 1802

After dinner, I took leave of Captain Hamelin and wished him a safe journey.
I think it apposite to point out that I had the pleasure of seeing only one of his
officers. Even then I think that he would not have appeared if Captain
Hamelin had not invited him to dine with us. As I left, I asked that they be
thanked for their politeness and told that I was very happy to have no farewells
to make to them.

In the evening we sighted a schooner heading for the anchorage and
which, in all probability, had come from Port Jackson. She dropped anchor aft
of the *Naturaliste* at about eight o'clock. As soon as I returned aboard [my
ship], I sent over to [the mineralogist] Citizen Depuch two sheep, 12 hens and
one pig from my store so that, with Captain Hamelin's assistance, I could help
keep him in fresh food supplies for as long as possible on the voyage, in view of
the poor state of his health.

I was extremely upset to see that the officers of that ship had preferred to use
the table money I had given them by spending it on useless trinkets and that they
had no supplies apart from a dozen pigs which they had had salted well before
their departure. If I could have foreseen such an abuse, I would have dealt with
them as I did with those aboard my own ship who wanted to follow suit, but I
was informed too late of some of the doings of the officers on the *Naturaliste*.

The short and apparently innocuous delay experienced by the *Naturaliste* was
to have significant political repercussions. The English schooner referred to by
Baudin was the *Cumberland*, whose captain, Charles Robbins, accompanied by

surveyor Grimes, boarded the *Naturaliste* shortly after Baudin had returned to the *Géographe*. They informed Hamelin that they had been sent by Governor King to prepare for the establishment of a settlement in D'Entrecasteaux Channel. History shows that the English did form a settlement in 1803. At this stage, however, it was simply a ruse: King wanted to pre-empt any plans the French might have for colonising Van Diemen's Land. Hamelin's delay was therefore particularly untimely from the French point of view, as it meant that he would now be carrying back to France the (premature) news of English settlement plans in Tasmania. Furthermore, Hamelin decided for some reason not to consult Baudin on this matter before he set sail the next morning. This, too, was unfortunate, as Baudin, upon receiving a similar visit from Robbins and Grimes later that day, shrewdly guessed the real intentions behind the *Cumberland*'s presence in these waters: his good friend Governor King wanted to keep a close eye on their activities.

## 9 DECEMBER 1802

At about nine o'clock we were joined by a dinghy sent from the schooner which had arrived the day before. When the men in it came aboard the *Géographe*, I was busy working in my cabin, which meant that I was quite surprised when an officer of the English Navy was shown in, accompanied by a geographer whom I had met at Port Jackson. After we had expressed our pleasure at meeting one another, I asked them to lunch with us and they accepted. This was when Mr Robbins, who was in command of this schooner, handed me a letter from Mr King, the governor of Port Jackson, and, soon after, his instructions as to what he had to do. After examining Mr King's letter, I read his instructions, with which I am probably not fully acquainted, for he won't have shown me everything. But the contents of Mr King's letter provided enough clarification for me to see the reason for his voyage – its sole purpose was to keep watch on us.

The following extract from King's letter to Baudin indicates the source of the governor's suspicions:

You will no doubt be surprised to see a ship following you so closely. You were aware of my intention to establish a settlement in the south, but this has been brought forward because of the information communicated to me immediately after your departure. This information is that the French wish to set up an establishment in Storm Bay Passage [D'Entrecasteaux Channel] or in the area known as Frederik Hendrik Bay. It is also said that these are your orders from the French Republic.

King went on to reassure his friend that he gave no credence to these rumours and would certainly have mentioned them to him if he had heard about them before Baudin's departure from Port Jackson. As it happens, there had indeed been some loose lips at work during the French stay in the new settlement at Sydney, and the culprit was none other than François Péron, who had been unable to resist the temptation to talk up the designs of the French, concerning Tasmania in particular. Whatever the intentions of the French may have been, Baudin was quick to note his reservations about the claims of the English.

## 9 DECEMBER 1802

The English claim on Van Diemen's Land was firmly stated in the instructions of the schooner's captain, but it was based on nothing more than

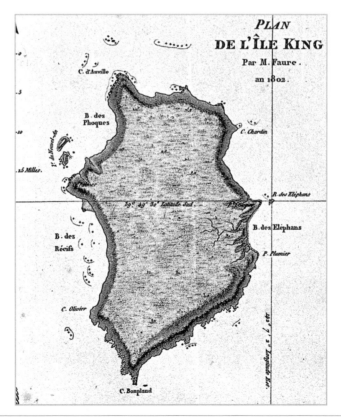

*Map of King Island*, Faure (1802). Published in the *Atlas* of the *Voyage de découvertes aux Terres Australes* (1811)

Captain Phillip's proclamation, the limits of which are recorded in what we know, from the outset, of the present settlement. Consequently, I am in no doubt that Governor King, going on whatever he may have been told, became afraid that I would have someone put on that land in order to occupy it first and it was this alone that prompted him to send a ship to keep watch on us.

Despite his comments, Baudin received all of this news with equanimity. It certainly did not prevent him from pursuing his work in Bass Strait. He had already despatched the *Casuarina* to study the Hunter Islands; likewise, Charles Baudin had been sent with the geographer, Faure, to circumnavigate King Island in the longboat. Tents were now set up on Sea Elephant Rock to facilitate the work of the scientists, about whom Baudin made ever-more disparaging remarks.

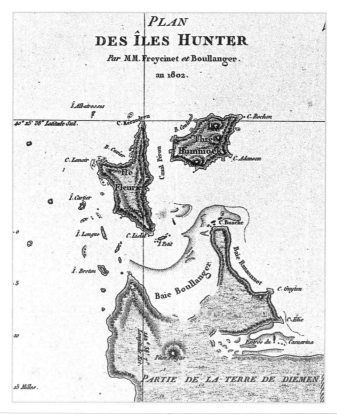

*Map of the Hunter Islands*, off the north-western tip of Tasmania, Freycinet and Boullanger (1802). Published in the *Atlas* of the *Voyage de découvertes aux Terres Australes* (1811)

## 10 DECEMBER 1802

> ... we sent out the longboat loaded with empty barrels. The large dinghy also departed carrying the scientists, their knowledge and their baggage, for these gentlemen never go anywhere without pomp and splendour. The cooks with their utensils – jars, saucepans and pots – took up so much room in the dinghy that they could not all fit in and some had to be put in the longboat. All this apparatus put me in such a bad temper that I went back into my cabin, feeling extremely annoyed that every one of them had not left on the *Naturaliste*.

His dealings with the men on the *Cumberland*, on the other hand, were more than cordial. In fact, Baudin showed himself to be most generous in helping them overcome their shortage of supplies.

## 10 DECEMBER 1802

> At three in the afternoon, the *Cumberland*'s boat came across with the captain and Mr Grimes, the geographical surveyor, who was with him. We dined together. Nothing much came up in our conversation and there was never any mention of the motive for their voyage, but they did point out to me that, having been sent out in great haste, they were short of many items and no one had thought even to give them a little gunpowder. Moreover, they had only one suit of very worn sails and no canvas to repair them in case of need – and of course neither thread nor needles. As they then asked me for several other articles, I invited them to send me a request in writing, promising to give them all that I could easily spare. They told me that they would make sure it reached me the following day. At seven o'clock we parted company and I had them taken back to their ship in one of my boats.

## 11 DECEMBER 1802

> In the morning, the *Cumberland* sent a boat over with a list of what she needed most. Her request was met in full and we sent over the following articles: one sounding lead, one 60-fathom cable, one length of canvas measuring 108 English yards, one pound of sail-thread, six needles, six padlock bolts and clamps.

The intervention of some bad weather forced Baudin out to sea, where the swirling winds and frequent bursts of thunder and lightning led him to affirm that this was one of the worst nights of the voyage. With the return of calmer conditions, he made his way back to Sea Elephant Bay, where he was surprised to find that the *Cumberland* had remained at anchor. Once again, Baudin was called on to provide Robbins with assistance, this time to repair an anchor. He also took the opportunity of going ashore, where an even more astonishing sight awaited him.

## 13 DECEMBER 1802

In the afternoon, we continued to head towards the land. It was not long before we sighted the islet where Bernier our astronomer was camped, and shortly after we saw the schooner *Cumberland* at anchorage, which greatly surprised us, for the weather we had had the day before gave us to believe that it was impossible for her to remain at anchorage. In other words, one could say that the captain in command was more fortunate than prudent. Perhaps, too, he was unable to get under way in easterly winds without incurring the risk of running aground, as he was right at the head of the bay and about a mile off shore.

## 14 DECEMBER 1802

At about nine o'clock . . . Mr Robin [Robbins] came aboard to ask me to have four iron rings made for one of his anchors; he had with him its stock, which had been broken. I gave the order that the rings be made for him and he then went ashore. As the weather was very fine during the morning, I made up my mind to go ashore. It was the first time that I had left the ship since our arrival on this coast, but I was very pleased that I would get to see our scientists who had been there for several days and find out what they were doing and how they were spending their time. I landed about midday. The captain of the English schooner was there, which did not surprise me since he had told me he was going ashore. But on the other hand, I was quite amazed to see an English flag in the exact spot where our tents were set up. I thought at first, judging from its position, that it had been hung out to dry, but after catching sight of a soldier in red uniform with a bayonet in his hand, I made inquiries about it. Our scientists then informed me that about an hour ago Mr Robin, who had come ashore to dine with them, had placed it there exactly as it was when I saw it and that they did not know what it meant, unless it was to inform us that the island belonged to him. I did not consider myself obliged to enter into any discussion on this matter, in that it was their fishermen who discovered and visited this island before we did; but if ownership falls to whoever circumnavigated it first, then it is patent that it belongs to the French.

At two o'clock, as the weather did not look too good, even though it was calm, I returned aboard, in great peace of mind, leaving Mr Robin and his flag in peace. He dined with our scientists. What he had just done did not seem to me an act of politeness. I do not know whether he was acting under orders, but these events confirmed that he had been sent to keep watch on us, rather than to hand me the trivial letter that Governor King sent me on that occasion.

Camp of the scientists at Sea Elephant Bay (King Island). To the left of the nearer tent can be seen a sentry sitting beneath the English flag. The inset shows the Union Jack in more detail. Charles-Alexandre Lesueur or Nicolas-Martin Petit. Muséum d'histoire naturelle, Le Havre – n° 18 036

This incident prompted Baudin to write two letters to King: the first an official missive addressed to the Governor of the English settlement in Port Jackson; the second a personal letter to King as a friend. They shed interesting light on the political games that were being played out and on Baudin's reactions to them. They also provide insights into the frankness and openness of his relationship with King.

> On board the corvette *Géographe*, King Island
> 23 December 1802
>
> Your Excellency,
> The arrival of the *Cumberland* would have surprised me by reason of the contents of the letter you were good enough to write me had not Mr Robbins, who is in command, revealed to me by his conduct the real motive for the precipitation with which he was dispatched; but perhaps he has arrived too late, for, several days before he hoisted his flag over our tents, we had left proof of the date of our visit on the four prominent sites of the island (for which I have retained your name).*

* Note by King in the margin: 'If Monsieur Baudin insinuates any claim from this visit, the island was first discovered in 1798 by Mr Reid in the *Martha*, afterwards seen by Mr Black in the *Harbinger*, and surveyed by Mr Murray in February 1802.'

The story you were told [regarding French settlement plans] and whose author I suspect to be Mr Kemp, captain in the New South Wales Corps, is completely unfounded. Nor do I believe that the officers and naturalists on board can have given rise to the rumour by anything they said; but, in any case, you can rest assured that if the French Government had ordered me to stop off for several days in the north or south of Van Diemen's Land, discovered by Abel Tasman, I would have stayed there, without keeping it secret from you . . .

The unofficial letter that Baudin wrote to King was much less circumspect:

Elephant's Bay, 23 December 1802

After having replied to your letter in your capacity as Governor General of the English settlement in New South Wales, I write to you in your role as Mr King, my friend, whom I shall always hold in particularly high regard. It is only on this account that I shall enter into various details with you and speak to you frankly of my way of thinking, but nothing that this letter contains bears any relationship to the policies of governments, and even less to your erroneous claims on Van Diemen's Land, with which you were no better acquainted than I when you included it, as a precaution, in the modest limits you set for your new territory. However, everyone knows that Tasman and his successors did not formally bequeath it to you, so you must expect that sooner or later they will probably tell you: *Sic vos non nobis nidificatis*, etc. [So you are not building a nest for us] . . .

I have no knowledge of the claims that the French Government may have on Van Diemen's Land, nor of its projects for the future, but I believe that its title would be no better founded than yours. However, if it were sufficient, according to the principle you have adopted, to have fully explored a land for it to belong to the first to have made it known, you would have no claim. To convince oneself that it was not the English, one only has to cast an eye over the theoretical maps drawn up by Arrowsmith, your geographer, and compare them with those drawn by Beautemps-Beaupré, which leave little to be desired.

I was convinced that the arrival of the *Cumberland* had a completely different motive from bringing me your letter, but I did not think that it was to fly an English flag in the exact spot where we had set up our tents well before. I must admit quite frankly that I am angry that it happened. That childish ceremony was ridiculous and was made even more so by the way in which the flag was hung, for it was upside down and its aspect was most unimpressive.

As I was on shore that day, I saw with my own eyes what I am telling you. I thought at first that it was a flag that had been used to strain water and hung out to dry, but when I saw an armed guard pacing round it, I was told of the ceremony that had taken place that morning. I took care not to mention it to your captain, but when our scientists dined with him they made jokes about it and M. Petit, whose talents are well known to you, drew a satirical cartoon of the whole thing. It is true that the flag sentry was worth a picture. I tore up the cartoon as soon as it was shown to me and forbade any further drawings of the sort.

The haste in which you obliged the *Cumberland* to leave is responsible for its complete lack of supplies. In spite of his choice to fly his flag above our tents, I gave Mr Robben [Robbins] all that he requested by way of gunpowder, sail cloth, thread, needles, lead and sounding line, old rope, etc. Our forge was employed for two days in work for him. I was unable to replace an anchor that he lost, having no other that was suitable . . .

I am very sorry that King Island bears your name in that it seems to me to be of no interest other than offering a temporary resource for the fishing of the sea lion and the seal the fishermen call sea elephants . . . It is all too apparent that in a short time your fishermen will have exhausted the resources that this island currently offers for the fishing of the sea lion and the sea elephant. Both will soon abandon their territory if you do not allow them time to recover from the losses that they sustain on a daily basis from the destructive war waged upon them. They are already becoming rarer than they were in the beginning and soon you will hear that they have disappeared altogether, if you do not put things to rights . . .

Kindly present my respects to Mrs King and remember me to her and to Miss Elizabeth and to all the others I had the pleasure of meeting at your home. I expect to receive a letter from you at Mauritius and I trust that we shall meet at a later stage in London or in Paris. In spite of the prevailing westerly winds, the *Naturaliste* has left to order dinner at your expense.

The comments relating to the future of the sea elephant colony show a remarkably modern concern with the conservation of nature. These stand in contrast to the attitude of Péron, among others, who saw a future in the seal trade in these parts and whose eagerness to talk up the prospects of French settlement doubtless contributed to the almost farcical events on King Island. Baudin also includes in this letter some similarly enlightened remarks on the process of colonisation and the treatment of indigenous peoples.

Sea elephants (King Island, 1802), *Mirounga leonina* (Linnaeus, 1758). *View of Sea Elephant Bay – Length of the seals: 25 to 30 feet*, engraving by Pillement & Duparc from a drawing by Charles-Alexandre Lesueur. Published in the *Atlas* of the *Voyage de découvertes aux Terres Australes* (1807)

By the end of December 1802 Baudin had finished the work he had set out to achieve in Bass Strait. He did not take very fond memories away with him of King Island: he had battled constantly with bad weather, losing his longboat in the process, and the work of the naturalists on the island had yielded meagre results. He could, however, have allowed himself to feel some satisfaction at the hydrographic achievements: as the first to circumnavigate King Island, the geographer Faure had fixed its position and outline, and, notwithstanding the fact that it had twice run aground, the *Casuarina*'s survey of the Hunter Islands had been similarly successful. With this work behind him, and having finally been rejoined by his consort, Baudin set off to cross Bass Strait once more, this time in order to conduct his expedition's second and more detailed survey of Kangaroo Island and the two gulfs.

# chapter eleven

# UNFINISHED BUSINESS

## The French Exploration of Kangaroo Island and St Vincent's and Spencer Gulfs, 2 January to 1 February 1803

Circumstances had prevented Baudin from conducting a thorough reconnaissance of Kangaroo Island and the two gulfs behind it on his first visit to these waters in April 1802. He had also been unable to land on the island and was therefore keen to return to complete what he considered to be unfinished

*Plan de l'Ile Decrès* (Kangaroo Island), L. & H. Freycinet and Boullanger (1802, 1803). Published in the *Atlas* of the *Voyage de découvertes aux Terres Australes* (1811)

business. He hoped that the *Casuarina*, with its shallower draught, would be able to conduct a close survey of the gulfs and of the island itself, whose south coast Flinders had been unable to chart. He was also looking forward to exploring the island and studying its natural history. However, when Baudin did return to Kangaroo Island in January 1803, his view of the southern coast was distinctly less favourable than his earlier impressions had been – a sentiment reiterated by Péron, who commented in his own account on the sterility and monotony of the terrain of Kangaroo Island and the continent of New Holland in general:

> . . . to the north-west the fertile isles of the Timor Archipelago met our astonished gaze with their high mountains, rivers, numerous streams and deep forests . . . to the south, we admired the sturdy vegetation of Van Diemen's Land and its lofty peaks rising up over the entire surface of that land . . . The scene changes; we reach the coasts of New Holland and for every point we make we shall henceforth have to reproduce those gloomy images which have already wearied the reader as often as they have astonished the philosopher and afflicted the navigator . . .
>
> In fact, in spite of its great size, Decrès Island [Kangaroo Island] contains no mountains in the true sense of the word, for it is entirely made up of hills that are quite high and whose peaks are almost all regular and uniform. All along the south coast they lie on a single plane about 200 to 300 feet high. Their slopes are so smooth that on their upper sections they appear to be slippery; but along the sea front these same hills form a sheer drop and rise up like ramparts almost everywhere. Their colours are dreary and wild; they vary from grey to brown or even a blackish colour; the patches which are not so dark are a dullish yellow ochre.

However emotionally charged Péron's description may be, the prevailing sentiment of disappointment is also echoed in the more sober prose of Baudin, whose journal paints in detail the sight that these navigators found so dreary on their second visit.

Profile of the western coast of Kangaroo Island showing Cape Borda (g) and the *Ravine des Casoars* (Cassowary Ravine) (h). Charles-Alexandre Lesueur. Published in the *Atlas* of the *Voyage de découvertes aux Terres Australes* (1807)

## 2 JANUARY 1803

On the morning of the 12th [Nivôse] we made an accurate sighting of the coast
of the continent of New Holland and also that of the south-eastern part of
Kangaroo Island. At daybreak we found ourselves about 3 leagues offshore,
with a perfect view of the channel, Cap l'Etoile [Land's End] and the headland
inside which I had anchored at the time of our first survey of this coast.

Since I had lost my longboat in the manner I described at the time of the
accident [on King Island], and since the one we were building on board was
still in the early stages, I decided to do the geographical survey of the southern
section of this island with the ship. Consequently, I ordered M. Freycinet, who
was in command of the *Casuarina*, to follow us, hugging the shoreline as
closely as he could and examining all the inlets which seemed likely to offer
anything of interest. In accordance with these arrangements, we ourselves
drew up alongside the south-easterly tip of Kangaroo Island . . .

The land that we sailed along during the morning is quite elevated and
falls away to the sea in a fairly gentle slope. The entire terrain is sandy and
treeless. All you can see are the occasional low tufts of heath, which are the
only decorative feature in these parts. It does not have anything like the
pleasant appearance of the opposite or northern side.

In the afternoon we entered a large bay whose bearings had at first seemed
to us very promising, offering shelter from the winds ranging from the south-
west to the north. But all we found here was a low, sandy coast without any
vegetation.

There was, however, a real satisfaction to be drawn from the survey in the fact
that its completion gave the expedition a claim to the discovery of an important
feature of the unknown coast. This also restored something of the sense of
purpose that Flinders' work had cast into doubt.

## 4 JANUARY 1803

Early on the 14th [Nivôse] we had finished our geographical work for the
whole of Kangaroo Island, which means that, although the English may have
the advantage over us of arriving here a few days earlier, we have the advantage
over them of having circumnavigated it and determined its geographical
position in a way that leaves nothing to be desired for the safety of navigation.

Baudin even declared upon the strength of his new survey that he now considered he had the right to rename the island, which he thereafter designated

as Borda Island, after the noted French mariner and mathematician – a name that would no more survive in the French account of the expedition published by Péron and Freycinet (who named it 'Île Decrès' in honour of the man who had become Minister of Marine by the time the expedition returned), than in the definitive attribution of the island's name, in which both Flinders' claim and Kangaroo Island's chief source of interest – its native fauna – were recognised.

On 6 January Baudin anchored inside Kangaroo Head, near present-day Penneshaw, and boat parties were sent to explore the shores of Eastern Cove in search of fresh water and timber for the new longboat. At first, Baudin was greatly disappointed by the little that that they were able to find. Another source of irritation was the discovery that five of six English convict stowaways who had been smuggled on to the *Géographe* in Sydney – and whom Baudin had ordered to be disembarked on King Island – were still on board. Two of them, at least, made themselves useful in supplying fresh meat to the company, thanks to their obviously well-practised skill in hunting kangaroos.

## 9 JANUARY 1803

> After I had sent out the dinghy I went ashore to explore a ravine near our anchorage where I was expecting to find water, judging by the fresh appearance of the plant life on this part of the coast. I also intended to sink a well if I did not find any running water. That is why I took some men with me and everything we needed to carry out this work. As soon as we landed, I went off to explore the place I have just mentioned and found nothing in this ravine: it was utterly dry. We dug five large holes which were completely useless, for less than two feet down, we hit the rock that no doubt forms the core of this island.
>
> The botanist, Leschenault, and the gardener's boy, who came ashore with me, as did Citizen Péron, went about their work and, when they rejoined us, after coming back almost empty-handed from their excursion, we thought about going back on board, for the only luck we had was one live kangaroo that our dog caught shortly before departure. I set off, leaving two Englishmen ashore to kill some kangaroos for us by lying in wait for them at night, as is their custom.

On 10 January Baudin and his consort separated, with the *Casuarina* departing to conduct a close survey of St Vincent's and Spencer Gulfs. During the three weeks of the *Casuarina*'s absence, the crew of the *Géographe* remained on Kangaroo Island constructing a new longboat and collecting specimens. Like Flinders and his men before them, the French were particularly struck by the

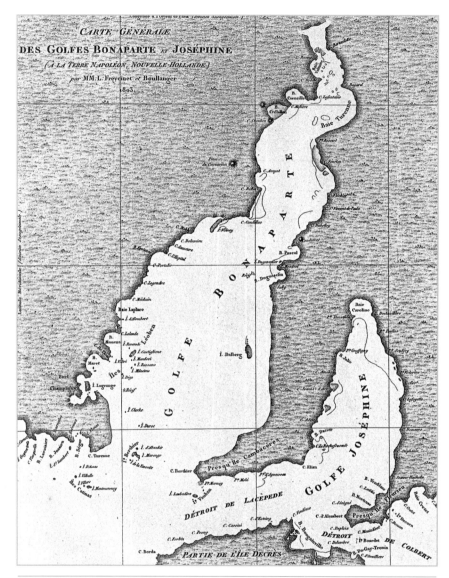

*Carte Générale des Golfes Bonaparte et Joséphine* (Spencer Gulf and Gulf St Vincent), L. Freycinet and Boullanger (1803). Published in the *Atlas* of the *Voyage de découvertes aux Terres Australes* (1811)

island's native kangaroos. Péron and the ship's engineer Ronsard both commented on the large numbers of them, expressing their anxiety that these numbers might diminish should present hunting techniques prevail. Péron was particularly concerned about the ease with which the dog killed the unsuspecting native animals.

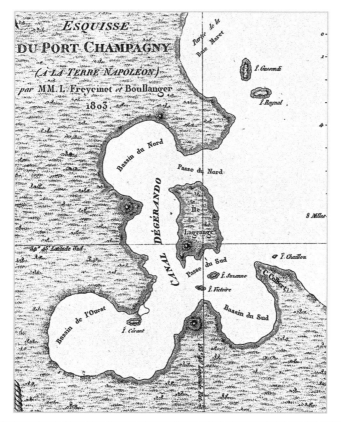

*Esquisse du Port Champagny* (Port Lincoln), L. Freycinet and Boullanger (1803). Published in the *Atlas* of the
*Voyage de découvertes aux Terres Australes* (1811)

[The dog] chased the kangaroos and, when he had caught up with them,
he killed them on the spot by tearing open their jugular arteries. Only the
presence and the shouts of the hunter could save the victim from certain death.
With a similar dog and hunting techniques such as these, there is no doubt that
a group of men established on Kangaroo Island would be able to obtain plenty
of food. One could even foresee that the innocent and helpless race of
kangaroos would inevitably be wiped out in a few years by several dogs of the
kind I mentioned . . .

Interestingly, while not part of the scientific staff, Ronsard was at pains to
establish the expedition's credentials for responsible practice in regard to the
long-term preservation of the native animal populations.

We have found, as did Mr Flinders, enormous numbers of kangaroos and, although we did but little hunting, the crew almost always did, if I may say so, with discretion. It was not the same with the emus; many were seen but we had only taken two which we brought aboard alive . . .

Western grey kangaroo (Kangaroo Island), *Macropus fuliginosus* (Desmarest, 1817), Charles-Alexandre Lesueur. Muséum d'histoire naturelle, Le Havre – n° 80 057

As commander, Baudin's concern for the kangaroos and emus was naturally dominated by his double responsibility to the expedition – firstly to see that his crew was supplied with fresh meat, but also to ensure that due care was taken of the live specimens which would be collected and properly housed on board for the long trip back to France. His journal nevertheless reveals that the scientific objectives of the expedition were uppermost in his mind: in successive entries, his admiration for the animals and his attention to their needs became manifest. Similarly, however critical his attitude may have been towards the particular scientists on board his ship, Baudin did record in detail the keen interest he took in their work. All of their results were faithfully kept, and Baudin was determined to ensure that their collections were preserved. Indeed, if the new specimens collected proved few in number or commonplace, he expressed not disapproval but disappointment – though he could not resist adding a dash of irony when recording the enthusiasms of the irritating Péron.

## 12 JANUARY 1803

The little dinghy, which had stayed behind to bring back Messrs Leschenault and Péron, did not get back to the ship until four in the afternoon. The first had had no luck on his excursion and brought back only two or three plants that were new to him, but Citizen Péron was delighted with his collection of three or four molluscs, two small lizards and half a dozen ear-shells like the ones that fill the sailors' sea-chests.

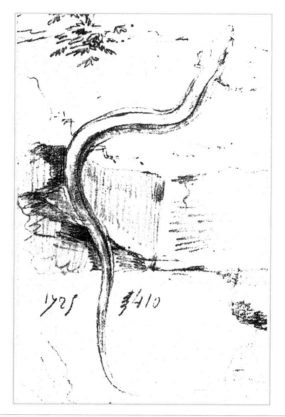

Lizard of the Scincidae family (Kangaroo Island), *? Hemiergis peronii* (Gray, 1831), Charles-Alexandre Lesueur. Muséum d'histoire naturelle, Le Havre – n° 78 130d

## 14 JANUARY 1803

As usual, the boats were sent out to fetch water and wood and, in the first, I dispatched one of my hunters to obtain some birds of a particular type which were described to us as having red tail-feathers and a grey body, and which were the size of a cockatoo and said to have a similar beak. The weather was fine all day. There was only a slight breeze from the south, variable to south-south-west.

At night the boats returned to the ship with little water and even less in the way of objects of curiosity. The red-tailed birds we had been promised turned out to be only black cockatoos with red patches in their tail-feathers and they were exactly the same as those we had obtained at Port Jackson. The best things they found were two golden-winged pigeons, which were in very good condition.

## 19 JANUARY 1803

During the day, the hunters who were on shore caught 12 giant kangaroos of various sizes with the help of the dogs. Seven of them, which we intended to take back alive, were caught and housed in pens on board the ship. Amongst those that we hope to take back home are three females with young that will perhaps grow to full size. Before we leave, I shall try to obtain a good twenty or so live ones, so that we shall have a better chance of keeping some alive throughout the voyage.

Baudin did not just keep a close eye on the work of the scientists, however. He was so anxious that the longboat be completed in good time that he was constantly checking on his carpenters to ensure that they were pursuing their work with a sense of urgency. So close was he to their centre of operations that he almost sustained serious injury.

## 21 JANUARY 1803

As I was constantly alongside the carpenters, urging them on, I was nearly crushed when a tree fell down in a different direction from the one we had calculated. When it fell it knocked me down and I was so entangled in the branches that it took me a long time to extricate myself. I escaped with only a few cuts to the head and other parts of the body. This fall caused me to spend the night ashore, where I could lie down easily enough, although I was in very great discomfort.

In the meantime, the two main tasks of the expedition continued unabated: the collection of water and supplies and the hunting of live kangaroos.

## 28 JANUARY 1803

Since I proposed getting underway as soon as the date set for the *Casuarina*'s return had expired, I began taking on branches of white casuarina as feed for our kangaroos which were doing very well. We already had 15; two of them had died because they had been too badly wounded by the dogs to recover.

Baudin's eagerness to collect a large number of specimens was justified. Some of the live animals did indeed survive the difficult conditions of the return journey. Among the specimens that eventually found their way into the collections of the Paris Museum and elsewhere were two of the species taken from the island – the western grey kangaroo and the dwarf emu of Kangaroo Island. The conservation of these specimens was the direct result of Baudin's attention to his scientific mission, but it came at the cost of further strain between the captain and his officers and scientists.

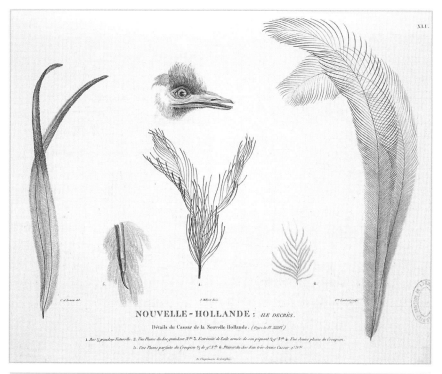

Details of the Cassowary of New Holland, Ile Decrès (Kangaroo Island), *Dromaius* sp. The term 'Cassowary' was used to refer to birds that modern nomenclature separates into the *Casuarius* and *Dromaeus* genera. Engraving by Milbert and Lambert from a drawing by Charles-Alexandre Lesueur. Published in the *Atlas* of the *Voyage de découvertes aux Terres Australes* (1807)

## 4 FEBRUARY 1803

At daybreak we found two of our kangaroos dead in their pens. I had no doubt at all that the bad weather had brought about their deaths for they were completely soaked by the rain and the continuous mist that we had had for the past three days, in spite of the great care we took to cover their pens with good tarpaulins. This accident convinced me that they should no longer be kept on the gangways, where they were housed. But in order to find somewhere else suitable I had to create two dissatisfied customers – or at least one, for he expressed his feelings to me in no uncertain manner, taking me to task for the fact that he was still aboard. According to him, it was all my fault, since I had refused to let him leave on the *Naturaliste*, as per the request he had made to me in writing at Port Jackson, etc.

'You are right,' was my reply, 'but I would not have gone to such lengths to urge you not to disgrace yourself if I could have foreseen that you were capable of preferring your own creature comforts and a few temporary conveniences to the greater success of the expedition and whatever may serve our country.' I nevertheless took the cabins of M. Leschenault, our botanist, and M. Ransonnet, which I needed to house the seven kangaroos which were exposed to all kinds of danger from the weather on our gangways.

While one may rightfully accuse Baudin of deriving some enjoyment from inconveniencing a man whose conduct irritated him, it is not certain that this grim satisfaction in any way matched the pleasure he felt in ensuring the integrity of his collections and the success of his mission. Indeed, Baudin was quite capable of putting aside the recriminations intended for his officers when a significant find distracted him, as it did on the final day on Kangaroo Island. The commander's satisfaction at the capture of two emus – a satisfaction that history would find to be well justified, since the Kangaroo Island dwarf emu was soon to become extinct – far outweighed the anger he felt over Louis Freycinet's failure to return at the appointed time.

### 31 JANUARY 1803

I should have set sail on the 11th [Pluviôse], for the maximum of 20 days I had fixed for the *Casuarina*'s mission had expired. Nevertheless, I spent this day still at anchor in the hope of seeing her return, but I wasted 24 hours for nothing . . .

The boat responsible for providing our water supplies returned with two pretty, live emus, which the men had caught with the help of the dogs. In spite of all our attempts, we had not managed to get close to them until now, even though we knew where they were to be found. This lucky prize lessened the regrets I felt over losing the day that I had just spent waiting for the *Casuarina*.

Emu (Kangaroo Island?), *Dromaius* sp., Charles-Alexandre Lesueur. Muséum d'histoire naturelle, Le Havre – n° 79 002

Baudin was of course not the only one to record his preoccupation with the mission of the naturalists on Kangaroo Island – they themselves left detailed descriptions of the specimens they eventually collected in good numbers. As well as the ever-present emus and kangaroos, they identified new species in groups ranging from seals and lizards to birds and fish. However, no frogs could be found, as Péron explains.

> On land which is without fresh water it is not surprising that we found no trace of toads, frogs or tree frogs; on the other hand, the lizard family, whose organisation adapts so well to arid and sandy places, accounted for a large number of new species: such as the black skink, *Scincius aterrimus*, N., the gecko *Pachyurus*, the gecko *Sphincturus*, the ocellate skink, *Scincoides ocellatus*, N., the Decrès Island iguana, *Iguana Decresiensis*, N.

Moreover, fish were found in smaller numbers than expected – a phenomenon which Péron explained by the presence of sharks, particularly in Nepean Bay:

> Of the different parts of New Holland which we were able to explore, Decrès Island [Kangaroo Island] seemed to us the least well supplied with fish; all our usual methods of fishing and all our efforts provided us with a mere 12

Péron's text designates this as *Gecko pachyurus – île Decrès* (Kangaroo Island), ? *Diplodactylus vittatus* (Gray, 1832). Charles-Alexandre Lesueur. Muséum d'histoire naturelle, Le Havre – n° 78 122g

species – new ones, it is true, but five or six of which are not usually eaten. Among them featured a wrasse which, by reason of its dirty, dull grey colours, seemed to me deserving of the specific name of *Squalidus*; a mackerel, rather like the European mackerel, but differing from it in its much smaller size and some of the details of its fins; a scad, with a beautiful azure-coloured back; a saury, 22 inches long and glittering with all the colours of the rainbow; a small reddish dorado; two barracuda; a flute-mouth; three trigger-fish, one of which is noticeable for its four brown lateral bands, another for its beautiful purple colour and pectoral fins, while the third, which is a *Balistacanthurus*, can be distinguished particularly by the black colour of its body and by the four large spikes arming its tail on either side.

But of all the fish of Decrès Island, the most amazing is a species of shark attaining a length of 15 to 20 feet and which is very common in Bougainville Bay [Nepean Bay]: day and night several of these monstrous creatures could be seen prowling around the ship in search of food, numbing with terror all those who saw them.

The seals caused them fewer problems than to Flinders' crew, and indeed were seen to be suitable for exploitation by the sealing industry. Péron, in apparent contradiction to the concerns he had expressed about the possible extinction of the kangaroo, spoke in favour of establishing such an industry upon the island. Among the seals inhabiting the shores of the island, a new species, *Otaria cinerea*, was found to hold the greatest commercial potential;

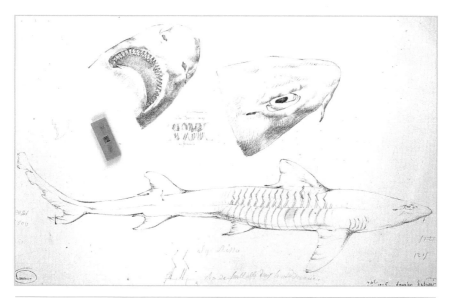

Shark designated as *Squalus Lesueur* (Southern Australia), *Furgaleus macki* (Whitley, 1943), Charles-Alexandre Lesueur. Muséum d'histoire naturelle, Le Havre – n° 76 796

three metres or more in length, with short coarse hair and a strong thick skin, the oil obtained from its fat proved both good and plentiful. For these reasons, the hunting of this seal and also several others, smaller but found in large numbers and possessing fur of good quality, appeared to Péron to offer valuable advantages. The island's other resources would also be useful: 'In the event of an industry of this nature, Spring Cove [Hog Bay] would provide the fishermen with enough water for their consumption, while kangaroos and emus would give them a healthy and inexhaustible food supply.'

The botanical results of the expedition were equally abundant, but Péron's remarks about the trees in particular seem to return to the theme of his overall assessment of Kangaroo Island, which is coloured by the notion of aridity and monotony. With the exception of Hog Bay, the lack of fresh water, which, according to Péron's descriptions, forced the kangaroos to come down to the sea to drink, and which determined the absence of human life from these shores, also dictated the 'unfortunate characteristic' of the island's forests and the poor quality of its timber.

> There are many of those trees, and especially the larger ones, that are so completely rotten inside that they could not be put to any sort of use. This damage seemed to me to be generally a result of the poor quality of the soil

Species of seal observed by Péron and Lesueur on Kangaroo Island, *Neophoca cinerea* (Péron, 1816).
Charles-Alexandre Lesueur. Muséum d'histoire naturelle, Le Havre – n° 80 676

which does not provide these plants with a sufficient quantity of nutritious
liquids, when, after growing to a great size, they need more moisture to keep
them in good condition. What shall I say of the unsuitability of the island's
forests when it comes to feeding man and beast? They have this unfortunate
characteristic in common with all the forests of New Holland and the islands
around it, a characteristic that is all the more inconceivable in that these distant
regions produce a very large number of magnificent plants.

In spite of the rich rewards that Kangaroo Island had yielded to the scientists,
the spirits of the ship's company had not been lifted dramatically by the time
spent on these as yet little known shores. Indeed, on leaving the island their
spirits would take a turn for the worse due to a navigational misunderstanding
beween Baudin and Freycinet that deepened the enmity between the commander
and his scientists and officers.

On 1 February 1803, the *Géographe* weighed anchor and headed west, its
captain now weary of waiting for its overdue consort to arrive.

## 1 FEBRUARY 1803

From four o'clock onwards on the morning of the 12th [Pluviôse], we
prepared to set sail as soon as the wind rose, as we had known it to do most
days while we were at this anchorage. We first started taking our three boats
aboard and then raised the ship's small bower anchor and hove short on the

other. Next the crew were given breakfast, after which we hoisted our topsails to the masthead, weighed anchor and headed off, leaving the *Casuarina* to her fate, as she had chosen to leave us to ours.

I intended to go and check out a landmass that the look-out men had reported to the west of Borda Island [Kangaroo Island], so I headed west and south once I was out of the bay in which we had been anchored and sailed along the whole of the north coast of this island for the third time, again identifying all the points that helped us draw up the chart, which seems to me to leave nothing to be desired.

In the afternoon, the winds were south variable to south-south-east, but it was blowing such a gale that we were obliged to take two reefs in the topsails and furl all our staysails. Although the wind was from on-shore, the sea was consistently rough and choppy.

At two o'clock we sighted the *Casuarina* on an easterly tack. I was expecting her to go on the same tack as us and to follow us as soon as she saw us. Consequently, when we were within cannon shot range of one other, I unfurled the mainsail, then furled it so that she would have less trouble keeping up with us. But that did not greatly concern her and she continued on her eastward tack with the result that by half past three we lost sight of her. It is unquestionably difficult to explain this manoeuvre on the part of Citizen Freycinet and I dare say he will tell us about it at our first meeting.

As I wanted to get to the outer side of the islands and rocks to the north of Borda Island, I continued on my way, preferring to wait for the *Casuarina* at the end of this island, rather than lose time chasing after her by heading back east. It could not be assumed that she would keep on that tack for very long, that is, if her intention was to rejoin us, of which I am not at all convinced.

Baudin's exasperation with Freycinet had reached its height. Although there is evidence from the other journals, such as that of Ronsard, to justify Baudin's actions in continuing on his westerly course, there is also evidence that Freycinet had indeed attempted to go about to meet the *Géographe*. Freycinet himself, in his account of this incident – which left the *Casuarina* desperately short of water and supplies until the two ships met up again on 17 February in King George Sound – denies that Baudin shortened sail in an attempt to reduce speed. Whether or not Baudin's account is to be believed, this episode clearly demonstrates that the trust which should have united all of the members of the expedition was now damaged beyond the point of all return and that loyalties were more divided than ever.

# chapter twelve

# AT THE END OF HIS TETHER

## *Baudin in King George Sound and on the Western Australian Coast, 17 February to 28 April 1803*

Had it not been for the controversial separation from the *Casuarina* on its return to Kangaroo Island, Baudin might have felt justly satisfied with the work conducted on the south coast. Although he had exceeded his allotted 20 days for the task, Louis Freycinet had completed a thorough survey of the two gulfs. This, combined with the circumnavigation of Kangaroo Island and the charting of the previously unknown coast, represented a considerable body of work and would indeed prove to be one of the most successful chapters of the expedition. Further success awaited Baudin as he made his way towards the rendezvous point of King George Sound: on reaching Nuyts Archipelago, he finally realised his ambition of passing between the islands of St Peter and St Francis and the mainland. In fact, having anchored in Denial Bay, he was able to conduct a much more thorough survey of this section of coast than Flinders had managed, leaving a lasting legacy in the place names that Péron and Freycinet would later confer upon its features: Cape Vivonne, Cape Thevenard, Tourville Bay, Murat Bay.

As he sailed past the islands at the western entrance of Denial Bay, bound now for King George Sound, Baudin finally allowed himself to express some measure of satisfaction.

### 11 FEBRUARY 1803

At these islands, we finished taking bearings of the south and south-western coasts of New Holland and I have no doubt that the chart we shall make of

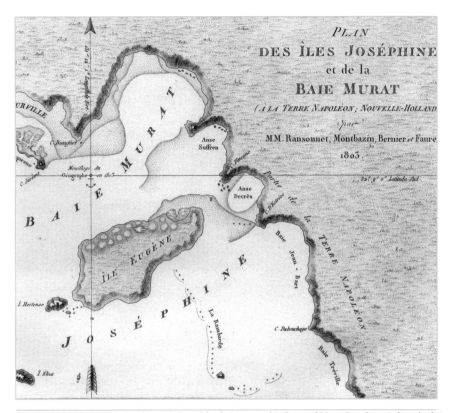

*Plan des Iles Joséphine et de la Baie Murat* (St Peter Islands, Nuyts Archipelago and Murat Bay, the main branch of Denial Bay. *Ile Eugène* is the island of St Peter), Ransonnet, Montbazin, Bernier and Faure (1803). Published in the *Atlas* of the *Voyage de découvertes aux Terres Australes* (1811)

them, together with the published map from d'Entrecasteaux's voyage, will provide accurate knowledge of this entire region which has remained unknown to Europeans for so long.

There was also a sense of triumph at having proved, contrary to the belief of the English, that the prevailing winds along this coast during the summer months were from the east.

## 12 FEBRUARY 1803

During the afternoon the fine weather continued and the winds varied from east-south-east to south-east. When I think about the winds that we have had since our departure from King Island, I have real difficulty in understanding how the English managed to convince themselves that nothing but strong westerlies and south-westerlies were to be encountered on the route I was to take. I in no way shared this opinion and, to back up my view, I mentioned the winds that I had encountered the previous year, but I could not make them see their error. I do not know what their authority is, since none of their ships has taken this route. It is thus likely that for a long time to come their ships departing from Port Jackson will prefer the route via Cape Horn over the route through Bass Strait, even though this is unquestionably the better one to take at this time of year.

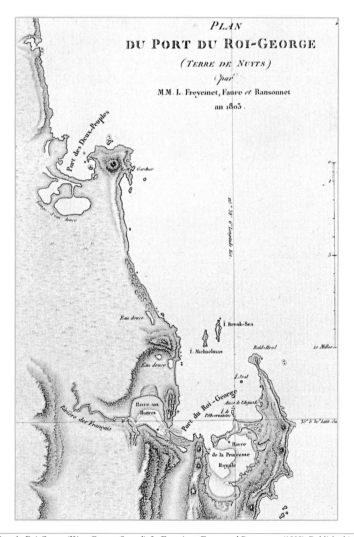

*Plan du Port du Roi-George* (King George Sound), L. Freycinet, Faure and Ransonnet (1803). Published in the *Atlas* of the *Voyage de découvertes aux Terres Australes* (1811)

While Baudin was conducting his brief but ground-breaking survey of Denial Bay, the *Casuarina*, in desperate need of water, had benefited from these pre-vailing south-easterlies, making good time to arrive at King George Sound on 13 February. The two ships were reunited when the *Géographe* arrived there on 17 February.

King George Sound, which offered the only safe anchorage on this vast stretch of coast, was unknown territory for the French, and Baudin was understandably keen to explore it.

At daybreak on the 29th [Pluviôse – 18 February] we put our boats out. One went straight out to reconnoitre the watering-place and the other was engaged in setting up our observatory on an island which was quite pleasant and which lay north-west by north of the ship.

When the dinghy returned from the watering-place, I was informed that the water was very good and easy to obtain. We found ten casks there belonging to the *Casuarina*, which we knew must be in one of the two ports; we were aware that she had arrived there first because of the flag she had placed on the summit of Seal Island. The day before, we had announced our own arrival by a cannon shot fired during the night, to which she had replied by sending up several flares. From these we learnt that she was in the Port de la Princesse Charlotte [Princess Royal Harbour].

At about eight o'clock we sighted the dinghy from this ship and, shortly after, her commander, Citizen Freycinet, arrived. When I asked him why he had not rejoined me at the time of our meeting off Borda Island [Kangaroo Island], he replied that he had not been able to do so and that furthermore I should have waited for him. I then pointed out to him the bad manoeuvre he had made – which seafaring men will be able to appreciate – but he remained nonetheless convinced that his had been better than ours and that ours alone had led to the separation I was complaining about. As I had told him that the islands of St Peter and St Francis were our first meeting-place, I asked him again if it were my fault that he had not gone there. He again replied that it was, since they were not in the latitude and longitude that I had indicated to him, in spite of the fact that we had gone to look them up in exactly the same place. What is more, he raised the objection that, having very little water, he had thought it more advisable to come to this port than to continue looking for me, given the uncertainty as to whether he would find me. Finally, he told me that his ship was in need of repairs and that he required caulkers and carpenters and that he had beached the ship in order to facilitate the work.

The details that M. Freycinet had just given me in no way excused his conduct, and to show him how dissatisfied I was, I responded only by saying that I would send a caulker and a carpenter across to his ship and that he could put them to work as he thought fit. Immediately afterwards, I set off in my dinghy to inspect the watering-place myself to see if it was as convenient and suitable as I had been told. After examining it, I found that it was indeed so, and I immediately had our tents set up there, with one reserved for our sick, then numbering four, and the other for the naturalists.

I also had a large reservoir made for washing the linen and the crew's hammocks, as I wanted to take advantage of this opportunity to do the washing.

Exploring the river that runs into Oyster Harbour, Baudin was pleased to find a further source of fresh water, along with two Aboriginal 'monuments'.

## 22 FEBRUARY 1803

At the first headland forming its entrance I met Citizens Faure and Bailly whom I took on board, in spite of the lack of room in my dinghy; we were in an arm of the sea, which we then followed upstream together. The lagoons that they had examined contain nothing but salt water that the high tide carries in through various little ravines that extend to the seashore. At one in the afternoon, having rowed about 1½ leagues inland, we stopped for dinner opposite a small stream which entered the river and in which we thought there must be fresh water. We went ashore to inspect it and indeed found a small amount which, although unpleasant in taste, we found very good, since our supply had run out.

While exploring the countryside surrounding the stream I have just mentioned, we found two rather remarkable and interesting monuments erected by the natives of the region – if only one could discover the purpose they served. The first one stood seven or eight feet from the stream, on a plot of bare ground three feet in circumference that was surrounded by finely-tapered spears painted red at the tip. There were 11 in all. On a parallel line with this trophy, on the other side of the stream, lay a plot of ground of similar form and planted with the same number of spears, but these spears seemed to be barring the passage from the left bank to the right, just as those on the left seemed to be blocking access from the right. As several people thought that the spears had been painted red with blood, we took one out to have a closer look and realised that this colour came from eucalyptus resin.

Everyone tried to guess what these monuments could be and we came up with various arguments. My opinion is that they are two graves in which lie two warriors of different tribes, who were buried there either after dying in single combat or in a war and who still appear to be challenging one another after death. I would not allow anyone to dismantle these tombs nor remove the spears adorning them, so as to ensure that any Europeans coming here can draw their own inferences from it, as their imagination dictates. However, I did put two medals and some glass beads on each one. In the surrounding area we also sowed some maize and other garden seeds.

Immediately after dinner, we got back in the boat and continued on our way up the river. I was intending to go far enough up-stream to find fresh water, but we were barely a mile further on when we found ourselves in shallow water, with the way blocked by dams that the natives of the area had constructed in the form of locks. These dams were built on each side of the river, in the middle of which was an island, which was linked to both banks by rocks that were part of the natural environment. But in the places where there were none and where the river bed had been hollowed out by the current, the natives had inserted stones which they had arranged skilfully and symmetrically side by side, which proves that they are not without intelligence. Until then we had never been in less than six fathoms of water and it was with great regret that we were forced to come to a halt in the middle of our excursion . . .

The banks of the section of the river along which we travelled are very pleasant to look at. The ground is high and well covered with tall trees. I collected various types of seed and a few flowering plants that were new to me. Everywhere we went we saw traces of fire and signs that the natives were occasionally to be found in these parts; but in the places where they had assembled, which were easily identified by the sites where they had lit fires,

Lizard (King George Sound), *Ctenotus labillardieri* (Duméril and Bibron, 1839), Charles-Alexandre Lesueur.
Muséum d'histoire naturelle, Le Havre – n° 78 127e

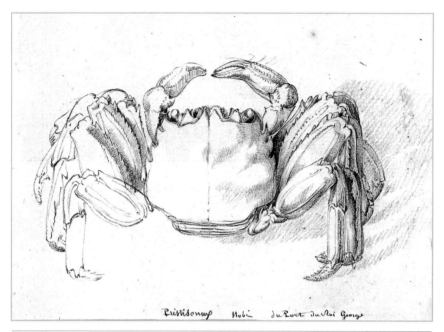

Crab (King George Sound), *Plagusia chabrus* (Linnaeus, 1758), Charles-Alexandre Lesueur. Muséum d'histoire naturelle, Le Havre – n° 73 109

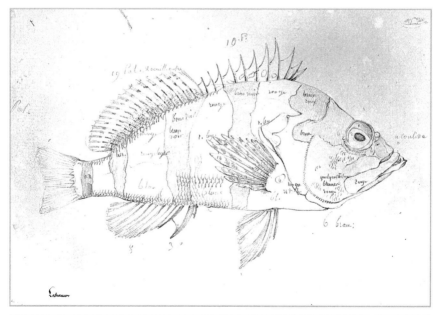

Fish of the Serranidae family (King George Sound), *Hypoplectrodes nigrorubrum* (Cuvier, 1828), Charles-Alexandre Lesueur. Muséum d'histoire naturelle, Le Havre – n° 76 379

we could not find the slightest indication of what their diet could have consisted of.

We collected several of their spears that were found propped up against the trees, as if they had been kept in reserve. These weapons of war were crudely made and much less sophisticated than the ones from Port Jackson.

At the foot of a high mountain-range running from north to south in the hinterland, we saw many separate columns of smoke, which made us think that the natives were momentarily in the vicinity; but they were too far away for us to try to get there, if it meant crossing an unfamiliar terrain where there were no food supplies. We gave up all thought of visiting them.

An unexpected meeting took place in King George Sound between the French expedition and an American sealer, the *Union*, under the command of Captain Isaac Pendleton. Sub-Lieutenant Ransonnet was the first to encounter the Americans, to the east of the Sound in a bay which he had been sent to explore and whose name commemorates the meeting – Two People Bay ('Port des Deux-Peuples'). Pendleton then sailed on to find Baudin.

## 23 FEBRUARY 1803

In the afternoon, the American captain, who had been told by his men that I was at this tent, came to see me. He informed me that he had left New York towards the end of last September and that he had been sent out on a sealing expedition, which so far had not brought him much luck, for, in the various places he had visited, he had only managed to obtain three or four hundred skins and he had twenty thousand to collect before even thinking of heading for China. He had decided to come to this port on the strength of the information provided by Vancouver, who saw plenty of seals when he was here. As his ship had sailed in from the east, he told me that he had spoken to the men in the boat commanded by M. Ransonnet, whom, as I mentioned, I had sent to reconnoitre the section of coast between Mt Gardner and Bald Island.

I invited the captain to dinner the following day and, after we parted company, I went back on board my ship.

Whatever pleasure Baudin may have had in meeting the American captain and providing him with charts and useful navigational advice, it did not distract him from the pressing task of replenishing his own expedition's supplies of wood and water. With growing testiness, however, Baudin noted that his companions did not appear to share his urgency of purpose.

## 24 FEBRUARY 1803

On the 5th [Ventôse] the *Casuarina* finally left the Port de la Princesse Charlotte [Princess Royal Harbour] and came and anchored opposite the watering-place where we were collecting her water and ours. I sent a boat across to find out if she were ready to take hers on board and Citizen Freycinet came over in the same boat to tell me that he was also out of wood and had not collected any in Princess Royal Harbour, in spite of the fact that he had been there for nearly a fortnight, swanning about and doing nothing. But it is more likely that he did not know exactly how much had been collected for him, for, according to the report of the carpenter whom I had sent over to work on his ship, his hold, in which there were only three or four casks, was so full that in order for them to find somewhere for the crew to sleep at night they had to send a fairly large number of them up on deck.

Be that as it may, we agreed that I should have some cut for him opposite the watering-place, although he claimed that there was none there. But since I had seen it for myself, I knew what to believe.

This officer remained smugly on board until eight in the evening, when I had to have one of my boats take him to his ship and make the return trip.

## 25 FEBRUARY 1803

The weather on the 6th [Ventôse] was fairly fine and so I manned the longboat to take over to the *Casuarina* the water and the wood I had had cut the day before. In order to get the job done, I went in the longboat myself and performed a task that my officers would have found most distasteful, had I instructed them to do it . . .

Since Citizen Freycinet had been advised the night before, by me in person, of the work that he had to do that day, I had presumed that he would be ashore to speed things up, especially since I had seen his dinghy making several trips to shore. But I was informed that he could not come, as he was having a dinner party that day and it was a large gathering. This conduct put me out of sorts, for all day I remained in charge of the work party and ensured the supervision of the men from the longboat. Seven of the *Casuarina*'s crew, who had been put ashore first thing in the morning without anyone to supervise them, had made off into the hills or gone fishing; consequently, they did not appear until dark and the longboat was unable to finish during the afternoon all the work that had to be done, since I was obliged to have everyone there collect the cut wood from the foot of the hill. I did not take things quietly and went back to the ship in my boat after dark, after giving the men from the longboat orders to sleep ashore so as to be better prepared for doing the work that remained to be done the next day.

When I arrived at the tents, I found no one but Citizen Guichenot, who was still busy with his plants and collections. I was told that Citizen Leschenault, the botanist, had gone to visit M. Bernier, and that the second doctor and M. Péron, our observer of mankind, had gone to dinner aboard the *Casuarina*. They all returned in the evening; but Citizen Freycinet did not appear, and it was a very good thing that he did not, for I was in a mood to teach him a thing or two about his duty and about not wasting his time partying when there is urgent work to be done.

According to his report, the gardener had collected more than 150 different species of plants during his stay ashore and had made up 68 pots of living specimens. This was all work and no talk.

No doubt Citizens Péron and Leschenault will have written 60 pages which, in inverse proportion, will be all talk and no work.

If Baudin did at least find some satisfaction in the work of the botanists, who would eventually collect about 200 new species during the stay in King George Sound, a further source of satisfaction was the news, brought by Ransonnet, of a friendly encounter with the Aborigines.

## 27 FEBRUARY 1803

At about three in the afternoon we learnt that M. Ransonnet's dinghy was on the way back. He was back on board ship around six o'clock. According to his verbal report, he discovered three harbours that were very suitable for ships of medium size, as they were 3¹/₂ to 4 fathoms deep at most. He also had the opportunity to communicate with the natives of the region, who did not appear unsociable; indeed, they were the first to demonstrate their friendly intentions, since they began by putting their weapons to one side before approaching the men from the dinghy, who did the same and then moved among them. Everyone communicated as best they could by signs and the greater part of the day was spent together on very good terms, but the natives would not allow anyone near the spot where they had confined their wives, who were three in number to their five. They made no fuss about eating and drinking all they were given and thoroughly enjoyed the sailors' cooking. As we had forgotten to put in the dinghy the presents that I normally intended for the natives whenever it was possible to communicate with them, our men could only give them their coat buttons, which were valued highly, handkerchiefs and a few jackets that were the worse for wear and which they did not like nearly as much.

Their work in King George Sound completed, the two ships then prepared to set sail. The instructions given to Freycinet by Baudin on 28 February are revealing, since they appear to leave the door open for the captain of the *Casuarina* to leave the expedition and return home in the event of another separation.

> To Citizen Freycinet, Commander of the schooner, *Casuarina*
>
> Citizen, you have already been advised in the last instructions I gave you at Borda Island [Kangaroo Island] that, when I left King George Sound, I would go to Geographe Bay in order to complete the remaining geographical work on that part of the coast.
>
> Before entering that bay, I intend to put in at St Allouarn Island for one day only so as to take accurate measurements of its latitude and longitude, which I believe to be extremely questionable on the French and English charts.
>
> If I have favourable winds and the weather is fine, I shall perhaps stay for three or four days on Rottnest Island and from there I shall go to Dirk Hartog Bay [Dampier Road] to obtain some turtles before heading further north. However, I draw your attention to the fact that these last two stops are more probable than certain.
>
> Whether they take place or not, I shall stop off for a while at the north-west point of New Holland in order to make absolutely sure that the place the Dutch named Willem's River is not an island, as I suspect. If we happen to become separated at sea while on our way there, this point will be a meeting place and the only one that I can indicate to you . . .
>
> From now on it is thus up to you and you alone as to whether you accompany me or not. I have always done everything in my power to prevent the two separations that have already occurred and that you were in a good position to prevent, either by your handling of your ship or by carrying out the orders I gave you. So you will be personally accountable to the government for the expenses incurred in the equipping of your ship, since they will have become a charge on the State and unnecessary for the expedition.

The two ships did indeed become separated, just one week later, when the *Casuarina*, sent to survey a section of coast close to shore, was slow in returning. Baudin's impatience with Freycinet was rapidly turning to exasperation.

On the 17th [Ventôse – 8 March] the winds changed from south-south-east to south, stiff breeze. We hauled in at the very spot where I had sent the *Casuarina*, but she was nowhere to be seen and I made the decision to continue on my way. It was quite enough to have wasted two days waiting for her to carry out a reconnaissance that was a simple matter of three hours, since I had given her express orders to come and report to me if the openings that I had indicated to her were the entrances to any ports or not. I had also forbidden her to stop there if the weather was fine.

This officer, who is insubordinate on principle, has been incapable up till now of discharging a single duty or even obeying the orders I have given him. So that is why, if he rejoins me at Rottnest Island, which I designated to him as a meeting place, there is every likelihood that I shall relieve him of his command to see if someone else will do better at carrying out the orders that I shall give him as circumstances dictate.

Baudin was anxious, in fact, to conduct a new survey of the coast north from Cape Leeuwin which he had first visited nearly two years earlier.

On the morning of the 18th [Ventôse – 9 March] we sighted Cape Leeuwin and at daylight we saw St Allouarn Island which we had tried to find in vain when we first examined this coast. From this we concluded that the point that we had taken to be Cape Leeuwin was not the one that corresponded to the name – at least, not according to the chart of Beautemps-Beaupré, the geographer.

In the morning we began a new survey of this entire coast, as we considered what had previously been done to be very poor.

Since I am accountable to the government for this time we have wasted, I am obliged to inform it that all our scientists were so inexperienced in their own particular fields that they were unable to be of any use until the expedition was nearly over – assuming that they were willing to work in order to acquire the necessary knowledge and especially the experience in this kind of work which, with all the theory in the world, will always be incomplete when it is being done for the first time and one's eye has not been trained to judge either the distance of a coast or the depth of a bay. This was definitely the case with our geographers, present and future. At a league off shore, the whole coast appeared to them to run in a straight line and on an even plane. As practice has improved their judgment since then, it is likely that the work they are doing now will be worthwhile and that their charts will be well drawn up.

This criticism of the previous survey done by his geographers was perhaps a little unfair, given that they had not been able to get as close to the coast as they would have liked.

Baudin was surprised, a few days later, to find the *Casuarina* at the rendezvous point off Rottnest Island.

## 13 MARCH 1803

At daybreak on the 22nd [Ventôse] we were about three leagues from the coast, which was definitely established as being Rottnest Island. As the weather was very fine and the sea calm, and as we were to the north of the island, I headed for the anchorage to wait for the *Casuarina*. I did so, having indicated it to her as a meeting place if the weather turned bad while she was away reconnoitring the section of the coast I had assigned to her – and where there was good reason to think she had stopped. But around seven o'clock we sighted her at the anchorage. After seeing us, she got under sail. This unexpected encounter brought me to the decision to go on, since this place had already been explored by the *Naturaliste* and it was not worth my while to stop off there. All that can be said of it, according to the report of Captain Hamelin and his officers, who stayed there for quite a long time, is that the anchorage is very poor and unstable; it is fully exposed to the winds from south-west to north-west and, in these conditions, the sea is very heavy. The Swan River, which was explored for 18 to 20 leagues up-stream, offers no resources at all. Fresh water was occasionally found in the streams that run into it, but they are very small.

Keen to head back to Shark Bay, Baudin sailed on, with Freycinet following close behind.

The six-day stay in Shark Bay was most notable for an encounter with a large group of Aborigines, most probably from the Nanda tribe, whose hostile attitude put great fear into the hearts of a French shore party and prevented them from landing. Undeterred, Baudin decided to send another party to shore the following day under the command of Sub-Lieutenant Bonnefoi, in order to make contact with these local people. This time, plenty of firearms were taken, though the instructions made it clear that bloodshed should be avoided. These precautions proved unnecessary, however, as the Aborigines had departed, abandoning their huts. Baudin was keen to have an accurate pictorial record of these huts, so he sent the ship's artist, Petit, to shore, accompanied by a number of the naturalists – among whose number was François Péron who, true to form, went off exploring with Petit and Guichenot, the gardener, delaying the return of the shore party and causing Baudin considerable concern.

*Native huts on Peron Peninsula, View of Bernier Island and part of Dorre Island*, engraving by Milbert, Pillement and Née from a drawing by Charles-Alexandre Lesueur. Published in the *Atlas* of the *Voyage de découvertes aux Terres Australes* (1807)

## 20 MARCH 1803

At sunset I was surprised to see that no one on the longboat was making any preparations for returning to the ship. But since I had given the officer on board express orders to be back before dark, I assumed that they were not yet all back at the boat and that he had been delayed by the absence of certain people – one of whom had to be Citizen Péron.

Whatever the case, at eight o'clock, when I saw that the same fires had been kept going from the day before, I gave the order to fire a cannon shot to call the boat back to the ship. At ten o'clock it had still not returned and we fired a second shot that had no more success than the first; consequently, I lost all hope of making the tour that I had planned for the following day in the south-west part of the peninsula. Since the absence of my longboat constitutes a formal act of disobedience to the orders that the commanding officer received from me, I have had thirty francs added to his account to pay for the two blank cannon shots that he obliged me to use up in calling him back.

Baudin had every reason to be annoyed – and concerned – as the following account shows.

## 21 MARCH 1803

By half past one the longboat had returned and was moored alongside the ship. The officer in command informed me that he had 600 pounds of excellent salt that had been collected from a saltwater pool, which was currently almost dried up. After the news of his duties on shore, I asked him why he had not complied with the orders I had given him to return at sunset the following day. He then informed me that he had been placed in a very awkward position by the absence of Citizens Péron, Guichenot and Petit, who had left him in the morning without telling him anything of their plans and had not reappeared in the afternoon. However, as they had set off without water or food supplies, he had assumed that they could not be far from the meeting place, unless they had become lost. He further told me that when he had still not sighted them by four o'clock, he had immediately sent out four armed men who had searched for them in different directions until dark and had come back without meeting up with them. Citizen Bonnefoi, fearing my reproaches if he did not bring everyone back and also knowing full well that he would be reprimanded for not returning, thought it best to spend the night waiting for them a little longer. Finally, at about nine o'clock in the evening, the three missing people reappeared, worn out and drained from hunger and thirst. Two of them lay down 12 or 15 feet from the tent and had to be carried to it.

After hearing more of the details, I learnt that Citizen Péron, the most irresponsible and thoughtless person on board, had persuaded the two others to cross the island from east to west, by assuring them that it was a league in width at the very most, that he had ascertained this from an examination of the chart and that, consequently, they had much more time than they needed for the excursion he was proposing. To help them make up their minds, he promised Citizen Guichenot he would be sure to make a large collection of new plants along the way and Citizen Petit that there would be many enjoyable things for him to do, which sounded good to him. Finally, they both agreed to fall in with Citizen Péron's plans and set off. They began by climbing up a slope to a fairly high point from which they could see the ship clearly. This same hill, with a tallish tree on it, was chosen as a landmark to which they were to return on their way back. This then was the point from which they took their bearings for the one league trek that they would make to cross the island.

After walking for about four hours straight, without the slightest break and in the heat of the sun, Guichenot, the gardener, said to Citizen Péron: 'The league that you told us about is getting very long and I think it's time to think about returning, for our walk back to the longboat must be as long as the one we've been on since we left.' Citizen Péron was certainly conscious of the soundness of this argument, but he got around it by saying: 'We haven't gone far enough to the left. That's what will have made our walk longer. Let's go in that direction now and we'll soon get to where we're going.' They followed him as if he were an experienced guide and, as they went on, several natives appeared, armed with spears. At first, they were frightened, as their only means of defence was a faulty gun that they had borrowed from the ship's steward and that would not fire, as they discovered when they tried it out. As the natives were still following them, they thought it would be better to impress them by putting up a bold front rather than to run away and so they decided to walk up to them.

The natives in turn stopped, but seeing that our men were still coming towards them, they also came forward. However, they did not walk as fast and our men drew near enough for them all to see one another clearly. The natives began by signalling our three fearful men to follow them – something which they were careful to avoid. As the two parties stood facing one another, all the natives except one moved aside. Our men thought he was the chief. This probably would have been the right time to approach him, but as they made no move in that direction, the native who appeared to be the chief took a few steps forward, signalled to them by broad gestures that they should go away and spoke very loudly. He was obeyed to the letter, for our wayward travellers, who did not consider their numbers adequate, left them and set out again in the direction that would lead them to the coast on the other side of the island, which they finally reached at one in the afternoon.

On this occasion, we missed the greatest opportunity that had arisen to communicate with the natives, and the artist, whom I had sent expressly to draw those we could get close to, did nothing but a view of the village inhabited by the people we encountered on our first landing on the island.

Rounded huts (Shark Bay), Charles-Alexandre Lesueur or Nicolas-Martin Petit. Muséum d'histoire naturelle, Le Havre – n° 16 033

After leaving the natives, they started looking for shells and brought back several that were absolutely the same as those that the *Naturaliste* had found and collected in great numbers. This thought alone should have been enough to remind them of the need to return, but the leader of the party – the citizen who, until now, has caused us nothing but trouble and anxiety when he has been ashore with no one to supervise and guide him – preferred to waste the remaining time fooling about on the shore rather than return. Consequently, they only set off when it was certain that they would not get back before the appointed time of departure, even assuming that they had taken the most direct route. At any rate, our travellers definitely thought far too late about returning, considering they had neither food nor water. Then night fell and added to their difficulties by causing them to get lost and wander completely off course. Pure chance was of greater use to them in this situation than the bearings they took, for they found themselves on the opposite shore just when their calculation of the distance that they had covered had them still three leagues away.

When Citizen Péron came to inform me of his return, he told me that he was not in a position to account to me for his actions and, before making his official report, he asked me to allow him the long rest that he no doubt greatly needed, since he could hardly speak or stand.

There is nothing much to report about the rest of the day. Guichenot, the gardener, did not find a single plant and was sick with exhaustion from having obligingly carried the whole way the 25 to 30 pounds in weight of worthless shells that had been collected with as much pleasure as care by Citizen Péron, who himself had to be carried back to the tent.

This is the third escapade of this kind that our learned naturalist has inflicted on us, but it will also be the last, for he shall not go ashore again unless I myself am in the boat in which he is travelling, and the limits that I shall set to his excursions will not allow him enough scope to delay the boat's departure or to wander too far away.

Baudin's next task was to conduct a more accurate survey of the long stretch of coast from North-West Cape to the Bonaparte Archipelago. However, as had been the case two years earlier, the numerous sandbanks and reefs made a close survey difficult. Baudin was also reluctant to allow the *Casuarina*, despite its shallower draught and Freycinet's willingness, to venture in behind the many offshore islands. In hydrographic terms, this second survey was nevertheless more successful than the first, with many features being charted in greater detail, correcting some of the inaccuracies contained both in the earlier Dutch maps and in their own 1801 charts.

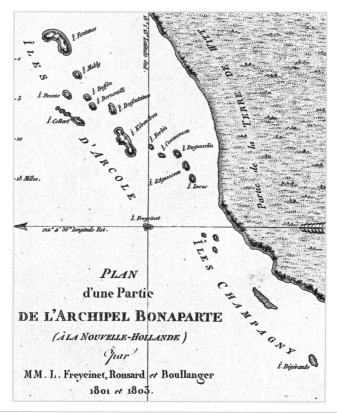

Map of part of the Bonaparte Archipelago, L. Freycinet, Ronsard and Boullanger (1801, 1803). Published in the *Atlas* of the *Voyage de découvertes aux Terres Australes* (1811)

The only other incident of note on this leg of the journey was an unusual encounter near Cassini Island.

## 25 APRIL 1803

At midday we again sighted our dinghy returning from the bay it had entered, and at two o'clock it was aboard.

The news that it brought us was quite extraordinary. The men had seen four big canoes which set sail at sunrise and headed towards the third island within our sight. They left from a sandy cove about 200 paces from where the dinghy was anchored. As soon as the men saw them, they set sail in pursuit to try to join them, but since the canoes moved much faster than the dinghy, with the aid of their paddles, they quickly drew away. While our men were off the point of the cove from which they had set out, they saw two more canoes, one setting sail and the other still at anchor. They then changed direction in order to join up with one of them. The one that had set sail escaped, but the third was finally pulled up when our men put on a show of strength by threatening to fire at it if it continued to row. When the canoe and the dinghy were alongside one another, our men were quite astonished to see that the five men on board the canoe were all of Malay origin and were dressed and armed entirely in the manner of the Timorese. Their dress consisted of a piece of cloth wound round their waist and between their thighs and tucked up at the back. Their head-wear consisted of a handkerchief tied around the head. All were armed with a dagger or a type of kris in the Malay style. Their canoe was long, raised at both ends and very well maintained; it was also freshly painted in black and white. At one end, in the stern, hung some bows, about four or five feet long, and several wooden boxes containing arrows.

At first the Malays were very frightened of our men, but they soon became more friendly when they saw that we only wanted to talk to them and that we did them no harm. Some of our men got into their canoe, while one of them boarded our dinghy.

The unlikelihood of making such a chance encounter meant that the men had no present to give them, so all we could exchange with them was some biscuit for turtles' eggs. The Malays made it clear that they wanted rum, but we told them they could only get some if they went on board the ship, which they were most reluctant to do. They offered the crew some water that they stored in a kind of jar similar to those that we had bought in Timor and very like the ones produced in most of the islands to the north of New Holland. They also beckoned to our men to follow them. However, as they were poorly armed and virtually defenceless – for the reason that I could not have imagined anyone visiting this island – they did not think they ought to trust their guide and preferred to return to the ship to tell me what had happened to them.

Baudin manned his large dinghy again and sent it, under the command of the master helmsman, Fortin, to follow the praus in the hope that he might be able to interview the Malay fishermen and find out more about their activities in these waters. Two days later Fortin returned with the news that the four large Malay praus were part of a sizeable flotilla of craft from Macassar on an annual expedition fishing for trepang. These were in great demand as aphrodisiacs in the markets of China.

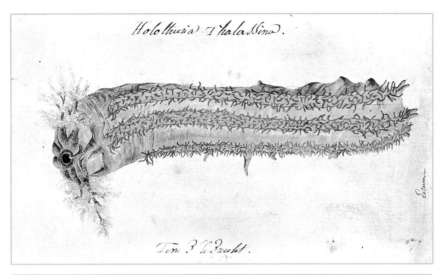

Sea cucumber (north-west Australia), *Holothuria* sp., Charles-Alexandre Lesueur. Muséum d'histoire naturelle, Le Havre – n° 74 079

Baudin's intention had been to press on and complete his survey of the north-west coast before making for the Gulf of Carpentaria. However, with his health deteriorating and the winds remaining frustratingly weak, he decided to break off and head once again for Timor, where the captain's physical condition, and his relations with the naturalists and the other officers, took further turns for the worse.

# chapter thirteen

# THE JOURNEY BACK

Northern Australia, Timor and Mauritius provided the stage on which a number of dramatic scenes were played out as both Baudin and Flinders wound up their expeditions and headed for home. Here again, some uncanny parallels can be drawn: neither captain would realise his ambition of conducting a thorough survey of Australia's north coast, though Flinders at least made it to the Gulf of Carpentaria; their visits to Timor left both expeditions with a legacy of serious illness; a stopover at the island of Mauritius was to prove fateful for Flinders and Baudin alike, albeit in different ways; and circumstances meant that neither captain was to bask in the glory of a hero's welcome back home.

## Cruel Twists and Bitter Conclusions: Baudin from Timor to Mauritius

On 29 April 1803 Baudin finally decided to interrupt his second survey of Australia's north-west coast and head for Timor. A key factor in this decision was the weather: weak winds not only made progress difficult, they also appeared to signal a change in the monsoonal season. A brief stay in Timor would allow the expedition some time to replenish supplies in anticipation of more favourable conditions. Baudin's thinking was no doubt also coloured by health concerns. Happily, and in contrast to their first survey of the north-western coast of Australia, the crew members on board the two French ships were not suffering from any outbreak of disease or illness – the lime juice taken on board at Port Jackson appears to have been effective in staving off the dreaded scurvy, in particular. The same could not be said, however, of their captain, who was by now experiencing severe chest pains and a nagging cough. Some respite from the duties and physical demands of navigation might therefore give him the chance to regain his strength for the next leg of the journey. Baudin's intention was indeed to resume his survey as soon as possible, paying particular attention to the Gulf of Carpentaria and New Guinea.

This second stopover in Timor, which lasted just one month, was considerably shorter than the first, but was no less rich in incident and drama. One particularly regrettable incident was a conflict that arose between Henri Freycinet and François-Michel Ronsard over the issue of seniority. Though engaged as an engineer, Ronsard had also spent quite a deal of time on watch during the course of the expedition and had enjoyed the challenge of these added responsibilities. He was particularly busy in Kupang Bay, maintaining order and supervising the movement of men and supplies to and from the *Géographe* in the absence of his captain, who had decided to stay on shore as much as possible. To all intents and purposes, he had for some time been fulfilling the duties of a first lieutenant and was beginning to feel aggrieved by Baudin's failure to acknowledge this officially. Added to this sense of frustration was the aggravation caused by the behaviour of Freycinet, who was independently performing some of the same functions at anchor in Timor, such as according shore leave. The absence of a clear line of authority and responsibility was a serious problem and one that should not have been allowed to arise. When Baudin finally decided to resolve the matter, he adopted a course of action that stunned everyone: he would put it to the vote.

> Tomorrow . . . I shall assemble the crew so that they can tell me which of the two of you they prefer to have as leader; their choice will be irrevocable, for it is only appropriate that men should be commanded by those who suit them best and in whom they have the most confidence.

The vote was heavily in favour of Henri Freycinet (60 to 12), which was hardly surprising given that Ronsard had been primarily responsible for discipline up to that point. Ronsard was understandably scandalised by the whole affair and decided then and there to take up Baudin's offer of permission to leave the expedition – an offer that was almost immediately withdrawn. That the saga left a bitter taste in his mouth was all the more unfortunate as Ronsard had shown himself to be both reliable and loyal. These were qualities that the captain felt all along to be in short supply.

Another episode of an altogether more comical nature provided a welcome contrast. François Péron decided to take advantage of the stay in Timor to embark on a crocodile hunt – not for sport but in the name of science. Accompanied by the artist Lesueur, he set off for the Babao marshes, where he soon found a suitable specimen. It fell to the artist to shoot the crocodile and the two Frenchmen then set about the task of skinning and dissecting it. However, in deference to the superstitions held by the local population with regard to these animals, Péron and Lesueur had to purify themselves by bathing twenty times in a trough of water, before donning Malay robes and attending a feast in their honour. Such a sight would no doubt have lifted the spirits of many among the officers and crew, and might even have brought a wry smile to the captain's face. By the time they made it back to port, the crocodile's skin had completely rotted and had to be discarded; the skeleton, on the other hand, eventually found its way to the Museum in Paris.

Based on the experience of the earlier stay in Timor, Baudin's principal concern would have been the health risks to which the visitors were likely to be exposed. Unfortunately, this second sojourn only confirmed the island's reputation as a hotbed of sickness and disease. When the expedition set sail on 3 June 1803, many of its members were already in the infirmary, struck down with fever or venereal disease. The fact that this did not lead to a repeat of the series of deaths that followed the 1801 visit would have offered at least some comfort had it not been for the one exception to this rule: on 5 June, the astronomer Bernier succumbed to fever, aged only 23. Baudin was deeply saddened by this loss – so much so, in fact, that it appears to have led to an aggravation of his own condition.

## 4 JUNE 1803

From the doctor's report I learnt that many of the crew had been struck down by venereal disease. Citizen Bernier, who had had a fever for the past four days, appeared to be coming down with a serious illness, as did the artist Petit. They had both been in very good health during the stopover and it was only two or three days before our departure that they began to feel slightly indisposed . . .

When I paid my visit to Citizen Bernier during the morning, I found him much worse than the day before and began to fear that he was coming down with a really serious illness, so depressed and haggard did he look – whereas the day before we chatted and talked together for more than an hour and he was very well . . .

During the afternoon the doctor came to inform me that Citizen Bernier had just shown the most disturbing signs that the end was near. He was convulsed with hiccoughs, and the changes in his pulse-rate were so violent and irregular that they gave us grave fears for his life. The doctor thought it advisable to apply the flies. I immediately went to see him, but found him unconscious, with the signs of death written all over his face. Incapable of being hardened to such a sight, I left the room. Besides, he had lost consciousness. I was so struck by the suddenness of the change that a feeling of sickness invaded my whole body and forced me to go to bed much earlier than usual. But for all that, I did not find the rest that I needed. During the night, I had bouts of spitting blood similar to those I had already had on two different occasions, and the sputum that I brought up was so thick that you would have said it was pieces of lung coming away from my body.

When the end finally came for Bernier, in the early hours of the following morning, Baudin was moved to note in his log:

## 5 JUNE 1803

This death, which can almost be regarded as a sudden death, had such an effect on me that it would be difficult to express all that I suffered. The loss of Citizen Bernier is an unhappy event, not only for us, but also for the government, for there is no doubt that he would have become a learned astronomer who was of service to his country. He had a natural aptitude for that science which had become for him both his occupation and a source of pleasure. Up till the day before his death, his work will no doubt have been in order and I am quite confident that the government will be pleased with it . . . I sincerely regret him on my own account and I have no hesitation in saying that, of all the scientists allotted to me, he was the one who worked the hardest, whether in acquiring new knowledge or carrying out the government's wishes.

While nothing could compensate for this tragic loss, some solace might be found in fulfilling the mission to chart the Gulf of Carpentaria. Unfortunately, this goal was ultimately to elude the French. Contrary to Baudin's expectations, the winds were not favourable to an easterly course; and this frustration was compounded by the slowness of the *Casuarina*, which frequently caused the *Géographe* to shorten sail and reduce its speed in order to wait for it. Conditions on board were also becoming decidedly uncomfortable due to persistent rain and a heavy swell. After persevering for a month, Baudin had made it no further than the middle of the Arafura Sea at a point a little east of Melville Island and present-day Darwin. On 7 July 1803, with the health of the animals on board deteriorating, and suffering himself from renewed bouts of coughing, Baudin finally resigned himself to abandoning his project and signalled to the *Casuarina* to turn round and make for Mauritius.

## 7 JULY 1803

During the morning I was informed that several of our quadrupeds and emus were very sick. The only reason we could find for this were the violent and increasing swells of the heavy sea, which did not allow them a moment's peace. This news was all the more unpleasant to me, in that I could see myself about to lose them after giving them the kind of care that should have earned them a happier fate. As the emus refused to eat, we force-fed them by opening their beaks and introducing pellets of rice mash into their stomachs. We gave them wine and sugar, as we also did to the sick kangaroos, and, although I was running out of these same things for my own use, I shall be very happy to have gone without them for their sake if they can help restore them to health.

On this same day I had a bout of spitting blood that was worse than any I had had before. I did not know what caused it, for I had not had an incidence of this problem for about a week and I thought I had shaken it for a while. Whether as a consequence of this illness, or for any other reason, this blood spitting was accompanied by such weakness in all the limbs that I was forced to take to my bed – which did not bring me much relief . . .

After midday the winds changed to south-east, and so we went about on a south-south-west tack. We held this course until eight o'clock, when we brought to in order to wait for the *Casuarina*, which did not catch up with us until ten o'clock. As it was a matter of absolute necessity to decide whether we sent her back and persisted in our attempt to reach the entrance to the Gulf of Carpentaria, or whether we gave up all hope of getting there and continued on in her company, I made up my mind to head for Ile de France [Mauritius] and gave her orders to steer south-west by west, taking the same course myself. I did not take this decision lightly. A thousand reasons should even have made me take it earlier, but without listing them all, I shall simply say that we had no more than a month's supply of biscuit, at the rate of six ounces per person, and two months' water, as a result of the water consumption of the birds and quadrupeds. Twenty men were in sick bay: several suffering from dysentery, the others unfit for duty because of serious venereal diseases contracted on shore. Nobody to replace me. The *Casuarina*, whose speed I have never managed to improve, in spite of all my efforts, and which is the one and only reason why I was not able to reach this gulf a long time ago, etc, etc, etc.

As disappointed as the captain was, the decision to head for Mauritius was welcomed with great joy and relief by almost everyone else on board. In fact, many of those on deck that night went regularly to check the compass, just to make sure it was true.

It took exactly one month for the *Géographe* to reach Mauritius, with the *Casuarina* arriving five days later on 12 August. During the first two weeks of this leg, they had enjoyed favourable conditions – a fact which, paradoxically, only added to the impatience of some of Baudin's officers as they felt the frustration of having to wait repeatedly for the *Casuarina* to catch up. The second half of the journey was far more unpleasant as they endured rain, heavy seas and a storm during which the two ships became separated, with the *Casuarina* also losing a man overboard. Two of Baudin's four emus had also died.

All the same, the arrival at Port Louis was a source of considerable relief and joy as the sailors were reunited with their compatriots, a number of whom they had met on the outward journey. They also found letters from friends and family at Mauritius, and were given some news of the *Naturaliste*, which had been forced to call there on its way home. The letter that Hamelin had left for Baudin contained the welcome news that, with the exception of the loss of a Samoan turtle, the animals and plants were generally in good health. Sadly, though, the mineralogist Depuch, who had been left behind at Mauritius, had recently succumbed to dysentery.

No further news of the fate of the *Naturaliste* was available at that time on the island. It would no doubt have cheered Baudin to learn that she had arrived home at Le Havre on 7 June with her cargo of animals and plants mostly intact. With the renewal of hostilities between France and England, however, Hamelin had been forced to spend ten days at Portsmouth after the captain of an English frigate had intercepted him and questioned the nature of his passport.

In Mauritius, Baudin's first concern was to arrange for the sick to be properly cared for. His own health continued to worry the doctors, but he remained defiantly confident that it was on the mend. He clearly wanted to give everyone a good rest before setting out to sea again, planning to stay on the island until December, when the change of season would ensure more favourable conditions for sailing. This would also be of benefit to the animals, birds and plants, whose welfare was of prime concern to Baudin. The success of the entire expedition would be measured in large part by the degree to which it had fulfilled its scientific mission, and Baudin was understandably anxious about the welfare of all his live specimens.

He took lodgings at Mauritius with a certain Mme Kérivel – a widow

*Port Louis: From the Eastern Side of the Harbour*. Published in T. Bradshaw, *Views in the Mauritius, or Isle of France* (London: James Carpenter & Son, 1832). Reproduced courtesy of the Royal Geographical Society of South Australia

who had become a good friend. In addition to the hospitality she gave to the French captain, she was kind enough to offer her garden as a place of refuge where the animals and plants could be properly cared for. Baudin took advantage of this stopover to catch up on some correspondence. Along with some letters of an official nature that he sent to the authorities in Paris, he wrote to his friend Governor King on 18 August 1803 to bring him up to date with the events that had taken place since his previous letter.

> I hasten to take advantage of an American ship which, after picking up some of its crew who had been left on Saint Paul and Amsterdam Islands, intends to make for Port Jackson to sell furs and other assorted objects that it is transporting to your country.
>
> Since I last had the honour of seeing you, I have spent nine months exploring the coast of New Holland, a task which is now finally completed but not without several gaps.
>
> During my second stay at Timor, I was informed of Mr Flinders' passage and of the poor state of his ship. I sincerely hope that he returned to you with no further accident.

The *Naturaliste*, after leaving King Island, took 41 days to reach Mauritius, from which it departed immediately. It must have arrived in France some time ago. Its collections of live animals and plants were in excellent condition. Mr and Mrs Thomson were well and had the most pleasant stay they could have wished.

At the entrance to the Gulf of Carpenteria I lost M. Bernier, our astronomer, whose death we all mourned and who was known to you. As for me, I have suffered two bouts of illness, and to such a point that the doctors often decided that my time was up, but they were wrong and, since my arrival, I have begun to recover.

I have set my date of departure for France for next December. They say that at the present time there are several political differences between your nation and mine, but I hope that the dark cloud that has appeared will be dispersed without our hearing the roar of the thunder. In any case, I commit myself to our friendship and trust you to believe that we shall always be friends.

Baudin's optimism regarding his health was to prove ill-founded: one month after writing this letter, on 16 September 1803, he was dead. It is perhaps not unsurprising, but nevertheless sad, to note that very few of the officers and naturalists showed any great distress at the loss of their commandant. Commander Milius seems to be one of the few to have shown an appreciation both of Baudin's selfless dedication to the expedition and of the sadness he must have felt at not being able to see it through to the very end: 'The Commandant must undoubtedly have suffered greatly to see himself thwarted in this way and he was even more sorely tried by his illness and spitting of blood.' He describes him as arriving at Mauritius 'overwhelmed by fatigue and devoured by worry', and notes his great spirit of sacrifice. Charles Baudin, in his journal, was another to show his emotion at the circumstances of Baudin's death and the pitiful send-off he was given.

His funeral was nothing less than dismal: he was universally detested. He had shown great strength of spirit in his last days. He had collected in a jar of spirits of wine the lungs he had brought up in the course of his untold suffering and he showed them to everyone who came to visit him.

There was nothing in the least bit gruesome or emotional in the matter-of-fact way in which his death was recorded by Péron and Louis Freycinet in the second volume of the official account of the voyage.

Since our arrival in the colony, his condition had become much worse; for a long time, all hope of a cure had been lost and the doctors' efforts were intended only to defer for a few days the end determined by the nature of his illness. At last the moment arrived and on 16 September 1803, around noon, M. Baudin ceased to exist . . . On the 17th he was interred with the honours due to the rank he held in the Navy. All the officers, all the scientists of the expedition were present at the procession, which was attended also by the principal authorities of the colony.

While Baudin did not survive the expedition, he would no doubt have hoped its achievements would ensure that his name would live on. However, he was to be denied his rightful place in the pantheon of great French navigators by the naturalist whose behaviour had been such a cause of irritation for him. In Volume I of the official account, published in Paris in 1807, François Péron contrived not to mention Baudin once by name. Referring to him only as 'our leader' or 'the commandant', he took every opportunity to denigrate Baudin as a sailor and as a man, thereby exacting further revenge for the disparaging remarks the captain had made about him. Whatever his shortcomings may have been, Baudin did not deserve to be written out of history in this way.

It was anticipated that Henri Freycinet would succeed Baudin as captain of the *Géographe*. To Freycinet's dismay, however, the colony's new governor, General Decaen, in consultation with Admiral Linois, chose Milius instead. Milius set about supervising the refitting and reprovisioning of the ship and, despite the difficulties caused by the obstructiveness of the island's administrators, he was able to set sail for home as planned on 16 December 1803, just one day before Matthew Flinders limped into Port Louis.

## The Long Way Home:
## Flinders from Port Jackson to England

The circumnavigation of Australia, completed in a leaky, barely seaworthy vessel, negotiating waters which were often treacherous and conditions which were at best unpredictable, not to mention the constant threat of disease, was an achievement of sustained heroism. But it was the attempted voyage home which was to provide the most acute instance of Flinders' bravery and his seafaring skill, and all that on a voyage on which he was a mere passenger.

Planning to return to England by sailing north and making passage initially to Batavia through Torres Strait, the *Porpoise*, under the command of Captain Fowler, was escorted by two merchantmen, the *Bridgewater* and the *Cato*.

Off the Queensland coast, disaster struck. During the night of 17 August 1803, the *Porpoise* ran onto a reef. A gun was fired to warn the other two vessels, but for the *Cato* it was too late, and it crashed onto the same reef. Flinders resolved to row a boat to the *Bridgewater* to discuss a rescue mission with its commander, Captain E.H. Palmer. In the darkness of night and amid strong winds, the task was impossible, so he waited. Morning revealed that, although the *Porpoise* was irreparably damaged, none of the crew was lost; the *Cato*, worse affected, was largely submerged, its crew crying desperately for help. On the positive side, they spied a sandbank sizeable enough to accommodate both crews, and the *Bridgewater* was still hovering in sight, its captain apparently contemplating a rescue. But Palmer, in a decision that showed brazen cowardliness, declined to attempt such a mission. After negotiating his way through patches of hazardous reef, he lay to one more night, then set sail for Batavia.

*View of Wreck Reef bank taken at low water, Terra Australis* (1803), William Westall. National Library of Australia

Flinders had little choice but to arrange his own rescue. He used a boat to retrieve the remaining crew of the *Cato* – three had drowned – and take them to the *Porpoise* where they could be fed and clothed. Provisions from the *Porpoise* were transferred to the dry sandbank. Later Flinders, having assumed command in his capacity as senior officer on the reef, gathered the 94 survivors together and proclaimed that all 'should be put on the same footing and united under one head'. A council of officers then agreed that Flinders should lead an expedition to Port Jackson in the large cutter to seek the governor's assistance in a rescue. On 26 August 1803 Flinders, accompanied by Captain Park and a crew of 12, set sail, leaving Captain Fowler to maintain discipline and preserve the sagging spirits of those left behind on what was aptly to be named Wreck Reef. They had a long wait ahead of them.

Governor King must have been taken aback when, during dinner with his family, the figures of Flinders and Captain Park, both presumably looking the worse for wear, appeared on his doorstep. So touched was the governor by the visitors' story of the tragedy of Wreck Reef, wrote Flinders later, that 'an involuntary tear started from the eye of friendship and compassion, and we were received in the most affectionate manner.' Like Flinders, King was not one to dally. He negotiated with the captain of the privately owned *Rolla*, which in any case was about to leave Port Jackson for Canton (now Guangzhou), to sail via Wreck Reef and pick up all those who preferred to return to England on that route. For those who wished to return to Port Jackson, the schooner *Francis* was despatched. As for Flinders himself, still eager to return to England without delay so as to negotiate the recommencement of his great voyage of exploration, the 29-ton *Cumberland*, at that time in service on the Hawkesbury River, was placed at his disposal. Small though it was, and unsuited to ocean sailing, Flinders planned to take it all the way back to England.

Together, the three vessels left Port Jackson on 20 September 1803 and arrived at the reef on 7 October, exactly six weeks after Flinders' initial departure on his rescue mission. The survivors no doubt thanked the heavens for Flinders' superb seamanship, but Flinders for his part had already cast his mind to the voyage ahead, selecting crew members to accompany him on the *Cumberland*. Little were they to know that, for the purpose of returning to their homeland, they would have been much better served taking the *Rolla* to China and making their way from there.

Given the size of the *Cumberland*, it was inevitable that she would need to make some stops for reprovisioning along the way. She followed the path of the *Investigator* through Torres Strait and then to Kupang. From there, ideally, she would have made a quick passage to the Cape of Good Hope, avoiding the French possession of Mauritius, as Governor King had explicitly suggested Flinders should do. But it seems that Flinders was condemned to make the most crucial of voyages during his career on vessels which were barely seaworthy. This certainly proved the case for the little *Cumberland*, especially after the call at Kupang, when only one of the two pumps could be employed to cope with increasingly heavy seas. It was in these circumstances that Flinders made his most fateful decision of all: in order to reprovision the *Cumberland*, to caulk it, and to pursue the possibility that he might find an alternative vessel to take him to England, Flinders decided to set course for Mauritius. Among a host of lesser reasons for calling there, he also listed: 'Learning some further intelligence on the *Géographe* and the *Naturaliste*.'

When Flinders had left Port Jackson, to the best of his knowledge the fragile Peace of Amiens still held. In fact, by the time he arrived in Mauritius, circumstances had changed; France and England were again at war, as he was soon to find out. Land was sighted on 15 December, and when the opportunity presented itself, the *Cumberland* followed a schooner into a harbour called the Baie du Cap. The reaction of the people on board the schooner surprised Flinders, as upon landing they fetched an army officer who, in the company of several men bearing muskets, approached the *Cumberland*. Flinders enjoined them to come on board, but they refused. Instead, one of Flinders' crew, Mr Aken, went ashore to show the French passport which Flinders had carried since the beginning of the *Investigator*'s voyage. He also carried letters from Governor King which were to be conveyed to the previous governor of Mauritius, General Magallon. All these documents were perused and returned; the French officer then boarded the *Cumberland* to speak with Flinders himself. It was only now that Flinders learned of the state of war. It occurred to him that the passport he carried was valid for the *Investigator* on its scientific voyage of discovery, not for the *Cumberland*. His wish was to leave Mauritius in haste, but a second French officer of a more abrasive demeanour appeared. Having observed that the passport was not for the vessel before him, he demanded that the *Cumberland* be piloted to the island's main settlement, Port Louis, so that Flinders might be brought before the Governor of Mauritius himself.

Flinders' apprehension could only have grown as he was guided into Port Louis harbour, though he could have had little premonition of what awaited him. He would have held the hope that news of the favourable treatment afforded the captains and crews of the *Naturaliste* and *Géographe* in Port Jackson not so long before might mean reciprocal treatment for him and his crew in Mauritius. As fate would have it, the *Géographe* had just left port and the meeting with the Governor of Mauritius did not go well.

Captain-General Decaen, the newly arrived governor of the island, was not a man to be meddled with. He immediately accused Flinders of being an impostor – the passport he bore was, after all, for another vessel; in time of war, Flinders' only possible motive had to be spying. Flinders was incredulous. The charts and documents he carried with him and offered to the governor for perusal were surely eloquent testimony to the scientific rather than military purpose of his voyage. The governor, though, was not to be persuaded, and neither the by now dead Baudin nor the departed crew of the *Géographe* were present to plead his case. Flinders returned to his ship angered and frustrated by the obvious injustice of his treatment, but still unaware that much worse was soon to follow.

Early the following morning, the *Cumberland* was boarded by Decaen's officers; Flinders and Aken were escorted away for further questioning. The interrogators on this occasion appeared to invest some credibility in the story told, and probably passed their views on to Decaen. As if to make amends for the initially shabby treatment of his guest, Decaen issued an invitation to Flinders to dine with him that evening in order, he said, to discuss the English captain's predicament in more convivial circumstances.

As far as Flinders was concerned, the insult already inflicted by the assault on his integrity was beyond redemption: 'the invitation accorded so little with my previous treatment, that I thought it to be a piece of mockery, and answered that I had already dined'. Decaen's envoy, Colonel Monistrol, urged Flinders to relent and accept the invitation, but Flinders only became more indignant. If the invitation was not prefaced with an unambiguous apology, Flinders said, he would not accept it.

> My reply was, that 'under my present situation and treatment, it was
> impossible; when they should be changed – when I should be at liberty,
> if His Excellency thought proper to invite me, I should be flattered by it,
> and accept his invitation with pleasure'.

Decaen took umbrage at such a sharp and ungracious response, and decided that he could not possibly apologise. More seriously for Flinders, his antagonistic attitude had sparked a deep and abiding hostility in the governor. All hope of Decaen and Flinders repairing their relationship was now lost.

Shortly thereafter the *Cumberland* was impounded, its stores put in the Port Louis arsenal and its crew placed on board a prison ship. Flinders and Aken were placed under house arrest in a squalid place called Café Marengo. Flinders protested vigorously at his treatment, but Decaen, who no doubt from his own viewpoint felt slighted by his prisoner, remained unmoved. When, in 1807, official permission to release Flinders finally arrived in Mauritius, Decaen refused to act on it.

His intemperate expression of grievance aside, it must be said that Flinders had made other mistakes which contributed to his downfall. He was carrying with him despatches from Governor King directed to the Secretary of State; other documents in his possession were from Lieutenant-Colonel Paterson, the Commanding Officer of Troops at Port Jackson. Consciously or not, Flinders was contravening the terms of his passport by carrying them, and thereby delivered Decaen grounds on which to incarcerate him. Decaen, for his part, seems sincerely to have believed that Flinders was implicated in British military designs on the island over which he had responsibility.

*Baie du Cap*. Published in T. Bradshaw, *Views in the Mauritius, or Isle of France* (London: James Carpenter & Son, 1832). Reproduced courtesy of the Royal Geographical Society of South Australia

The months passed, and Flinders' health began to suffer due to the conditions in Café Marengo. Eventually he was transferred to more agreeable circumstances in the Maison Despeaux, otherwise known as the 'garden prison'. Unhappily, he lost his beloved cat and constant companion, Trim, under mysterious circumstances: Flinders despaired that it was 'but too probable that this excellent unsuspecting animal was stewed and eaten by some hungry black slave'.

When his fellow prisoner, Aken, was freed in 1805 – an act later followed by the release of all other war prisoners on the island except Flinders himself – his sense of frustration and despair plumbed new depths. The only sop offered in return was that he was granted more liberal living conditions. After nearly two years he was permitted to take up residence in the middle of the island at the home of a certain Mme d'Arifat. He enjoyed greater freedom of movement than hitherto, along with more congenial circumstances in which to brush up his French and to work on his account of his travels and his precious charts, though these were not completed and published until well after his return to England. It must have irked him enormously that during his captivity the official French account of Péron and Freycinet, the *Voyage de découvertes aux Terres Australes*, appeared – replete as it was with false and exaggerated claims about the hydrographic achievements of the French expedition, especially as they concerned the previously 'unknown' coast, now transformed into Terre Napoléon.

Freedom did not finally come to Flinders until June 1810, and he did not set foot on English soil until 23 October of that year. Ironically, the *Investigator*, abandoned in Port Jackson because of its putative unseaworthiness, had returned five years earlier. Altogether, Flinders had spent six and a half years in his island prison.

It is tempting to blame his captivity at the hands of the French for the decline in Flinders' health since his departure from England nearly a decade earlier. No doubt Mauritius did contribute to that decline; in its own way, the island was as fateful for Flinders as it had been for Baudin before him. But the origins of Flinders' ill health in all likelihood lay much earlier in his career. The symptoms may have appeared earlier, but it was on Mauritius that he reported attacks of a painful complaint which he called 'the gravelly', and which was caused by crystals in the bladder. In Flinders' case, it seems likely that the condition was brought on by gonorrhea, which he might have contracted during his early voyage aboard the *Providence* under William Bligh. The voyage had taken in the Fiji islands, where the young Flinders may have contracted the disease as a result of a sexual encounter with one of the local women. The ship's records, in any case, suggest that he purchased from the surgeon large amounts of mercury – in those days the preferred means of relief from gonorrhea, but one which could not offer a permanent cure. Flinders' most recent biographer, Miriam Estensen, has suggested that the disease which eventually contributed to Flinders' renal failure was scurvy. In either case, the hazards of life at sea seem squarely to blame.

Flinders' period back in England, joyful though it was for the reunion with his wife and the birth of a daugher in 1812, was marred by ill-health and a sense of anti-climax. By 1810 the concerns of the day were very much focused on events in Europe, where Napoleon was aggressively pursuing his imperial designs, and not on the achievements of an expedition to the other side of the world which had set out more than a decade earlier. The praise he received from his patrons was fulsome, but it was not accompanied by the fanfare that his return would have attracted in 1804. Flinders devoted himself to his family, his financial woes – a promotion to post-captain was back-dated a miserly six months – and his magnum opus. As his health worsened, he must have become increasingly aware that the book, with its narrative, its charts and its illustrations, would be his testament. So committed was he to its completion that it was written and eventually printed at his own cost.

His last days in 1814 were accompanied by great pain. His doctor pre-scribed calcined magnesia to ease the condition, but in reality the treatment merely exacerbated it by crystallising in the urinary system. By March he was needing to urinate as often as 52 times a day, as he once counted, passing more crystals enveloped in mucus and blood than urine. In the end there was a sort of poetic injustice in the timing of his demise. His publisher rushed the first bound copy of *A Voyage to Terra Australis* to Flinders at his premises in London Street, only to find that he had drifted into an unconsciousness from which he never awoke. A day later, on 19 July 1814, he died at the age of 40, leaving the task of perpetuating his memory, and above all his achievements, to the book he never quite got to see.

part two

# LEGACIES

# REPUTATIONS

By any measure, the expeditions led by Nicolas Baudin and Matthew Flinders rank as remarkable voyages of discovery. In terms of navigation and geography, the two expeditions were ground-breaking, with both contributing significantly to the completion of the map of Australia and to its refinement. More generally, their expeditions also led to great advances in scientific knowledge about Australia's peoples, flora and fauna. We can still marvel today that so much information eventually made it safely back to port, when we know how many of the expeditioners did not.

The meeting of Baudin and Flinders in Encounter Bay is now celebrated in Australia as a symbol of the shared success and joint contribution of the two expeditions. For the British and French authorities of the day, however, this meeting was seen to symbolise lost opportunities. The administrations to which Baudin and Flinders had to answer appeared disappointed by their endeavours, particularly by the failure of either captain to win the race to chart the unknown south coast. Because of the prevailing political circumstances, it would clearly have been contrary to each nation's interests to draw inspiration from the conduct of two sea captains who, upon meeting in Australia's southern waters, rose above their own disappointment to share the information they had gleaned and to recognise each other's work.

It was as though Baudin and Flinders were fated to be swallowed up by the geo-political strategies that were the backdrop to their expeditions and which, in their meetings, they had both sought to transcend. Since the voyages continued well after the encounter, the two captains could reasonably have expected that their many other achievements would temper any official disappointment at the shared discovery of the unknown coast. They would certainly have hoped for a timely return home and a warm reception. The reality was far more cruel. They both met a tragic fate on Mauritius, the island that was a pawn in British and French imperialist games of the Napoleonic era.

Had they encountered one another again at Mauritius, the story may well have been different. We know from the letter Baudin left with Governor King that he had wished to recommend Flinders to the administration of Mauritius, in return for the generosity shown to him in Port Jackson. If Baudin had been able to plead Flinders' case personally, it would surely have eased tensions between Flinders and Governor Decaen. This in turn would have helped to curb early rumours that the French were conspiring to prevent Flinders from publishing his results first. But the French commander died before Flinders' arrival. Subsequently, Flinders' detention was not only a personal and professional disaster for the Englishman, whose behaviour in the circumstances was frowned on by his mentor Joseph Banks, but it also reinforced international bad feeling about the French and, by extension, the Baudin expedition. Mauritius – and the missed encounter – thus proved near-fatal for the reputations of both navigators.

Baudin and Flinders appear to have been destined to follow rigorously parallel paths until they died, their lives blighted by the international conflict through which they sailed, their health compromised by the rigours of their voyage. However, to see them as helpless victims of fate is to overlook the decisions that they themselves made along the way. Much of the interest in their parallel stories lies in the fact that they were both self-made men who embarked on a voyage that they saw as their chosen path to enduring glory. Men of intelligence and sensitivity, they also had the courage of their convictions. They were aware that their own choices might occasionally lead them into difficulty, but they knew they had the willpower to keep themselves going in the face of adversity.

Both men derived their strength of character from their status as outsiders – to the establishment in general and to the navy in particular. They attained their rank through their own hard work and determination, but also thanks to their prior service in long and difficult voyages. We know little of the formative years and ambitions of Baudin, but a great deal about those of Flinders. He set his mind on achieving greatness as a very young man and then pursued his goal with a remarkable single-mindedness. He was determined to escape the narrow provincialism of middle class life in Donington and knew – perhaps because James Cook had already shown it to be true – that a career in the navy offered the chance to transcend his origins. More particularly, and again perhaps because of the model of Cook, he saw the role of explorer as conducive to his goals, as he once explained most candidly in a letter to Joseph Banks.

> I have too much ambition to rest in the unnoticed middle order of mankind. Since neither birth nor fortune have favoured me, my actions shall speak to the world. In the regular service of the Navy there are too many competitors for fame. I have therefore chosen a branch which, though less rewarding by rank and fortune, is yet little less in celebrity.

Such self-belief sustained him in the face of many disappointments. Yet it could not prevent the establishment from rejecting him when he returned from Mauritius without accomplishing all he had set out to do. His reception upon his eventual return to England was at best an exercise in indifference; though he was received politely in society, his achievements were consigned to an already half-forgotten past. He was shunned in the years of illness and near penury, refused back-dated promotion to post-captain, and obliged to complete work on his precious charts and his official account on half pay. After his death, his widow Ann lived on in genteel poverty, while the very grave of Flinders was obliterated. The outsider had been firmly rejected and would remain so until his achievements were recognised by the new nation that he had helped to explore and in which the outsider was often a figure to be revered.

Baudin, too, was shunned by his nation's authorities in death. After the attempts to blacken his reputation in Mauritius, his name was all but omitted from the official account of his own voyage, written by François Péron and Louis Freycinet. On the other hand, his so-called incompetence was not. The history of his life's work was rewritten to cast him in the worst possible light.

It is clear that part of the motivation for this revision of history by Péron and Freycinet was to save the expedition from oblivion, and not just to preserve their own reputations and careers. However, the strategy they employed to obtain government support backfired – on them and on the expedition's reputation. By consistently designating Baudin as a villain, they succeeded in convincing officialdom that all faults lay with their commander and all virtues with his officers. But this was not an appropriate tactic when it came to salvaging the reputation of the expedition, especially since the criticisms were piled on so thickly – in Péron's account, the expedition came over as a complete fiasco. Moreover, the naming of the unknown coast as Terre Napoléon caused them serious embarrassment with the English. For those errors of judgment Péron and Freycinet were entirely responsible.

To ensure that the scientific results of the expedition survived, the professors of the Museum of Natural History had supported them, through Antoine-Laurent de Jussieu, the Museum's director, and Georges Cuvier, the renowned naturalist and member of the Institut de France. Initially, Jussieu had been Baudin's friend and ally, and he was the recipient of regular letters from Baudin during the voyage; on the expedition's return, he seemed more intent on preserving the scientific specimens than to defend Baudin against Péron's accusations. Jussieu's scientific associates from the Museum – Riédlé, Maugé and Levillain, who were close friends of Baudin – had died on the expedition. This meant that Jussieu had little information with which to defend Baudin, had he thought it wise to do so.

Baudin was likewise without personal supporters in the navy; there had been a change of minister and, in any case, Baudin's detractors, the Freycinets and Bougainville, had much better connections than their commander, who was neither of noble birth like them, nor a navy careerist. It is conceivable that much of the initial hostility to Baudin displayed by the midshipmen came from their distrust of a complete outsider, whose future patronage would be of little use to them. As the voyage progressed, this enmity only became more pronounced, with the result that the captain eventually became an outsider on his own ship. Baudin's disgrace might then be seen as partly a question of class – the very question that had dogged his early career. Always the outsider, he was finally treated by the establishment and navy as though he had never existed.

Both Baudin and Flinders saw the voyage to Terra Australis as an opportunity to establish their reputations and change their status forever. Sadly, neither lived to enjoy such recognition. Yet it was their need to prove themselves and their will to endure that sustained them as they struggled to complete their voyages. For Flinders, the case is clear: he was a man of courage, an indomitable spirit. How else could one explain his willingness to travel from one side of the world to the other in a leaking boat, then circumnavigate a continent the size of Australia in that very same vessel? Or how else could one account for his selflessly heroic actions on Wreck Reef off the Queensland coast?

Baudin, on the other hand, is not often cast in the same heroic mould. He was, of course, 20 years older than Flinders and seriously ill for a greater part of his voyage. In his early career, however, he led by example, in much the same way as Flinders. The botanist Ledru's account of Baudin steering the *Belle-Angélique* through a violent storm conjures up a classically heroic image – that of the captain who refuses to abandon his ship and his crew, and who triumphs against impossible odds. On the expedition to Terra Australis, Baudin's ship was never in such dire distress. The captain did, however, show endurance and courage, particularly when faced with difficult human issues. In Timor, for instance, he managed to defuse Picquet's violent challenge to a duel; during the outward journey, he stonewalled the administrators of Mauritius when they tried to keep his ships in port; and he kept his calm when he was hit by a rock during a tense scene with the Tasmanian Aborigines.

It is nevertheless true to say that Baudin's courage more often took the form of stoicism – a quality that became even more important in the latter stages of the expedition, when he had to endure the solitude of his command following Hamelin's departure, not to mention the suffering caused by his deteriorating health. Knowing that he was in the final stages of tuberculosis and coughing up his very lungs, he managed to make light of it – by marvelling that he could live without lungs. His self-deprecating humour was obviously part of his philosophy of resistance and endurance.

In the final stage of his journey, Flinders too was obliged to add to his natural courage a strong dose of stoicism. The prolonged detention on Mauritius destroyed his naval career, but it also ended any opportunity he might have had to achieve greatness on the terms he himself had set. In other senses, though, Mauritius was the making of Flinders as a complex and tragic human being. Typically he kept as busy as he could on the island, undertaking long walks, learning languages, working on his charts and account, and reading voraciously. Detention inevitably enforced a kind of contemplativeness on him which sometimes took the form of melancholy, but which also enhanced his capacity for self-reflection and rumination. In his *A Voyage to Terra Australis*, Flinders adopts a matter-of-fact tone that makes it difficult to obtain insights into his personal feelings; his correspondence, on the other hand, is much more revealing. It was from Mauritius, for example, that Flinders wrote a letter to Ann which plainly indicated that he had become a humbler person:

> I shall learn patience in this island, which will perhaps counteract the insolence acquired by having had unlimited command over my fellow men. You know my dearest that I always dreaded the effect that the possession of great authority would have upon my temper and disposition. I hope they are neither of them naturally bad; but when we see such a vast difference between men dependent and men in power, any man who has any share of impartiality must fear for himself. My brother will tell you that I am proud, unindulgent, and

hasty to take offence, but I doubt whether [Midshipman] John Franklin will confirm it, although there is more truth in the charge than I wish there were. In this land, those malignant qualities are ostentatiously displayed. I am made to feel their sting most poignantly. My mind has been taught a lesson in philosophy, and my judgment has gained an accession of experience that will not soon be forgotten.

This lesson in philosophy would also have helped Flinders as he later lay dying, like Baudin, in great suffering. Neither man died in solitude, however. They were not abandoned by their friends or loved ones, for both, throughout their troubles, had displayed the capacity to inspire friendship and loyalty. For Flinders, it almost goes without saying. He cultivated comfortable relations with officers and crew aboard the *Investigator* and other vessels under his command, and when on land in England, Australia or Mauritius he seems to have mixed as readily with friends as he did with high society. The respect in which he was held by his crew became most evident when the *Cumberland* made its fateful landing in Mauritius – even when given the opportunity to leave, many chose to remain with their captain. Indeed, his personal servant John Elder stayed with him on Mauritius until ill-health forced him to leave in 1807.

With Baudin, the case is, as always, more complex. There is no doubt that his gruff exterior, coupled with his dry humour, was off-putting to most of his officers, especially those who were of noble birth, and to a number of the scientists, who were rarely permitted to see beyond it. Those who did, such as his companions from the *Belle-Angélique*, had learned to take his memorable grumpiness in their stride. Riédlé may have had the occasional disagreement with his captain, but no damage was ever done to their excellent working relationship, which was based on a strong mutual respect; Riédlé's trust in Baudin was a given, for he named his captain in his will. Baudin also came to appreciate other scientists whom he met for the first time on the voyage to Terra Australis. The kind words he had for Bernier, the astronomer, showed that he himself could see beyond the tough exterior of others and appreciate them for their innate qualities. He generally became deeply attached to those who were competent and disciplined professionals and who pulled their weight – though the converse was equally true.

The sick were a source of great concern for Baudin. From his journal we can see that he consistently offered kindly advice to those who were ill or suffering and, apart from the aberration of the second Tasmanian survey, when he himself was suffering from the effects of scurvy, he was attentive to his duty of care. His remarks on the mineralogist Depuch, who went ashore in spite of his illness, show how the captain cared even for someone he described on occasion as 'unreasonable'. Surgeon Harris in Port Jackson witnessed Baudin's visits to the hospital and commented on his great humanity. This did not always mean that Baudin's words were received as they were intended, for his manner was sometimes awkward or his humour misplaced. But there can be no doubt about the sincerity of his feelings.

Baudin's reputation has suffered also from the accusation that he was socially inept. The scientists on board certainly considered that he treated them with too great a degree of familiarity. Perhaps he did, since he clearly distinguished between what was suitable behaviour on board, among men, and what was appropriate in high society. With the members of the Institute, the Ministry or the Museum he was held in great esteem before the voyage; significantly, he had shown that he was polished enough to present his project to Napoleon Bonaparte and to win his approval. Upon first meeting Baudin, Ledru, the botanist who would soon accompany him on the *Belle-Angélique*, commented to Jussieu on his courtesy and refinement. Baudin later won the friendship and patronage of Jussieu, and his letters to his patron showed a command of polite and formal language that did not exclude warmth and sincerity.

Before concluding that the commander had no social graces, we should therefore remember that the officers and scientists had decided he was uncouth before the voyage had even started. Not that they themselves were 'reasonable', as Charles Baudin, one of their number, readily admitted. They often quarrelled among themselves, and in the most infantile manner, requiring an almost parental intervention on the captain's part. While this may at times have been a source of irritation for him, Baudin generally managed to view such incidents with a healthy dose of irony. Early in the journey, for example, the sight of Péron, dripping with blood after losing a fight with the ship's surgeon over who should have the heart of a shark they were dissecting, caused Baudin more amusement than annoyance. He resolved their spat by promising Péron he could have the next shark.

What did upset Baudin was that the young officers and scientists, who apparently treated one another without distinction of rank, should have subjected men such as Riédlé to social or personal prejudice. Baudin noted that the scientists did not think a simple gardener was worthy to be one of their number; in spite of his requests, they did not bother to help him write a Latin epitaph for Riédlé's tomb.

On the other hand, Baudin was prepared to give total respect to anyone who, in his eyes, had earned it. His own loyalty, then, was absolute. He made a vow that he would do his utmost to preserve Riédlé's collection of plants, as a monument to his work. Baudin's grief at losing Riédlé, then Levillain and Maugé, was intense. What affected him most deeply was the thought that it was their loyalty to him that had led them to their deaths. Ledru, the only member of the team from the *Belle-Angélique* who had been unable to accompany Baudin to Terra Australis, remained equally faithful to his former captain: his was the lone voice defending the memory of Baudin following the return of the expedition. It is thus the story of these loyal companions that needs to be told when one judges Baudin on his capacity for friendship.

Neither should it be forgotten that Baudin made new friendships during the expedition, and that he could also rely on old ones, particularly in Mauritius when all seemed to conspire against him. On the journey out he was able to obtain supplies and continue on his way thanks to his old friend, the Danish consul. Throughout the expedition Baudin's relationship with Hamelin, the captain on his consort ship, was one of great confidence. They consulted one another frequently about routine matters, as well as difficult cases, and Baudin seemed more relaxed during the times he was in regular contact with his affable companion. His relief at being reunited with the *Naturaliste* at Port Jackson overrode any negative feelings he may have had about Hamelin's decisions during their lengthy separation. Similarly, Hamelin's own bewilderment at some of his commander's actions does not seem to have been of great consequence in their relationship. The clearest expression of Hamelin's attachment was given at the moment of their final parting, when his sorrow was equalled only by Baudin's distress.

On that occasion, Baudin's spirits were already low for having just said farewell to an unexpected friend, Governor King. This friendship went beyond the camaraderie that linked Baudin and Hamelin. It seems to have been a meeting of like minds, as well as a sharing of similarly difficult professional situations. Baudin's famous letter to the governor from King Island revealed the French commander as he was rarely seen by others and rarely represented – a man of strong conviction, humanity and compassion, who also practised what he preached. His criticism of the colonial process and of its treatment of indigenous peoples was in harmony with the policy of non-violence that he had rigorously enforced during his stay in Terra Australis.

It is an endearing trait that men of action such as Baudin and Flinders were sensitive to the finer emotions, but as men of ambition they were not shy to put themselves forward or to exert their authority – which made them at times infuriating to their superiors or to their subordinates. Flinders could be given to impetuousness, a blemish which surfaced quite early in his naval career. The consequences were not serious, but Flinders' actions on the so-called 'Glorious First of June' in 1794, when, against the orders of his captain, he fired as many guns as he could into a passing French three-decker, showed that he could succumb to the heat of the moment. That blemish was to reappear many years later with far graver consequences. It was a certain rashness, allied perhaps with a streak of hubris, that led to Flinders' fateful falling out with his nemesis Charles Decaen in Mauritius. Affronted by his unfriendly reception on the island, Flinders unwisely declined Governor Decaen's dinner invitation and exacerbated an already tense situation by insisting on an apology. In so doing, he assured himself of a prolonged detention when a more diplomatic swallowing of pride might have led to a speedy reconciliation and an early release.

If pride sometimes turned to arrogance in Flinders, ambition could also bring a hint of servility to the fore. He was known to curry favour with those he thought capable of furthering his career. Thomas Pasley, William Bligh and John Hunter all slotted into the role of patrons at various points. But it was to Joseph Banks that Flinders sagely assigned the role of mentor-in-chief. The tone of the Flinders correspondence with Banks reeks at times of an unseemly reverence for the great man. Immediately upon his return to England aboard the *Reliance* in September 1800, Flinders fired off a fawning missive to Banks in which he played explicitly on their common heritage, and pleaded

> . . . in behalf of any informality there may be in thus addressing him, that almost constant employment abroad, and an education amongst the unpolished inhabitants of the Lincolnshire fens, have prevented me from learning better; but not from imbibing the respect and consideration with which the Right Honourable president of the most learned society in the world will always be held by his most devoted and obedient servant.

Whether such reverence was required is a moot point: Banks had long been impressed by the work of the young man. Flinders knew exactly where to go to get what he wanted.

Flinders' flaws, inseparable from the energetic traits that allowed him to achieve so much, were compensated by his great qualities as a leader of men. He may have irritated Banks and others, such as his brother, but he experienced few difficulties with his crew. As a disciplinarian he was driven by a sense of justice and of the common good. Above all, he could lead through example; his past exploits were well known, his valour and industry aboard the *Investigator* plain for all around him to see.

Surprisingly, given the reputation of the French commander, the description also fits Baudin – if only partially. From his journal, we note that he had few disciplinary problems with the ordinary seamen; the punishments he meted out were reasonable for the time, but he would not persist if there were any doubt about the veracity of the allegations or the fitness of a sailor to receive punishment. His problems lay with the excessive number of opinionated officers and scientists on board – a situation that arose despite his best advice and that stands in stark contrast to the experience of Flinders. At times, Baudin's officers were insubordinate and even close to mutinous – a fact which may later have caused them serious difficulties if Baudin had survived. The captain's problems with the naturalists, on the other hand, did leave a lasting legacy: on the strength of this experience, the French Navy would subsequently do its utmost to avoid taking on large contingents of scientists for such expeditions.

In these trying circumstances, Baudin managed to avoid any real challenge to his authority, even though it came at the human cost of his isolation from his staff. Hamelin, on the *Naturaliste*, fared better – by keeping his temper and his distance, and sheltering behind an affable exterior. In contrast, Baudin reacted to any challenge by standing on his rank. He found the task of disciplining his officers distasteful, and this led him to send them curt notes rather than expressing his dissatisfaction face to face. He would relieve them of their duties, often taking them on himself – which would have done nothing to diminish his annoyance.

However, for all his irritability, Baudin ultimately showed great forbearance. Péron, despite his lack of discipline, was not taken severely to task for the many times he wandered off into the bush; and it is by no means certain that Baudin would have made unduly unkind remarks about Péron's behaviour had he lived to complete the fair copy of his journal or the official record of the expedition. In the small portion of the fair copy that Baudin wrote, Péron is given the benefit of the doubt in terms of his scientific abilities. His extensive report on Geographe Bay is transcribed in full by Baudin; there is no attempt to vilify him, although his foibles are certainly noted in other parts of the captain's log. To the unbiased reader, Baudin's attitude to Péron appears justified and his comments relatively mild in comparison to the treatment that Baudin's reputation later received at the hands of Péron.

In terms of leadership, history distinguishes Flinders from Baudin. Flinders clearly brought out the best in his crew and officers alike, while Baudin became mired in the unpleasantness that reigned on board his ship. Yet for all Baudin's grumpiness, he was not the incompetent manager of shipboard life he is often made out to be. In his practices he was not very different from Flinders, who is seen as a paragon of virtue. Both imposed a strict order, along with the application of a regime of hygiene and a diet of anti-scorbutics. Péron accused his captain of not following the instructions given to him by the chief medical officer, but this was a patent falsehood. Baudin's journal shows he was most attentive to his orders on hygiene. The anti-scorbutics he took were modelled on the example of Cook; fresh meat was obtained from the livestock carried on board, and fresh salad was grown by Riédlé. Baudin also respected the advice given by Bernardin de Saint-Pierre about regular exercise and morale. One can only imagine the spectacle of the grumpy commander imposing evening dancing and gaiety on board, but it did happen, and is mentioned in the journal on the long voyage out.

Scurvy broke out nonetheless, but was it as widespread as Péron claimed? And was Baudin's seamanship a contributing factor, as Péron also asserts? Historian Frank Horner definitively refutes the accusation that Baudin took the wrong route around the Cape of Good Hope. In so doing, he debunks the idea that Baudin wilfully prolonged the journey to Mauritius and carelessly put his men at risk of scurvy. In fact, he took the route used by several illustrious precursors, including Cook. Besides, it was not until much later, after the stopover in Timor, that serious illness broke out. Most of the deaths incurred by the Baudin expedition were a direct result of the dysentery and fevers picked up on that island; scurvy accounted for no more than three fatalities during the course of the voyage. The overall death toll was not even high for long voyages of the period: in all, Flinders lost just over one-fifth of his original complement, as opposed to Baudin's 13.5 per cent. (It is true that the loss of Thistle and his companions off the unknown south coast affected Flinders' statistics.) Baudin's health and safety record is therefore extremely respectable, especially when one considers that for Cook (on the *Endeavour*) and d'Entrecasteaux the figures were closer to 40 per cent.

Baudin took a keen interest in the problem of scurvy and adapted his practices as new information came to light. Two modern French doctors, Guicheteau and Kernéis, have shown that Baudin devoted his time in Port Jackson to a thorough examination of the question. He learnt that the long periods at sea were chiefly to blame and thereafter was careful to break the voyage more frequently. He also took on lime juice to replace the powdered lemon juice with which the French authorities had originally supplied his ships, and whose effectiveness was questionable.

Baudin's only real lapse in his duty of care was in prolonging the second survey of the Tasmanian coast when his men were already affected by scurvy – an act of obstinacy for which the only explanation seems to be that Baudin was himself stricken by it and not in full possession of his faculties. The incident did reveal that Baudin, like Flinders, had to choose between two competing sets of instructions – to finish the survey or allow rest for his men. Both at times felt the drive to complete their allotted tasks all too keenly.

If Flinders was eventually granted recognition, it was not just because he had achieved so much in terms of the naming and circumnavigation of Australia; more importantly, he had lived long enough to publish his own version of what he had achieved. Eventually, too, he became a suitable icon for the young Australian nation seeking, at the beginning of the twentieth century, to distinguish itself from Britain and to establish its own historic tradition. Eventual recognition should also have been part of Baudin's story, as modern Australia moved towards embracing the multicultural aspects of its history and origins, and France took a keener interest in its role in the Pacific. But even in France there have been few to champion Baudin's cause, whether in the 1800s or now, so persistent has been the legend created by Péron. And yet, on reading Baudin's own story of his voyage, it is clear that his foibles were relatively minor and that his achievements greatly outweighed them. Like Flinders, his greatness was by no means untainted, but perhaps in his case too we can come to accept that history is made by human beings with all their virtues, their flaws, and their foibles.

# chapter fifteen

# SHAPING AUSTRALIA

One of the most distinctive and recognisable symbols of any nation is the outline of the country its citizens inhabit. Determining the shape of Terra Australis was a process in which mariners over many centuries played a role. Even after Flinders and Baudin, who in the end were unable to fulfil their respective goals, the map was not entirely complete – parts of the coastline had still been filled in with only a tremulous hand. But it was thanks to the joint efforts of Flinders and Baudin in 1802 that the one large piece then missing from the Australian puzzle was finally added – namely, the stretch of coastline that corresponds roughly to the coast of present-day South Australia. It was not merely a matter of filling in the details of an unknown stretch of coast; it was also a matter of confirming once and for all that they were dealing with a single, massive continent. Baudin and Flinders were among those who had speculated that there might be a strait running from the unknown coast in the south to the Gulf of Carpentaria in the north, separating New Holland from New South Wales. Together, on 8 April 1802, they established from each other's experience that no such strait was to be found.

Baudin seemed well placed to emerge the winner of the race to finish the map, having been the first to set out on his mission. But we now know only too well that his advantage was soon lost and that his lasting contribution to the definitive map was relatively small. Moreover, the tragic end to his life and the eventual settlement of Australia by the English ensured that he would not have the opportunity to compete with Flinders when it came to naming the continent whose shape he had helped to define. There have been so few opportunities in history to name a new land that Baudin and the French might be considered to have lost heavily on that score. Baudin's death also cost him naming rights

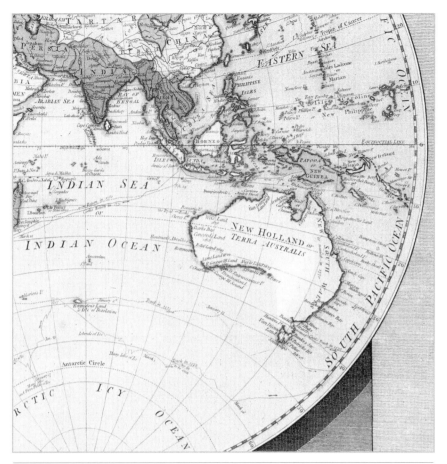

Detail of Laurie & Whittle's *New map of the World* showing Terra Australis as known in November 1800.
State Library of New South Wales

for the geographical features that he identified in the rough charts made during the voyage.

Many French names still survive in parts of Australia that the Baudin expedition charted. However, in most cases these are the names used by Péron and Louis Freycinet on the maps published in the official account of the voyage, and not those originally given by the commander himself. To make matters worse, Péron and Freycinet themselves featured prominently in the resulting nomenclature, while Baudin's own name was as pointedly omitted from the map as it was from the written record of the voyage. Admittedly, Baudin might well have adopted a similar approach, had he been given the chance. There was little in the way of flattery or homage to his officers in his original nomenclature; one can therefore imagine that Baudin's faithful companions, such as Riédlé or Maugé, would have received more recognition from him than the likes of Péron and Freycinet.

Be that as it may, circumstances would probably have forced Baudin, like Péron, to revise his nomenclature to account for other considerations than personal point-scoring. The same bureaucratic and political factors that influenced Péron's choices would certainly have weighed heavily on the commander in his review of the names in his drafts. After all, the official cartographers at the Ministry of Marine would have had some say in the matter. It is also a constant fact of life that Ministers change and that the new incumbents require some form of flattery to ensure that funds continue to flow. Baudin did not have to face that particular dilemma; it was Péron, and later Freycinet after Péron's death in 1810, who had to deal with the political obstacles that impeded publication of the voyage's map and official account.

One of Péron's strategies was to name a relatively large number of features after prominent political figures of Napoleon's regime. Some of these were the cause of a certain amount of embarrassment even before the Freycinet map of Terra Australis appeared – particularly the twin gulfs of what is now South Australia, which were named after Napoleon and his by then repudiated spouse, Josephine. However, since it was Flinders who had first charted and named the two gulfs, he had every reason to object, as he later did, to the ill-inspired nomenclature of Péron and Freycinet.

Baudin was, of course, long gone before controversy erupted over the political ramifications of the French nomenclature. Péron had not just chosen to name the French expedition's discoveries after political figures, but he had also assigned politically inspired names to Flinders' section of the unknown coast. As if this were not bad enough, of these names Napoleon's was the one that was guaranteed to cause the deepest offence to the English. When the first volume of Péron's account appeared in 1807, the English reacted most angrily to the naming (and implied claiming) of the entire unknown south coast as Terre Napoléon.

It is hard to imagine that Baudin would have been party to this, even under pressure. From the conversations and exchanges of information between Flinders and Baudin, we know that both captains were scrupulous about noting what the other had done – and that this was to serve as the basis for their final maps. Flinders found it hard to believe that this etiquette had been breached and that his own discoveries on the south coast had deliberately been ignored by Péron, whom he would have known well from the stay in

Port Jackson. The case against Péron was, in fact, so damning that Freycinet felt the need to remedy the situation in the second edition of the *Voyage de découvertes aux Terres Australes*, published in 1824 – although he took care to distance himself from the controversy, attributing the original nomenclature to Péron alone. In defence of his deceased colleague, however, Freycinet stated that Péron had not intended to claim as discoveries the features he wrongfully named; he had simply not known the names Flinders had given, since the English map was published much later, in 1814. Once Flinders' names were known, the French accepted them without question.

Unfortunately, despite these disclaimers, the nomenclature issue placed Péron and Freycinet in a poor light. And other incidents show that, for all their professional and personal qualities, neither Péron nor Freycinet was always entirely respectful of the truth or maritime ethics. In Péron's case, we have only to recall the malicious and manifestly untruthful portrayal he made of his commander in the official account. The case against Freycinet is less clear-cut, but his ambition seems to have marred his judgment on more than one occasion. For example, Freycinet wished to remove from Dirk Hartog Island the ancient plate commemorating the seventeeth-century voyages of Hartog and Vlamingh. He was thwarted in this by his captain, Hamelin, in 1801, but Freycinet returned to Shark Bay in 1818 as commander of his own voyage of discovery and this time succeeded in taking the plate back to France – where it remained until its rediscovery in 1940 and subsequent return to Australia. In this case, as in Péron's, the preoccupation with glory seemed paramount, although Freycinet, who was from a privileged background, was perhaps simply used to having his own way.

Both young men were certainly focused on their future careers – careers that they feared their 'incompetent' superiors had compromised – rather than on a strictly professional code of ethics. Later in his successful naval career, Louis Freycinet learned to comply, but Péron's death in 1810 meant that he did not become fully aware of the furore his lapses had caused. Perhaps he would not have understood. Thrust into his responsibilities at a young age, during a time of intense national rivalry, the non-seafaring Péron was insensitive to the constraints that dictated the decisions of experienced mariners like Flinders and Baudin and that united them in professional solidarity.

It is thus unlikely that the two captains would have fallen into disagreement over the delicate issue of prior rights. In fact, in naming generally, they adopted similar practices. Their charts bore homage to celebrities, often maritime figures, as in the case of Cape Borda on Kangaroo Island, named by

Baudin after the eighteenth-century French naval officer and mathematician. The French expedition's major discoveries were also commemorated in other ways. The captain's ship, for instance, provided the inspiration for the naming of Geographe Bay in Western Australia. To prominent landmarks Baudin often gave names that corresponded to their physical appearance. This was also a conventional category, in that it signalled recognisable features to future explorers – a practice illustrated by Baudin's 'Ile du dragon' (Dragon Island) off the Victorian coast, now known more prosaically as Lawrence Rock.

Baudin's names sometimes went a little further than mere appearance. The steep columns he saw at Cape Hauy in Tasmania led him to adopt the name 'Cap des Organistes' (Organists' Cape) in an attempt to describe the grandiose nature of the spectacle, with its tall columns reminiscent of organ pipes, rather than just evoke the sheerness of the cliffs. In another category, Baudin also conformed to conventional usage by conferring names that reflected incidents on board ship. Of course, he could not refrain from adding the occasional dash of his characteristic humour and sarcasm – though, not surprisingly, the humorous names disappeared entirely from the list of Péron's names, which overwhelmingly favoured the use of clusters of philosophers and scientists. While the commemoration of such celebrated figures is an interesting heritage that reminds us of the scientific nature of the Baudin expedition, it does not entirely compensate for the loss of such colourful names as those that Baudin gave to parts of Geographe Bay: 'Anse des Maladroits' (Cove of the Clumsy – today Wonnerup Inlet – where Baudin's longboat was grounded) or 'Cap des Mécontents' (Cape of Discontent – now Cape Naturaliste – where Baudin reprimanded Sub-Lieutenant Picquet for his failure to land).

While there is no definitive record of place-names comparing the names conferred by Baudin with those that finally appeared on Freycinet's charts, it is clear that both lists draw to a similar extent on the conventional categories. The differences are to be found in the relative frequencies of certain categories, but these can be telling. Péron and Freycinet used more proper names, whereas Baudin's nomenclature reflects a more evenly balanced use of the various naming principles. On the other hand, his use of descriptive names was no more conventional than the man himself. This fact alone may have caused him later problems with the official cartographers, had he lived to supervise his map.

However, another factor makes it certain that he would not have exercised quite such control over the final product as did Flinders, for French hydrographic practice at the time of the voyages differed greatly from that of the English. Since this has a bearing on how the achievements of the Baudin expedition are perceived, it is important to highlight some of these differences. On board, Baudin did not draw up his own charts, whereas Flinders did so, with meticulous care. Baudin's scientific and creative energies went principally into making a fair copy of his journal, whose remaining fragments, edited by Jacqueline Bonnemains and published for the first time, in French, in November 2000, indicate a work of exceptional interest. He did, however, comment liberally on the surveying that was done in preparation for drawing up the rough charts.

Naturally, Baudin could see the humorous side to charting, as he could to most things, informing us, for example, that his geographer Boullanger was so short-sighted that he could only take bearings when the land was right under his very nose. But the subjects of his humour were not always the subject of his disdain; he did not think any less of his geographer for this particular shortcoming. Indeed, he entrusted the reliable Boullanger with great responsibilities. Both of the geographers – Boullanger on the *Géographe* and Faure on the *Naturaliste* – conducted between them all of the initial survey work, often in dangerous conditions. Since two ships were involved in surveying at any one time – a practice that continued when the *Naturaliste* was replaced by the *Casuarina* – the charting was a collective task and not the exclusive domain of Baudin.

The commander nevertheless kept a close eye on the work accomplished. He was aware, for example, when the surveying was so patchy that it required more work, as was the case when he tried to locate Cape Leeuwin correctly upon first landfall in 1801. It was not until his return to western Australia in 1803 that the problem was solved – although, ironically, despite this correction, Freycinet later erred in placing it on the final map. Similarly, Baudin was anxious to have a detailed survey made of the South Australian gulfs during his second visit to those waters, in order to complete the work he had begun during his earlier reconnaissance. The work was so thoroughly done that this section of coastline featured as one of the most accurate parts of Freycinet's final map.

Both examples reveal that, despite the collective nature of the hydrographic enterprise, Baudin was sensitive to his personal responsibility for the final product, whose quality reflected on his leadership. If it is customary to attribute to Baudin the shortcomings as well as the achievements of his team, this is because that is how he and his own superiors saw it. It is certainly not a reflection on Baudin's abilities to point out that the captains of the other ships – the *Naturaliste* or the *Casuarina* – accomplished better surveys than he did, especially since the geographers were on different ships at different stages of the journey and Baudin was at times without a geographer at all. Besides, his own ship, the *Géographe*, was not considered a suitable vessel for taking running surveys. It was of a deeper draught than the others and therefore unable to run so close to shore. Critics of Baudin's survey work, including Flinders and Freycinet, did not fully allow for this. Even Péron had no criticisms of his commander's failure to run close to shore during the dangerous passage through the islands of the north-west coast. And, of course, unlike Flinders and Freycinet, Baudin did not run aground at any time during a voyage that for him lasted nearly three years, all of which shows the danger in measuring merit against one single criterion.

Yet if Baudin had his limits as a hydrographer, his expedition was not without merit on that score. Its contribution to world knowledge was not limited to the discovery of a section of the south coast, important as that discovery was in determining the shape of the Australian continent. The French expedition's surveys of south-eastern Tasmania and the circumnavigations of Kangaroo Island and King Island were a spur to the development of the sealing trade and to the future settlement of South Australia and Tasmania. In Tasmania, important corrections were made to existing maps, with the discovery that 'Tasman Island' was in fact the second of two connected peninsulas. Similar discoveries were made in Shark Bay, namely in establishing that Middle Island was a peninsula – eventually named after Péron. Conversely, in Western Port, Hamelin and his men determined that the piece of land that George Bass, and Francis Barrallier after him, had taken to be a peninsula was actually an island that now bears the name French Island.

Hamelin's close survey work on the western Australian coast and in Bass Strait, and Freycinet's along the southern coast and in western Australia, filled in missing details that Flinders' own trip, for a variety of reasons, had not managed to encompass. Nor was Baudin's personal contribution meagre: he ensured that the essential surveying work was done, and redone, often to such a point that he enraged his colleagues with his obsessiveness. In consequence, in some places – in Tasmania or on the north-west coast, for example – the map of the Baudin expedition was far more accurate in its detail than that of Flinders. For this, Freycinet deserves much of the credit. He proved to be a cartographer of real talent; as the cartographic specialist Geoffrey Ingleton points out, the draughtsmanship of his maps was of great elegance. If some details are sketchy, it is because that was where the survey work was less detailed, often due to bad weather. In assessing the contribution of Baudin's expedition to the final map of the Australian continent, it would be no fairer to omit the name of its commander than it would to overlook Louis Freycinet – or Boullanger, Faure, Hamelin or Bernier the astronomer, or indeed any of those who set out on foot to identify coastlines and other geographical features.

On the English side, in contrast to French practice, the hydrographic work was conducted by Flinders himself, who was as well qualified as anyone of his day to bestow a shape on the southern continent. For European explorers, the science of navigation had made great leaps forward even in the time since Flinders' hero, James Cook, had charted the Pacific and many of its islands. Indeed, on Cook's first great voyage of exploration, during which he had famously sailed up the eastern coast of Australia, he did not even have the use of time-keepers, which made it very difficult for him to fix positions precisely. Flinders, in contrast, was blessed thirty years later with state-of-the-art astronomical and surveying instruments, including a sextant made by Jesse Ramsden and chronometers by Arnold and Earnshaw. The Admiralty also provided him with a full set of charts relating to Australia – including of course Cook's – as copied by the hydrographer Alexander Dalrymple. Even more importantly, perhaps, the Admiralty furnished Flinders with instructions confirming that the meticulous charting of the Australian coast was to receive his undivided attention.

> You are to be very diligent in your examination of the said coast, and to take particular care to insert in your journal every circumstance that may be useful to a full and complete knowledge thereof, noting the winds and weather which usually prevail there at different seasons of the year, the productions and comparative fertility of the soil, and the manners and customs of the inhabitants of such parts as you may be able to explore; fixing in all cases, when in your power, the true positions both in latitude and longitude of remarkable headlands, bays, and harbours, by astronomical observations, and noting the variation of the needle, and the right direction and course of the tides and currents, as well as the perpendicular height of the tides . . .

Flinders rightly prided himself above all on his hydrographic achievement. His maps were ultimately dearer to him than his written account or than the collections his scientists gathered – wherein lies a real contrast with Baudin, who no doubt saw himself first and foremost as a scientific voyager and chronicler.

If Flinders were to choose just one document by which to be remembered, then it would surely be his map of Terra Australis. So meticulous was his work that some of his charts of the Australian coastline were still being used well into the twentieth century.

Not that Flinders accomplished all that he set out to do. The fact that he was consigned a leaky vessel to perform his task meant that in the end much was left undone. He was unable to survey any of the vast western coastline of Australia, for instance. The north-western part of the continent, known only in outline despite Baudin's efforts, had to await the arrival of Phillip Parker King – the son of Governor King – who was commissioned in 1817 to survey that part of the coast which Flinders had left unexamined.

If Flinders himself had a weakness as a hydrographer, then it was in his search for rivers puncturing the coastline. Even before the *Investigator* voyage he had managed to miss the mouth of the Clarence River on the far north coast of New South Wales, although he had anchored off it in the *Norfolk*, and he failed to see where the Brisbane River emptied into Moreton Bay on the coast of southern Queensland. But above all Flinders, like Baudin at about the same time, sailed unwittingly past the entrance to Australia's grandest river, the Murray. To have found it would have gone a long way toward explaining why no great channel stretching from north to south was to be found – rivers like the Murray were sufficient to drain the inland plains of a single vast continent. It might also have saved later explorers a good deal of effort, since it was not until 1830 – nearly three decades later – that Charles Sturt followed the Murray to its mouth.

However, what Flinders discovered and charted was far more considerable than what he missed. Furthermore, the originality of so much of Flinders' hydrographic work meant that he became one of the great providers of Australian place-names, leading his first biographer, Ernest Scott, to label him the 'Great Denominator'. Where Cook had added 103 place names on his chart of the continent's east coast, Flinders added nearly 300 around the country, most of which still apply to this day. Of these, some were added during the voyage itself and appear in his logs, but most were the product of much longer deliberation.

In bestowing names Flinders, like Baudin, was faithful to the practice of the day. This meant that no attention was paid to any names that might have been given by the indigenous population. Like the French, the British assumed that it was their right to bestow their own names upon this antipodean *tabula rasa*.

Flinders appears to have been driven by a combination of custom, prag-matism, altruism and at times also a touch of sentimentality. In many cases, he named places for prominent British public figures, particularly those who, as patrons, were well placed to help him in his career. Hence the two great gulfs explored along the 'unknown coast' became – and have remained – Spencer's Gulf (generally referred to today as Spencer Gulf) – named 'in honour of the respected nobleman who presided at the Board of Admiralty when the voyage was planned' – and the Gulf of St Vincent (now more commonly called Gulf St Vincent) – named 'in honour of the noble admiral' who was head of the Admiralty when the *Investigator* departed from England's shores.

Some pragmatism is evident in his choices of names that might help fellow mariners identify coastal features. For example, Streaky Bay was so called because of 'much seaweed floating about'; the name Thorny Passage prepared all who neared it to be wary of dangerous rocks; while Mount Lofty speaks for itself. Flinders' altruism is evident in the fact that he named no feature of the coastline after himself. True, he named a Flinders Island, but that was after his brother Samuel. Other features bearing the name Flinders were named not by him but by others some time later. On the other hand, Flinders was happy to immortalise the scientific gentlemen aboard the *Investigator*: Brown and Westall had mountains named after them; Ferdinand Bauer is remembered in Cape Bauer; Allen's Island in the Gulf of Carpentaria is named after the 'miner' or geologist John Allen. Nor did he ignore the ship's crew. Cape Catastrophe and Memory Cove recall the place off the unknown coast where a boat was lost with all hands. The names of those drowned are recalled in nearby islands, including Thistle Island, named for the sorely missed Master of the *Investigator*, John Thistle, whom Flinders had known for several years.

A certain sentimental provincialism seems to inform the spate of names Flinders gave to features in and around Port Lincoln. The arid landscape itself can hardly have reminded Flinders of the fertile fens of his native Lincolnshire; perhaps it was the harbour's natural beauty that led him, in hindsight, to commemorate his northern home by naming this part of the southern coast after it. Apart from the generous harbour of Port Lincoln itself, shielded in part by Boston Island, names such as Bicker Island, Surfleet Point, Stamford Hill, Spalding Cove, Grantham Island, Kirton Point, Point Bolingbroke, Louth Bay and Isle, Sleaford Mere, Lusby Isle, Langton Isle, Kirkby Isle, Winceby Isle, Sibsey Isle, Tumby Isle, Stickney Isle, Hareby Isle and Revesby Isle were all taken from the map of Flinders' native province. In this way, a small part of Australia will remain forever Lincolnshire.

On other stretches of coast, many names had already been provided by Europeans who had been there before him. That applied to his fellow Englishmen, but also to Dutch explorers of many years earlier, to French navigators such as d'Entrecasteaux and even to his French contemporary Nicolas Baudin. However, Baudin was less fortunate than Flinders in that fewer of his original claims were respected. It is also ironic that one of the few places at which the name 'Baudin' appears on the Australian map has much more to do with Flinders than Baudin. Baudin's Rocks are just north of Robe, on the stretch of southern coastline first charted by Baudin. Respecting the French prior discovery, Flinders initially named the rocks Geographe's Rocks. The name was one of just 14 he applied to features of the South Australian coast in his original log books. By the time he constructed his atlas and wrote his official account, however, the name was changed to Baudin's Rocks. Subsequently, the feature has officially been renamed Godfrey's Islands, but in local parlance the French connection, with Flinders' help, has been preserved – albeit in a somewhat 'naturalised' form, the rocks in question being commonly referred to as 'the Bodins'.

Flinders was therefore understandably peeved that Péron and Freycinet, in their naming of Terre Napoléon and its features, did not accord him the same respect as he had shown them. Although he generously surmised that Péron had in all likelihood been subjected to pressures from above, Flinders felt much aggrieved. As irksome as it was, however, this conflict over naming rights was always going to be resolved in favour of Flinders given the British settlement of the continent. On the other hand, Flinders was not to have his own way on an even weightier matter of nomenclature, at least not in his own lifetime. At issue was the bestowing of a name for the very continent he had circumnavigated, and his opponent was not a Frenchman but none other than his mentor, Sir Joseph Banks.

Since he had established beyond doubt that New Holland and New South Wales were one and the same continent, it was Flinders' view that a new name embracing the entire land mass had to be applied. The name he suggested was Australia, drawn from the much older Latin name Terra Australis ('southern land'), originally formulated to give a label to a land which, as Europeans had speculated for centuries, simply must exist in order to balance the land mass of the northern hemisphere. Flinders was not the first to apply the word 'Australia' to the southern continent – George Shaw used it in 1794. But Flinders the cartographer was more influential than the naturalist Shaw. He began using the word 'Australia' in his correspondence from the year

1804, first in a letter written from Mauritius to his brother Samuel on 25 August.

> I call the whole island Australia, or Terra Australis. New Holland is properly that portion of it from 135° of longitude westward; and eastward is New South Wales, according to the Governor's patent.

Flinders first used the word 'Australia' publicly in 1807, in an essay he wrote in French, curiously enough, about the likely fate of La Pérouse. In this essay, written for the Société d'Emulation in Mauritius and subsequently published in Paris in 1810, he wrote that he thought it convenient to bring together New Holland and New South Wales 'under a common designation which will do justice to the discovery rights of Holland and England, and I have with that object in view had recourse to the name Austral-land or Australia.' Flinders felt it would be unjust, in naming what was now proven to be a single land mass, for Cook's New South Wales to be absorbed in the New Holland of the Dutch – and vice-versa. His proposed nomenclature would solve the problem by giving precedence instead to the continent's southern or austral location.

Banks had known of Flinders' preferences in this regard long before the issue came to a head. On the last day of 1804, Flinders wrote to Banks about his 'general chart of Australia'. When he finally arrived back in England in February 1810, he wished to commence his account of his voyage and thus broached the topic with Sir Joseph directly for the first time. Banks did not like 'Australia', and the cartographer Arrowsmith also had his objections – he had always used 'New Holland' in his charts. By 1813 Flinders thought that he had brought his old patron round to his view; indeed, in correspondence with Banks he pleaded that the latter had accepted the name in front of witnesses. Banks, however, appears to have had no such recollection and remained adamant: 'Australia' was unacceptable, though he did at least agree to 'Terra Australis'. This, then, was the name used in both Flinders' charts and his account. In accepting the directive of Banks, Flinders nevertheless took the licence of including his own preference, labelling his map 'General Chart of Terra Australis or Australia'. Flinders explains his preference in a cautiously worded footnote in *A Voyage to Terra Australis*: 'Had I permitted myself any innovation upon the original term, it would have been to convert it into Australia; as being more agreeable to the ear, and an assimilation to the names of the other great portions of the earth.' Only after the book's publication in

1814 – and thus after Flinders' death – did the name he so vigorously championed begin to come into general use.

In the end, the Great Denominator was denied recognition in his lifetime for the name that corresponded to his life's ambition, just as Baudin the frustrated denominator was denied – not by Flinders, but first and foremost by his own countrymen – the honour of naming very much at all. But Flinders was avenged by history, and Australians now honour his name by bestowing it on towns, streets, institutions, motels and even a pop star. Baudin, whose part in shaping Australia was honourable by any standards, has yet to be recognised as a folk hero in the same way, even though his status as a courageous and oppressed outsider is very similar to that of Flinders. Baudin is rarely acknowledged in his own right: while his name is often associated with that of Flinders, it always stands in a relation of inferiority. A good example of this is the way in which their names are used within Australia: an Adelaide street named after Baudin – Baudin Avenue – is in a suburb called Flinders Park. Only when his name independently adorns more than the odd rock or street will Baudin's rehabilitation be complete. There are some signs that the process has commenced, some two hundred years after his death.

# chapter sixteen

# THE ARTISTIC RECORD

By the time Flinders and Baudin undertook their Australian voyages, it had become standard practice for expeditions of exploration and discovery to have artists allocated to them. In the age before cameras, there needed to be some means of recording the new worlds made visible to the European eye. So close was the relationship between the artists and the scientists that one almost conventionally speaks of a 'fusion of art and science'. The description is apposite enough, especially as it stems from no less a being than Johann Wolfgang von Goethe, who, perhaps more than any other intellect of the day, could claim to have mastered the fusion himself.

The artists in question typically played the role of handmaidens to the scientists and hydrographers. They sketched and painted what they were told to sketch and paint, and that meant above all landscapes and coastal profiles as well as zoological, botanical and anthropological specimens. Even if, in practice, their work accorded closely with the aesthetic preferences of their day – which themselves were informed by colonialist visions and desires – objectivity was as much a duty as it was an ideal. The highest artistic achievements of the two expeditions – the botanical sketches of Ferdinand Bauer, the marine animals of Charles-Alexandre Lesueur and the Aboriginal portraits of Nicolas-Martin Petit – were indeed the extraordinary products of this duty and ideal.

Naturally, the art of the two voyages varied greatly in focus and flavour, being the result of specific projects, talents and human tensions that demanded entirely different responses from their artists. It is no surprise to learn that the story of the artists who accompanied Nicolas Baudin on his voyage is as colourful and as tinged with controversy as the expedition itself, at least in the early stages. With more than 20 scientists on board the two ships, there was always going to be plenty of artistic work required in the service of geographic discovery and scientific enquiry. Accordingly, three artists were engaged by the French government to undertake this important task: the 32-year-old landscape artist Jacques Milbert and the 30-year-old draughtsman Louis Lebrun on board the *Géographe*; and the 47-year-old genre artist Michel Garnier on the *Naturaliste*. In addition, Baudin engaged on his own account two young artists, Nicolas-Martin Petit and Charles-Alexandre Lesueur. Officially appointed as assistant gunners, their real function was to provide illustrations for the captain's personal log.

In view of what transpired, the decision to engage Petit and Lesueur was a particularly felicitous one. The outward journey from Le Havre to Mauritius proved too much for the three official artists who, like a number of their scientific colleagues, were unused to the rigours of a long sea voyage. They abandoned the expedition in Mauritius on the grounds of ill health. However, as with those scientists and other crew members who likewise withdrew from the expedition at this port of call, ill health appears in most cases to have been nothing more than a pretext. News that the official artists had decided to leave was poorly received in France, where one journal, the *Magasin Encyclopédique*, made scathingly ironic comments.

> The flourishing state of the colony [Mauritius] and the riches which its inhabitants generally enjoy placed these artists in a position to exercise their talents with success, and all the more so as the distance from Europe, depriving that island of the presence of men who cultivate the arts, meant that they had no competition to fear. It appears that the combined effect of these circumstances allowed them to earn a great deal of money in a short space of time.

Baudin, for his part, does not seem to have been perturbed by the loss of his three official artists. Lebrun had been responsible for an altercation with the *Géographe*'s medical officer, Lharidon, on the docks in Tenerife and was much disliked. Milbert, too, had caused his captain concern, though of a different kind. Baudin, in a letter to the Minister of Marine, had made disparaging remarks about the scientists and artists on board the expedition. While this was nothing more than a gentle jibe about the excessive number of them that he had been forced to take on, the rumour quickly spread that the captain was sending slanderous and malicious reports about their work. When Milbert learned of this, he fell into a state of deep melancholy and depression, apparently fearing that the authorities would surmise from the captain's letter that he was not doing his job and withhold his wife's share of his salary. Baudin, once he became aware of Milbert's state of mind, did his best to retrieve the situation and to cheer him up, but the seed of doubt had been sown. More disturbingly, this affair revealed to Baudin that some on board, including a number of his officers, were reading his official correspondence and working already to undermine his authority.

If Milbert reacted in this manner to what was a very mild and generalised comment on the artists and scientists as a group, it is difficult to imagine how he would have felt if he had seen the letter that Baudin subsequently sent to Jussieu, the Director of the Muséum d'histoire naturelle in Paris, from port in Mauritius. In this letter, Baudin singled out for praise the illustrations that 'his' artists Lesueur and Petit had already begun to produce of the molluscs and other marine animals collected by the naturalists. In doing so, he suggested that they would be 'more useful to the expedition and . . . more deserving of national recognition than all the well-known artists who were chosen and who were so over-praised that they looked on work which would have done them honour as beneath their dignity'.

How greatly did the expedition suffer from the loss of three such well-established artists? Their departure certainly affected the nature, if not the quality, of the pictorial record of the French expedition. The paucity of illustrations of Australian scenery, for example, may be attributed to the absence of Milbert, who was said to be 'gifted in the subject of landscape' – though Lesueur and Petit proved quite capable at producing coastal profiles and Lesueur was a gifted landscape painter, as we can see from some of the background details of his Port Jackson or Tasmanian sketches. Indeed, on his return to France, Lesueur was to go on to make a series of sketches of the countryside around Paris. The lack of botanical sketches from Baudin's journey of discovery can similarly be attributed, at least in part, to the loss of Garnier and Lebrun, both of whom had established a reputation for drawing plants and flowers. The botanist Leschenault did produce some botanical sketches but, because of his illness and late return to France, these did not feature in the atlas of the voyage.

We can, of course, only speculate on the quality of the work the official artists would have produced if they had remained on the voyage. Back in France, Milbert did eventually assist with the final engravings for the atlas, suggesting changes to the Aboriginal portraits that would bring their proportions into line with academic convention. This gives us some idea of the role that all three official artists may have played. After all, they had been recommended by

The Château de Jœurs near Etampes (south of Paris), Charles-Alexandre Lesueur. Muséum d'histoire naturelle, Le Havre – n° 35 068

the Commission of the Institute in Paris and were products of the French academic tradition. Lebrun, in fact, was a student of the great French neo-classical painter Jacques Louis David. Commentators have suggested that the official artists' representations of Australia's flora, fauna, landscapes and peoples would have carried at least traces of the aesthetic preferences of the French Academy – preferences which, at the end of the eighteenth century, were heavily influenced by a revival of interest in the classical Greek model. Baudin's artist Nicolas-Martin Petit was also a student of Jacques Louis David but, being less advanced in his career, he was, we suspect, freer to react to his subjects than his well-established colleagues may have been.

Nevertheless, these young artists were not working within a void. Previous voyages of discovery, most recently those of Bougainville, d'Entrecasteaux and Cook, had established a practice, if not a tradition, of artistic representation to which it was now their turn to contribute. This practice included the drawing of coastal profiles, human subjects and scientific specimens. Both Petit and Lesueur were young, enthusiastic and anxious to heed the advice they received from the scientists about scientific draughtsmanship and realistic representation. The fact that the work fell to two unheralded artists who did not carry with them the full weight of the academic tradition – with all of the aesthetic preconceptions that this implies – guaranteed that the drawings would have a fresh and lively quality.

The work of Lesueur and Petit soon confirmed, at any rate, that they were worthy of their sudden and unexpected promotion to official artist status. Moreover, if the expedition benefited greatly from their efforts, Lesueur and Petit equally had good cause to be grateful to Baudin for choosing to include them on it. As is demonstrated by the biographical research of Philippe Manneville and Jacqueline Bonnemains (the former curator of the Lesueur collection in Le Havre), their participation in this voyage of discovery would be a defining moment in their careers and would change their lives forever.

This is particularly true of Lesueur, whose life, at the time he was singled out by Baudin, was at a loose end. In the summer of 1800, the 22-year-old Lesueur's interest was piqued by the preparations that were being made in the port of his native Le Havre for this expedition to the Antipodes. An ardent supporter of the Revolution and the new French Republic, he had participated during his youth in a number of naval and military training exercises only to find himself declared unfit for military conscription in 1799 because of an umbilical fistula he had suffered since birth. With no immediate career prospects, he was living from one day to the next with his grandmother and

Portrait of Charles-Alexandre Lesueur, pen drawing by V. Gribayedoff, after an oil painting by C.W. Peale (Academy of Natural Sciences, Philadelphia). Muséum d'histoire naturelle, Le Havre – n° 64 062.2

his younger brother – his mother had died when he was 16 and his father was frequently in Paris for business reasons. He stood ready to serve his country in its hour of need, but was unsure what path destiny had laid out for him. The frenzy of activity in the port where he lived seemed to be calling him to his fate.

While it is easy to imagine why Lesueur sought to enlist on the expedition, what prompted Baudin to take him on and to employ him as an illustrator is less clear. No record of any artistic training has been found, and there is no mention of art classes in the curriculum of his school. Jacqueline Bonnemains notes that there existed in Le Havre a School of Hydrography, created in 1791, whose mission was to provide training in draughtsmanship and graphic techniques for young men hoping to join the navy. Anyone over the age of 13 who could read and write was permitted to attend these classes, and it seems that many young hopefuls did, including two of Lesueur's cousins. Only a small number went on to sit for the formal examination, however, and given that records exist solely for those who did so, there is no documentary evidence that Lesueur benefited from such training.

Whatever means he found for developing his draughtsmanship, the young man's talents were, we must assume, sufficiently impressive to attract the attention of Baudin. Although Lesueur was officially enlisted as an assistant gunner, Baudin's intention from the outset was to employ him in a private capacity as an illustrator for his personal log. This is made clear in the correspondence between Lesueur and his father in the weeks leading up to the departure of the expedition on 19 October 1800. On 10 August, he seeks to reassure his father about the duties that will be expected of him: 'As I will be in the employ of the Captain, he has promised to take care of me . . . I will not be assigned to ship duty.' He reiterates this point in a letter dated 20 August 1800: 'Have no fear for my fate. I have so far been on good terms with Captain Baudin who intends to employ me and some other of my friends in a useful manner, without being obliged to perform ship duty. Our lot will instead be drawing.'

The 23-year-old Nicolas-Martin Petit, whose life is known to us through the research of Jacqueline Bonnemains, seems to have been an equally enthusiastic recruit. Like Lesueur, he was living in uncertain circumstances in 1800 when he learned of the Baudin expedition. His situation, like that of many young men of the time, was unsettled because of the effects of the Revolution. Born in Paris into a family of artist fan-makers, Petit would normally have expected to pursue a career in that trade. In the troubled post-revolutionary period, however, there was little call for such specialised luxury items;

fan-makers were in low demand and unemployment levels among them were particularly high. On a more positive note, the revolutionary authorities wished to encourage technical artists, in order to support the needs of industry.

Petit, who had already shown an aptitude for painting, came to frequent David's school at the Louvre. The great artist was a fervent admirer of Napoleon Bonaparte, so there is every chance that it was in David's studio that Petit first heard talk of a new scientific expedition to be sent to the little-known Terra Australis. A taste for adventure, perhaps, combined with concern about being conscripted for military service, led Petit to enlist on Baudin's voyage. Though engaged, like Lesueur, as an assistant gunner, it was his artistic talent that similarly caught Baudin's eye. He, too, was assigned to work on the illustrations for the captain's personal log.

For both Lesueur and Petit, the Baudin expedition offered the opportunity to develop their talents and to resolve, at least for a time, some of the uncertainties in their lives. They were quick to repay the favour, showing a particular talent for drawing the many and varied marine animals that were hauled up from the Atlantic during the journey down to the Cape of Good Hope. They immediately excelled in the art of realistic representation. In his personal log, Baudin records his early impressions of their work: 'The coloured drawings in my log that have been made by Citizens Martin Petit and Lesueur leave nothing to be desired in terms of regularity and precision'. These early drawings are indeed remarkable, both for their attention to detail and for the sense of movement that they manage to suggest. The captain's illustrated log consequently became an object of great curiosity and wonderment, as the zoologist from the *Naturaliste*, Bory de Saint-Vincent, records during the stopover in Mauritius.

> I looked over the commandant's log in admiration: it was a huge hard-bound volume, lying open on the table in his apartment, and it could apparently be handled without causing offence, since [the gardener] Riédlé and [the zoologist] Maugé felt free to consult it and to show it off to visitors. This log contained a multitude of drawings in which molluscs, fish and other objects of natural history were painted with an incomparable perfection and trueness to life.

As impressive as they were, these early illustrations nevertheless drew one criticism from the otherwise enthusiastic Bory de Saint-Vincent: they did not show all of the features required for a full scientific study.

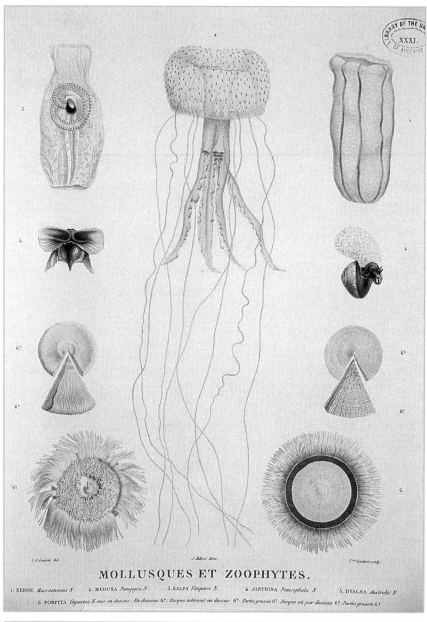

MOLLUSQUES ET ZOOPHYTES.

1. BEROE *Macrostomus N.*    2. MEDUSA *Panopyra N.*    3. SALPA *Vivipara N.*    4. JANTHINA *Penicephala N.*    5. HYALEA *Australis N.*

6. PORPITA *Gigantea N. vue en dessus : En dessous* 6² : *Disque intérieur en dessus*  6³ : *Partie grossie* 6⁴ : *Disque vû par dessous* 6⁵ : *Partie grossie* 6⁶

*Molluscs and zoophytes*, engraving by Milbert and Lambert from a drawing by Charles-Alexandre Lesueur. Published in the *Atlas* of the *Voyage de découvertes aux Terres Australes* (1807)

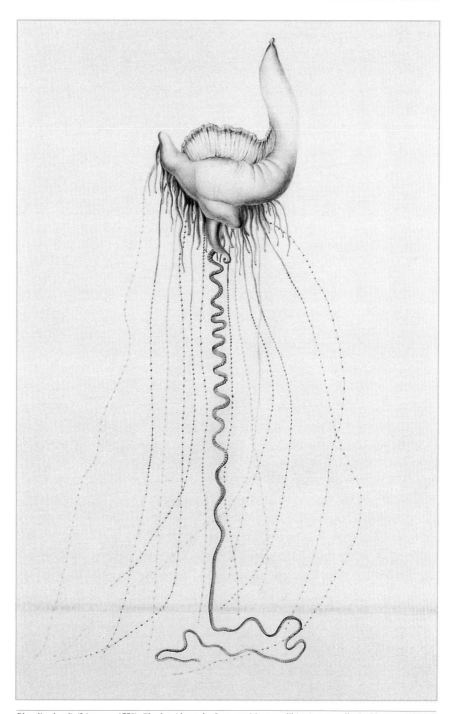

*Physalia physalis* (Linnaeus, 1758), Charles-Alexandre Lesueur. Muséum d'histoire naturelle, Le Havre – n° 70 067

I regretted that these drawings had not been supervised by a naturalist; in that way, they would have left nothing to be desired, but as it was, they showed no anatomical details; the painter had not always represented the animal on the side that exposed its specific features . . .

It was not long, however, before Petit and Lesueur began to incorporate these additional anatomical features in their illustrations. As the voyage progressed, and particularly after their promotion to official artist status, they worked more and more closely with the naturalists and soon developed a deeper understanding of what was required for their work to be of benefit to science. While they showed themselves ready to work with all of the scientists on the expedition, they also began to develop their own particular specialties: Lesueur became increasingly interested in the study of animals, whereas Petit devoted

Starfish, *Archaster angulatus* (Müller and Troschel, 1842), Charles-Alexandre Lesueur. Muséum d'histoire naturelle, Le Havre – n° 74 060

himself more to the important tasks of producing the coastal profiles and drawing portraits of the native peoples encountered during the voyage.

Their collaboration with the naturalists meant that the two artists were essential members of the various shore parties that were undertaken. An especially productive partnership developed between Lesueur and Péron, with the result that the artist became more and more interested not just in the depiction of animals but in the science of zoology itself. He demonstrated his capabilities during the stay in Sydney where, according to Péron, he 'killed and prepared no less than 200 birds, and had amassed in our repositories 68 quadrupeds' – all of this in addition to his artwork.

It was also at Sydney that Lesueur turned his hand to drawing topographical sketches of the burgeoning British settlement. With few exceptions, these drawings fulfil an essentially utilitarian function: as art curator Susan Hunt has pointed out, they appear to indicate a preoccupation not so much with the picturesque qualities of the landscape but with the more political issue of obtaining an accurate pictorial record of the new colony. The natural features of the land are all but ignored in the majority of these drawings, which focus attention instead on the settlement itself and on the various signs of human presence: the tents and the buildings, particularly those of military interest or which constitute the infrastructure of the colony (the powder magazine, the army barracks, Government house and so on). The precise location of these constructions is also indicated with meticulous care on a number of plans that were drawn of the township. These drawings serve a practical purpose, in the

Aborigines in front of their hut, Charles-Alexandre Lesueur or Nicolas-Martin Petit. Muséum d'histoire naturelle, Le Havre – n° 16 023

sense that they provide information, in much the same way as the cartographic records. It is not too difficult to imagine, however, that the gathering
of this information reflected the strategic purpose of obtaining a progress
report on the colonial project of a political rival with whom France had
recently been at war.

In that sense, the topographical sketches of Sydney may be seen as one of
the few exceptions to the dominant pattern of scientific observation in the
expedition's artwork. The plan of Sydney, in particular, is a hybrid work,

*Port Jackson – New Holland* (1802). This view of Sydney shows the barracks, powder magazine, officers' quarters,
church and windmills. Charles-Alexandre Lesueur. Muséum d'histoire naturelle, Le Havre – n° 16 069

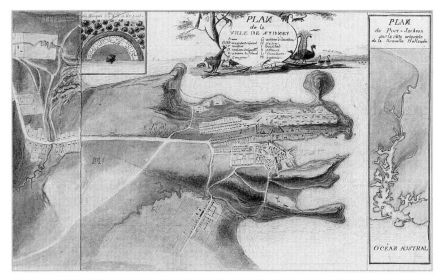

*Plan of the Town of Sydney* (1802), Charles-Alexandre Lesueur (from bearings taken by Charles-Pierre
Boullanger). Muséum d'histoire naturelle, Le Havre – n° 16 074.2

containing details of the coastline supplied by the hydrographer Boullanger, a detailed plan of the township, but also animal figures and, incongruously, a drawing of the Aboriginal sacred grove from Geographe Bay in Western Australia. As such, it remains a summary of the principal scientific subjects of the artists – the geographical, zoological and ethnographical – while at the same time responding to a strategic objective.

As the close collaborator of Péron, who later claimed to have been on a mission of espionage at Port Jackson, Lesueur was no doubt encouraged to add this political dimension to his work. Petit's finished work, on the other hand, does not appear to have touched upon the political or the strategic. We do know that he drew a cartoon of the farcical English attempt to claim King Island in 1802, because Baudin asserts that he tore it up. The sketch of the incident that remains – depicting the British flag hanging upside down as the French scientists go peacefully about their work – is certainly a political statement, but it cannot be attributed to Petit with any certainty. This is one of the many cases where it is difficult to distinguish between his work and Lesueur's. Clearly, both young artists were willing, and able, to attempt any of the artistic tasks required of them.

Petit's main achievement was in the ethnographical domain. In his Aboriginal drawings, he sought consciously to achieve a form of representation that corresponded to the scientific ideas and objectives of his day. When the expedition set out, one of the key principles established by the emerging science of anthropology was the need to study native peoples in their natural environment and to record as faithfully as possible their customs and behaviour. Petit had shown an interest in the subject at Tenerife, where he had made a number of drawings of the local women dressed in costumes that reflected their social status. He similarly made sketches depicting the various social categories of the Malay inhabitants of Timor.

But it is the pictorial record of Australia's Aborigines that stands as one of the most durable contributions made by the artists on this voyage, and by Petit in particular. His drawings include portraits as well as illustrations of huts, canoes, weapons and other artefacts of great interest to ethnographers both then and now. Social customs such as dances and other ritual gatherings are carefully depicted. Lesueur, too, was interested in such scenes. He made one of the earliest drawings of a corroboree, and also left an unfinished series of scenes from Aboriginal life, several of which took on strong subjects (including the massacre of a woman).

Petit excelled in the portraits of Aborigines, and in these we can discern a

Woman from Tenerife. The zoologist Levillain noted that this costume was worn by rich women on the island who had reached an 'advanced age'. Nicolas-Martin Petit. Muséum d'histoire naturelle, Le Havre – n° 14 004

Aborigines dancing near a fire, Charles-Alexandre Lesueur. Muséum d'histoire naturelle, Le Havre – n° 16 008

*Van Diemen's Land – Bara-Ourou*, bust showing scarifications and necklaces, engraving by Milbert and Roger from a drawing by Nicolas-Martin Petit. Published in the *Atlas* of the *Voyage de découvertes aux Terres Australes* (1807)

clear and interesting progression. The visual record he left of the native inhabitants of Maria and Bruny Islands, in south-east Tasmania, is precious in itself, since these groups were soon to be decimated, the victims of British colonisation. While the portraits do reveal a strained quality, the fixed smiles or the occasional intense frown being no doubt related to the nervous tension that the French attributed to the Tasmanians in general, they are also the portraits of individuals with dignity and personality.

As an 'observer of man' Petit incorporated valuable ethnographical information into his work, paying careful attention to head and body shape, hair, facial features and bodily markings such as paint and scarification. Clothing and ornaments were painted in minute detail, as were poses that were seen to be characteristic, such as a woman sitting in a crouching position or the one commented on by Baudin, when he remarked that the men had the habit of standing on one leg holding their foreskin.

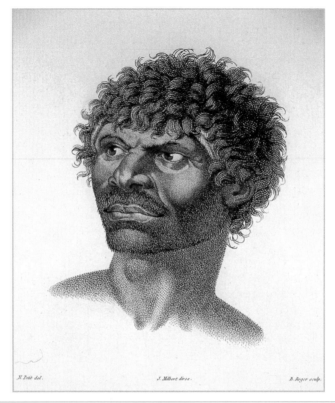

*Gnoung-a-gnoung-a, Mour-re-mour-ga (called Collins)* (Port Jackson), engraving by Milbert and Roger from a drawing by Nicolas-Martin Petit. Published in the *Atlas* of the *Voyage de découvertes aux Terres Australes* (1807)

Petit continued to emphasise the ethnographical when the expedition moved on to Port Jackson, where he sketched the social and sexual habits of the indigenous inhabitants. The human subjects in Petit's Port Jackson portraits are also more individualised; they have an inner life that is difficult to detect behind the fixed smiles of his Tasmanians. Nonetheless, he did not idealise the body shapes or proportions of his subjects nor greatly engage in sentimentality – except perhaps in his portrait of a child whose almost entreating expression is in contrast with the distance retained by his adult subjects. However, his Port Jackson portraits do reveal a return from the uncomfortable distance that marked the expedition's relationship to the Tasmanians as well as a renewed enthusiasm for his mission as ethnographical artist. There seems little doubt that this evolution mirrored the experience of François Péron who, from his contact with the Port Jackson Aborigines, abandoned the notion of the 'noble savage' and put his faith in the civilising power of European society.

*Bādgi Bādgi* Young man *from the Gwea-Gal Tribe* (New South Wales) Nicolas-Martin Petit Muséum d'histoire naturelle, Le Havre – n° 20 041.1

We do not know whether Petit's ideas were directly influenced by Péron's, but since Péron was the self-appointed anthropologist of the expedition, as well as its chief naturalist by the journey's end, the case seems likely. On the other hand, we do know of Péron's influence on the work of Lesueur. Under the guidance of his friend, Lesueur would produce the huge quantity of animal illustrations – almost 1000 – that is the other great artistic achievement of the Baudin expedition. It was entirely complementary to the scientific bounty that was collected in the form of over 2500 new animal species. From the scientist's point of view, Lesueur's paintings of Australia's native fauna are admirably precise. Every platypus hair, every echidna spine, every bird feather is drawn with meticulous care.

Perhaps the most astonishing of the zoological drawings are those depicting marine life – fish, molluscs, jellyfish, gastropods, zoophytes of such colour and profusion that we can only concur with Baudin when he says that, even with the evidence of pictures, it is hard to believe they exist. In addition to their morphological characteristics, these illustrations of even the tiniest marine animals have an evanescent quality that makes them eerily beautiful. The study of marine life was clearly the subject of Péron and Lesueur's greatest enthusiasm and zeal. Baudin was right to have seen that the long period spent at sea would reap rich rewards in terms of the collection of marine animals, and he greatly encouraged the artists and naturalists who were engaged in preserving them. He was to marvel at their beauty and also to affirm that the drawings gave a finer description of them than words alone could convey.

Lesueur's Australian birds and animals are also a source of admiration, though not all of them show the essential characteristics that would help to identify them precisely – his drawings and engravings of emus being perhaps the most famous case in point. In one particular instance, we cannot be certain

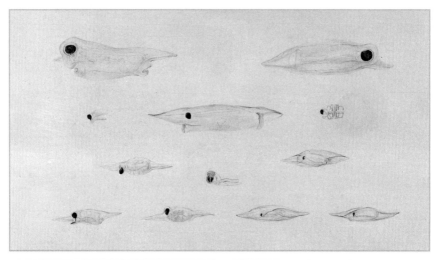

Salps, *Salpa maxima* (Forsskål, 1775) and *Salpa fusiformis* (Cuvier, 1804), Charles-Alexandre Lesueur. Muséum d'histoire naturelle, Le Havre – n° 75 007

whether the animal represented is the extinct emu of King Island or of Kangaroo Island, although the images in question are so finely executed that the aesthetic satisfaction is sufficient reward for the observer. Conversely, his watercolour of possums that neatly incorporates into the picture itself those skeletal remains that are often set apart in his more obviously scientific sketches aims to fulfil every aspect of his brief. At the same time, in capturing the animal in full flight, he has completely transcended it. Like Petit, Lesueur did much more than warm to a practical task. The attentive observer also created his own universe.

It is all the more regrettable, then, that the two artists should encounter so many frustrations and material difficulties on their return to France in March 1804. Fate was particularly cruel to Petit. No sooner had the *Géographe* docked at the Breton port of Lorient than he received news of the death of his father, just nine days earlier on 16 March. His own health was also showing the strains of such a long sea voyage. When he was granted paid leave of one year by the Minister of Marine, it was as much to help him recover physically as it was to allow him to complete his drawings. Tragically, he would have time to do neither: an apparently anodine injury to his knee caused by a fall in a street in Paris quickly turned gangrenous and, weakened no doubt by his bouts of scurvy and the general fatigue of the voyage, he succumbed in a matter of days, on 21 October 1804.

Lesueur was more fortunate, though he did suffer a number of frustrations and disappointments. After such an intrepid voyage he had been hoping to return home to an enthusiastic welcome, particularly on the part of the scientific community. The reception was, however, much cooler than he had anticipated: the innuendo and rumours spread by Baudin's enemies had already significantly undermined both the captain's reputation and the achievements of the expedition. Lesueur, determined to gain proper recognition for the scientific work he had helped to carry out, decided to continue his collaboration with Péron. Working together in Paris, they wrote up the details of their many discoveries, eventually publishing a number of their findings in scholarly journals and preparing the official account of the voyage for publication. Soon after the publication of the first volume of the *Voyage*, however, Péron's health began to deteriorate, and on doctor's advice he headed for the sunnier climate of the south of France. Lesueur accompanied him on this trip, during which they pursued further zoological work together. Their productive partnership was brought to a sad end in 1810, when Péron died. The sorrow Lesueur felt at the death of his close friend and collaborator was compounded by a decision that would leave an especially bitter taste in his mouth: the job of completing the account of the expedition was entrusted not to him but to Louis Freycinet.

When the Napoleonic era came to an end in 1815, Lesueur set out for further adventure, this time as part of a scientific voyage to the United States of America led by the philanthropist William Maclure. There he continued to pursue his two principal interests – art and science – with a particular focus on ichthyology (the study of fish). It was not until 1837 that he returned to France, where he spent his time, between Paris and Le Havre, working on further artistic and scientific projects. In 1845 he was awarded the Legion of Honour in recognition of a lifetime of devotion to these twin pursuits, and in the following year he became the first curator of the new Museum at Le Havre. Nine months later, on 12 December 1846, he suddenly died.

The voyage to Australia was indeed a defining moment in the life of Lesueur. Not only did it provide him with the opportunity to confirm and develop his artistic talent, but it also allowed him to nurture his passion for science. The fusion of art and science, held to be the guiding principle of naturalist painting, became the characteristic of Lesueur's life, as well as his work. The quality and the enduring value of the drawings produced by both Lesueur and Petit, whether as documents for scientific study or objects of aesthetic contemplation, also confirmed beyond doubt that the role of artists on such voyages of discovery was not a luxury but a necessity.

The artwork of Matthew Flinders' voyage would prove the same point, even though it was produced by artists of different standing and qualifications from Baudin's young assistant-gunners-made-good. Like their French counterparts, the artists on board the Flinders expedition were standing on the very tall shoulders of their illustrious predecessors. Of particular significance was the work of the artists on James Cook's three great expeditions. On the first of those voyages – the one on which Cook charted the eastern coast of New South Wales – were two artists, Alexander Buchan and Sydney Parkinson, who above all tended to the botanising activities of the young Joseph Banks. Banks was distraught when Buchan died in Tahiti, but the Australian work of Parkinson – a trained botanical draughtsman – was of such range, quality and quantity as to offer an impressive record of the expedition's achievements. Generally answering to the wishes of Banks, Parkinson produced altogether 955 drawings of plants in the form of sketches and finished drawings. He also produced drawings of people and places as well as of coastal profiles.

So positive was Banks's experience with Parkinson aboard the *Endeavour*, and so central was Banks's role in the preparation of Flinders' voyage, that there was no question that there would be a complement of artists on the *Investigator*: a botanical artist would assist the botanist Robert Brown, while a landscape artist would devote his attention to coastal profiles and landscapes so as to complement Flinders' own hydrographic work.

In the appointment of the botanical draughtsman, Banks pulled off a stroke of genius. His choice was Ferdinand Bauer, an Austrian-born artist who, together with his brother Franz (or Francis), had been attracted to England by the presence of none other than Banks himself. Ferdinand's reputation as a botanical draughtsman was cemented by a journey he undertook to Greece in 1786 in the company of John Sibthorp. It was Bauer who provided the finished drawings for Sibthorp's seminal *Flora Graeca*. In 1800, and for a fee of £300 per annum – supplemented by rations and a servant – Bauer agreed to join the *Investigator* as botanical draughtsman. In doing so, he entered a professional relationship with Robert Brown that is unequalled in the history of the botanical sciences. Sadly Bauer, like Baudin, was destined to become a largely forgotten figure in his own lifetime and beyond, the scientific importance and the aesthetic quality of his work recognised only by a small but ardent circle of admirers confined to his original and adopted homelands of Austria and England.

Bauer's work on the Flinders expedition began long before its arrival in Australian waters. As early as during their brief sojourn in Madeira, Brown recorded that Bauer drew a turtle which Flinders had managed to capture. Similarly, the Cape of Good Hope offered an opportunity for Bauer and the scientists to engage in some serious field work. Bauer was particularly struck – as he recorded in a letter to his brother – by the range and beauty of the orchids to be found there. But it was in King George Sound at the end of 1801 that his real work began, as he assisted in the gathering of plants and animals, often in the course of arduous excursions into the interior. In that way a pattern was set that was to be repeated on numerous occasions over the following months. The most extensive of the inland excursions took place during the prolonged stay in Sydney, which took Bauer and his companions as far as the Blue Mountains.

It was only after the rigours of the collecting or the hunt that Bauer could settle to his primary task of creating a visual record of the collection to complement the living specimens taken on board. At that early stage, Bauer devoted himself to creating sketches to which he would add, in a characteristic manner, a series of numbers to indicate which colours should be employed in later working the sketch into a full colour representation.

Both Bauer and Brown chose not to return to England with Flinders aboard the *Porpoise* and thus were spared the dramas of Wreck Reef. Wisely, too, they did not seek passage on the *Cumberland*, preferring to continue their work in New South Wales with the express permission of Governor King. Bauer, it seems, continued to undertake excursions within New South Wales to continue his botanising work with Brown. After Brown's departure for Tasmania, Bauer made for Norfolk Island, where he collected and sketched for some eight months before returning to Sydney and then to England. The return voyage was aboard the maligned *Investigator*, which delivered both Bauer and Brown without incident to their destination in 1805, years before their erstwhile captain finally made it.

According to a report written by Sir Joseph Banks, who took possession of Bauer's collection, there were 2073 sketches – 1541 of Australian plants, 263 of Australian animals, the rest of plants and animals on Norfolk Island, Timor and at the Cape of Good Hope. It was Banks's wish that Bauer be employed to make finished drawings from his sketches according to a selection made by Brown and Banks himself, and that Bauer and Brown collaborate on the publication of their findings. The two of them were still devoting themselves to their task when Flinders, finally returned from Mauritius, sought out his former companions. Bauer was able to produce some 300 watercolours derived from his Australian sketches, making use of his colour-coding system. Unfortunately, Brown's 1810 work, *Prodromus Florae Novae Hollandiae et Insulae Van Diemen*, was unillustrated, and Flinders' two-volume *A Voyage to Terra Australis*, finally published in 1814, contained only ten plates of Bauer's illustrations. For his own efforts on his *Illustrationes Florae Novae Hollandiae*, Bauer was able to gain tragically little encouragement or support, with the result that the project was abandoned with only three parts appearing in tiny editions that remained vastly under-valued until our own time. Eventually Bauer returned to Austria, where he died in 1840.

Bauer's drawings, as one admirer suggests, reveal a complete mastery of the problems of botanical draughtsmanship. In part this is attributable to Bauer's own intimate knowledge of botany, gained before the expedition and then refined over the course of a long working relationship with a true luminary in the field. But in part it was also because of an unrelenting attention to the finest detail employed with the dual goal of showing his subject's scientific structure but also its innate beauty. Ultimately his art was about much more than the naturalistic recording of the surface of things, whether plants or animals. What is distinctive of many of his illustrations, of plants in particular, is the detailed representation of reproductive organs (that is, their stamen and pistils) and of floral and seed structure. His art evinces a scientific curiosity that wants to reveal the inner structure of living things and to establish how they work, not merely how they appear. In this sense, even Bauer's finest and most conscientious attention to detail ultimately served also the utilitarian task of making nature amenable to human needs – before it could be tamed, the natural world needed to be understood, not simply admired.

The utilitarian dimension of the art produced as a result of Flinders' voyage is perhaps even more evident in the case of the landscape artist William Westall. Like Bauer, Westall soon learnt aboard ship that he was expected to work hand-in-glove with his scientific colleagues, though he does not seem to have generated the same level of enthusiasm for the task as Bauer so evidently did.

Indeed, Westall was not the first choice for the position of landscape artist on the voyage. That honour had gone to William Daniell, who managed to disqualify himself for service by becoming engaged to Westall's sister. When Westall was invited, he was a mere 19 years of age and a probationary student at the Royal Academy, where he was becoming well versed in a neo-classical tradition. The offer of a place on a major voyage of discovery held the promise not only of establishing his artistic career but also of taking him to exciting and exotic parts of the world. For those reasons, it is hardly surprising that he accepted.

With the benefit of hindsight, however, it might well have been an offer Westall would have refused. Australia by no means conformed to his expectation of the exotic – as he was to put it, its subjects could neither 'afford pleasure from exhibiting the face of a beautiful country, nor curiosity from their singularity'. His disappointment was expressed forthrightly in a letter to Joseph Banks in which he claimed that he had been duped, that he had been led to believe that the expedition would travel to other, more rewarding parts of the world than the barren Australian coast. As compensation for having to endure such prolonged periods of unrelieved dullness, he suggested that he be sent to the South Sea Islands. That offer was bluntly refused, but after leaving the Flinders expedition he chose to travel to China and India in search of what he regarded as the more genuinely exotic. By that point, he had completed merely some 140 watercolours and sketches of Australia, a woeful output compared with that of his older colleague Bauer.

As was the case for his French counterparts, one of Westall's key briefs was the preparation of coastal profiles – that is, profiles of the coast made when Flinders quite deliberately positioned his vessel at an appropriate distance out to sea so that his artist might record the precise appearance of land formations made from a meticulously recorded place at a particular time. The coastal profiles were published in black and white in Flinders' *A Voyage to Terra Australis*, but in some cases were also produced in more attractive form as watercolours. They are testament to Westall's quite considerable artistic skills, but at the time they were conceived and received above all as a form of navigational aid. Used in conjunction with Flinders' detailed charts, they would assist future navigators in negotiating natural harbours or potentially treacherous stretches of coastline.

Westall complemented the work of Bauer by making some sketches of Australian flora and fauna. They were noteworthy for the obvious influence of his older colleague. In addition, he produced some portraits of Aborigines, initially employing a neo-classical style which had them resembling Greek Gods.

*Port Jackson – An Old Blind Man* (1802), William Westall. National Library of Australia

His central achievement, though, was his landscapes, which invariably began life as sketches made during the voyage. In some cases, they were later worked – with Westall's collaboration – into engravings for publication in Flinders' *A Voyage to Terra Australis*; some were similarly transformed into oils painted after his eventual return to England in 1805.

These engravings and oils stand very much in the tradition of what art historian Bernard Smith calls 'the typical landscape'. For Smith, it is a genre with a clear ideological underpinning. As he puts it: 'The European control of the world required a landscape practice that could first survey and describe, then evoke in new settlers an emotional engagement with the land that they

*Port Jackson – Grass Trees* (1802), William Westall. National Library of Australia

had alienated from its aboriginal occupants.' For Westall and other proponents of the genre, it was not merely a case of recording landscapes as they actually were – and in this sense Westall's landscapes went a step further than the coastal profiles. The painter of the typical landscape felt empowered, as it were, to mix and match, creating a combination of elements that might not actually exist in reality but might nonetheless be ascribed typicality.

This can be seen, for example, in Westall's painting of King George Sound. It derives from an early coloured landscape sketch, to which he added a couple of new components. It does not appear to have perturbed Westall in the least that the grass tree he added was derived from sketches he had made at Port Jackson, while a tree adjacent to it stemmed from a sketch made in Spencer

*Spencer's Gulf – Eucalyptus* (1802), William Westall. National Library of Australia

Gulf. The various components, he presumably reasoned, were at least from the same continent. The fanciful nature of these composite images was not lost on the more scientifically minded Flinders, who commented, for example, on the egregious use of artistic licence in Westall's *View of Wreck Reef*. Flinders wrote of the painting that it 'represented the corals above water, to give a better notion of their forms and the way in which they are seen on the reefs; but in reality, the tide never leaves any considerable part of them uncovered'.

These engravings and oil paintings dating from the post-exploration period, and in some cases even from decades later, have a serene, almost arcadian quality and convey nothing of the disappointment Westall felt at the time. Temporal and geographical distance, it seems, had made the art grow fonder. Moreover, the mature Westall moved away from a formulaic neo-classicism with its clean lines and contrived sense of order, and toward a sense of the picturesque with a (sometimes equally contrived) sense of the slightly disordered, and even the romantic. In some of his works, Westall seems almost in awe of a natural world unsullied by European civilisation.

Beyond his development in the realm of the aesthetic, Westall remained a willing worker in the colonial cause. In the 1830s he became associated with a group pushing for the establishment of a colony in South Australia. He contributed to a pamphlet recording his own recollections of the place and agreed to produce six engravings of South Australia for Robert Gouger, one of the principals of the South Australian Association. *The First Report of the Directors of the South Australian Company*, published in 1836, contained a view

*King George's Sound – View from Peak Head* (1801), William Westall. National Library of Australia. (See Plate 31 for a colour reproduction of this scene.)

of Port Lincoln drawn and engraved by Westall. Whether his work gave potential colonists an informed view of what might await them in the antipodes remains a moot point. One such colonist, a certain John Newcome, who was obviously familiar with Westall's illustrations in Flinders' *A Voyage to Terra Australis*, was struck by the distinction between Westall's contrived landscape and the more sober reality which confronted him when he approached Adelaide by ship for the first time.

> The absence of the seals, kangaroos and emus, that enliven the views in Flinders' work, and were consequently mixed up in my mind with all sea-side scenery in this part of the world, took from it in my opinion its Australian character, the more so, as no black men or women were gazing in wonder at our noble vessel as she sailed majestically along, nor could I detect any columns of smoke rising from their fires, over the thickly-wooded hills.

Westall's typical landscape, it seems, had provoked the same dashing of expectations he himself had experienced decades earlier.

In many ways, then, Westall's role as landscape artist set him apart from both Bauer and the young French artists on the Baudin expedition. Where these naturalist painters were bound in their artwork to respect the requirements of science – impartial observation and accurate representation, whether sketching on board or working from specimens back in Europe – Westall, in his depiction of Australia's scenery, had more licence. As a result, preoccupations of a different order were able to come into play in his artwork – the ideological purposes behind the contrived landscapes, for example, or the more personal feelings of desolation and disappointment that perhaps led to the production, by compensation, of idealised images of Australia's land and peoples. In contrast, it was their connection with natural history and their understanding of the symbiotic relationship between art and science that characterised the work of Bauer, Lesueur and Petit. Bauer's keen interest in botany as a science was as surely an integral part of his artistic production as Lesueur's passion for zoology or Petit's commitment to the principles of the new science of anthropology were to theirs. In this respect, it is perhaps pointless to regret that the French artists did not produce more botanical sketches or that Bauer did not turn his hand more frequently to illustrations of marine life. Their zeal led them to work with a care and dedication that could not be duplicated in equal measure across all branches of scientific enquiry.

# chapter seventeen

# THE SCIENTIFIC PROJECT

To gain a sense of the centrality of scientific endeavour in the French and British voyages two centuries ago, we need look no further than the names given to the ships: the *Investigator*, the *Géographe* and the *Naturaliste*. Baudin and Flinders sailed as much in the service of science as in the cause of promoting the glory of their respective nations. They both quite consciously represented the values of the Enlightenment with its central belief that empirical observation, combined with reasoned thinking, could make the world knowable. Under the guidance of their enlightened captains, the 'men of science' on the expeditions of discovery set themselves the task of observing a part of the world which had hitherto largely escaped the enquiring gaze of Europeans.

The expeditions were contributing to a grand project, conceived and carried out when the ambitions of European science were at their greatest. With such wide-ranging goals in mind – nothing short of an encyclopædic gathering of knowledge about the world and even its smallest constituent parts would do – it was little wonder that they were pursued in a spirit of collaboration that evidently transcended the political and even military rivalries of the day. It could not be said, however, that the Enlightenment somehow transcended the values of its time: though many of its devotees were quite oblivious to its practical ends, the task of knowing the world was in fact inextricably tied to the goal of controlling it.

Whether they were conscious of it or not, the scientists who set out on the Flinders and Baudin expeditions were observing a natural world whose riches their governments sought to exploit. Science was thus crucial to the process that led from observation to possession. That notion was indeed written into the instructions of the Baudin expedition. Following the advice setting out the scientific ideal of 'research of all kinds that can contribute to perfecting the natural sciences and increasing the sum of human knowledge' came the instruction to bring back 'useful animals and plants' that could be acclimatised at home. The scientific administrators who sponsored the voyages were thus juggling with national imperatives that had the potential to clash with the interests of science in general or with their own discipline in particular.

Of all the scientific figures connected with the two voyages, none exemplified that clash better – or dealt with it more successfully – than the English botanist Sir Joseph Banks. His defence of the internationalist principle of science had helped many a European scientist in distress – ironically, he even secured the release of Milius who, after the return of the Baudin expedition, was on active naval service and became a prisoner of war. But Banks was also a patriot, and his name was intimately linked to the colonisation of New South Wales. The apparent conflict seemed not to have troubled him. His influence, in time of war, had secured the return of the d'Entrecasteaux collections to France, as well as the passports for Baudin's successive expeditions; but it was also his support that allowed the Flinders voyage to set out so quickly to Terra Australis, as though in pursuit of the Baudin expedition. Banks is thus at the intersection of the English and French scientific projects, and it is with him that the scientific history of the rival voyages must start.

Though the custom was by no means unknown earlier, it was in the time of James Cook, and in large part because of Cook, that the equipping of exploratory voyages with scientists – and specifically with naturalists and their artist-assistants – established itself. Joseph Banks made his mark as botanist aboard the *Endeavour* on Cook's first great voyage of discovery in 1768–1771. Banks in turn had been swayed by the work of the Frenchman Charles de Brosses who, in his 1756 treatise *Histoire des Navigations aux Terres Australes*, underlined the central role of naturalists and of natural history draughtsmen on voyages of exploration. The naturalist Philibert Commerson had accompanied Bougainville on his Pacific voyage in the years 1766–1769, but it was Banks who set the standards for scientists of all nationalities to follow. Even more crucially, perhaps, he used his reputation, along with his very considerable organisational skills and political nous, to promote the cause of science. Banks was able to do this in part through Royal patronage – it was on the wish of George III that Banks established at Kew Gardens a huge collection of exotic plants from all over the world. In part, also, it was because of his membership of such bodies as the Linnean Society, the Horticultural Society, the British Museum, the Board of Longitude, the Committee of Trade of the

Privy Council and, most importantly, the Royal Society, that he was able to pull the strings of British colonial scientific endeavour. He was a central figure in the push to settle New South Wales and indeed corresponded with all the governors from Arthur Phillip through to Lachlan Macquarie during the first three decades of the colony's existence. In England he was without question *the* authority on New South Wales, about which he assembled a knowledge that extended well beyond the botanical.

Recognising Banks's potential as a patron remarkably early, Flinders was the one who sought out his assistance in mounting the case for a thorough exploration of the Australian coast. It was a wise move to dedicate his account of his 1798 circumnavigation of Tasmania to the great man. The ensuing approach – by letter – played heavily on Banks's well-established commitment to the cause of science in his recently established capacity as 'Right Honourable president of the most learned society in the world', by which of course Flinders meant the Royal Society. By the time a meeting followed, it seems that Banks was already convinced that he had found the man for the job description that Flinders had in effect written for himself.

If Flinders acted sagely in appealing to the scientist to make his voyage possible, Banks equally did well in settling on a man of obvious scientific bent to lead it. Flinders came from a scientific background himself – both his father and his grandfather had been surgeons. His abilities in the discipline of hydrography were proven through the survey work he had already carried out on the Australian coastline; moreover, his acuity of observation was evident to all who read his account of his Tasmanian exploits. This was significant because, even in an age of increasing scientific specialisation, much work would fall to the commander. Flinders would not only have to carry out observations of his own, he would have to facilitate the work of others, supervise and guarantee the safety of the collection of botanical and zoological specimens, enable the artists to create a visual record of the expedition's discoveries and, beyond all that, himself furnish its narrative record.

The latter is itself ample testimony to Flinders' innate skills as a scientific observer. It is true that many of the observations recorded in *A Voyage to Terra Australis* are confined to matters of a quite utilitarian nature. His comments on plant-life, water availability or soil and rock formation, for example, are motivated by a need to assess the continent's potential as a colony. But in some passages, such as the following, in which he presents his observations of a coral reef, he gives free rein to a talent for meticulous observation which transcends any purely pragmatic purpose.

In the afternoon, I went upon the reef with a party of the gentlemen; and the
water being very clear round the edges, a new creation, as it was to us, but
imitative of the old, was there presented to our view. We had wheat sheaves,
mushrooms, stags horns, cabbage leaves, and a variety of other forms,
glowing under water with vivid tints of every shade betwixt green, purple,
brown and white; equalling in beauty and excelling in grandeur the most
favourite parterre of the curious florist. These were different species of coral
and fungus, growing, as it were, out of the solid rock, and each had its
peculiar form and shade of colouring; but whilst contemplating the richness
of the scene, we could not long forget with what destruction it was pregnant.
(9 October 1802)

If his two-volume account were not enough to establish his scientific credentials, Flinders undertook research of his own in a number of areas. He was
interested in the action of the tides and in the relationship between wind direction and marine barometer readings – a topic he explored even during his
imprisonment in Mauritius. Over many years, he had noted that the barometer
rose just before there was a change from a land breeze to a sea breeze; corre-
spondingly, a wind change in the other direction was preceded by a falling
barometer. A paper he wrote on the topic – arguing that wind changes could be
predicted with a barometer – was conveyed to England, where it was read by
Banks before the Royal Society and then published in the Society's *Transactions*
in 1806. Flinders was similarly intrigued – and, in his own navigational work,
troubled – by the influence of a ship's iron on compass deviation. Eventually the
problem of interference was solved through the introduction of compensatory
devices, including the so-called Flinders bar, its name an open acknowledg-
ment of Flinders' invaluable contribution to developing it.

Just as it was Joseph Banks who arranged for Flinders to command the
expedition of scientific discovery, so it was Banks who recruited most of its
scientific staff. There was a botanist in Robert Brown, a botanical draughtsman
in Ferdinand Bauer, a gardener in Peter Good, a landscape artist in William
Westall and a miner in John Allen. To round out the full complement of
'scientific gentlemen', there was also an astronomer, John Crosley, though
he was appointed not by Banks but rather by the Admiralty and the Board of
Longitude. With the exception of Cook's second voyage, this was the largest
scientific party on a British expedition since 1760.

Though it was not to be foreseen, Crosley was an unfortunate choice. His
health broke down early in the piece, with the result that he did not proceed

beyond Cape Town. As no replacement was to be had there, the burden of his responsibilities, along with the instruments to perform them, was transferred to Flinders himself and his younger brother Samuel. Their relationship could have done without the added strain, and more than once Matthew had to chastise Samuel for failing to wind the clocks; but the accuracy of survey work suggests that Crosley's departure was adequately covered.

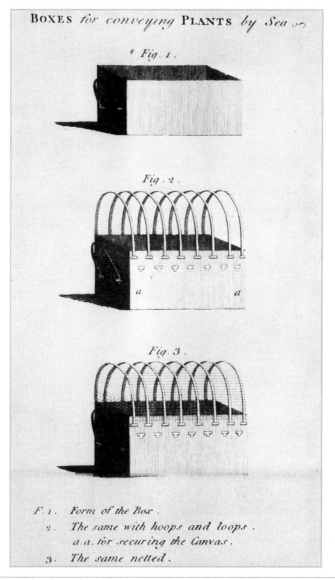

*Boxes for conveying plants by sea.* Plate 3 in J.C. Lettsom, *The Naturalist's and Traveller's Companion* (1799)

Peter Good and Robert Brown were a successful team. The aptly named Good, as the official gardener, had the task of caring for all the plants and specimens brought aboard ship. This he did with much-admired devotion until his death. Good was one of those who fell ill after the visit to Kupang. He made it back to Port Jackson but died a short time later, prompting Flinders to record in his journal: 'Peter Good, botanical gardener, a zealous worthy man . . . regretted by all.'

Fortunately Good's boss, Robert Brown, was made of tougher stuff and managed not only to complete the voyage but to go on to make his mark in the annals of botany. Banks had been lucky to secure him for the expedition. At

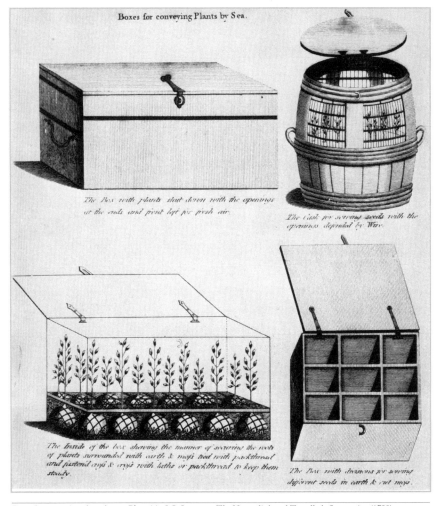

*Boxes for conveying plants by sea.* Plate 4 in J.C. Lettsom, *The Naturalist's and Traveller's Companion* (1799)

the time he approached Brown, the latter was serving as a surgeon's mate in the Scottish Fifeshire Fencibles in Ireland. His colonel had objected to Brown's proposed departure, so that only Banks's direct approach to the Lord Lieutenant of Ireland had won the young, medically-trained Scotsman for the *Investigator*. Flinders had good reason to be grateful for Banks's crucial intervention, as Brown was to prove himself the ideal botanist–explorer. Frequently, Flinders would accompany Brown and the other 'scientific gentlemen' on their botanising expeditions into the Australian hinterland, or he would climb mountains with them in order to gain a vantage point over the surrounding territory. In recognition of the quality of his work and of his enthusiasm for it under trying circumstances, Flinders named one such mountain – located near the head of Spencer Gulf – after his botanist.

Brown proved a zealous collector during his travels. Part of his collection came to grief on Wreck Reef while being transported in the *Porpoise*, but Brown himself had wisely chosen to remain with the artist Ferdinand Bauer in Sydney. There they shared a house until Brown departed for the south where he spent nine months, mainly in Tasmania. It must have been with some trepidation that he eventually accepted a return passage to England for himself and his by now supplemented collection aboard the *Investigator*: the ship was at one point condemned as unseaworthy, but, by 1805, it had been recaulked and prepared for the perils of a long voyage. Happily, not only Brown but most of its cargo of flora and some fauna this time made it safely to Liverpool, and from there to London.

The plant collection numbered approximately 4000 specimens, almost half of which were hitherto quite unknown. The Australian wildlife he took with him included kangaroos, a platypus, an echidna, various birds, fish, reptiles, insects and a male wombat. The latter was given into the possession of a certain Sir Everard Home, who noted that it adapted remarkably well to its new environment.

> It burrowed in the ground whenever it had the opportunity, and covered itself in the earth with surprising quickness. It was quiet during the day, but constantly in motion in the night: was very sensible to cold; ate all kinds of vegetables; but was particularly fond of new hay, which it ate stalk by stalk, taking it into its mouth like a beaver, by small bits at a time. It was not wanting in intelligence, and appeared attached to those to whom it was accustomed, and who were kind to it.

Gould's goanna, *Varanus gouldii* (Gray, 1838), Ferdinand Bauer. Naturhistorisches Museum, Vienna

Kangaroo foetus, *Macropus* sp., Ferdinand Bauer. Naturhistorisches Museum, Vienna

Bustard, *Eupodotis australis* (Gray), Ferdinand Bauer. Naturhistorisches Museum, Vienna

An episode of gout prevented Banks from greeting the arrival of Brown's collection with the rapturous welcome it deserved, but he did arrange for Brown to continue his work on it at the government's expense. In this way, Brown was able to commit to paper the results of his botanising carried out often in the face of privation and discomfort on the other side of the globe. In 1810 he would become librarian to Banks – a post he held even beyond Banks's death a decade later. The terms of Banks's will left Brown with an annuity of £200 and a lease of the house in Soho Square so that he could continue work on Banks's expansive collections – at least until they were transferred into a specially created department of the British Museum under the direction of none other than Brown himself. In this post, Brown's botanical interests quickly spread far beyond the analysis of Australian botany, but he never abandoned the Australian connection. His last work was an appendix to Charles Sturt's 1849 *Narrative of an Expedition into Central Australia*.

The published results from the voyage to Terra Australis confirmed Brown's reputation as one of the eminent botanical scholars of his day. His *Prodromus Florae Novae Hollandiae et Insulae Van Diemen*, published in 1810, is rightly regarded as a classic of a nascent discipline. That it was written in Latin was by no means an elitist gesture but rather a symptom of Brown's belief that science transcended national borders; he was writing as much for his continental colleagues as for his British peers, and in those days Latin was still the universal language of science. But Brown also published in English a lengthy appendix to Flinders' two-volume account under the wordy title 'General Remarks, Geographical and Systematical, on the Botany of Terra Australis'. Whether the use of the vernacular tongue made his keen scientific analysis more accessible to the layperson is for the reader to judge; in any case, it helped to establish his reputation as the originator of the science of plant geography – a reputation that soon spread far beyond British shores. The great German scientist Alexander von Humboldt, who once described Brown as the 'Botanicorum facile princeps', was one of his most ardent admirers in continental Europe.

In his great work, Brown covered 464 genera and about 1000 species of plants. The names of 187 new genera were proposed, most of which still stand today. The naming of one genus, notwithstanding its accidental misspelling, *Lechenaultia* (Goodeniaceae), was generous in its commemoration of the work of Leschenault, the botanist on the Baudin expedition. An eminent British botanist, Joseph Dalton Hooker, labelled Brown's study 'the greatest botanical work that has ever appeared'. Its reputation is based in large part on its contribution to overturning the established Linnean system of botanical tax-onomy – though Brown remained an active member of the Linnean Society, of which he was eventually to become president. In the Linnean system, used almost exclusively in Britain until Brown's day, plants were classified according to the numbers and the arrangement of sexual organs. As a result of his Australian experiences, however, Brown came out firmly in favour of the 'natural system' of botanical classification advanced by the French scholar Antoine-Laurent de Jussieu – a system that rejected the rigidities of the Linnean system by taking into account as many attributes of the plant as possible, not just the flower and its sexual system. It was a paradigm shift that encountered trenchant criticism but helped to revitalise botanical science.

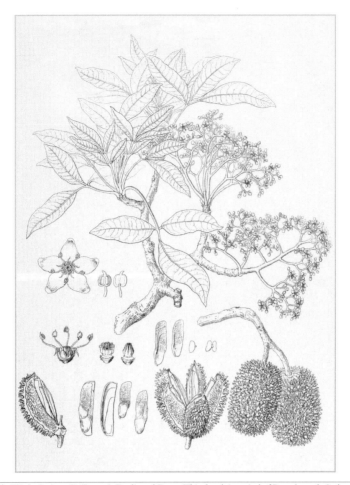

Crows Ash, *Flindersia Australis* (Brown), Ferdinand Bauer. This sketch is typical of Bauer's work. It shows all of the attributes of this plant which Brown collected at Broad Sound in Queensland and later named after his captain. Published in *A Voyage to Terra Australis* (1814)

Brown's work also provided a good example of the intertwining of the scientific projects of the French and the English and of the intellectual links that they maintained throughout the Napoleonic wars. In affirming Jussieu's system, Brown was not just participating in the collective march of European science, he was also building upon the system of a botanist who was the patron of Nicolas Baudin and who, in many ways, was to the French expedition what Sir Joseph Banks was to Flinders' voyage. Jussieu, who was Professor of Botany and director of the Muséum d'histoire naturelle of Paris, had supported and facilitated Baudin's voyage of discovery. Given Baudin's reputation as a botanical voyager and Jussieu's own intervention in the choice of the voyage's botanical staff, the eminent botanist might well have hoped that from the French expedition to Terra Australis a great scientific work would emerge. It was no doubt disappointing to him that this honour fell instead to Robert Brown. In spite of Jussieu's efforts to secure the means for Brown's French counterpart, Leschenault, to write up his results, this would occur far too late to secure for French botanists the recognition that counted – in scientific nomenclature and publication.

Not that the botanical harvest from the French expedition was meagre. On the contrary, the scope and variety of the French collections were impressive by any standards. Jussieu wrote to Banks in 1810 that specimens from the Baudin voyage had greatly enriched the herbarium of the Jardin des Plantes in Paris. He had already noted in his report of 1804 that, in addition to the plants and seeds brought back by the sole surviving gardener Guichenot, there were the collections prepared and sketched by Leschenault, which included 600 new species. Even though Leschenault eventually published a report in the second volume of the official account that appeared in 1816, the timing meant that Brown's work was already well known.

This tardiness can readily be attributed to a series of discouraging – one might say overwhelming – accidents: the death of Riédlé, the head gardener whom Baudin had designated as irreplaceable right from the start; the death of Sautier, the gardener's assistant; the illness that delayed Leschenault's return to France until 1807. Yet the efforts of Riédlé and Leschenault were not in vain. Scientist and historian of the Baudin expedition, Michel Jangoux, has determined that much of the Baudin collection is still to be found in the herbarium of the Muséum and he leads a team involved in the identification and description of the specimens that remain. Late recognition is thus still possible for Baudin's zealous botanists. Furthermore, we know that certain of the seeds and plants collected by the botanists on the Baudin expedition were soon propagated and acclimatised in the south of France, with the effect that they were of immediate 'usefulness', in accordance with the expedition's instructions.

However, for botany, as for the other areas of natural science, the lack of contemporary interest in the expedition was the most serious impediment to the proper and speedy dissemination of results. For this, the political turmoil that greeted the expedition on its return was much more to blame than the competence of its surviving scientists or its institutional patrons such as Jussieu. Since this situation affects to a greater or lesser degree all of the scientific results of the voyage, it is of interest to examine the circumstances to which

Baudin's men of science returned in 1804 before attempting to judge the lasting value of their achievements.

We have already noted that the expedition returned to France with a poor reputation and to heightened political tension that made the French authorities unwilling to pour additional resources into a purely scientific endeavour. The peace treaty of Amiens had been broken and French–English hostility reignited. With the French Navy blocked by British forces in the Channel and the defeat of Trafalgar soon to confirm, in 1805, that naval glory was not to belong to Napoleon, the return of the expedition was yet another reminder of frustrated maritime ambitions. Besides, in 1804 naval resources were tight, which meant that the senior officers of the expedition, such as Milius and Hamelin, were needed for active service rather than as chroniclers of the voyage of discovery. The fact that they seemed to have thought it prudent to accept naval duties is perhaps yet another indication of the expedition's poor standing.

Indeed, Baudin's supporters in high places had effectively been marginalised – the scientific community wielded less influence since Bonaparte had become First Consul in 1802 and was on his way to becoming Emperor in 1804. He no longer relied on the support of the scientists to establish his intellectual and philosophical credentials. Besides, Napoleon's ambitions were now clearly centred on the European scene and the Baudin expedition had lost much of its relevance. Forfait, the Minister of Marine who had originally authorised the voyage, had been replaced by Decrès, already angered by reports of Baudin's behaviour in Mauritius on the journey out. The career officers who had deserted at Mauritius had also contributed to turning the tide of opinion against Baudin and, most importantly, in hardening the attitude of Decrès, who would systematically oppose or delay any form of funding to the expedition – either for back pay or for publishing the voyage's official account. The politically poisoned climate of Mauritius continued to influence Baudin's destiny; even after his death, charges of irregular accounting were laid against him in that colony. To these recriminations were added those of François Péron who, in a letter to Decrès written immediately upon his return in 1804, implied that Baudin had sought to sell part of the expedition's collection of live animals in Mauritius.

It is difficult today to give credence to any of these accusations, as Frank Horner has so convincingly demonstrated. Péron's tactic of blackening the commander's name did little to enhance the expedition's scientific reputation or the Minister's eagerness to salvage it. Even the enthusiastic report on the scientific collections that Jussieu addressed to Decrès could do little to sway the

Minister's steely resolve to confine to oblivion what he considered a national embarrassment. Baudin's dissident scientists and officers had obviously been more successful than they had intended.

How then was science to emerge with honour? It was only when Péron's extraordinary energy and persistence were put to the defence of science rather than politics that official channels began to open. For two years Péron's pleas to Napoleon, to the Empress and to Decrès for permission and support to publish the expedition's findings fell on deaf ears. However, it was clear that zoological specimens had been brought back in huge numbers – including over 2500 new species – and that they would yield spectacular results. When Péron pleaded his case once more to the Museum, this time it was the zoologist Cuvier who sprang to his defence in a letter addressed, not to Decrès, but to the Minister of the Interior.

Georges Cuvier was a distinguished scholar credited with founding the disciplines of comparative anatomy and palaeontology. Like Jussieu, he had been influential in the preparation of the expedition and he was also the mentor of Péron, whose appointment he had recommended. His support was crucial – and effective: in August 1806, Napoleon approved the plan for Péron and Lesueur to write the official account of the voyage. The first part was to be completed by the end of the same year. Yet it is in this decision that further disappointments lay ahead in terms of the dissemination of Péron's scientific results. Péron had published some of his own findings while awaiting a decision on the voyage's fate, but Napoleon's decision meant that his energies would now be directed exclusively to the publication of the record of the journey itself. Consequently his study of the zoology of New Holland would never be completed, and most of his papers would be unavailable to science until the late nineteenth century.

In 1810 Péron died of tuberculosis before he could finish writing either the official account of the voyage or his own substantial findings. His partner, Lesueur, attempted to carry on their joint work, but when Lesueur was overlooked as the chronicler of the voyage in favour of Louis Freycinet, he was so incensed by the injustice that he eventually decided to pursue his career as an artist–zoologist in America. It was not until after Lesueur's death in 1846 that many of Péron's papers, as well as Lesueur's, were bequeathed to the Muséum d'histoire naturelle in Le Havre. The sour legacy of the Baudin expedition and of the politics that engulfed it was not only illness, death and bitter disappointment; it was also the failure to produce results in the very domain where the expedition deserved most to excel.

But recognition could not be withheld entirely. Péron's contribution to the historical records of the voyage was considerable and the first volume of the *Voyage de découvertes aux Terres Australes* that he did publish in 1807 contained many scientific observations of his own, as well as summaries of those made by his colleagues in other disciplines. The atlas that accompanied the first volume also contained a valuable record of the visual documents drawn by Lesueur and Petit to support the observations of the scientists. Péron did not receive due scientific recognition for this particular work which, along with the subsequent volumes completed and published between 1811 and 1816 by Louis Freycinet, provides a fascinating glimpse of the breadth of the zoological results that might have been attributed to Péron and his collaborator, Lesueur, the artist whom he helped to become a scientific illustrator extraordinaire but also a zoologist in his own right.

Nowhere are the combined gifts of the two zoologists more evident than in their studies of jellyfish, a much neglected area of scientific inquiry prior to the Baudin voyage. This was one of the few areas where they had managed to publish results, and even though there were complaints that they published the descriptions without the illustrations, which made the ground-breaking nature of their study hard to appreciate in their own time, it greatly impressed Cuvier. This opinion has been confirmed by modern science, which now has access to Lesueur's illustrations and to Péron's papers, with the result that they are credited with the discovery of 18 new species. Cuvier may well have been frustrated that these precious documents were not available to him, but this did not prevent him and his colleagues from working on the zoological specimens available to them in the Museum, which resulted in further attributions, many to Cuvier himself. In spite of all of the obstacles, the zoological results were impressive by any standards.

Of course, we should be wary of attributing these to Péron and Lesueur alone, and neglecting the role played by those who died in the course of the voyage. It would have been difficult for the Museum to continue its work after Péron's death without, for example, the specimens prepared early in the voyage by Maugé, an expert taxidermist. In other scientific disciplines, there had also been significant contributions. Riédlé the gardener had been tireless in the collection and preservation of his plants and would also have greatly assisted his botanist colleagues at the Museum if he had survived. Depuch the mineralogist had worked hard and well, as his various reports revealed, but, unfortunately, his journal was lost, and along with it many of the expedition's mineralogical findings. Bernier the astronomer was greatly respected by his captain and left

Jellyfish, *Toxorchis thalassinus* (Péron & Lesueur, 1810), Charles-Alexandre Lesueur. Muséum d'histoire naturelle, Le Havre – n° 70 022

other reminders of his presence than just his calculations – he notated, for instance, along with Lesueur the three Aboriginal chants that were published in the atlas of the voyage.

Baudin himself, whom Péron had so unfairly branded the enemy of science, must figure prominently among those who did not survive to reap the rewards of their efforts. Although self-educated, he had strong scientific interests and even credentials to rival those of Flinders: his history shows his passion for collecting botanical specimens; he was a member of the Society of the Observers of Man; he had even invented his own oscillometer, to measure the roll of the ship. During the voyage, he had always been at pains to protect the integrity of the natural history collections – insisting, for example, that Levillain's collections, sold and dispersed to the crew after his death in

*New Holland – New South Wales. Aboriginal music 1° Chant, 2° Dance melody, 3° Rallying cry*, notated by Lesueur and Bernier. Muséum d'histoire naturelle, Le Havre – n° 16 059.1

Tasmania, be returned then and there to the expedition. He had ensured that the live animals were given the utmost care and attention to guarantee their survival – even if it meant housing them in the scientists' cabins.

Baudin was also known to concern himself with the problem of classifications. His opinions inspired confidence in some of his subordinates; Hamelin was in the habit of consulting his commander on the value of natural history specimens. In the later stages of the voyage, Baudin's competence seemed to evaporate, as we see from his difference of opinion with Péron over teeth found in Shark Bay. Influenced no doubt by Dampier's earlier assessment of a similar find, he was convinced that they belonged to a hippopotamus, while Péron rightly asserted that they belonged to a dugong. Nevertheless, Baudin's journal was a precious and reliable source of information on the scientific matters raised during the voyage. It contained information that would assist in identifying the now extinct Kangaroo Island emu, and it is fitting that the species, recently identified, should bear Baudin's name. It was he who had acquired the live emus and his instructions had been vital in preserving them. This concern extended to all of the expedition's natural history collections, which arrived safely back in France in such spectacular numbers. The results of the expedition would most likely have been even more impressive had Baudin been able to write up the official account, leaving Péron free to disseminate his results and perhaps placing him under a greater obligation to keep the expedition's documentation intact.

Baudin also had an important role to play in the other area of research that was to bring lasting – although far from immediate – recognition to his voyage. This was in the domain of anthropology. Previous expeditions, including those of Cook, Bougainville and d'Entrecasteaux, had collected ethnographic data, but none had set out to do so in quite the way prescribed by the instructions for Baudin's voyage. These had been prepared by prominent members of the Society of the Observers of Man, and they recommended the study of primitive peoples in all of their social and cultural manifestations. Joseph-Marie Degérando, one of the Society's early members who is now considered a pioneer of the discipline of anthropology, had also transmitted an essay on anthropological method to Baudin. His approach was based upon the Enlightenment ideal of a common humanity. For Degérando, 'primitive' peoples were simply at a different stage of development from their European counterparts. In order to understand these peoples, he recommended the detailed study and recording of their social and cultural practices, according particular importance to language.

Degérando's ideas were, however, already in competition with another tendency that would later dominate nineteenth-century anthropology and that was illustrated in the second set of anthropological instructions given to the Baudin expedition – by Georges Cuvier. Cuvier's interest lay less in the study of social context, as recommended by Degérando, than in the anatomical features that were postulated as characterising different races.

While the expedition did not systematically adhere to either set of instructions, it was serious in its attempt to gather the kinds of social and physical information required, particularly on the peoples of Tasmania. As such, its records, both written and visual, are precious documents for the study of the now vanished peoples of Maria and Bruny Islands. These include the reports of both Baudin and Péron, Petit's drawings, Péron's vocabulary lists and the results obtained by Péron with his dynamometer – an instrument designed to measure muscular strength. They also collected information and drawings from their encounters with the original inhabitants of Port Jackson and Western Australia, as well as various ethnographic objects and artefacts, such as canoes and spears – including a collection of objects from the South Seas donated by George Bass to the planned museum of the Society of the Observers of Man.

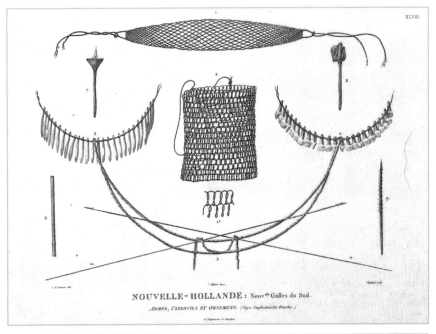

*New Holland – New South Wales, Weapons, utensils and ornaments.* Charles-Alexandre Lesueur, Muséum d'histoire naturelle, Le Havre – n° 16 036

In spite of these riches, the anthropological contribution of the voyage was overlooked for many decades. Once again, the politics of Empire were to blame. During the absence of the voyagers, the second class of the Institute had been disbanded by Bonaparte and, when the expedition returned in 1804, the Society was in its last days. Partly for this reason, and partly because the expedition had originally been instructed to collect artefacts for Josephine, the entire collection of ethnographic objects was sent to her property at Malmaison. The collection was partly destroyed in 1814 by invading troops; the rest was dispersed and sold in 1829.

The written and visual records were fortunately retained for posterity and their value was to increase over time. This anthropological material was largely the work of François Péron, although the variety of his scientific activities during the voyage meant that he did not devote himself exclusively to the task and needed at times to be prompted by Baudin to do so. François Péron described himself as the expedition's anthropologist, but his interest in the question was relatively recent, which probably explains why the commander refers ironically to Péron as 'our observer of Man'.

In fact, Péron had been appointed to the expedition as a trainee zoologist, even though he had requested a place as a student of medicine and anthropologist. The essay he had submitted to support his claim stressed how the study of other peoples could lead to useful information in the treatment of disease. At this point, his preoccupations were not inspired by Degérando's views but by his own medical studies; even though he would respond to some of Degérando's recommendations, the anthropological research which he undertook more systematically than any other was in line with his original ideas. The main thrust of his field-work was thus to test the relative strengths of the peoples he encountered, expecting to confirm the superior strength of 'savage' man and hence the superiority in physical terms of the 'primitive' lifestyle. When his results did not confirm his expectations, any more than did his contacts with the Tasmanians, Péron moved away from the Enlightenment assumptions on which his experiment had been based and towards the position of his mentor, Cuvier. He not only abandoned any notion of the 'noble savage' and the inevitable progress of all peoples towards civilisation but, as anthropologist George Stocking points out, he also seemed to support the notion of racial difference. This change reflects the reasons for the disappearance of the Society, whose humanist precepts were no longer in fashion; physical anthropology would eventually provide the basis for the inegalitarian theory that flourished in the nineteenth century.

As an anthropoligist, Péron stood at the intersection of eighteenth and nineteenth-century thought. But herein lies an essential difference between himself and Baudin. It has been well argued by commentators, firstly F.C.T. Moore and later Miranda Hughes, that Baudin, in his reports on the peoples of Tasmania, was a better practitioner of the methods of Degérando than was Péron. His observations were not so inclined to speculation as were those contained in the lyrical prose of the 'observer of Man'. Baudin also remained firmly within the bounds of Enlightenment philosophy. We already know from his letter to Governor King that he saw no justification for dispossessing the Tasmanians of their land. His observations of their life and customs had not led him to believe that they would benefit from the 'civilising' influence of the Europeans, as Péron believed the Aborigines of Port Jackson had done. In spite of the field-work conducted by Péron, we do need to ask ourselves, upon reading Baudin: who was the more rigorous anthropologist? Regardless of the response, we can see that it was not only temperamental differences that distinguished them; they were separated just as effectively by the philosophical differences that made them men of different centuries.

The study of science thus reveals all of the reasons for the grandeur and misery of the Baudin expedition. There was no room for two such dominating personalities on the one ship, a situation that meant conflict until one winner emerged to impose his version of events and his achievements. History initially designated Péron, who chose to efface the memory of his rival. With all the records available to us, we can no longer accept that single point of view. From these, we can see that Baudin deserves to stand alongside the men of science whose work he encouraged. Critics have often pointed to the excessive number of scientists aboard as one of the principal reasons for the commander's difficulties. The Flinders expedition, with its more modest dimensions, had been better focused; botany was a clear winner, thanks to the diligence of Robert Brown and the patronage of Joseph Banks. The lines of authority were clear. But was not another reason for Baudin's difficulties to be found in the extraordinary personality of François Péron, and the battle for scientific authority that, unlike the battle of wills, remained largely unspoken?

# chapter eighteen

# THE CLASH OF CULTURES

Baudin and Flinders were both well aware that their voyages in Australian waters would necessarily lead to encounters with indigenous people. Neither captain wished that the inevitable 'clash of cultures' would take the form of open violence and bloodshed – indeed both genuinely worked hard to retain the peace. At the same time, the balance of colonial pragmatism and scientific altruism on the two expeditions was different. Where Flinders' behaviour was driven by a recognition that to understand the local populations and to cultivate harmonious relations would ease the process of settlement, Baudin and his men were not so far advanced or implicated in this same process. They could pursue a more disinterested engagement with the Aborigines, applying the theories of the day and nurturing the new 'science' of anthropology. Whether in the end the French scientific approach offered a more enlightened understanding of Australia's Aborigines is a moot point – as we have seen, anthropology, like the other scientific disciplines, had its place in the Europeans' imperial endeavours. For both expeditions, the potential for misunderstanding was thus great.

In the early nineteenth century British and French expectations of encounters with indigenous people in the Pacific and elsewhere were framed by a mixture of stereotypes, drawn largely from fantasy on the one hand and previously recorded experience on the other. Often there lay a yawning chasm between the two that could be filled only by renewed direct experience.

The most widely disseminated stereotype of the time was that of the 'noble savage'. Many Europeans had been struck by the apparent generosity and nobility of indigenous people living on Pacific Islands such as Tahiti or Fiji, and by their perception of a society living in harmony with nature. In fact, those perceptions had as much to do with what Europeans wanted and hoped to find there as with the reality before their eyes. Though prevalent above all in the eighteenth century, 'noble savage syndrome' in a Pacific context could be traced back at least as far as the Spanish navigator Pedro Fernández de Quirós who, in the early seventeenth century, had set off in search of a presumed great southern land. When he stumbled across what is now known as Vanuatu he was quite sure he had found it. His descriptions of what he labelled 'La Austrialia del Espíritu Santo' and its people were nothing less than rapturous, with the result that many attempted to follow him in his search for this southern arcadia.

Against the inspired visions of Quirós, with their flimsy foundations, were the experiences of navigators whose discoveries extended to the real Australia. Flinders would have been familiar with the writings of his country-man, William Dampier, who had twice visited the coast of New Holland in the late seventeenth century. Dampier's experience of the indigenous population could hardly have been more different from that of Quirós.

> The Inhabitants of this Country are the miserablest People in the World . . .
> setting aside their Humane Shape, they differ but little from Brutes. They are
> tall, strait-bodied, and then, with small long Limbs. They have great Heads,
> round Foreheads, and great Brows. Their Eyelids are always half closed, to
> keep the Flies out of their Eyes . . . They are long-visaged, and of a very
> unpleasing Aspect, having no one graceful Feature in their Faces. Their Hair
> is black, short and curl'd, like that of the Negroes; and not long and lank like
> the Common Indians: The Colour of their Skins, both of their Faces and the
> rest of their Body, is Coal-black, like that of the Negroes of Guinea.

In the age of Enlightenment, too, sailors often found that local populations adopted less than noble standards of hospitality in dealing with their European interlopers. James Cook's experience was somewhat ambivalent. With an implicit reference to Dampier, he wrote of the Aborigines he encountered at Endeavour River that 'they may appear to some to be the most wretched people upon earth', but then went on to observe that 'in reality they are far happier than we Europeans'. On that first of his three great voyages of exploration, Cook was equipped with a set of instructions infused with Enlightenment ideals about the brotherhood of all humankind. Thus he was enjoined to bear in mind that the native peoples he would encounter . . .

… are natural, and in the strictest sense of the word, the legal possessors of the several Regions they inhabit. No European Nation has a right to occupy any part of their country, or settle among them without their voluntary consent.

Conquest over such people can give no just title; because they could never be Aggressors.

They may naturally and justly attempt to repell intruders, whom they may apprehend are come to disturb them in the quiet possession of their country, whether that apprehension be well or ill founded.

Therefore should they in a hostile manner oppose a landing, and kill some men in the attempt, even this would hardly justify firing among them, till every other gentle method had been tried.

In practice, Cook found it difficult to persevere with gentle methods of persuasion and, against the Royal Society's advice, did not go to much effort to consult with the Aborigines before claiming New South Wales for Britain.

The French experience was similarly ambivalent. The fate of the navigator Marion-Dufresne, the victim of cannibalism in 1773, was well known to his successors. The *philosophes* of the eighteenth century may well have acquainted navigators of their time with the concept of the 'noble savage', but experience taught them to be deeply sceptical of it – as La Pérouse's example shows. After one of his landing parties was ambushed in Samoa and 12 Frenchmen lost their lives, he noted bitterly: 'I am a hundred times angrier at the philosophers who praise them … than at the savages themselves. Lamanon, whom they massacred, was saying the day before that these men were worth more than we are …'

History had therefore taught Baudin and his men to approach the indigenous populations of New Holland with great caution. The commander's preconceived ideas of the inhabitants of western Australia seemed to be closely influenced by those of Dampier, whose *Voyage to New Holland* was part of the ship's library and which Baudin often quoted in his log entries for 1801. Apprehension was the dominant mood when, in June 1801, a series of encounters took place in Geographe Bay. The lone figure whom Baudin saw fishing inspired little in the way of confidence – the commander described his expression as 'very unpleasant'. The feeling was no doubt mutual, since the Aborigine first signalled to the Europeans to go back to their ship and then fled without showing the slightest interest in the trinkets he was offered.

In the second encounter, Lesueur tells of the fear that he and his companion inspired in an Aboriginal couple. The man fled, but the pregnant woman had no means of escape. Refusing all overtures of friendship, she remained paralysed with fear until they departed. The news of the white men's arrival must then have spread because, in the third encounter, the French were greeted by men armed with spears. Frightened as they were, the French refrained from using their guns, even to repulse their potential assailants. As Depuch, the mineralogist, reported to Baudin:

> Hard pressed as we were, we had either to open fire on them and perhaps kill one of them to intimidate the others, or make an orderly retreat to the spot where we had disembarked, without turning our backs on them for a single moment. As you can well imagine, we preferred the latter course, even though we were quite determined to respond to the first spear by a charge of shot, to the second by a few bullets. The philanthropic sentiments that formed the basis for our conduct in this circumstance will have your approval, Citizen Commander, we know. The advantage that the superiority of our arms gives us over these men is already too considerable to allow us to refuse them, or even envy them, the advantage of striking the first blow. If everyone had made it his duty at all times to employ such moderation, how many fatal combats we could have avoided, how much innocent blood would not have been spilt, as in the case of that inhabitant of New Caledonia who caused so many pious tears to be shed by Cook, and by Forster and the other philosophers accompanying that famous circumnavigator . . .

In spite of their own fear, Baudin's companions had been well instructed in the behaviour they must adopt in their dealings with the inhabitants of New Holland. The restraint they showed here in the use of firearms was maintained throughout the entire voyage. Guns were taken ashore and they were displayed and even fired as a deterrent, but they were always considered a weapon of the last possible resort. Baudin must take some credit for having impressed these 'philanthropic sentiments' on his men, as Depuch's remarks clearly show.

But this 'philanthropy' did not always come without a cost. At Geographe Bay, Baudin himself was consumed by fear that his men had been overpowered by natives when, insufficiently armed and prepared, they had been forced by rough weather to spend the night ashore. He remarked in his log that he had wept 'bitter tears' while anxiously awaiting their return. However, they did return and, if there was loss of life, it was by accidental drowning, not by aggression from the people the French had expected to be 'brutes'. The only incident that resulted in any violence in New Holland was at Shark Bay, in July 1801, when a midshipman from the *Naturaliste* was injured by a fire-stick. During the survey of the western Australian coast, indeed during the entire voyage, no Aboriginal casualties were recorded. The commander's constant reminders to his men to be prudent in their behaviour and 'philanthropic' in their manner served them well.

Depuch's remarks also reveal that the French were aware of how they wished to measure up to the English: namely, to be seen as more 'philan-thropic' than their colonial rivals. From altruism, but perhaps also because of future colonial designs, they were at pains to leave a good impression in New Holland. It is a fact that Baudin cast a pragmatic eye upon the inhabitants of the as yet unexploited western coast. In his letter to the Minister he assessed its inhabitants unfavourably as partners or subordinates in any future enterprise; he could not see them as traders or labourers, for example.

In many ways, then, the New Hollanders conformed to the expectations the French had formed even before setting out on the expedition. The encoun-ters were too brief and inconclusive to give them any real insights into the customs and lifestyle of those whom they had the duty to study. There was also little opportunity for the artists to do more than sketch the empty huts. Baudin, as an 'observer of man', would go no further in his assessment than the scarce details would permit; as the commander, he was relieved to have left unfriendly shores without incident.

On the other hand, François Péron was always prepared to advance a few speculations and did so in an impressive scientific report on Geographe Bay that Baudin included in the fair copy of his journal. Baudin was in no way sarcastic about the work finally produced. Indeed, here, as during the subse-quent sojourn in Tasmania, he may have been anxious to ensure that Péron should devote more of his considerable energies to anthropology. Péron had no contact with the Aborigines himself in Geographe Bay, but he had made a discovery for which he claimed great significance – a carefully designed and decorated space that he took to be a 'sacred grove'. There appeared to be many semi-circular meeting-places in the area – Baudin briefly describes them – but none of these corresponds to the site that Péron later had illustrated in the official account of the voyage. He attributed such importance to it that he had it included as an inset for the map of Geographe Bay and for the plan of Sydney Town.

Unfortunately there are no other witnesses to Péron's discovery, as he had wandered off into the forest on his own, but there is no reason to doubt the interest of what he saw. The spectacle of an amphitheatre encircled by paper-barks and decorated with mysterious symbols stirred his imagination. He wondered whether the riverside amphitheatre was a place of worship and compared the Aborigines to the Egyptians who venerated the river that sustained them. Even more importantly, he was led to speculate on their relationship with the natural world and on their capacity for finer feelings.

> Everything about the grove, its coolness, its simple and touching decoration, its situation, the grassy bench, this greenery, these clear and limpid waters, everything about it indicated that it had been consecrated by men who were gentle and good. It could not possibly be part of any mystery involving iniquity or the spilling of blood . . . crime always seeks refuge in darkness.

Unlike his fellow travellers, Péron refused to conclude that the New Hollanders were 'savages' or 'brutes'. He preferred to leave the question open, declaring:

> we know nothing certain about the moral character of these men nor could we have any concrete knowledge on that question . . . for how could we determine such a delicate matter in a few instants after having seen only a few men whom we did not understand, who did not understand us and whom we could not approach; it was impossible . . . Moreover, it was most unfortunate that the expressions of friendship our men lavished on them were no more effective than their presence had been at overcoming their prejudice, or rather their indifference, which I find quite extraordinary and whose cause it would be most interesting to ascertain.

Péron obviously remained optimistic that further study would reveal the New Hollanders as 'gentle and good' children of nature, in other words as 'noble savages'. In his speculations on the religion and on the symbolic writings of the Aborigines of Geographe Bay, Péron was at odds with the findings of his fellow voyagers who had seen little of this 'gentle' nature. While his exalted conclusions did him great honour, for they preserved the humanity of the people he had not yet seen, they ill prepared him mentally for the real and significant contact that would soon take place.

It was in Tasmania, after a prolonged stay and many shared observations, that the anthropologist and his fellow scientists and voyagers came to reconcile their views. They had all expected to establish friendlier relations with the native populations of Van Diemen's Land than with the New Hollanders, thanks largely to the positive reports brought back by the d'Entrecasteaux expedition; it was here that Péron believed he would find the answers to the questions that had intrigued him in Geographe Bay. The first contacts with the Tasmanians comforted him in his optimism. Péron himself encountered a family group at Port Cygnet and was impressed by the maternal feelings displayed by a mother towards her baby, as well as by the friendly innocence of a young girl called Ouré-Ouré and by the air of affection and trust that marked the entire encounter. Baudin and others had had similar experiences, after which the commander concluded that there was 'nothing unpleasant' about these people. Unhappily, the feeling was short-lived.

The very next day, Maurouard, one of the midshipmen, was injured by a spear without there having been the slightest hint that anything was amiss. While Baudin remained calm about the incident and sought to find a rational explanation for it – namely that Maurouard may have unwittingly humiliated one of the men by defeating him in a wrestling match – Péron's positive feelings seem to have evaporated. The description of his next encounter with the Bruny Islanders was coloured by the impression that he was dealing with a potentially treacherous and hostile group. Although the meeting was friendly, Péron was under no illusion that mutual trust had been established; he also drew attention to the repugnant appearance of the women and to the anger and jealousy of their 'ferocious spouses'. His position regarding the noble savage had been suddenly and radically altered by the tense encounters with people whom he had intended to glorify. Their reluctance to accept any familiarity seems to have disappointed him bitterly, indeed even wounded and offended him, so greatly did his language and attitude change in comparison with his report on Geographe Bay. Even though Péron was no different from his companions when he concluded that the Tasmanians were not noble savages after all, it is surprising that his open-minded benevolence had so rapidly deserted him, unless we see in his change of heart the reaction to the collapse of all that had inspired him to request a place on the expedition. Perhaps if he had made contact with the New Hollanders, like his companions, the shock would not have been so brutal.

This change in attitude did not prevent Péron from collecting valuable data during the stay in Tasmania, but it did have some effect on his motivation: he needed some reminding to approach his anthropological duties as systematically as his other scientific collecting. Baudin was obliged to prompt Péron to devote his full attention to a study of the Tyreddeme people of Maria Island, in south-east Tasmania – he rose to the task by completing a detailed series of observations. Péron added to the vocabulary compiled by La Billardière, the botanist and chronicler of the d'Entrecasteaux expedition, and noted many details of the customs of the Maria Islanders.

He also undertook what is often described as a first in terms of anthropological field research, its serious errors notwithstanding. With his dynamometer, an apparatus intended to measure the strength of the subject's arms and upper legs, Péron set about testing, or questioning, his original hypothesis that civilisation was a corrupting and degenerative influence on mankind. He had intended to demonstrate this Rousseauist principle by proving that primitive peoples were physically stronger than those who lived in civilised society. In line with his change of views about the noble savage, he managed to prove exactly the opposite. When Péron completed his survey by comparing the strength of the Timorese, the Europeans, the New Hollanders and the Tasmanians, the order of superiority descended from the Europeans to the Tasmanians – even though there was a strong case for invalidating the Tasmanians' results (they had scored so poorly partly because they were reluctant to participate). The results were clearly more indicative of Péron's new philosophy than they were of the relative strength or 'humanity' of the Tasmanians. Since he now considered that humanity was the product of civilisation, he could no longer see any virtue at all in the lifestyle of the children of nature he had once so lavishly praised.

Aboriginal tomb on Maria Island (Tasmania), Charles-Alexandre Lesueur or Nicolas-Martin Petit. Muséum d'histoire naturelle, Le Havre – n° 18 019

It seems ironic today that the great achievement of Péron as an anthropologist was not his initiation into the living culture of the Tasmanians but his discovery of their cult of the dead. On Maria Island, Leschenault, the botanist, and Péron separately discovered tombs that contained cremated human remains in different stages of decomposition. Péron is generally credited with the discovery, since it was his description, accompanied by Petit's and Lesueur's drawings, that ensured that the details of burial practice amongst the islanders were preserved for the benefit of later researchers. As the anthropologist Rhys Jones points out, the bark linings of one of the tombs were covered in symbols that were later found to be related to body cicatrices and hence to group identity. Péron in his own reports did not speculate on them in the same way that he had done for the symbols of the 'sacred grove'. Even if he puzzled over the existence of religious sentiment among the Tasmanians, his fervour and his idealism had deserted him: nothing could sway his opinion of the people for whom he later postulated different racial origins from the Aborigines of the mainland.

The third series of encounters with Aborigines that took place in Port Jackson confirmed for Péron the lessons of the Tasmanian sojourn. His experiments with the dynamometer continued to 'prove' that the Tasmanians were physically more degenerate than the mainlanders, while the easy contacts with the inhabitants of Port Jackson also added grist to his mill concerning the beneficial influence of civilisation. He himself did little more in the way of field work, although he mentions Aboriginal mythology and rock art a propos of a trip to the Blue Mountains. Other vital ethnographical records, as we have seen, were assembled by various members of the party, especially the artists. Among the artworks there are also some examples of Aboriginal drawings – whether these were done by Aborigines themselves, to whom the French gave pencil and paper, or whether they are copies, by Petit or Lesueur, of Aboriginal rock art, has been the subject of some discussion. Current opinion would have it that they are indeed drawings done by Aborigines, which would make them unique historical documents. In any case, their existence confirms that the artists were fascinated by what they saw in Port Jackson and made concerted efforts to reproduce images of a social and cultural life that appeared richer to them than that of the Tasmanians.

In other words, the evolution of the expedition's artists paralleled closely that of its anthropologist. Nowhere is this more evident than in the Aboriginal portraits executed by Petit. As we know, the initial contacts in western Australia were too fleeting to allow Petit the time to make portraits; the only Aboriginal figures included in the scenes of native life in Geographe Bay were drawn from imagination. In Tasmania, the artist was obliged to sketch his subjects during tense encounters; in one of these, on Bruny Island, his drawing was snatched from his hand, as his activity aroused suspicion and even hostility. After Petit snatched it back, the group began to throw large stones, one of which hit Baudin on the hip. Although the incident had no other consequences, because of Baudin's policy on firearms, it was indicative of the difficult conditions under which the artist worked. Consequently, his portraits of the Tasmanians, although remarkable in their ethnographical detail, do not reveal mutual trust and understanding. Behind their fixed smiles, the subjects remain unknowable, in spite of attempts to 'humanise' them by the attribution of names and familiar gestures, such as the young boy holding out his hand or the mother carrying her child.

*Shelters (Van Diemen's Land)*, engraving by Lesueur from drawings by Nicolas-Martin Petit. Published in the *Atlas* of the *Voyage de découvertes aux Terres Australes* (1807)

In the atlas of the voyage, the figures are dehumanised still further – several of the individual portraits are inserted into a 'family' group assembled around a campfire, at which point the figures clearly become the representation of social types and ethnographic subjects. By contrast, the Port Jackson portraits reveal a series of knowable and dignified human subjects. In spite of features that make them exotic, they are not 'noble savages' in either anthropological or philosophical terms; the subjects no longer belong to a 'savage' or pristine environment. Petit's Port Jackson subjects, in contact with civilisation and drawn in comfortable conditions, have more 'human' features than those of Tasmania. While remaining ethnological subjects, whose body markings designate them as 'other', the Aborigines featured in the Port Jackson portraits have a demeanour and gravity that make them familiar and, in many cases, endearing; the proof that contact with civilisation has 'tamed' them is the disappearance, in most cases, of their bared teeth and strained features. But these have been replaced by a perceptible sadness. Petit's art, in spite of the nobility it captured and the empathy it displayed, augured no better for the survival of the 'savage' than did the anthropological work of François Péron. Petit, whether consciously or not, had captured in the melancholy of his

*Norou-gal-derri going out to fight* (Port Jackson), engraving by Milbert and Roger from a drawing by Nicolas-Martin Petit. Published in the *Atlas* of the *Voyage de découvertes aux Terres Australes* (1807)

subjects something of his commander's concern for the Aboriginal peoples in contact with European civilisation.

What, then, was the attitude towards 'natural man' of the other 'observer of man' on the *Géographe* – its captain Nicolas Baudin? He certainly remained attached to his 'philanthropic sentiments'. We have observed that he maintained his stance over firearms throughout the voyage, in his anxiety to preserve the lives both of his crew and of the Aborigines they encountered. In Tasmania he went even further in his restriction of guns, fearing that much ammunition was being wasted on hunting by his men. From this we can also assume that he saw no real danger coming from the Aborigines, even though he practised and preached great vigilance. When sudden attacks occurred, such as the spearing and stone-throwing incidents, he was at great pains to seek a rational explanation that would justify the assailants' behaviour. In that he was unlike Péron, who was frequently subjective in his assessment. For example, Péron saw the use of fire by the Tasmanians as a manifestation of their destructiveness, whereas Baudin ventured different explanations throughout the length of the French stay, showing a far greater curiosity for what he rightly saw as a different cultural practice; he noted the burning out of shelters in large trees, and hypothesised on the use of fire to signal combat, to erase footprints or to facilitate hunting.

On another issue, sexuality, Baudin offers a more factual approach than Péron in describing the interest that both groups – the French and the Tasmanians – took in the other's behaviour. One suspects that the reputed friendliness of the Tasmanians may have led the French to imagine that it would extend to sexual encounters, as in the well-known Pacific voyages. Part of their displeasure with the people they actually encountered could even be related to such a frustration. Péron mentions many aspects of the sexual question – the first happy meeting with the 'flirtatious' Ouré-Ouré seemed promising, for example. But hostility was soon the dominant tone; he notes the jealousy of the men when they saw their wives making 'flirtatious' overtures to the Europeans. Later he tried to discover whether they were in the habit of kissing and was struck by the fact that it appeared unfamiliar to them; he also refers to the wish of the Tasmanians to undress the white men and particularly to see their genitals. He concludes, after noting the Aborigines' astonishment at seeing a young sailor growing an erection during the course of one such inspection, that their surprise stemmed from the fact that they were less virile, their sexual behaviour being more akin to the cyclic activity of the animal. Again, Péron's judgments on the inferior status of his subjects intruded on his observations.

On the question of sexual relations between the European men and the Tasmanian women, however, there is silence. It was clearly a controversial topic; official prudery meant that the drawings made by Petit and Lesueur of sexual acts between Aborigines were not published in the official account of the voyage. However, we can also ask whether Péron thought that sexual relations with the Tasmanians were below contempt, since he, and others, described the women as extremely repugnant. Baudin, for his part, seemed untroubled by the possibility that some of his men might have had sexual encounters with the Tasmanian women and was willing to state the facts as plainly as convention would allow. He noted all of the incidents reported to him involving the undressing of the sailors and was indeed subject to one such request himself, consenting only to have his chest inspected. He did not gloss over the explicit advances of the women and reported that Heirisson, one of the sub-lieutenants, had been taken off into the forest by a woman who 'may have completely satisfied her curiosity'. Since Baudin specified that the Aborigines were interested in both the form and function of the male organ, there is a strong possibility that intercourse took place. Baudin commented that the women may already have had sexual encounters with Europeans. He noted not only that they had trinkets of European origin but also that there was a child whose appearance gave the impression that he was of mixed origin. Given that the Aborigines had been in contact with navigators and sealers by that time – as their familiarity with the power of firearms confirms – this seems a reasonable supposition.

Baudin has rightly been described as a better anthropologist than Péron; his reports were full of detail and were neither judgmental nor prone to theorising. If Baudin was disappointed, like Péron, by the behaviour of the Tasmanians, he did not allow it to affect his world-view. Nor did he take the opportunity to pass judgment on the Tasmanians, whose hostility was no doubt triggered by their recent contacts with whalers and sealers. In the report he sent to the Minister of Marine from Port Jackson, he commented on the hostility of the Tasmanians, mainly because he was anxious to correct the impression created by La Billardière in his account of the d'Entrecasteaux expedition, in which it was suggested that they were gentle and peaceful. His prime duty as a representative of the government was to report on possible obstacles to future trade, travel or settlement. However, his disappointment did not cause him to abandon his philosophical position nor to alter the tone with which he described his encounters with a people he surely considered 'primitive', but nevertheless part of the human race.

Baudin well understood by the end of his stay in Tasmania that its people had good reason for distrusting Europeans. More importantly, he eventually came to defend their right to live in peace. He left only one document relating to the evolution of his thinking about the Tasmanians, but it is an extraordinary one – his famous letter to Governor King from Bass Strait in December 1802. After learning of the decision to settle Tasmania, he accused the English of dispossessing a people who were no more savage than the Scots or the peasants of Brittany. His thinking had been deeply affected by his stay in Port Jackson, and in a way that radically opposed him to Péron, who became an enthusiastic supporter of the penal colony. Baudin saw the convict settlement as having retarded the progress of civilisation, as well as having brought disease to the native population; worse still, it had inspired in the local Aborigines such aversion to the white man that they sought to move away rather than mix or inter-marry with the coloniser. Of all that he saw, and in spite of his enduring affection for Governor King, Port Jackson inspired in him the strongest political and emotional reaction by offering him a view of the new world in which inequality and racism would prosper. In the inevitable clash of cultures that would ensue, he explicitly predicted the disappearance of the Aborigines.

But what was the Aboriginal view of these sombre predictions? Although the Baudin expedition is not known to have left a specific impression on the Tasmanians with whom they had spent anxious times, d'Entrecasteaux and his men left tree carvings in Recherche Bay that Baudin later saw and that the Bruny Islanders associated with the spirit of death. Anthropologist Rhys Jones suggests that the white men were also considered ghosts or spirits, which would explain why the Tasmanians were anxious to cover them with powdered charcoal. The European, with his ghostly skin and his gun, was associated with death, however well intentioned he may have been. There was thus apprehension on both sides: the French were undoubtedly keen to avoid clashing with the Tasmanians, who in turn were anxious to ensure they did not precipitate their own destruction at the hands of these potentially malevolent spirits. Baudin himself, while sensing the Tasmanians' distrust, was far from imagining the extent of their fear.

In his observations of the peoples of Australia, Baudin was nonetheless more prescient than all of his companions and more bound to the egalitarian principles of the Enlightenment, which were also those of the Revolution. His men were happier than he to adapt to the new world that they saw at Port Jackson, where they seemed less aware than Baudin of the effects of colonisation on the native population. By his philosophy and his actions, Baudin sought to avoid the clash of cultures, whereas Péron in particular saw no harm in European civilisation exercising domination over 'natural man'. However, once the British decision to colonise was known to him, Baudin was also freed from all pragmatic concerns and implications regarding the potential settlement of Tasmania by his own nation. He was thus able to head for home with his philosophy intact.

Matthew Flinders, for all his good intentions, and despite some promising early contacts, was not always so fortunate in his dealings with Australia's indigenous peoples. Ever the pragmatist, Flinders was well aware of what might happen should relations with the Aborigines spiral out of control. In that regard, the fate of his great idol, James Cook, murdered by natives in 1779 in Hawaii, provided a negative model. By the time he sailed on the *Investigator*, Flinders had already managed to collect a good deal of experience in immediate contact with the Aborigines in Australia, both during his previous stay in Sydney and on his voyages of exploration. Most of it had been positive, due in no small part to Flinders' capacity to hold his nerve in circumstances that a more tremulous spirit might have found intimidating. One incident during the voyage of the *Tom Thumb* has entered Australian folklore. At one point, the tiny boat capsized and had to be beached on the banks of a small creek. A group of Aborigines came to observe the intruders making repairs and drying their clothes and stores. To nip in the bud any possibility that resentment at an intrusion might escalate into violence, Flinders pulled forth a pair of scissors and entertained the Aborigines by clipping their hair and beards.

As commander of the *Investigator*, Flinders was armed with instructions from the Admiralty requiring him to record 'the manners and customs of the inhabitants of such parts as you may be able to explore'. There was no anthropologist among his complement of 'scientific gentlemen', so, in effect, the Admiralty was inviting Flinders himself to step into the role, albeit as a layman. Furthermore, in order to smooth the path to cordial relations in a well-tried manner, the *Investigator* was equipped with very large numbers of 'trinkets'. The method did not always yield the results expected. In spite of the offering of gifts and other friendly overtures, the Europeans encountered shyness on the part of the Aborigines; Flinders was frequently disappointed at their elusiveness.

As the account of Flinders' sojourn in King George Sound demonstrates, the expedition's initial experiences were harmonious enough and set the tone for much of the voyage. Wherever closer contact was established, Flinders was able to step into his role of amateur anthropologist. Inevitably, perhaps, his natural inclination was to compare the local inhabitants in the places he visited with those he already knew from around Sydney. He was often struck by similarities in both appearance and manner. Drawing on the scientific expertise at his disposal, he had his surgeon, Hugh Bell, take a set of anatomical measurements of one of the 'best proportioned' King George Sound Aborigines, recording height but also cranial proportions. Flinders also took a keen interest in the question of Aboriginal languages. However, in contrast to his observations on the similarity of their mannerisms and physical characteristics, he soon came to the conclusion that there existed a high degree of linguistic diversity among the groups of Aborigines he encountered in his travels. In western Australia, for example, Flinders collected a list of words, compared them with what he knew from Port Jackson, and found not the hint of similarity.

Determined though he was to provide an objective account of the local inhabitants and to cultivate cordial relations with them, Flinders hardly subscribed to any notion of racial equality. As we have seen, he set about demonstrating to the Aborigines of King George Sound their inferiority in a quite theatrical way, ordering the complement of marines aboard the *Investigator* to display their full regalia. Instead of inspiring the expected solemn sense of awe, however, this display provoked in the spectators a fit of glee and a counter-performance demonstrating a capacity for mimicry.

There were other signs too that, rather than being cowed into fear by the sight of armed men, the Aborigines went so far as to question their visitors' very masculinity. A seaman aboard the *Investigator* by the name of Samuel Smith recorded his version of contact in western Australia in which, if anything, he appears the more intimidated party.

> . . . their Features are Quite awfull having such large Mouths & long teeth every part Exhibits the Attitudes & Manners of A compleat Savage, their spears are from 8 to 12 Feet in Length, after paying us Visits several times; they Begun to Examine our people; supposing, they thought us to be of the feminine Gender, but finding their Mistake, they pointed to their Women they left in the Bush, this being their constant practice, while the Men came up to the Tents, they then rubb'd their skin against ours; expecting some mark of White wou'd apear upon theirs but finding their mistake they appear'd surprised; & soon afterwards went off Quite satisfied.

In the end, one can only speculate as to how the Aborigines perceived the exotic intruders on their shores. No written records or directly recalled experiences can provide their side of the story of contact. There are, however, a couple of clues to an Aboriginal perspective, one of them stemming from the performance of Flinders' marines. Philanthropist Daisy Bates, it seems, while working in South Australia later in the nineteenth century, once witnessed a corroboree whose origins lay on the other side of the Nullarbor. Her investigations, according to the historian H.M. Cooper,

> revealed that this colourful display, presented by strange new people arrayed in bright and vivid uniforms and carrying strange weapons, made a lasting impression on the mind of one of the appreciative audience who, later as an old man, wandered eastward into South Australia. Here he described, no doubt with skill and embellishment of his own, for the native is a born mimic, that wonderful scene to members of the local tribe and with such good effect that it became the theme of a new corroboree, passed on from generation to generation and witnessed by Mrs Bates in later years.

The other clue is a recorded song sung by an Aboriginal woman at Yardea, also in South Australia. The song tells of a beautiful white bird that flies across the ocean, then stops and folds its wings and is tied up so that it cannot escape. With its origins among the Aboriginal population of the Denial Bay area, behind the Nuyts Archipelago, the song almost certainly refers to the arrival in the region of a sailing vessel. It seems likely that the vessel in question is either the *Investigator* or the *Géographe*, since both visited the area. From an Aboriginal perspective, no doubt the Europeans all looked alike.

Though Flinders sighted some Aborigines along the unknown coast, he had merely fleeting contact with them. This disappointed Flinders, who nonetheless, like Baudin, sought rational explanations for their cautious attitude. That the Aborigines should avoid contact was, under the circumstances, entirely natural behaviour. He mused on what would happen if the roles were reversed.

> On the arrival of strangers, so different in complexion and appearance to ourselves, having power to transport themselves over, and even living upon an element which to us was impassable; the first sensation would probably be terror, and the first movement flight. We should watch these extraordinary people from our retreats in the woods and rocks, and if we

found ourselves sought and pursued by them, should conclude their designs to be inimical; but if, on the contrary, we saw them quietly employed in occupations which had no reference to us, curiosity would get the better of fear and, after observing them more closely, we should ourselves seek a communication.

In Port Lincoln there was not time to wait until the Aborigines made the first move. But when he arrived in Sydney, Flinders took a step designed to promote contact with local inhabitants during the rest of his voyage. He took on board two Aborigines, Bongaree (or Bungaree) and Nanbaree. Bongaree was already well known to Flinders from his voyage north on the *Norfolk* in 1799; he was known to be blessed with a pleasant nature and a sharp sense of humour, which he at times turned against the Europeans. It was said that he could imitate the gait and the mannerisms of every Governor of New South Wales. By agreeing to sail with Flinders again in 1802, Bongaree became the first Aborigine to circumnavigate Australia; he went on to sail extensively with the next great surveyor of the Australian coastline in Phillip Parker King. Nanbaree, whom Flinders describes as 'a good-natured lad', also sailed north aboard the *Investigator* but returned to Sydney aboard the consort *Lady Nelson* in October 1802.

Whether in reality Bongaree did much to ease contact with the Aborigines of northern Australia is unclear. The western Australian experience might have suggested to Flinders that there was no single indigenous language, and sure enough Bongaree's linguistic skills were as good as useless at any distance from Port Jackson. But the mere presence of a black man might have appeased local inhabitants and encouraged them to come forth and make contact. Sailing north from Sydney, the first such contact was made at Sandy Cape. Flinders describes it as follows:

> Several Indians with branches of trees in their hands were there collected and, whilst they retreated themselves, were waving to us to go back. Bongaree stripped off his clothes and laid aside his spear as inducements for them to wait for him; but finding they did not understand his language, the poor fellow, in the simplicity of his heart, addressed them in broken English, hoping to succeed better. At length they suffered him to come up, and by degrees our whole party joined; and after receiving some presents, 20 of them returned with us to the boats, and feasted upon the blubber of two porpoises, which had been brought on shore purposely for them. At two o'clock the naturalists

*Bungaree – A Native of New South Wales* (1826), Augustus Earle. National Library of Australia

returned, bringing some of the scoop nets used by the natives in catching fish; and we then quitted our friends, after presenting them with hatchets and other testimonials of our satisfaction.

A couple of weeks later, relations with the Aborigines reached new heights. A couple of the *Investigator*'s crew went missing overnight, having been seen earlier in the company of Aborigines. The following morning a search was organised, but the two sailors returned quite unharmed and probably better fed than if they had spent the night on their vessel. Having become disoriented the previous day, they had spent the night in a mosquito-infested mangrove swamp, but in the morning fell into the company of some 25 Aborigines who took them to a fireplace. Flinders recounts:

> A couple of ducks were broiled; and after the wanderers had satisfied their hunger and undergone a personal examination, they were conducted back to the ship in safety. Some of the gentlemen went to meet the natives with presents, and an interview took place, highly satisfactory to both parties; the Indians then returned to the woods, and our people were brought on board.

Sadly, relations were not to remain so harmonious, and a terrible tragedy occurred early the next year on a small island in the Gulf of Carpentaria. A wooding party came across a group of men from the Yolngu people of Blue Mud Bay. Flinders' account has it that a Mr Whitewood from the wooding party approached the Aborigines with friendly intent, but their first inclination had been to retreat. Later, however, a contact did occur, leading to the spearing of Mr Whitewood. According to the story gleaned by Flinders, Whitewood

> ... put out his hand to receive a spear which he supposed was offered; but the Indian, thinking perhaps that an attempt was made to take his arms, ran the spear into the breast of his supposed enemy. The officer snapped his firelock, but it missed, and he retreated to his men; and the Indians, encouraged by this, threw several spears after him, three of which took effect. Our people attempted to fire, and after some time two muskets went off, and the Indians fled; but not without taking away a hat which had been dropped.

Flinders himself had only heard the commotion and the firing of muskets from the distance of the *Investigator*, and had suspected that his own people had probably been the aggressors. His instructions to his master were that if the Aborigines had made an unprovoked attack then as punishment their canoe was to be confiscated; thereafter he himself would take appropriate action. Beyond merely securing the canoe, the master also sent the wooders to intercept the Aborigines. At dusk they came across three of them on the other side of the island. The Aborigines sought to flee in a canoe, but the Europeans fired on them, hitting one, while the others leaped from the canoe and swam away. A sailor then swam to the canoe to find the apparently lifeless body of the Aborigine, who allegedly wore the straw hat of a sailor. While both canoe and hat were recovered, the body was dumped into the water.

By his own account, Flinders was 'greatly displeased' at this turn of events. The next day he sent a boat to recover the body, 'the painter being desirous of it to make a drawing, and the naturalist and surgeon for anatomical purposes'. Sure enough, a body was found at the water's edge, but with 'the posture of a man who was just able to crawl out of the water and die'. Flinders speculated that there may have been a second death and that this may have been the body of one of those who had dived from the canoe in flight.

> He was of the middle size, rather slender, had a prominent chest, small legs, and similar features to the inhabitants of other parts of this country; and he appeared to have been circumcised! A musket ball had passed through the shoulder blade, from behind; and penetrating upwards, had lodged in the neck.

The gruesome details of what was done with the body are recorded in the journal of Seaman Smith: 'Being hoisted in the Surgeon Cut off his Head & took out his Heart & put them in Spirits: most of his bones seem'd to have been broke, & his beard Very long.'

Flinders did not say much more about the tragedy. He does not appear to have punished the sailors for disobeying orders, and then he named the island – Morgan's Island – after a sailor who died of sunstroke. Fortunately Willliam Westall has left something of a record in the form of a sketch of the recovered body. Although found face down, Westall's sketch shows it lying face up, with an unlikely covering over the genitals and a similarly improbable twig clutched in the right hand, perhaps a sign of reconciliation akin to an olive branch. Most unlikely of all though is the bullet hole in the chest – Flinders' own account reveals the uncomfortable fact that the man was shot in the back while attempting to flee.

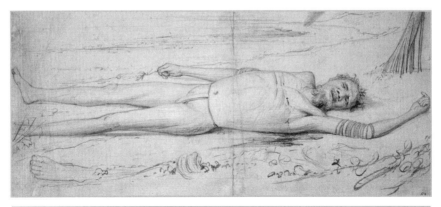

*Blue Mud Bay – body of a native shot on Morgan's Island* (1803), William Westall. National Library of Australia

Regrettably it was this isolated incident rather than the otherwise peaceful dimensions of the encounters between Europeans and Aborigines which prefigured the course of the clash of cultures in Australian history. Flinders and Baudin showed that relations could be conducted on a basis of empathy and mutual understanding. In contrast to the fleeting contact which distinguished the exploration of Flinders, Baudin and others, colonisation meant enduring contact, competition for land and other resources, and eventually for the Aborigines it meant dispossession and repression. The goodwill that both Baudin and Flinders had brought with them on their voyages of exploration was not and perhaps could not be preserved when exploration gave way to settlement.

As the goodwill died, so too did the idea of the noble savage. To conceive of native populations as essentially noble was to put them on a par with Europeans and render their subjugation unjustifiable. If the Europeans needed an ideology that would assure them of their own superiority and of the importance of their civilising project, then the idea of the noble savage just would not do. Worse than that, the inferiority of the Aborigines could not stem solely from cultural differences, which after all would be readily overcome with the arrival of the West. To establish an unbridgeable gap between colonisers

*Tombs of the Natives, View of a part of Riédlé Bay and Oyster Bay (Maria Island), of Cape Bernier, Marion Bay and the entrance to Frederick-Hendrick Bay (Van Diemen's Land)*, engraving by Milbert, Pillement and Duparc from a drawing by Charles-Alexandre Lesueur. Published in the *Atlas* of the *Voyage de découvertes aux Terres Australes* (1807)

and colonised, the differences had to be much more fundamental than that – they had to be based on the indelible differences of race. This regrettable and even fateful transition from a cultural to a racial paradigm of understanding the differences between colonisers and colonised occurred at precisely the time of the Flinders and Baudin expeditions.

The two voyages had been clearly entrapped in the same dilemma, which they articulated in different ways, all leading to the same conclusion. Whether they approved of the outcome or not, the expeditioners all could have guessed who would emerge victorious in the clash of cultures that would escalate in the wake of their voyages – and even because of their voyages and the information they had brought back to their respective colonial masters. In that sense, one of the engravings of the Baudin voyage stands as the clearest symbol of the outcome of that clash. The famous engraving of Péron, removing bones from the burial site and master of a landscape from which the living inhabitants are absent, stands as an ominous signal of what was to come for the Tasmanians. But the anthropologist was not to blame; his thinking and his acts were symptomatic of the colonial project. If he had thought differently about those he judged as an inferior race, it would not have changed the course of colonial history. But it is tragic that the views that held sway were not closer to those of Baudin.

# CONCLUSIONS

## *From Mind Games to Endgame:*
## *the Battle for the Southern Seas*

In the aftermath of the Baudin and Flinders expeditions, the rival colonial aspirations of Britain and France continued to play a significant role in the exploration and settlement of Australia, as the two nations jostled to position themselves strategically in the southern oceans. The generosity and nobility of spirit that the two captains had displayed in their dealings with one another appeared out of step with the temper of the times. Moreover, despite their many navigational and scientific achievements, the two expeditions quickly became embroiled in the politics of the day.

The expeditioners, it must be said, were not entirely blameless in this. Shortly before he left Mauritius to return home on the *Géographe*, François Péron submitted to Governor Decaen a report in which he asserted that the scientific aims of the Baudin expedition had been 'merely a pretext' and that its real purpose was to gather information about the current position and future plans of the English in the southern seas. This was of course completely fanciful. All the same, the report, modified versions of which were delivered to the new director of the Museum in Paris, Fourcroy, and to Count Fleurieu himself, contained quite detailed information on the settlement at Port Jackson. In it, Péron claimed that the defence capacity of the new colony was weak and that it would be a simple matter for French ships to blockade the narrow entrance to Port Jackson. He even went so far as to urge his government to destroy the colony, assuring the authorities that any invading force would have local support in the form of the Irish, who were said to be ready to rebel. In this way, Péron suggested, the French could put an end to the expansionist plans of the English in the Pacific.

As an exercise in espionage, Péron's report is amateurish to say the least. The information it contains is often circumstantial and much of it was already widely known. Superficial as it may have been, the report nevertheless suited the purposes of the man who had requested it – Governor-General Decaen. As one of Napoleon Bonaparte's generals, he was known for his hostility towards the English; but as the governor of a small island in the Indian Ocean, he had a particular axe to grind. His aim was to persuade the First Consul of the necessity to invade India, where the French had already lost considerable ground. This would help to restore some balance in the southern seas and make French possessions such as Mauritius less vulnerable. The flourishing state of the settlement in New South Wales and the possible establishment of further settlement sites in Australia meant that the English now had a base from which they could strengthen their position in the Pacific. This in turn would allow for the development of new commercial and military ties with the subcontinent, thereby adding to their influence in the Indian Ocean. In Decaen's view, an attack on India would put a stop to the expansionist designs of the English in the region.

Unfortunately for the governor of Mauritius, the invasion of India was not to be. Though Napoleon did show some interest in the idea, his energies were focused on a project much dearer to his heart: the invasion of England itself. In the event, Decaen's worst fears were eventually realised when, in 1810, Mauritius was taken by the English. This was shortly after Flinders had been released from his detention on the island. As fate would have it, Flinders was called upon to play a part in the invasion of Mauritius – though he may have drawn little satisfaction from this, despite his treatment at the hands of Decaen. On his passage home, Flinders stopped off in Cape Town where the commander-in-chief, Vice-Admiral Bertie, summoned him to provide information on the island he was preparing to attack. Flinders at first refused, pointing out that this would be in breach of his parole. But the Vice-Admiral insisted and Flinders eventually yielded, feeling he had no alternative. He supplied details of the island's defences and its topography – including, inevitably, a map. In this way, Decaen's prolonged detention of Flinders on Mauritius contributed, in however small a way, to the loss of the island to the English. The Baudin and Flinders expeditions, organised under the banner of scientific inquiry and conducted in the spirit of international cooperation, also left a political legacy.

Flinders, the reluctant spy, and Péron, the enthusiastic would-be spy, had each in their own way become involved in the events that unfolded in the Indian Ocean. But this was not the end of the story of Anglo-French rivalry in the southern seas, where Australia was still a prize waiting to be more fully explored and settled. Ironically, it was when the two nations had made their peace, after the defeat of Napoleon in 1815 and the restoration of the monarchy in France, that they once again became sparring partners in Terra Australis. It seems that for every French action there would be a more determined and opposite reaction on the part of the English. Governor King's earlier decision to establish a settlement in south-east Tasmania in 1803–1804 had been due in no small part to the interest shown by Baudin during his visits there. The rumours spread by Péron in Port Jackson about the supposed settlement plans of the French in D'Entrecasteaux Channel had caused some alarm. Such a scenario seemed all the more plausible as France had shown a predilection for insular territories, which it felt would be easier to defend. Baudin's visit to King Island in 1802 raised further concerns about possible French interests in Bass Strait, prompting King to move to settle Port Phillip. Whenever the French appeared to show their hand, the English responded in decisive fashion. This was a pattern that would be repeated over the next 25 years or more.

After the end of hostilities in Europe, the French renewed their interest in scientific exploration. And once again, with each new expedition science would increasingly become submerged by politics. News that the French were planning a round-the-world voyage that would take in western Australia coincided strangely with the decision to despatch Phillip Parker King, the son of the former governor of New South Wales, on a fresh hydrographic mission aimed at filling in the gaps left by Flinders in his charting of the continent. During his famous 1817–1822 surveys, he paid particular attention to the north-western coastline, the precise outline of which Baudin's cautious approach had not enabled him to determine. Because of the prompt action taken by the English, King arrived in these waters one year before the *Uranie*, under the command of Baudin's former sub-lieutenant Louis Freycinet, anchored in Shark Bay. Although Freycinet's mission was purely scientific – to set up an observatory in order to study the earth's magnetic field and gather meteorological data – the reappearance of the French in western Australia fuelled new rumours about their intentions.

As it happens, these rumours, while speculative, were not entirely baseless. In 1819 plans were indeed being considered in Paris for the colonisation of south-western Australia. The Swan River and King George Sound were favoured as potential sites for a convict settlement. A short time later, two expeditions were sent to the Pacific, with instructions that included a fact-finding visit to these areas. For different reasons, neither of these expeditions complied with their orders: both Duperrey (1822–1825) and Hyacinthe de Bougainville (1824–1826) – another of Baudin's former officers and the son of the great Pacific explorer – chose to by-pass south-western Australia. Nevertheless, the alert was given. The French were closing in and pre-emptive action was required. Accordingly, Governor Brisbane sent a contingent under the command of Major Lockyer to occupy King George Sound. The English contingent landed near present-day Albany late in 1826, but not before yet another French explorer, Dumont d'Urville, had called in at King George Sound. There was no need for concern, however – by now the French had turned their attention to New Zealand and the Pacific. Dumont d'Urville had stopped on the coast of Australia only because bad weather had forced him to interrupt his journey to New Zealand's north island. Nevertheless, to be on the safe side, the British colony was duly established at the Swan River in 1829, effectively extending that nation's claim to the whole of Terra Australis. Because of the French, Australia had become entirely British.

## *The Shared Legacy*

The territorial outcomes of the long sequence of French and British explorations in Australian waters were one-sided. But in scientific and cultural terms the honours were more evenly shared, with the French playing a much greater part than is often acknowledged. The achievements of Nicolas Baudin and Matthew Flinders, though different in a number of respects, exemplify this joint contribution. Two hundred years after the voyages of Baudin and Flinders, the conventional wisdom is that their legacies are complementary – most would assert that Flinders' legacy was richest in cartography and botany, Baudin's in anthropology and zoology. There is indeed much wisdom in this point of view, which duly gives credit where credit is due, but which also attempts to distinguish between the different priorities assigned to the two commanders by their political and scientific leaders and to allow for the different obstacles they faced in pursuing their goals. It is all part of an impartial process of evaluation that measures the achievements of each voyage against its objectives. Such an outcome indeed seems a logical consequence of the approach that we ourselves have adopted when comparing the results of the two voyages across the range of activities in which they were engaged. However, to conclude simply at the end of the process that Flinders was the greater navigator or Baudin the more enlightened 'observer of man' is not our intention – to establish such a 'report card' on the voyages is to continue, consciously or unconsciously, to situate them within a context of rivalry.

This is not to deny that the legacies of the voyages are in great part complementary, it is rather to affirm that establishing a hierarchy makes little sense when one is judging extraordinary achievements. As we have seen, the Baudin expedition made a far greater contribution to cartography than the mapping of the small portion of the unknown coast that is commonly attributed to it; Flinders also took far greater interest in the Aboriginal question than is commonly acknowledged. Robert Brown's immense contribution to botanical science should not consign to oblivion all of the efforts of Baudin's gardeners and botanists; a series of accidents meant that Baudin's expedition would not gain scientific recognition for all the specimens it collected, yet the specimens and the living plants it brought back to Europe were of great importance for the progress of botanical science. Similarly, no one would seriously claim that the exquisite zoological drawings executed by Bauer for the Flinders expedition are of lesser interest than Lesueur's equally exquisite gallery of zoological subjects; although not as numerous as his botanical drawings, Bauer's animals and fish are an important contribution to scientific knowledge and to the history of Australian art. From these and many other examples, we must therefore conclude that the exploits of the two voyages are as intertwined as they are complementary. Historically, the two captains may well have been rivals, but they have passed down a joint legacy that places them, for posterity, in a relationship of scientific collaborators rather than in a race for supremacy – a relationship, unwitting or not, that continues to enhance the reputation of both voyages.

And yet, in spite of this belated recognition, Nicolas Baudin is not honoured as a hero in the way that Matthew Flinders continues to be: when it comes to choosing new place names or erecting statues, Baudin runs a very distant second to the English navigator. In fact, he seems even to have been outdistanced by Flinders' cat, Trim. Leaving aside the question of Baudin's nationality or the misrepresentation of his achievements – factors that become less influential with the passing of time – it would seem that his lesser status might still be attributed to a negative perception of his character. Even though the positive results of Baudin's voyage are now more readily acknowledged, his mistakes or his difficult relations with his officers are still often cited in the same breath as his achievements. His perceived flaws are held against him, while those of Flinders are not seen to cast a long shadow over his heroic status. Yet, as we have seen, Flinders and Baudin both had failings as human beings and, at times, both pressed on with their voyage at great cost to their men – all in the name of their mission as discoverers. It is fascinating to learn of such failings, in the name of historical accuracy and a good story, but heroes are not usually tainted by them – indeed, their very flaws can enhance their standing. Flinders' clumsy beginnings to his voyage largely offset a grating careerism by revealing a touching and human vulnerability; Baudin's sarcasm is often a sane response to the arrogance of his young officers, and one which defused many a tense confrontation. The impetuosity of Flinders or the laconic humour of Baudin cannot be dissociated from their achievements – they are part of the personality that gave them the means to endure and hence that made them heroes. When Australians today read without preconceptions or misconceptions the narratives of the two explorers, it is even possible that the particular heroism of Baudin – namely his forbearance and dry humour in the face of adversity – might have a profound appeal to them as a quality now enshrined in their national character.

# LIST OF ILLUSTRATIONS AND MAPS

## 1  The Journey Out

## 2 Charting the Western Coast

Page 42: *Terre de Leeuwin* (Leeuwin's Land), detail of the French map of New Holland (1804). Published in the *Atlas* of the *Voyage de découvertes aux Terres Australes* (1811)

Page 43: Coastal profiles of Cape Leeuwin, Charles-Alexandre Lesueur or Nicolas-Martin Petit. The coastal profiles are most likely the work of Petit, though some plates are signed by Lesueur. This set of profiles is from Baudin's personal journal. French National Archives, Paris

Page 44: Starfish, *Uniophora aff. granifera* (Lamarck, 1816), Charles-Alexandre Lesueur. Muséum d'histoire naturelle, Le Havre – n° 74 048

Page 45: *Map of Geographe Bay*, L. & H. Freycinet, Montbazin and Boullanger (1803). Inset: Aboriginal ceremonial ground (possibly a sacred grove). Published in the *Atlas* of the *Voyage de découvertes aux Terres Australes* (1811)

Page 51: *Plan des Iles Louis-Napoléon et de la Rivière des Cygnes* (Rottnest and Garden Islands and the Swan River), L. Freycinet and Heirisson (1801, 1803). Published in the *Atlas* of the *Voyage de découvertes aux Terres Australes* (1811)

Page 55: *Carte de la Baie des Chiens-Marins* (Shark Bay), L. Freycinet and Faure (1801, 1803). Published in the *Atlas* of the *Voyage de découvertes aux Terres Australes* (1811)

Page 56: Striped wallaby (Shark Bay), *Lagostrophus fasciatus* (Péron and Lesueur, 1807), Nicolas-Martin Petit. Muséum d'histoire naturelle, Le Havre – n° 80 055

Page 56: Bird of the Meliphagidae family (Western Australia), *Meliphaga virescens* (Vieillot, 1817), Charles-Alexandre Lesueur. Muséum d'histoire naturelle, Le Havre – n° 79 007

Page 57: Fish of the Synodontidae family drawn from a specimen caught in Shark Bay, *Saurida undosquamis* (Richardson, 1848). Charles-Alexandre Lesueur. Muséum d'histoire naturelle, Le Havre – n° 76 188

Page 58: Front view of a fish of the Scorpaenidae family (found in the northern half of Australia, down to Rottnest Island), *Pterois volitans* (Linnaeus, 1758). Charles-Alexandre Lesueur. Muséum d'histoire naturelle, Le Havre – n° 76 320

Page 58: Left profile of *Pterois volitans* (Linnaeus, 1758). Charles-Alexandre Lesueur. Muséum d'histoire naturelle, Le Havre – n° 76 321

Page 59: Fish of the Mugiloididae family drawn from a specimen caught in Shark Bay, *Parapercis nebulosus* (Quoy and Gaimard, 1825). Charles-Alexandre Lesueur. Muséum d'histoire naturelle, Le Havre – n° 76 274

Page 59: Various gastropods from north and north-west Australia, *Terebralia sulcata* (Born, 1778), *Conus victoriae* (Reeve, 1843), *Aplustrum amplustre*

## 3  Surveying the South-West

## 4  Colonial Prospecting in Van Diemen's Land

Page 86: Aboriginal woman in a crouching position (Van Diemen's Land), Nicolas-Martin Petit. Muséum d'histoire naturelle, Le Havre – n° 20 012

Page 91: Fish of the Batrachoides family said by the French to inhabit the coasts of Tasmania, but no longer found there, *Batrachoides diemensis* (Lesueur, 1824). Charles-Alexandre Lesueur. Muséum d'histoire naturelle, Le Havre – n° 76 276

Page 91: Dorsal and abdominal views of a species of ray the French found in abundance in D'Entrecasteaux Channel. It was a welcome addition to their table because of its 'tender and delicate' flesh. *Urolophus criciatus* (Lacépède, 1804). Charles-Alexandre Lesueur. Muséum d'histoire naturelle, Le Havre – n° 76 751

Page 92: Shark caught by the French in Adventure Bay (Bruny Island), with details of teeth and caudal fin, *Notorynchus cepedianus* (Péron, 1807). Charles-Alexandre Lesueur. Muséum d'histoire naturelle, Le Havre – n° 76 793

Page 92: Shark caught in North-West Bay (D'Entrecasteaux Channel), designated here as 'Squalus Daubenton', *Emissola antarctica* (Günther, 1870). Charles-Alexandre Lesueur. Muséum d'histoire naturelle, Le Havre – n° 76 828

Page 94: Aborigine sitting before his fire (Van Diemen's Land), Nicolas-Martin Petit. Muséum d'histoire naturelle, Le Havre – n° 20 005

Page 95: Portrait of 'Parabéri' (Van Diemen's Land), Nicolas-Martin Petit. Muséum d'histoire naturelle, Le Havre – n° 20 018.1

Page 98: Portrait of 'Arra-Maïda' carrying a child on her back (Van Diemen's Land), Nicolas-Martin Petit. Muséum d'histoire naturelle, Le Havre – n° 20 022.3

Page 101: Portrait of an Aboriginal boy (Van Diemen's Land), Nicolas-Martin Petit. Muséum d'histoire naturelle, Le Havre – n° 20 021.4

Page 105: A species of butterfly common to Tasmania and mainland Australia. The artist has drawn the caterpillar and the chrysalis as well as dorsal and ventral views of a female specimen. *Belenois java teutonia* (Fabricius, 1775). Charles-Alexandre Lesueur. Muséum d'histoire naturelle, Le Havre – n° 73 009

Page 106: Canoe on a shore; a few spears (Van Diemen's Land), Nicolas-Martin Petit. Muséum d'histoire naturelle, Le Havre – n° 18 004

Page 107: Seashell found in North West Bay (D'Entrecasteaux Channel), *Phasianella australis* (Gmelin, 1791). Charles-Alexandre Lesueur. Muséum d'histoire naturelle, Le Havre – n° 72 059

Page 108: Seashell found in North West Bay (D'Entrecasteaux Channel), *Bassina disjecta* (Perry, 1811). Charles-Alexandre Lesueur. Muséum d'histoire naturelle, Le Havre – n° 72 067

Page 109: Map of Maria Island showing Great Oyster Bay (*Baie des Huîtres*) and Riédlé Bay, Boullanger (1802). Published in the *Atlas* of the *Voyage de découvertes aux Terres Australes* (1811)

## 7 *False Discoveries*

## 9 *The Encounters of Port Jackson*

Page 237: Lizard of the Scincidae family (Kangaroo Island), *? Hemiergis peronii* (Gray, 1831), Charles-Alexandre Lesueur. Muséum d'histoire naturelle, Le Havre – n° 78 130d

Page 239: *Details of the Cassowary of New Holland, Ile Decrès* (Kangaroo Island), *Dromaius* sp. The term 'Cassowary' was used to refer to birds that modern nomenclature separates into the *Casuarius* and *Dromaeus* genera. Engraving by Milbert and Lambert from a drawing by Charles-Alexandre Lesueur. Published in the *Atlas* of the *Voyage de découvertes aux Terres Australes* (1807)

Page 241: Emu (Kangaroo Island?), *Dromaius* sp., Charles-Alexandre Lesueur. Muséum d'histoire naturelle, Le Havre – n° 79 002

Page 242: Péron's text designates this as *Gecko pachyurus – île Decrès* (Kangaroo Island), *? Diplodactylus vittatus* (Gray, 1832). Charles-Alexandre Lesueur. Muséum d'histoire naturelle, Le Havre – n° 78 122g

Page 243: Shark designated as *Squalus Lesueur* (Southern Australia), *Furgaleus macki* (Whitley, 1943), Charles-Alexandre Lesueur. Muséum d'histoire naturelle, Le Havre – n° 76 796

Page 244: Species of seal observed by Péron and Lesueur on Kangaroo Island, *Neophoca cinerea* (Péron, 1816). Charles-Alexandre Lesueur. Muséum d'histoire naturelle, Le Havre – n° 80 676

## 12  At the End of His Tether

Page 247: *Plan des Iles Joséphine et de la Baie Murat* (St Peter Islands, Nuyts Archipelago and Murat Bay, the main branch of Denial Bay. *Ile Eugène* is the island of St Peter), Ransonnet, Montbazin, Bernier and Faure (1803). Published in the *Atlas* of the *Voyage de découvertes aux Terres Australes* (1811)

Page 248: *Plan du Port du Roi-George* (King George Sound), L. Freycinet, Faure and Ransonnet (1803). Published in the *Atlas* of the *Voyage de découvertes aux Terres Australes* (1811)

Page 251: Lizard (King George Sound), *Ctenotus labillardieri* (Duméril and Bibron, 1839), Charles-Alexandre Lesueur. Muséum d'histoire naturelle, Le Havre – n° 78 127e

Page 252: Crab (King George Sound), *Plagusia chabrus* (Linnaeus, 1758), Charles-Alexandre Lesueur. Muséum d'histoire naturelle, Le Havre – n° 73 109

Page 252: Fish of the Serranidae family (King George Sound), *Hypoplectrodes nigrorubrum* (Cuvier, 1828), Charles-Alexandre Lesueur. Muséum d'histoire naturelle, Le Havre – n° 76 379

Page 259: *Native huts on Peron Peninsula, View of Bernier Island and part of Dorre Island*, engraving by Milbert, Pillement and Née from a drawing by

## 13  The Journey Back

Plate 6: Bridled, golden-eyed or small brown leatherjacket (southern coast of Australia), *Acanthaluteres spilomelanurus* (Quoy and Gaimard, 1814), Charles-Alexandre Lesueur. Muséum d'histoire naturelle, Le Havre – n° 76 131

Plate 7: Spiny-tailed or Brown's leatherjacket (southern Australian waters – this specimen caught at King George Sound, Western Australia), *Acanthaluteres brownii* (Richardson, 1846), Ferdinand Bauer. Natural History Museum, London

Plate 8: Jellyfish (Shark Bay area of Western Australia), *Zygocanna purpurea* (Péron and Lesueur, 1810), Charles-Alexandre Lesueur. Muséum d'histoire naturelle, Le Havre – n° 70 031

Plate 9: Weedy or common seadragon (southern Australia – these specimens caught at King George Sound, Western Australia), *Phyllopteryx taeniolatus* (Lacépède, 1804), Ferdinand Bauer. Natural History Museum, London

Plate 10: Fish common to the entire Indo-Pacific, from southern Africa to Japan, *Dactyloptena orientalis* (Cuvier, 1829), Charles-Alexandre Lesueur. Muséum d'histoire naturelle, Le Havre – n° 76 858

Plate 11: Butterfly cod (specimen caught at Strong Tide Passage, Queensland), *Pterois* sp., Ferdinand Bauer. Natural History Museum, London

Plate 12: Display of eight frogs from Port Jackson, *Litoria* sp., Charles-Alexandre Lesueur. Muséum d'histoire naturelle, Le Havre – n° 77 001

Plate 13: Southern bell frog (south-eastern Australia – this specimen may have been collected on Kangaroo Island, South Australia), *Litoria raniformis* (Keferstein, 1867). Ferdinand Bauer. Natural History Museum, London

Plate 14: Several platypuses by the edge of a pond, *Ornithorhynchus anatinus* (Shaw, 1799), Charles-Alexandre Lesueur. Muséum d'histoire naturelle, Le Havre – n° 80 034.1

Plate 14: Common wombat, *Vombatus ursinus* (Shaw, 1800), Charles-Alexandre Lesueur. Muséum d'histoire naturelle, Le Havre – n° 80 069.1

Plate 15: Platypuses (specimens collected at Port Jackson), *Ornithorhynchus anatinus* (Shaw, 1799), Ferdinand Bauer. Natural History Museum, London

Plate 15: Common wombat, *Vombatus ursinus* (Shaw, 1800), Ferdinand Bauer. Natural History Museum, London

Plate 16: Two kangaroos, *Thylogale thetis* (Lesson, 1827), Charles-Alexandre Lesueur. Muséum d'histoire naturelle, Le Havre – n° 80 061

Plate 17: Black-footed rock wallaby (Recherche Archipelago, Western Australia), *Petrogale lateralis hacketti* (Gould, 1842), Ferdinand Bauer. Natural History Museum, London

Plate 32: *General chart of Terra Australis or Australia*, Matthew Flinders. Published in *A Voyage to Terra Australis* (1814)

Page 279: *Baie du Cap*. Published in T. Bradshaw, *Views in the Mauritius, or Isle of France* (London: James Carpenter & Son, 1832). Reproduced courtesy of the Royal Geographical Society of South Australia

## 15  Shaping Australia

Page 297: Detail of Laurie & Whittle's *New map of the World* showing Terra Australis as known in November 1800. State Library of New South Wales

## 16  The Artistic Record

Page 312: The Château de Jœurs near Etampes (south of Paris), Charles-Alexandre Lesueur. Muséum d'histoire naturelle, Le Havre – n° 35 068

Page 313: Portrait of Charles-Alexandre Lesueur, pen drawing by V. Gribayedoff, after an oil painting by C.W. Peale (Academy of Natural Sciences, Philadelphia). Muséum d'histoire naturelle, Le Havre – n° 64 062.2

Page 316: *Molluscs and zoophytes*, engraving by Milbert and Lambert from a drawing by Charles-Alexandre Lesueur. Published in the *Atlas* of the *Voyage de découvertes aux Terres Australes* (1807)

Page 317: *Physalia physalis* (Linnaeus, 1758), Charles-Alexandre Lesueur. Muséum d'histoire naturelle, Le Havre – n° 70 067

Page 318: Starfish, *Archaster angulatus* (Müller and Troschel, 1842), Charles-Alexandre Lesueur. Muséum d'histoire naturelle, Le Havre – n° 74 060

Page 319: Aborigines in front of their hut, Charles-Alexandre Lesueur or Nicolas-Martin Petit. Muséum d'histoire naturelle, Le Havre – n° 16 023

Page 320: *Port Jackson – New Holland* (1802). This view of Sydney shows the barracks, powder magazine, officers' quarters, church and windmills. Charles-Alexandre Lesueur. Muséum d'histoire naturelle, Le Havre – n° 16 069

Page 320: *Plan of the Town of Sydney* (1802), Charles-Alexandre Lesueur (from bearings taken by Charles-Pierre Boullanger). Muséum d'histoire naturelle, Le Havre – n° 16 074.2

Page 322: Woman from Tenerife. The zoologist Levillain noted that this costume was worn by rich women on the island who had reached an 'advanced age'. Nicolas-Martin Petit. Muséum d'histoire naturelle, Le Havre – n° 14 004

Page 322: Aborigines dancing near a fire, Charles-Alexandre Lesueur. Muséum d'histoire naturelle, Le Havre – n° 16 008

## 17 The Scientific Project

## 18  The Clash of Cultures

# SELECT
# BIBLIOGRAPHY

## Works Cited

The following is an alphabetical list of the reference works that are the source of the comments attributed to the authors cited within this book.

Baker, S. J., *My Own Destroyer: A Biography of Matthew Flinders, Explorer and Navigator*, Sydney: Currawong, 1962.

Bonnemains, J., 'Les Artistes du "Voyage de Découvertes aux Terres Australes" (1800–1804): Charles-Alexandre Lesueur et Nicolas-Martin Petit', *Bulletin Trimestriel de la Société Géologique de Normandie et des Amis du Muséum du Havre*, tome 76, fascicule 1, 1989.

Brown, A. J., 'The Captain and the Convict Maid. A Chapter in the Life of Nicolas Baudin', *South Australian Geographical Journal*, 97, pp. 20–32.

Cooper, H. M., *The Unknown Coast: A Supplement*, Adelaide: s.n., 1955.

Duyker, E., 'In search of Mme Kérivel and Baudin's last resting place', *National Library of Australia News*, September 1999.

Estensen, M., *The Life of Matthew Flinders*, Crows Nest: Allen & Unwin, 2002.

Guicheteau, T. and Kernéis, J.-P., 'Medical Aspects of the Voyages of Exploration, with particular reference to Baudin's expedition, 1800–1804', in J. Hardy and A. Frost (eds), *European Voyaging towards Australia*, Canberra: Australian Academy of the Humanities, 1990, pp. 67–69.

Horner, F., *The French Reconnaissance. Baudin in Australia 1801–1803*, Carlton: Melbourne University Press, 1987.

Hughes, M., 'Philosophical travellers at the ends of the earth: Baudin, Péron and the Tasmanians', in R. W. Home (ed.), *Australian Science in the Making*, Cambridge: Cambridge University Press, 1988, pp. 23–44.

Hunt, S., and Carter, P. (eds), *Terre Napoléon. Australia through French Eyes*, Sydney: Historic Trust of New South Wales/ Hordern House, 1999.

Jangoux, M., 'Les zoologistes et botanistes qui accompagnèrent le capitaine Baudin aux Terres Australes', *Australian Journal of French Studies*, XLI, 2, 2004.

Jones, P., 'In the Mirror of Contact: Art of the French Encounters', in S. Thomas (ed.), *The Encounter, 1802. Art of the Flinders and Baudin Voyages*, Adelaide: Art Gallery of South Australia, 2002, pp. 164–175.

Jones, R., 'Images of Natural Man', in J. Bonnemains, E. Forsyth, B. Smith, *Baudin in Australian Waters. The Artwork of the French Voyage of Discovery to the Southern Lands, 1801–1804*, Melbourne: Oxford University Press, 1988, pp. 35–64.

Jouanin, C., 'Les Emeus de l'expédition Baudin', *L'Oiseau et La Revue Française d'Ornithologie*, V, XXIX, 1959, pp. 169–203.

Manneville, P., 'Charles-Alexandre Lesueur, sa famille, son enfance – Jean-Baptiste Denis Lesueur', *Annales du Muséum du Havre*, 14, 1979.

Moore, F. C. T. (ed.), J.-M. Degérando, *The Observation of Savage Peoples*, London: Routledge and Kegan Paul, 1969.

Parker, S. A., 'The extinct Kangaroo Island Emu, a hitherto-unrecognised species', *Bulletin of the British Ornithological Club*, 104, 1984, pp. 19–22.

Smith, B., *European Vision and the South Pacific*, 2nd ed., Sydney: Harper & Row, 1985.

Stocking, G. W. Jr., 'French Anthropology in 1800', *Isis*, 55, 2, 180, 1964, pp. 134–150.

## Works Consulted

In addition to the works cited, the following works were consulted in the course of our research and considered to be indispensable references.

### Primary sources
#### 1. Manuscripts

Lesueur Collection, Muséum d'histoire naturelle, Le Havre.

Baudin Journals , originals held in the Centre Historique des Archives Nationales, Paris (Marine Series – sea log: 5JJ 36, 37, 38, 39, 40A; fair copy: 5JJ 35, 40 B-D); reproduced on microfilm in the State Library of South Australia (ARG Series 1, Reels 11–14).

Flinders papers, Mitchell Library, Sydney

## 2. Published accounts and documents of the expeditions

Bladen, F. M. (ed.), *Historical Records of New South Wales*, tome 4, Appendix: Baudin Papers, pp. 941–1009, and tome 5, Sydney: Government Printer, 1892–1901.

Bonnemains, J. (ed.), *Mon voyage aux Terres Australes. Journal personnel du commandant Baudin*, Paris: Imprimerie Nationale, 2000.

Bonnemains, J. (ed.) and P. Haughel, *Récit du Voyage aux Terres Australes de Pierre-Bernard Milius*, Le Havre: Société havraise d'Etudes diverses, 1987.

Bory de Saint-Vincent, J.-B., *Voyage dans les quatre principales îles des mers d'Afrique, avec l'histoire de la traversée du capitaine Baudin jusqu'à Port-Louis de l'Ile Maurice*, Paris: 1804.

Brunton, P. (ed.), *Matthew Flinders: Personal Letters from an Extraordinary Life*, Sydney: Hordern House/State Library of New South Wales, 2002.

Cornell, C., *The Journal of Post-Captain Nicolas Baudin*, Adelaide: Libraries Board of South Australia, 1974.

Edwards, P. I. (ed.), 'The Journal of Peter Good, Gardener on Matthew Flinders' Voyage to Terra Australis 1801–1803', *Bulletin of the British Museum (Natural History), Historical Series*, vol. 9, 1981.

Flinders, M., *A Voyage to Terra Australis; Undertaken for the Purpose of Completing the Discovery of that Vast Country, and Prosecuted in the Years 1801, 1802 and 1803, in His Majesty's Ship, the* Investigator, 2 vols and Atlas, London: G. & W. Nicol, 1814.

Martin, R. (ed.), 'François Péron, Mémoire sur les établissements anglais à la Nouvelle Hollande, à la Terre de Diémen et dans les archipels du grand océan Pacifique', *Revue de l'Institut Napoléon*, 176, 1, 1998.

Monteath, P. (ed.), *Sailing with Flinders, the Journal of Seaman Samuel Smith*, North Adelaide: Corkwood Press, 2002.

Péron, F. and Freycinet, L., *Voyage de découvertes aux Terres Australes exécuté par ordre de Sa Majesté l'Empereur et Roi, sur les corvettes le* Géographe*, le* Naturaliste*; et la goélette le* Casuarina*, pendant les années 1800, 1801, 1802, 1803, et 1804*, Paris: 1807–1816, comprising the following volumes:

*Historique*, vol 1, by François Péron, 1807.

*Historique*, vol. 2, by F. Péron, continued by Louis Freycinet, 1816.

*Atlas*, 1st part, by Lesueur and Petit, 1807.

*Atlas*, 2nd part, by L. Freycinet, 1811.

*Atlas, Navigation et géographie*, by L. Freycinet, 1812 (sic: appeared December 1814).

*Navigation et géographie*, by L. Freycinet, 1815.

Thomson, S., 'Narrative of the proceedings of *Le Géographe* and *Naturaliste*, sent on a voyage of discovery of the French government in 1800', in John Turnbull, *A Voyage of Discovery Around the World in 1800, 1801, 1802, 1803 and 1804*, London: s.n., 1813.

Vallance, T. G., Moore, D. T. and Groves, E. W. (eds), *Nature's Investigator: The Diary of Robert Brown in Australia, 1801–1805*, Canberra: Australian Biological Resources Study (Flora), 2001.

## Secondary sources

Ageorges, R., *Ile de Ré, Terres australes: les voyages du capitaine Baudin, marin et naturaliste*, Sainte-Marie-de-Ré: GER, 1994.

Blackman, M. (ed.), *Australian Aborigines and the French*, University of New South Wales: French-Australian Research Centre, Occasional Monograph 3, 1990.

Bonnemains, J., Forsyth, E. and Smith, B., *Baudin in Australian Waters. The Artwork of the French Voyage of Discovery to the Southern Lands, 1801–1804*, Melbourne: Oxford University Press, 1988.

Brown, A. J., *Ill-starred Captains: Matthew Flinders and Nicolas Baudin*, Hindmarsh: Crawford House Publishing, 2000.

Chittleborough, A., Dooley, G., Glover, B. and Hosking, R. (eds), *Alas, for the Pelicans! Flinders, Baudin and Beyond*, Kent Town: Wakefield Press, 2002.

Cooper, H. M., *French Exploration in South Australia*, Adelaide: s.n., 1952.

Cooper, H. M., *The Unknown Coast. Being the Explorations of Captain Matthew Flinders R. N. along the Shores of South Australia 1802*, Adelaide: s.n., 1953.

Eisler, W., *The Furthest Shore. Images of Terra Australis from the Middle Ages to Captain Cook*, Cambridge: Cambridge University Press, 1995.

Findlay, E., *Arcadian Quest: William Westall's Australian Sketches*, Canberra: Australian National Library, 1998.

Fornasiero, J. and West-Sooby, J., 'Baudin's Books', *Australian Journal of French Studies*, XXXIX, 2, 2002, pp. 215–249.

Gascoigne, J., *Science in the Service of Empire. Joseph Banks, the British State and the Uses of Science in the Age of Revolution*, Cambridge: Cambridge University Press, 1998.

Goy, J. and Breton, G., 'Les Méduses de François Péron et Charles-Alexandre Lesueur (1775–1810 et 1778–1846), révélées par les vélins de Lesueur', *Bulletin Trimestriel de la Société Géologique de Normandie et des Amis du Muséum du Havre*, XVII, 2, 1980.

Hardy, J. and Frost, A. (eds), *European Voyaging towards Australia*, Canberra: Highland Press, 1990.

Ingleton, G. C., *Matthew Flinders Navigator and Chartmaker*, 2 vols, Guildford: Genesis Publications Ltd., 1986.

Mabberley, D. J., *Ferdinand Bauer: The Nature of Discovery*, London: Merrell Holberton Publishers and Natural History Museum, 1999.

Mabberley, D. J., *Jupiter Botanicus: Robert Brown of the British Museum*, London and Braunschweig: British Museum and J. Cramer, 1985.

Marchant, L. R., *France australe*, Perth: Scott Four Colour Print, 1998. (Artlook Books, 1982).

Perry, T. M., *The Discovery of Australia: the Charts and Maps of the Navigators and Explorers*, London: Hamilton, 1982.

Perry, T. M. and Simpson, D. H. (eds), *Drawings by William Westall: Landscape Artist on Board H. M. S.* Investigator *during the Circumnavigation of Australia by Captain Matthew Flinders R. N. in 1801–1803*, London: The Royal Commonwealth Society, 1962.

Plomley, N. J. B., *The Baudin Expedition and the Tasmanian Aborigines 1802*, Hobart: Blubber Head Press, 1983.

Sankey, M., 'The Baudin Expedition in Port Jackson, 1802: Cultural Encounters and Enlightenment Politics', *Explorations*, 31, December 2001, pp. 5–36.

Scott, E., *Terre Napoléon, a History of French Exploration and Projects in Australia*, London: Methuen & Co, 1910.

Scott, E.,*The Life of Captain Matthew Flinders R.N.*, Sydney: Angus & Robertson, 1914.

Thomas, S., *The Encounter, 1802. Art of the Flinders and Baudin Voyages*, Adelaide: Art Gallery of South Australia, 2002.

Tiley, R., *Australian Navigators*, East Roseville: Kangaroo Press, 2002.

Tindale, N. B., *Aboriginal Tribes of Australia*, Canberra: Australian National University Press, 1974.

Watts, P., Pomfret, J.-A. and Mabberley, D., *An Exquisite Eye: The Australian Flora and Fauna Drawings of Ferdinand Bauer 1801–1820*, Sydney: Historic Houses Trust of NSW, 1997.

# ACKNOWLEDGMENTS

The authors are deeply indebted to the many individuals and institutions without whose assistance and support over the past five years this book may not have come into being. We would firstly like to express our gratitude to Alexander Downer, whose initial advice led us to qualify for a grant from the Department of Foreign Affairs and Trade which enabled us to conduct the archival research necessary to our project, both in Australia and overseas. Our task of identifying sources of information would have been made infinitely more difficult without the amiable and expert advice of Jacqueline Bonnemains, Curator of the Lesueur Collection of the Muséum d'histoire naturelle of Le Havre, Paul Brunton, Senior Curator, Mitchell Library, Sydney, and Valerie Sitters, Librarian of the Royal Geographical Society of South Australia. The unfailing assistance of the librarians in charge of the specialised collections relating to Pacific exploration and explorers in the Universities of Adelaide and Flinders was equally essential to our project: we would like to thank most warmly Susan Woodburn and Elise Bennetto, Special Collections, Barr Smith Library, University of Adelaide, and Gillian Dooley, Flinders Collection, Flinders University Library. Sarah Thomas, Curator of Australian Art at the Art Gallery of South Australia, was particularly helpful with questions relating to the artwork of the two expeditions, but also with practical matters concerning the illustrations of this book – as was Georgia Hale, also of the Art Gallery. For access to vital documents, special thanks to Jeff and Dorothy Pash; for invaluable advice on textual matters, we are greatly indebted to Celia Jellett. We are also most grateful for advice from Philip Jones of the South Australian Museum, Kevin Jones of the South Australian Maritime Museum, and Robert Sexton, to whom we give particular thanks for the precise and elegant drawing of the *Investigator*, which he has kindly permitted us to reproduce in this book. And not least, we would like to thank the team at Wakefield Press for their enthusiasm for this project and for the attention to detail that has brought improvements too numerous to mention to every aspect of this book.

# INDEX

Wakefield Press is an independent publishing and
distribution company based in Adelaide, South Australia.
We love good stories and publish beautiful books.
To see our full range of titles, please visit our website at
www.wakefieldpress.com.au.